# SOCIETY AND CULTURE

# Theory, Culture & Society

*Theory, Culture & Society* caters for the resurgence of interest in culture within contemporary social science and the humanities. Building on the heritage of classical social theory, the book series examines ways in which this tradition has been reshaped by a new generation of theorists. It also publishes theoretically informed analyses of everyday life, popular culture, and new intellectual movements.

EDITOR: Mike Featherstone, *Nottingham Trent University*

THE TCS CENTRE
The Theory, Culture & Society book series, the journals *Theory, Culture & Society* and *Body & Society*, and related conference, seminar and postgraduate programmes operate from the TCS Centre at Nottingham Trent University. For further details of the TCS Centre's activities please contact:

Centre Administrator
The TCS Centre, Room 175
Faculty of Humanities
Nottingham Trent University
Clifton Lane, Nottingham, NG11 8NS, UK
e-mail: tcs@ntu.ac.uk
web: http://tcs.ntu.ac.uk

# SOCIETY AND CULTURE

## Principles of Scarcity and Solidarity

Bryan S. Turner and Chris Rojek

SAGE Publications
London • Thousand Oaks • New Delhi

SAGE Publications Ltd
6 Bonhill Street
London EC2A 4PU

SAGE Publications Inc
2455 Teller Road
Thousand Oaks, California 91320

SAGE Publications India Pvt Ltd
32, M-Block Market
Greater Kailash – I
New Delhi 110 048

HM
621
, 187
2001

Published in association with *Theory, Culture & Society*,
Nottingham Trent University

**British Library Cataloguing in Publication data**

A catalogue record for this book is available
from the British Library

ISBN 0-7619-7048-7
ISBN 0-7619-7049-5 (pbk)

**Library of Congress catalog record available**

Typeset by Mayhew Typesetting, Rhayader, Powys
Printed and bound in Great Britain by Athenaeum Press,
Gateshead

# CONTENTS

# ACKNOWLEDGEMENTS

The idea for this study emerged over the last fifteen years, following the publication of an earlier study *The Body and Society*. More recently, the basic framework of the dynamic of solidarity and scarcity grew out of a series of lectures that were given at York University, Toronto, Canada. We want to acknowledge an intellectual debt to John O'Neill and Egin Isin at York University.

The critique of decorative sociology emerged during the development of this volume and a version of the argument was published by *Sociological Review* (2000). Chapter 1 on the discipline of sociology was initially given as a lecture at the University of Liverpool and we are grateful to Gerard Delanty for his critical comments on the original formulation. Chapter 2 on the organic analogy was originally given at the University of Aberdeen to celebrate five hundred years of its history. Mike Hepworth helped to organize the seminar and assisted the development of the argument. The chapter on rights evolved out of a comparison of Heidegger, Lyotard and Rorty from *The Politics of Jean-François Lyotard*. Chapter 8 on intimacy emerged from research conducted with Anne Riggs, Deakin University Australia in the middle of the 1990s. Aspects of the argument about ageing and intimacy have been published previously. The argument about cosmopolitan virtue was developed at a 1998 conference organized by Engin Isin at York University on the city and citizenship. The chapters on 'Disorder', 'Choice' and 'Solutions' benefited from the TCS seminar programme at Nottingham Trent University. We wish to acknowledge the contributions of Roger Bromley, Stephen Chan, Mike Featherstone, Sandra Harris, Joost Van Loon and John Tomlinson. In particular, Roger Bromley's work on the politics of 'new belonging' and John Tomlinson's study of 'globalization and culture' were helpful. We also wish to acknowledge the seminar programme held at Charles University, Prague in April 2000, which helped to clarify many aspects of the argument on 'Solutions'. The conclusion of our account depends on a view of the role of religion and citizenship in modernity. Aspects of these arguments will appear as 'The Erosion of Citizenship' in the *British Journal of Sociology* and as 'Cosmopolitan Virtue: Religion in a Global Age' in the *European Journal of Social Theory*. A version of Chapter 5 appeared as 'Scarcity of means and solidarity of values' in "*Osterreichische Zeitschrift für Soziologie*" 2000, volume 6, pp. 239–56. A version of Chapter 8 appeared in A.K. Carlstrom, L. Gerholm and I. Ramberg (eds) (2000) *Embodying Culture* Tumba, Sweden: The Multi-cultural Centre pp. 15–45.

Bryan S. Turner, University of Cambridge
Chris Rojek, Nottingham Trent University

# PREFACE

Our study is an attempt to rebuild contemporary sociology around the classical theme of social action, but action understood from the perspective of embodiment. Our aim is to rejuvenate the sociological imagination from a theoretical standpoint that takes the human body seriously, and that draws out the connections between environmental politics and the vulnerability of human embodiment. This account of sociology in terms of the vulnerability of the social actor provides a sociological perspective on 'the human condition'. In order to restore what we take to be the central issues of sociological theory, it is necessary to adopt a critical attitude towards many contemporary trends in sociology. Although we believe that sociology has to include the study of the cultural dimensions of social life, as a discipline sociology has, through the so-called cultural turn, been devolved and dissolved into a series of related fields – cultural studies, women's studies, urban studies and media studies. We intend to show that the pedagogic merits of multidisciplinarity very neatly satisfy the managerial needs of the commercially driven higher education system rather than a deeper commitment to scholarship. Our critical stance is directed against a contemporary tendency that we call 'decorative sociology', namely a sociology that is obsessed with the immediacy of commercial and popular cultures, has no sense of historical depth, does not engage in comparative research, and has little political relevance.

Our argument is that social analysis from the standpoint of human embodiment provides a foundation from which sociology can regain its original concerns with economics, politics and ethics. We need a sociological viewpoint that can facilitate understanding of large-scale historical processes that have shaped modern societies – war, industrialization, reproduction, the nation state, technology and secularization.

Sociology has at its best sought to comprehend social change and provide solutions to its negative consequences. Decorative sociology has detached sociological theory from both ethics and politics, and thus our agenda is to provide a general sociology of modern societies that is driven simultaneously by a respect for classical sociology and an intellectual concern that it must forever address contemporary issues with critical responsiveness and openness to new ideas. This study provides both an overview of the key issues of classical sociology and a catholic engagement with contemporary developments (such as postmodernism, reflexive sociology, risk society and globalization theory). We engage with Marx, Weber, Durkheim and Simmel, but also evaluate the contributions of Bourdieu, Elias, Giddens and Castells. Although this list is obviously a list of men, our interest in embodiment has drawn upon feminist analysis of the ethnics of embodiment, care and voice. We draw much of our inspiration from Mary Douglas, Juliet Mitchel, Rosi Braidotti, Carol Gilligan, Luce Irigaray and various feminist philosophies of the body. Our approach to embodiment does however diverge importantly from much feminist epistemology of deconstruction. Whereas feminist theory has been concerned to problematize the body by an examination of its representational politics, we are more concerned with the phenomenology of embodiment that has its roots in Feuerbach, Marx, Heidegger and Lukács, namely with an approach that attempts to grasp the alienation of human embodiment in social institutions – the family, religion, law, labour and war – and the possibilities for freedom and justice.

Our account opens with classical social science. We start with the view, central to Max Weber's sociology, that the social sciences are primarily sciences of social action and interaction. Action and interaction are the basic stuff of the discipline of sociology, that is the endless actions of human beings in satisfying their needs, creating social relations and institutions, building meaningful systems of culture and interpretation, and establishing communal life forms. This stuff of social interaction, exchange and reciprocity we call 'social life'. In short, sociology is a science that begins with the social relationships of everyday life and the conditions that shape it.

The origins of nineteenth-century sociology can be found in a continuous criticism of the individualistic and rationalist assumptions of economics. Our contention is that Talcott Parsons's *The Structure of Social Action* (1937) closed the classical period of sociology and opened the contemporary debate about action and structure, sentiments and actions, values and meaning. Parsonian sociology was a critique of marginalist economics, because it argued that rational actors in pursuit of their ends would, in a context of scarcity, employ fraud and force to satisfy their needs, other things being equal. Such a theory of rational action cannot produce a convincing theory of society, because it cannot explain social order. How do co-operation and solidarity exist if economic rationalism is the only or principal guide to action? Conventional economics artificially solved the problem by inventing explanations that could be derived from their basic rationalist assumptions – such as the hidden hand of history or sentiment. Parsons solved the problem of order by arguing that human beings can engage in economic activity without destroying society, if they share common values and norms. The solution of economic and social order was to be found in culture and institutions, not in the psychology of Economic Man. Social actors are socialized into a common system of values when their social actions are psychologically rewarded. Our study of society and culture can be understood as an attempt to understand the structure of social action from the perspective of a post-Cartesian view of human embodiment and action.

Parsons developed an interdisciplinary model of the social sciences within which economics is a science of scarcity. It is essentially a study of the rational application of effort to the satisfaction of wants in an environment of competitive scarcity. Sociology by contrast involves the analysis of the conditions of social solidarity through shared rituals, common values and consensual norms. For sociology, religion (especially religious rituals and ceremonies) has been the fundamental social cement of social existence. Psychology is the study of the motives and drives that underpin commitment to society and motivation to act. Finally, politics is a discipline that studies the coercive element in the allocation of goals. In the work of the mature Parsons, society is a complex dynamic between two requirements: allocation of scarce resources (politics and economics) and the integration of society (sociology and psychology). The social science disciplines exist in an intellectual division of labour within which they consider different elements of social action. In this sense, Parsons's interest in social systems was always an interest in action-systems.

Our study takes the dynamic contradictions between solidarity and scarcity as the driving force of social organization. Human beings are exposed to problems of scarcity (of resources), but the social roots of scarcity are more profound. Critical theorists, like Herbert Marcuse, provided a powerful analysis of how capitalism creates artificial wants and stimulates needs through advertising and other means of sales promotion. Although economics has traditionally assumed that scarcity is a function of natural shortages, the sociological tradition claims that scarcity is a function of social closure whereby powerful social groups attempt to establish monopolies. We treat social stratification, primarily social class, as the essential element of scarcity. In this sense, we live in a state of social competition that was first fully stated by Thomas Hobbes, according to whom rational men in conflict over scarce resources form a social contract in order to avoid the violence of the state of nature. We use the word 'men' here deliberately since classical politics and economics largely assumed that the public domain of exchange and power was occupied by men. In the psychoanalytic version of Hobbes, men fight over women as a scarce resource in the competence struggle to reproduce and ensure their continuity.

Sociologists, generally speaking, have been critical of social contract theory. Parsons, drawing upon Durkheim, argued that social contracts would not be binding without the prior existence of shared values and beliefs, and therefore the social contract that creates the state to enforce civilized society has in fact to presuppose the existence of society. Social contract theory was thus circular. Parsons laid the foundations of contemporary sociology by demonstrating the failures of utilitarian economic theory and Hobbesian theories of the state. Parsons's sociology has rightly been subject to persistent criticism, much of which was driven by the view made popular by C. Wright Mills that Parsons's sociology was abstract and conservative. By contrast, we see the weakness of Parsons's sociology to lie in his treatment of action theory. Parsons's social actor is capable of affective responses to social situations. For example, Parsons distinguished between the cognitive orientation to the social situation in terms of the actor's definition of interests and the cathetic orientation that involved the gratification of the actor. Nevertheless, Parsons's social actor remained strangely disembodied. In fact Parsons regarded the human body, at least in his early work, as part of the conditions of social action. Our principal criticism of the classical tradition of sociology is its failure to come to terms with embodiment of social actors, and it is this criticism that opens the way into our study of sociological understanding of the main dynamics of modern social life. We draw heavily on Martin Heidegger's far more robust and vibrant account of social existence and embodiment through his critique of metaphysics.

Much of this study involves an attempt to define embodiment. We prefer the notion of 'embodiment' to 'body', because we want to suggest that the corporeal existence of social actors is a process that changes throughout the life cycle rather than a static phenomenon, and secondly we want to recognize that embodiment takes place within the social world rather than in 'nature'. We derive this notion of embodiment from many classical sources in philosophy and social theory – Feuerbach, Marx, Nietzsche, Heidegger and Merleau-Ponty. Our use of the term is not primarily rooted in biology. In fact it is closely related to Marx's analysis of labour and alienation in the Paris Manuscripts. Human beings in order to exist must labour on their environment in the collective satisfaction of their wants. They are sensuous and practical agents who, in satisfying their needs, constantly transform their environment and transform themselves. Marx rejected mechanistic versions of materialism in *The Poverty of Philosophy* (1847). Marx claimed that history was nothing other than the continuous and constant transformation of human nature.

By claiming that human beings are embodied, we, like Marx, do not want to embrace a reductionist form of materialism in which the biological characteristics of human beings determine their history. We are quite hostile to the claims of contemporary versions of Darwinism and evolutionary psychology. The principal feature of any social action theory is the premise that social relationships require individuals who make choices between alternative courses of action and are therefore reflexive about their social being. In Weber's sociology, intentionality and self-reflexivity distinguish action from mere behaviour. Social actors have agency and in order to exert that agency they require identity and memory. Consciousness of past actions is a precondition of memory without which purposeful and coherent activity would be impossible. We have to be self-reflexively aware of ourselves as individuated social actors in order to engage meaningfully with others as other individuated social beings. Successful embodiment also goes along with what we will call the process of enselfment, that is the process by which human beings become self-reflexive, purposeful and individuated social agents. Socialization into selfhood (or enselfment) is continuous and contingent. The capacity for memory is eroded with the process of ageing, and memories have to be constantly reconstructed to match the vicissitudes of one's passage through time. We do not posit a fixed or coherent self. Enselfment is a precarious process, but against postmodern notions of flexible selfhood, we argue that some consistency across the life course is a condition of effective or successful social action. The idea of a reversible self is simply incompatible with social life.

Our view of embodiment has been influenced by Heidegger's *Being and Time* (1962). From Heidegger, we have developed a sociological awareness of the embodiment of social actors in the everyday world. Heidegger employed the term *Dasein* (literally There-Being) to describe existence. From this term, we have developed the obvious point that embodiment has always to be embodiment in time but also in a specific place. Sociologists have been somewhat neglectful of the specificity of place in their analysis of social action. Perhaps only Erving Goffman had a clear sense of the setting of social action in his notions of fronts, stages and behind the scene activities. For example, the management of the back stage is crucial for Goffman's discussion of the presentation of self (Goffman, 1959). We call this aspect of social relations 'the emplacement of action' to indicate the placing of acts in a physical and social context. Emplacement is an important corrective to contemporary utopian writing about the social consequences of the internet as a means of social intercourse. The body is always present in virtual reality, and embodiment limits the scope of virtual communities. Building a home and creating a garden remain, in an age of breathtaking technology, fundamental activities of everyday life.

A core notion behind our attempt to rebuild sociological theory around embodiment is vulnerability. Human beings are vulnerable because they are exposed to disease, sickness and the ageing process. This frailty is central to our humanity and a bond that unites human beings, regardless of social differences in status and wealth. While much has been made of the cultural relativism of the emotions in modern social theory, this neglects the moral solidarity that is possible because there is a bond of frailty. *The Merchant of Venice* has it perfectly – if you prick us do we not bleed? if you tickle us do we not laugh? Although we are persuaded by the force of the argument for human rights from an assumption about the commonality of our frailty, in this study we prefer the term 'vulnerability', which suggests our openness to the world and our capacity to respond to that openness in ways that are creative and transformative. World-openness is an idea developed by Peter Berger and Thomas Luckmann to register the fact that human beings must work together to fashion a cultural world to manage their vulnerability. Because human beings are not determined in some mechanical fashion by their instincts, they stand in a flexible relationship to their biology and immediate environment. This world-openness is, however, biologically and psychologically intolerable, and thus human beings construct stable structures through their own collective activity. The creation of social institutions is the core of this world-constructing activity (Berger, 1980: ix).

Shortly before completing this study, we were fortunate to read Alasdair MacIntyre's *Dependent Rational Animals* (1999). In this new work, MacIntyre criticizes Western philosophy for its neglect of two central facts about human beings – their vulnerability and their afflictions. He goes on to argue that vulnerability explains our dependence on others for protection and sustenance. Vulnerability is derived intellectually from the legacy of Aristotle's view of animality. Although MacIntyre's view of vulnerability is compatible with the approach taken in this sociological study, we note certain important points of departure between the two arguments. Our own approach, as we have suggested, is part of a legacy of sociological analysis that includes Karl Marx, Karl Löwith, Arnold Gehlen, Peter Berger and Thomas Luckmann rather than Aristotle and Aquinas. While MacIntyre (1999: 6) quotes Merleau-Ponty with some approval to suggest that 'I am my body', our approach is concerned to explore 'embodiment' as a process rather than 'body' as a phenomenon. Our view of the vulnerability of our embodiment is connected with a notion of the precarious nature of institutions and the interconnected nature of the social world. We wish to develop a general sociology of everyday life based on embodiment, institutions and social networks that in turn lays the foundation for the justification of human rights. We locate this discussion of vulnerability and rights within a global social system, where the hybridity and fragmentation of culture brings us to a discussion of cosmopolitan virtue. While MacIntyre also employs 'vulnerability' to sustain an analysis of virtues, his approach is derived from the Aristotelian tradition.

The concept of 'vulnerability' derives from the Latin *vulnus* or 'wound'. It is instructive from our point of view that 'vulnerability' should have such an obviously corporeal origin. In the seventeenth century, vulnerability had both a passive and an active significance: to be wounded and to wound. To 'vulnerate' is to wound, but in its modern usage it is solely the human capacity to be open to wounding. Again in its modern form, vulnerability has become, in one sense, more abstract: it is the human capacity to be exposed to psychological or moral damage. Our openness to wounding is part of what Peter Berger has called our 'world-openness', namely that we do not live in a biologically determined or species-specific environment. To be vulnerable is to possess a structure of sentiments and emotions that enable us to steer a passage through the social order. Our vulnerability is also part of our capacity to draw sensual pleasures from our openness to experiences. In our view, therefore, Marx rather than Aristotle offers a more promising starting point for a study of our wounding, because he points to the sensual, practical and active components of the structure of social action. We depart from MacIntyre's position (with its exclusive emphasis on disability and affliction) in wanting to argue that vulnerability is not merely passive.

While attempting to avoid a wholly melancholic social science (Lepenies, 1992), we recognize that the world that human beings fashion collectively to form social worlds is inherently and alarmingly precarious. The social arrangements we create are never entirely perfect or reliable. We live in a world of perpetual, ceaseless social change, with the result that our associational world is never perfectly suited to human needs and intentions. The social world is contingent and unstable, so it is unpredictable. We live in an institutional setting where management strategies constantly demand the amalgamation, restructuring and reorganization of the corporate world. The risky character of social arrangements is particularly evident under conditions of rapid modernization. There is no perfect blueprint for institution building, and we are all subject to the whimsical outcomes of action. We live in a world of unanticipated consequences. In the words of Robert Burns, the best laid schemes of mice and men often go awry.

The uncertainty of life is a function of the vulnerability of our embodiment and the precariousness of social institutions, but nevertheless social life persists. Human beings as individuals and social groups have a surprising capacity for recovery, survival and renewal. Any account of the divisions and conflicts that surround the scarcity of means to the achievement of ends (in economic theory) must also take note of the co-operation, reciprocity and sharing that are the building blocks of social existence. In addition to social conflict over resources, there is also a celebratory quality to social relationships which we find in ceremonials, rituals and festivals. In our secular society, we have lost touch with what we might call the elementary forms of the ecstatic life so characteristic of shamanism and early religion. Ecstasy, or the experience of being outside ourselves, is perhaps glimpsed in modern sport, and it stands as a reminder of the religious roots of the social. We call this propensity for social reciprocity and interpersonal relatedness in social life 'interconnectedness'.

We have a dynamic view of social relations where embodiment, enselfment and emplacement refer to the necessary preconditions of social action. They are in this sense the 'pre-structures' of action. The social actor in these prestructural conditions is characterized by vulnerability and frailty, and social action takes place in a context of the precariousness of social institutions. This picture of social life might suggest a pessimistic model of society, somewhat related to the dilemma of Malthus's population theory in his 1798 *Essay on the Principle of Population* (1976). In the Malthusian world, life is precarious because the sexual drive to reproduce results in over-population where it is not restrained by morality, and hence famine, disease and warfare reduce population density. Because population outstrips food supply, human beings must live in misery.

This negative view of social conditions is, in our approach, offset by the necessary and always present interconnectedness of social actors, and by their sensuous capacities for resistance, innovation and change. This view of the social actor, as we have said, is compatible with the materialism of Marx in which human beings labour collectively to produce social life. Marx's view of praxis and human ontology emerged from his encounter with Ludwig Feuerbach's *The Essence of Christianity* of 1841 in which

Feuerbach had attacked the abstract idealism of Christian theology by celebrating the sensuous existence of humanity (Feuerbach, 1957). It was Feuerbach who on reading the medical materialism of Moleschott declared, punning on 'to eat' (*essen*) and 'essence' (*Essenz*), 'Man is what he eats'. Although these theological debates are now primarily matters of historical interest, Feuerbach's vision of the importance of our sensual existence should not be neglected (Wartofsky, 1977). As sensuous and practical agents, we are open to the ecstatic possibilities of the shared life. The structure of social action is organized around the dynamic of scarcity and solidarity.

While we start our account of sociology in terms of social action, we agree with Durkheim's definition of sociology in *The Rules of Sociological Method* as the science of institutions (Durkheim, 1958). Sociologists are interested in the shape or pattern of social actions and the conditions under which they take place. Durkheim, in *De la méthode dans les sciences* of 1909, declared that the three principal branches of sociology were the study of religious, legal and economic institutions (Traugott, 1978). One can see how Durkheim selected these institutions to illustrate his notion of social facts, that is institutional structures that are independent of individuals and exercise normative constraint over their actions. Our study of society is also organized around an interest in what we call 'the institutions of normative coercion' and we have attempted to illustrate these arrangements through reference to religion, law and medicine. These institutions exert a normative organization over action at the micro level and in this respect they are not unlike Michel Foucault's notion of governmentality – the micro regime of normative regulation and production of social life. These institutional norms are an important part of the conditions of social action.

However, we are also aware that in contemporary society globalization and the information revolution have brought about a radical transformation of society. The nation state that was the taken for granted in the context of social theory in the nineteenth century has been challenged by globalization and information technology. While we do not think that the sovereignty of the state has been removed by the globalization of the economy, these changes do raise profound difficulties for classical sociology. Our argument is however that our social action framework does provide an effective analytical paradigm for connecting everyday life to global society, especially through the notion of embodiment. Technological and industrial change has brought about a profound degradation of the environment, destroyed many aboriginal cultures, and compromised the authority of different civilizations through processes of standardization and McDonaldization. There is therefore an immediate connection between our embodiment and the globalization of environmental risk. Our emplacement as illustrated by the management of our urban garden connects us automatically with commercial exploitation through global horticulture. The planting of buddleias connects us to the extraction of booty from the Americas and the creation of a global economy, because 'Picturesque England' (Pevsner, 1955) has been an important part of the system of colonial power since Quaker merchants brought plants back to England from Pennsylvania and Virginia. These circuits of power and culture in the global system create a systematic linkage between the individual and society through embodiment and intensify the dynamic between vulnerability and precariousness. An understanding of the necessary connections between environmental politics, institutional precariousness and embodied vulnerability provides an analytical platform upon which ethics and politics can be reintegrated in modern sociology.

# 1

# DISCIPLINE

Our purpose in this book is to give a general account of sociology that places the embodiment of human beings at the centre of social theory. Although there has been a considerable amount written on the body in the last twenty years, the importance of the issue of embodiment is still often obscured or misunderstood in the literature. A focus on human embodiment leads, through an understanding of human sensuousness and vulnerability, to a defence of universalistic human rights and thus, to a critical social theory. By defending a foundational theory of the human body, we attempt to furnish sociology with a powerful perspective on our humanity and on human rights.

Our argument is obviously influenced by Martin Heidegger's thought on care, being and his critique of technology. Heidegger borrowed central aspects of his phenomenology from Husserl. Husserl attempted to isolate fundamental and constant features of being in response to the challenge of historicism which, in its most extreme form, read everything as historically determined. Heidegger recast features of Husserl's phenomenology and presented it as a new ontology of being. We share this concern with isolating fundamental and constant features of being, and argue:

1   Being in the world is always sensual, since anxiety, pleasure and frailty always require our sensual engagement with life. Marxian sociology was right to set such store on the sensual foundation of labour. For Marx, labour is the means of self-expression and he correctly presented the urge to labour as a universal category of being human. But it is a Victorian conceit to privilege labour over all other categories of human experience. In this respect the conflation of labour with creativity in Marxian sociology is a mistake. Our original and inescapable relation to the world is one of openness. This is the cause of our vulnerability and our desire to impose control.

2   Being-in-the-world is always socially interconnected. Anxiety, frailty and pleasure can only be fully understood sociologically. The body is not a natural condition, but an accessory of society. The patterning of behaviour in individuals is fundamentally interconnected with social patterning.

3   There is always a tension between being and society, for we can never be entirely comfortable in the world. We require a collective response to the brutal material fact of human frailty, since we must depend upon

others in sickness, old age and at the hour of our death. Nor, as Freud (1936) argued, can the pursuit of pleasure be unregulated.

4   The political and economic solutions that attempt to unify being and society are unsatisfactory. None deals adequately with the problem of unintended consequences. As Weber understood, technological and cultural innovations which are intended to increase human happiness and security, have the unanticipated effect of posing new threats to humans, and in this way contribute to the tension between being and society.

Without wishing to minimize the importance of Heidegger for our argument, we ultimately reject his conservative approach to technology and politics in favour of a revised interpretation of culture and civilization in classical sociology. Further, we reject Heidegger's sense of frailty and sensuousness because, we hold, it was dominated by a masculinist paradigm. As an alternative, we outline an approach which is consistently sociological in that it is based in the recognition of human interdependence, the effect of inequalities of power, and the necessity to conceive of human activity in historical and processual terms. The consequence of this is a return to the roots of sociological theory.

The implicit argument in this framework is that the understanding of social relations depends significantly on a cluster of disciplines, in particular on sociology, economics and politics. These disciplines provide the substantive framework within which ethical debate can properly take place. To defend sociology against erosion by a culturalist or literary interpretation of society as a text, we also offer a defence of the idea of disciplinarity as a necessary foundation for knowledge before multidisciplinarity or inter-disciplinarity can occur. This study as a whole therefore is structured by two simultaneous debates – a defence of the discipline of sociology and an exposition of the connections between body, self and institutions.

### Intellectuals and politics

This intellectual programme for rebuilding contemporary sociology has to promote a particular view of the role of the intellectual in contemporary society. Bauman (1987) has provided a powerful analysis of the problem of the relationship between intellectuals, the state and culture. Said's (1994) work on intellectuals and representation is also important. Following Foucault, Said recognizes that the notion of intellectual neutrality is a myth. He argues that intellectuals occupy 'strategic locations' in relation both to the object of study and to the discursive formations which address the field, including the discursive formation to which they belong. In *Orientalism* (1978: 246) he noted the drift from 'an academic to an instrumental attitude' to social analysis. He links this with what he terms 'the seductive degradation of knowledge' (1978: 328).

Elias (1956) also recognized this problem with his cautionary analysis of 'involved' positions in sociology in which researchers are emotionally cathected to the object of study. He advocated the cultivation of detachment, and clarified what he meant by detachment in colloquial terms, as a 'standing back' from the object of enquiry. In our view, this is not much clarification at all. Elias crucially failed to present a methodology for achieving detachment. Moreover, the absence of political discussion in his work, together with his (1978b) championing of the sociology of Auguste Comte, has led some readers, perhaps wrongly, to conclude that he is, in methodological terms, a closet positivist (Layder, 1992).

Interestingly, Said (1993, 1994) also presents distance as a requisite of intellectual labour. He does not use the term 'detachment', but prefers the more emotive term, 'exile'. In the context of the postcolonial debate, Said's understanding of exile is that intellectuals must be both inside and outside the cultures in which they are located. Metaphorically, Said uses the concept to propose a preferred attitude in intellectual labour both to the object of study and to the traditions in which one is situated.

Critical sociology accepts the requirement for a degree of emotional distance from the object of enquiry in academic work and we also condone the recent defence that reflexivity is a proper aspiration for relevant sociology (Beck et al., 1994). The form of action theory that we are interested in defends the researcher's political engagement with the object of enquiry while placing the responsibility for reflexivity on the researcher's shoulders and, of course, on the shoulders of the wider research community in which the researcher is located. The term that best captures this for us is 'engaged detachment'. By this we mean an attitude to research which recognizes that intellectuals are citizens of societies and therefore have conscious and unconscious attachments to the human formations which they study. In addition, these attachments should be no less the subject of critical, detached scrutiny than the relations and processes that constitute the object of study. Our position is clearly a further reflection on Weber's notion of 'vocation'. While the value-neutrality argument is typically misunderstood to indicate that academics should remain remote from political involvement, we argue that his concepts of value-relevance and value-analysis described engaged detachment. Sociology is, apparently more than other social science and humanities disciplines, prone to fashion and intellectual crisis. These fashions in theory unfortunately obscure what we perceive to be the cumulative nature of sociological enquiry. As a response to the 'cultural turn', we recognize the cumulative achievements of substantial research on cultural history from Elias on the civilizing process, Bourdieu on the cultural field, and Sennett on public space and architectural culture. For us, the attempt to resecure the social also requires a particular political orientation, which we have termed 'engaged detachment'. If sociology is to survive as a viable discipline, it must provide public intellectuals with a detached perspective and engaged practices towards *communitas*.

## Postdisciplinarity as Postmodernity

Disciplinary boundaries and borders are changing rapidly under the impact of new information technologies, the postmodernization of culture, and above all the changing relationship between the university, the national culture and the nation state. These changes are in turn features of the emergence of a global economy and the globalization of culture. Post-disciplinarity corresponds to postmodernity, because the authority of disciplines is breaking down, and there is a fragmentation of knowledge. Notions of overarching paradigms and binding epistemology are now very much out of fashion. Academics have grown inured to the premise that a state of multiparadigmatic rivalry exists in the study of social and cultural life, and that nothing much can be done about it. This, together with the expansion of student numbers, has left its mark on pedagogy. At under-graduate level, flexibile knowledge has replaced cumulative knowledge, a concern with cultural relevance has overshadowed comparative and histori-cal study and the emergence in the British university system of the research exercise as a way of evaluating productivity has militated against long-term research because such research usually requires a long lead time before investigation can be translated into publishable findings. University curri-cula, at least in the social sciences and humanities, often resemble a super-market where concern with consumer sovereignty means that knowledge is served up on an academic smorgasbord.

Disciplinary coherence is the product of a dominant national culture which is confident in the authority of its own high culture. In 1869, writing of culture as the best that can be thought in a society, Mathew Arnold (1969) was able to assume the moral authority of English high culture and the role of intellectual as its spokesman and defender. Arnold could also propose that a strong national culture required a powerful state to impose its hegemonic force at home and abroad.

We now know that Arnold's confidence was a delusion. The fragmen-tation of modern cultures and the growing hybridity of national traditions have reinforced the feeling among public intellectuals, not only that there are no final vocabularies, but that all perspectives are partial. The rise of multiculturalism in the West imposes a significant detachment or decentring from one's inherited culture. Academics and other professionals often feel more connection with taste cultures which share their predispositions in other countries and faculties. The very idea of national disciplinary unity is now questioned – just visit any national annual conference of sociologists, or better still the meetings of the International Sociological Association, which occur every four years, to witness the limits of 'one world' thinking. While this thinking has considerable power at the rhetorical level, it is in no sense an accurate description of the current state of sociology. Postcolonial-ism has emphasized the hybrid character of the self-image of the West and the categories of classification and hierarchy underpinning Western government.

The intellectual context of English culture in relation to the rest of the world has changed radically since Arnold's day, and these changes impact significantly on a cluster of interrelated roles and institutions, in particular the state, the university, the economy and the intellectual. Like Mathew Arnold's response, our answer to these changes appears somewhat conservative. We hold that it now seems important to protect disciplinarity as a basis of study and research against postdisciplinarity as the final outcome of multidisciplinarity.

## Disciplinarity

We turn first to some definitional issues about disciplinarity. In Western cultures, the concept of 'discipline' has an inevitably religious connotation. In the traditional sense, a discipline may be defined as an organized perspective on phenomena which is sustained by academic training or the disciplining of mind. Like the related notions of cultivation and culture, a discipline requires disciplinary practices, and a rhetoric of competence, if a certain type of mentality is to be sustained over time among a community of scholars. Disciplines of mind and body within a monastic context were, in Michel Foucault's sense, technologies of the soul. Some disciplines appear to be less concerned with the transmission of a body of knowledge than with a set of methodological practices, such as an ethnographic imagination. In some cultures, such as Buddhism, these intellectual or spiritual disciplines more explicitly involve the disciplining of bodies. A fundamental discipline is one which provides the basis for a cluster of applied or interdisciplinary fields. Following Pierre Bourdieu, we argue that these practices of knowledge are constituted by power relationships and social structures within the academy. The rise and fall of disciplinary regimes is the consequence of powerful alliances which marshal the distribution of rewards within a field of academic practice. Disciplines are periodically fragmented and dispersed by internal intellectual struggles and by external conflicts with adjacent disciplines. Some disciplines – homoeopathy or astrology – are never fully accepted into the academy, while certain areas of study – Soviet studies – may disappear. Disciplines through internal specialization – human and physical geography – may fragment and divide, and as a consequence disciplines which are held together by the requirements of an external professional body may be more resistant to internal fragmentation.

‹ Sociology has enjoyed neither the professional benefits (and limitations) of external regulation nor the comfort of internal disciplinary coherence. Sociology has struggled to gain acceptance in the academy, with elite universities still having an ambivalent view of its relevance. The discipline has been fragmented by paradigmatic rivalry, which at times made some sociology departments resemble a field of internecine warfare. Disciplines are obviously artificial constructs; they are not naturally occurring intellectual divisions which refer to divisions of the mind. They are socially constructed perspectives constituting a particular slice of reality and as such they can always be either reconstructed or deconstructed. Disciplines can also be merged or integrated with related fields to construct, for example, interdisciplinary studies. A sociology of knowledge is necessary to study and understand them.

As we have just indicated, while Soviet studies has largely disappeared from the university system, European studies is a growing area of teaching and research. Women's studies, while often claimed by radical feminists to be a discipline, in fact consists of multidisciplinary studies rather like the social sciences. Talcott Parsons's analysis of the four subsystems of the social system (the famous AGIL formulation) was an attempt to provide an intellectual justification for the particular configuration of disciplines in the Harvard interdisciplinary programme on social institutions (Parsons, 1951). It attempted to show how economics, sociology, social psychology and politics could be complementary disciplines in the social sciences. A cluster of related disciplines traditionally forms a faculty, of which historically there are only two – the arts and science. Finally, a set of faculties forms a university as an institution which seeks to offer a universal education in human knowledge of the world through the enforcement of discipline.

### Companionship (*socius*) and bread (*panis*)

Classical sociology emerged as an intellectual response to economic theories of society and ethical worries about the effects of population growth. Its early formulation of class analysis, its development of theories of social change and its understanding of cultural phenomena were responses to the limitations of economic theory. In particular, sociology denied that marginal utility theory was an adequate explanation of human motivation or an adequate account of value. Early studies of religion were attempts to understand magic and religion without assuming that they represented faulty versions of utilitarian rationality.

Similarly, Chadwick's interventions into public health in the 1830s and 1840s focused on delivering health to the expanding urban-industrial centres. The fight against physical pollution was often reconceptualized as a war against moral pollution. In this sense, the first management-oriented sociologies were fully cognizant of the problem of difference. They merely treated it as something to be purified (Stedman Jones, 1971). This, in turn, created a whole series of critical debates about the proper ethical limits of intervention. Sociology emerged as the study of companionship (*socius*), and companionship indicates the importance of sharing resources such as bread (*panis*) if fellowship is to be sustained. Sociology's preoccupation with the symbolic realm of human culture, namely religion in its broadest significance, has been based on a concern to understand how social bonds are formed and sustained, despite rather than because of economic exchange. Sociology was 'conservative' only in the sense that it regarded industrial capitalism as a threat to the possibility of community.

The study of companionship was also the study of brothers and sisters and communities and strangers, friends and foes, specialists and amateurs. Because sociology had to come directly to terms with the divisive effect of social values, and the inclusionary and exclusionary boundaries of companionship, it was unusually prone to registering difference in its methods and theoretical propositions. Borrowing from Bourdieu (1986), it is appropriate to interpret the paradigmatic rivalry in sociology as an expression of competing taste cultures. For example, Durkheim's emphasis on *collective conscience* and *collective representations* was not only an attempt to expose the limitations of economic essentialism, it was also an attempt to rebut the Kantian notion of the individual. Durkheim saw himself as standing in the Enlightenment tradition of creating a scientific understanding of society that would rise above what he regarded as the obscurantism of philosophy and the misplaced concreteness of economics. In doing so, he created a distinctive taste culture in sociology, which privileged 'social facts' in sociological study.

Weber did not explicitly set out to create an antithetical tradition to the Durkheimian influence. However, his emphasis upon casual adequacy and 'rendering intelligible' subjective meaning opened up a contrasting modern tradition of studying the social. It was one which revived aspects of Kantian thought.

In general terms, sociology as a discipline has been concerned with the relationship between two dimensions of human collectivities, namely scarcity and solidarity. It recognizes that scarcities, which are predominantly economic and political aspects of society, are inescapable features of all human existence, and that somehow societies have to cope with and respond to scarcity. Scarcity does not disappear with increasing economic prosperity, because paradoxically it exists amongst plenty (Bataille, 1991). As prosperity increases, new goods became desirable, and hence they become scarce. The development of social arrangements to cope with scarcity is mundane and ubiquitous. For example, the formation of a queue is a basic response to scarcity, because it sets up an orderly method of managing the limitation of a desirable good. However, the precise nature of the queue has important cultural components: is the principle first come, first served, or the elderly and the needy to the front, or the strongest to the front? How do we get people to accept and enforce queuing as a legitimate solution to scarcity? Alongside the fact of scarcity, sociologists have argued that society needs some level of social order if it is to survive. The question of solidarity has been a specifically sociological interest, and it is this analysis of social order which has driven sociologists into an exploration of the functions of language, symbolic systems, communication and values, namely culture.

### Sociology as a discipline

It is important for sociology to retain a concern for the dynamic tensions between scarcity and solidarity. An emphasis on questions relating to scarcity often leads to an accusation of 'economic reductionism', whereas the opposite emphasis on solidarity raises objections about a conservative bias or even 'idealism'. Sociology as a discipline can function effectively as the scientific study of society when it is concerned to probe the contradictions, ambiguities and tensions between scarcity and solidarity, that is between patterns of inequality and relations of co-operation. The Marx–Weber dialogue was beneficial to the rise of sociology because it explored these paradoxes of social struggle and co-operation in the period of the development of European industrial capitalism. The debates about status and class, religion and capitalism, ideology and knowledge, intellectuals and hegemony, and sociology and political economy can in retrospect be seen as explorations of the scarcity/solidarity dichotomy. In this respect, the analysis of social citizenship can be seen as at least one outcome of this legacy, because in T.H. Marshall's formulation citizenship mediates between scarcity (in the form of class inequalities) and the need for solidarity (in the redistribution of resources to contain class conflict and promote social solidarity). The result of those debates was a rich legacy of theories, concepts, methodologies and empirical findings which constituted sociology as a discipline.

Parsons's structural functionalism has often been criticized for its conservative bias, as a sociology which explained social order by reference to shared values and as a result neglected issues relating to scarcity. This criticism is somewhat misleading and exaggerated, because in fact Parsons's account of the social system was an attempt to understand two crucial dimensions of any society, namely the dimensions of allocation and integration. The allocative function required an analysis of how scarce resources are distributed; the integrative function, of how social integration is secured. In the allocative functions there were political decisions about the ends or goals of society, and economic decisions about how, within the political framework, society can produce goods and services. In the integrative function, there is the motivation of individuals to achieve necessary goals and objectives, and finally there is the need to maintain values and norms to resolve social conflicts and tensions. This scheme was intended both to produce an interdisciplinary programme and to defend sociology as a discipline within the action frame of reference. The specific task of sociology within social systems theory was to understand how values contribute to maintaining social solidarity through an analysis of action. According to Parsons's principle of voluntary action, people make choices between different courses of action with respect to scarce resources in terms of values and norms.

The Parsonian solution to the relationship between scarcity and solidarity was never entirely successful. The Parsonian paradigm was heavily attacked by so-called conflict theory, which claimed that Parsons's sociology neglected issues to do with scarcity such as class structures and inequality. With the breakup of the influence of Parsonian sociology after his death in 1979, no paradigm has emerged as dominant and in the postwar period there have always been various trends in sociology (symbolic interactionism, ethnomethodology, conflict sociology, rational choice theory and so forth) which have sought to correct the (alleged) problems of the Parsonian paradigm. There have also been attempts to restore a Parsonian approach in the form of neo-functionalism (Alexander, 1985). The failure of sociology to resolve these intellectual disagreements has produced further fragmentation and uncertainty. Indeed with the rise of postmodernism and cultural studies, there have been arguments to suggest that the very concept of 'the social' was historically limited. The practice now is to accept that we live in a world of multiparadigmatic complexity and to abandon theoretical interest in universalism.

The implication is that the end of 'the social' is also the end of sociology. However, to put our own stress on the importance of a comparative and historical approach into practice, we should note here that, in some respects, the crisis of English literary studies in American universities has been far more profound than in British and Commonwealth universities. In America during the Cold War, a unified curriculum for literary studies was important, to differentiate Western from Soviet culture. With the collapse of the 'communist menace', American literary studies as a coherent university programme began to fall apart. Again, we are reminded of the pitfalls of establishing disciplinarity around cultural relevance. The emphasis on multiculturalism and the recognition of difference ruled out any normative or canonical curriculum. The impossibility of a unitary programme of literary studies created an academic vacuum which was quickly and effectively filled by cultural studies. The study of media, communication and culture became dominated by a power/knowledge problematic which, with one or two notable exceptions, was explored almost exclusively first at a textual level and later at a digital level. These disciplinary changes also need to be seen within the context of a growth in the corporatization and commercialization of the university system. Literary studies does not sit easily within a university system which needs to generate significant injections of investment funding from private industry. By contrast, cultural studies can claim to have some relevance to the growth of the communications and consumer industries.

In a period of state intervention in the regulation of the economy and the creation of a welfare state, the discipline of sociology could legitimately claim to have relevance to the creation and professional development of policy analysts, civil servants and professional workers in the service sector. During the 1960s Marshall's theory of social citizenship provided an intellectual framework for both social policy and social work. It was an obvious bridge between Weberian sociology and applied social science. With the erosion of a centralized welfare state and the growth of neo-liberalism, there has been a marked departure from social Keynesian policies, with the result that the traditional place of sociology with respect to training in social policy has been undermined. With the spread of cultural studies and the decline of centralized welfare policies, sociology has often become subsumed under 'social theory' and/or 'cultural studies' as a general or liberal education.

Much contemporary sociology that is concerned with the analysis of cultural institutions is unsatisfactory because 'reading' all social relations as cultural relations, apart from its other difficulties, leaves out the tensions between scarcity and solidarity, being and society, as the intellectual terrain on which the social sciences function. Cultural studies has marginalized not only the questions traditionally addressed by Marxist political economy, but also Weberian sociology as a general framework for the analysis of patterns of scarcity and solidarity.

We can define Weber's principal analytical interests as the problem of scarcity (especially a scarcity of meaning with secularization), the political scarcity of resources (which underlies the division between class, status and power), the sources of social solidarity in common religious systems, and finally the problem of social change within a dynamic of scarcity and solidarity. Rationalization can be interpreted as a process which attempts to resolve the historical problem of scarcity and solidarity through secular regulation. These political-economy dimensions in both Marx and Weber are lost in cultural studies, which we can criticize as apolitical culturalism.

There is a case for defending the legacy of Marx and Weber in classical sociology, and further, a need to defend the ideas of theoretical cumulation and social intervention. However, this argument has been marginalized by the cultural turn, because the study of society has been eclipsed by the study of culture. Because in modern societies culture is diversified into multiculturalism there is a greater sense of the hybridity of modern cultural forms. Because there cannot be an authoritative or unified culture, we need to protect and respect different cultures, especially those which are perceived to be threatened or at risk from stronger cultural traditions.

This argument in its own terms is perfectly valid, but by implication it also argues that morality is fragmented and relativized. It does not begin to think its way out of the impasse implicit in terms like 'ambivalence', 'difference' and 'self-reflexivity'. Instead it celebrates these conditions as self-ordaining boundaries of the field. Students are left wondering precisely what ethical values are being defended and what politics is being advocated. Too often, the debate around multiculturalism ends in utopian and pious declarations of 'one world' imperatives and 'rainbow coalitions' between identity groupings. These coalitions are sociologically unconvincing because they recognize that identity is nuanced around difference, without locating a compelling basis for achieving transcendence or principles of care for the vulnerable. Durkheim's injunction that social facts exist, and that they possess 'priority', 'externality' and exercise 'constraint' over individual choice and action, already provides a sociological basis for rejecting cultural relativism. Durkheim believed that social facts were the distinctive objects of sociological study. The discipline was ultimately founded on them.

In a period when multidisciplinary cultural studies have flourished, arguments in favour of disciplinary training must appear (and are) inherently conservative. We submit that there are at least four critical responses to contemporary multidisciplinarity. The first is that multidisciplinarity must presuppose strong disciplines as the foundation for cross-disciplinary co-operation. The second is that multidisciplinarity is in fact weak interdisciplinarity, because it makes no assumptions about what might be appropriate combinations of study. Thirdly, multidisciplinarity is perfectly compatible with the McDonaldization of the university curriculum, because it suggests that in a perfect world of borderless multidisciplinarity everything is compatible with everything else. Fourthly, multidisciplinarity makes a virtue of eclecticism and what appears on the curriculum is often what is calculated to attract students, rather than to reflect fruitful, or potentially fruitful combinations of knowledge and research traditions.

The disciplinary basis of the social sciences is worth defending on the grounds of cumulative depth and progression through a body of knowledge. Sociology makes an important contribution to the study of scarcity and solidarity in modern societies. To remain a discipline it requires an awareness of, and commitment to, the pecularities of its own historical tradition.


## Postmodernism and the cultural turn

In social theory postmodernism has been a critical challenge to the reigning rationalist epistomologies of the social sciences and the humanities which continue to assume an objective world which can be understood by neutral, rational inspection. The major issue in this critical debate has been the nature of representation. Postmodern theory has been significantly influenced by developments in literary studies and critical studies within which the idea of deconstruction and social construction have been major elements. These deconstructionist techniques attempt to show, for example, that the devices which are employed implicitly in writing philosophy and science are as methodologies no different from texts in fiction or imaginative writing. Barthes (1970, 1975), who was in many respects an important forerunner of postmodernism, even suggested that there is an equivalence between the reader and the writer. He went on to denounce language as 'fascist', in the sense that it is impregnated with ideological presuppositions (Calvet, 1994). The result was to boost the significance of emotional responses and aesthetic judgement in social and cultural analysis. If no means of communication could be trusted, because all means of communication are ideologically impregnated, and if epistemology provides no basis for adjudicating between different positions, the only way that the

Hobbesian war of all against all can be avoided is by turning towards gesture, rhetoric and style in analysis and debate.

In practice there is little significant difference between postmodernism and poststructuralism as theories about reading the world of cultural objects. Deconstruction has been a critical technique closely associated with the work of writers like Jacques Derrida and Paul de Man, who have used deconstructive techniques to proselytize a new reading of language, philosophy and literature. The deconstructive approach to literary theory was, for example, also associated with feminist criticism which noted a strong patriarchal set of assumptions in literary theory within which men were the only source of literary talent.

In sociological theory, the postmodern turn first challenged the dominance of the so-called founding fathers of sociology (all of whom were obviously male). It moved on to suggest alternative approaches in sociology which use discourse analysis, critical literary methods and radical hermeneutics as approaches to the analysis of social texts. Postmodern social theory therefore tends to regard society as a social text which can be read using deconstructive methodologies. Postmodernists tend to argue that the data which sociologists attempt to make sense of (questionnaires, letters, archives, biographies, official reports, histories, criminal statistics and so forth) are in fact all texts. Sociology offers an interpretation (reading) of these social texts. It is not unlike literary analysis or hermeneutics (a science of interpretation). A postmodern defence of society as text claims that mainstream sociology has not learnt the lesson of modern theories of language and representation which have challenged the simplistic representational theory of language. Sociological research and sociological theory have to be read as texts within a framework of deconstructive techniques. The commitment to empirical research, a hallmark of classical sociology, has diminished because there is no agreement about the character of social reality or what constitutes 'proof' in any debate between positions.

Postmodern theories suggest that there are no universal meanings for concepts such as rights, corruption, community, *socius* or the self, but rather that the meaning of action and belief is deeply contextual and has to be understood within the context of local rather than global or universalistic categories. For example, different societies have very different approaches to the meaning and value of the human body. Monastic institutions denied the body; modern advertising celebrates the body. If postmodern theory could be read therefore as a radical hermeneutics, then this suggests at least that there might be a close relationship between the traditional anthropological approach to local knowledge and postmodern deconstructive techniques and Max Weber's notion of 'understanding' in sociological methodology. This relationship between local knowledge within anthropological and ethnographic approaches and postmodernism has been noted in the work of writers like Vattimo (1988), who says there is a profound crisis in postmodern culture which has negative (nihilistic) trends.

In recent years postmodernism has begun to have a major impact on anthropological theory and practice. Although writers like Richard Rorty have been tempted to regard postmodern anthropology as merely an extension of the interpretive anthropology of analysts like Clifford Geertz, postmodern anthropology advocates a more radical break with the past, suggesting that in the context of the decolonization of the third world, a new type of anthropology is required which is more systematically sympathetic to the needs and requirements of local cultures. A key text in this development of radical postmodern anthropology is Clifford and Marcus (1986). Traditional anthropology has been dominated by the quest to describe and understand the meaning of the cultures of native peoples. Radical, postmodern anthropology suggests that you can only understand these cultures in their own, local, contextual terms. This approach throws in doubt the possibility of universal values or institutions. Meaning is local, and therefore cannot be generalized.

The attempt to defend and develop a postmodern ethnography has been challenged by philosophers like Ernest Gellner (1992). Gellner treats postmodernism as merely a modern version of traditional forms of relativism: he sees it as a movement in anthropology which gives a special emphasis to the local, contextual and textual importance of meaning. For Gellner, postmodernism challenges any universalistic notion of knowledge, and so he concludes that we can criticize and reject postmodern forms of relativism on the same grounds that he has rejected classical relativism, namely that it is a contradiction in terms. Any claim for relativism would itself be relativistic and therefore open to doubt, criticism and finally rejection.

It is important to recognize that there is a light-hearted almost frivolous form of postmodernity which enjoys challenging what it regards as the serious and sombre nature of rational universalistic modernism. Postmodernists enjoy the challenge represented by ironic criticism. A primary illustration of this approach is to be found in the work of Jean Baudrillard, who has argued that the traditional forms of representation and understanding have been destroyed by the development of mass society and mass culture based upon advanced forms of electronic communication. He suggests that the social has imploded as a consequence of the velocity and density of modern communications. Because the social is dead, the traditional forms of representing it in the social sciences are hopelessly obsolete. Much of Baudrillard's own work assumes a very poetic style of argumentation and presentation, utilizing irony, parody, provocation and allegory as principal means of discussion. This approach is well illustrated by two of his influential works on America (Baudrillard, 1989, 1990). Both adopt the ironic argument that American society is utopia realized, and that the aimlessness and hopelessness of American culture is a product of the very success of the American democratic revolution.

Baudrillard's work is clearly controversial, especially his argument that the Gulf War was merely a media event, yet his approach to social theory has proved to be influential in the elaboration of a postmodern position (Rojek and Turner, 1993). Baudrillard's most significant argument is probably that contemporary society and culture are simply simulations and that the realities that stood behind modern society have evaporated in the welter of advertising and promotion which typifies modern life. For example, in con-temporary film, fictional representation, documentary footage and actual history are often blended in a way which confuses the line between reality and representation (Denzin, 1991). Of course the advertising industry is well aware of the arguments in the social sciences that advertising produces a simulation of reality. Contemporary advertisements are often conscious of the use of parody and have become highly self-referential in their approach to customers. Competition in the soft drinks market for a teenage audience has produced even more explicit, self-conscious, self-reflexive sexual imagery relating to the mouth (Falk, 1994).

### Globalization

The debate about postmodern methods in anthropology has indicated a significant context of postmodernization: namely the tensions between the process of the globalization of culture and local resistance to both Westernization and globalization. The postmodern debate in methods and theory can be seen as a consequence of a set of broad changes in world culture which has been described in terms of globalism and globalization (Robertson, 1992; Turner, 1994c). At one level, the process of globaliza-tion simply means that the world is more systematically connected together. The bonds of connection include contemporary processes of electronic transformation and communication of information; the development of a world economy; the emergence of world systems of military communication and defence; the growth of global legal arrangements such as the human rights movement; the development of a world system of tourism; and the elaboration of intellectual communication between universities brought together within a system of global education.

There is little to object to in the argument that economic growth, mass transport systems and telecommunications have combined to increase connectivity between nations and social actors. At a more controversial and profound level globalization refers to a change in consciousness, parti-cularly the awareness of societies of their involvement in the process of globalization and the impact of globalism. Globalization therefore relates to the forms of self-reflexivity which have been discussed by Giddens and Beck. Globalism is self-reflexivity of the world as 'one world'. Globalism undermines assumptions, forcing communities to interpret and understand their own identity. For example, North American native tribes typically referred to or called themselves 'The People'. Globalization forces modern communities to realize that they are (at best) 'a people' or merely 'some people', not with capital but lower-case letters.

The paradox of globalization is that it is closely and inevitably connected with consciousness of localism and localization. That is, the globalization of culture threatens the very existence of local practice and belief, which become engulfed in a unifying process of cultural integration. The need to defend localism is a response to the impact of cultural globalism, particularly through such processes as tourism and multinational investment. The attempt to protect local knowledge, culture and practice is thus associated with anthropological postmodernist and hermeneutic emphasis on textuality, locality and indigenous meaning. It immediately establishes cultural relevance and appears to demonstrate in compelling ways what is at stake in the politics of cultural domination and resistance. Indeed, the process of globalization within religious and intellectual systems has given rise to a strong nationalist local and indigenous response. For example, within fundamentalist Islam there is a strong movement which is referred to as the Islamization of knowledge. This can be seen as a response to globalization and the integration of Islam as a local culture into a world system.

The processes of decolonization have produced a variety of critical responses to imperial culture and authority. For example, within the Indian sub-continent there has been a profound reaction against the dominance of (English) literary studies, which has imposed a Western canon of literature on Indian culture. The decolonization of literature has involved a critique of this canon, an emphasis on the value of local literary traditions, and the evolution of alternative forms of literary expression (Rajan, 1992). This decolonization of literature was associated with a broader rejection of Western claims to universalism in the work of Edward Said, specifically in his critique of Orientalism (Said, 1978) and imperialism (1993). These critical movements in cultural theory are closely related to the debate about postmodernism because they have one basic characteristic in common: a critical rejection of the idea that Western forms of representation and reasoning can be construed as a global or universalistic discourse embracing human culture as a whole. Just as postmodernism has rejected the idea of the legitimacy of the 'grand narrative' (Lyotard), so subaltern studies and other forms of decolonizing protest have rejected the legitimacy of the Western grand narrative to determine cultural hierarchies and cultural authenticity. The critical literature of decolonization claims that the local tradition has the same stature and value as the imperial tradition which assumes global significance, because imperial power has been able to impose its autonomy.

To summarize, postmodernism as a theoretical movement has challenged the dominance of traditional canons of knowledge. Specifically, patriarchal and class-based canons of knowledge have been undermined. Further, it has disrupted cultural hierarchies by mixing high culture and kitsch, and neutralized the authority of traditional reason by a variety of literary strategies such as irony, simulation, provocation and parody. These theoretical strategies of course reflect much of the transformation of modern culture within which the mass media have indeed mixed together various forms of culture to present a cocktail of cultural taste, habit and attitude.

Postmodern theory also reflects a significant change in the social authority and status of intellectuals within the cultural market place. Throughout the academic world there is a profound sense of the crisis of the intellectual who has lost authority as a legislator over the authenticity of high culture (Bauman, 1987). The retreat of the sociologist from the public sphere is an example of this. In the 1970s and 1980s much of the advanced, cutting edge theory produced and discussed by sociologists was unintelligible to the general public. Sociologists began to sever their connection with the public sphere, which was the source of their hard-won status earlier in the century. Gouldner's (1970) pejorative description of 'newspaper sociology' was designed to show the limitations of instant analysis and topical cultural relevance. In many respects, newspaper sociology anticipated the negative traits in cultural studies and decorative sociology that we have described above. In the ferment of expansion in student numbers in the 1960s and early 1970s, Gouldner's minatory analysis was unheeded. It was only in the late 1990s that it became all right to talk about comparative and historical exerience again. The acclaim given to Castells's (1996, 1997, 1998) trilogy is perhaps a measure of the frustrations within the discipline with the pre-eminence of postmodernism. Sociologists celebrated the fact that, at last, someone was writing about something 'real' again, and with an impressive quantity of comparative and historical data to back up the argument.

The roots of postmodernism lie in the intellectual crisis of Western Marxism. Central to this crisis was the collapse of communism and the intellectual ossification of feminism. Both of these movements claimed advantage over other approaches on the basis of rigorous materialist analysis of social and economic conditions. After 1968 both fell foul of apparently irrevocable materialist realities. Proletarian revolution never occurred in Western societies. Where it did happen, *contra* Marx, it was as the aftermath of mass warfare or as the consequence of imperialist forces. This absence of class-driven revolution in Western capitalism raised doubts about the validity of Marxist historical materialism both as a scientific theory of socio-economic change and as a form of political practice. The dominant ideology thesis was challenged (Abercombie et al., 1980) on the grounds that the evidence of ideological/cultural hegemony was weak, and that the emphasis on ideology was actually incompatible with Marx's notion of historical materialism.

Feminism revolutionized understanding of power and subjectivity. It opened up the themes of marginality, difference and sexual identity; it also connected significantly with debates in decolonization and subaltern studies, which became decisive in the formation of postcolonialism. Yet it never achieved the transcendence it promised. One strain within radical feminism regarded male involvement in *any* aspect of theorizing or practising gender as intrinsically suspect. This tendency produced a largely fruitless impasse in feminist responses to the Foucauldian view of power and the micro-politics of difference articulated under postmodernism. The theory of patriarchy became a stale and repetitive analysis of hierarchical power. Feminism reacted to rather than provided new paradigms in the emerging areas of the sociology of the body (Turner, 1984) and the sociology of the emotions (Barbalet, 1998). While some feminists embraced Foucault's emphasis on micro-politics they rejected his analysis of the crisis in radical politics as over-pessimistic. Feminism still retained a conviction in the necessity of social transcendence, but is not convincing about the levers of change.

However, Foucault's emphasis on the arbitrary 'order of things' clearly struck a chord with many feminists. In particular it was influential in the work of feminist writers who struggled to recast the concept of heteronormativity in response to the challenge of subjectivist approaches such as queer theory. This produced a new set of fissures among feminists. More widely, generational divisions emerged. Younger feminists, who had grown up with the postmodern emphasis on fragmentation, diversity and identity politics, became increasingly disillusioned with the *dirigiste* mentality of the 1960s and 1970s generations who dominated feminism in the academy. Few feminists today postulate woman as a 'universal collective subject'. The work of Butler (1990), Braidotti (1991) and hooks (1991) suggests a new form of 'decentred' feminism which embraces aspects of the postmodern and practises the politics of ambivalence. This left the agenda and common ground in feminism more disputed than ever before.

A sense of frustration with the difficulty of answering the question 'What makes a social theory a feminist social theory?' emerges with clear force in Jacqueline Stevens's (1998) recent review essay in which she rejects the possibility of a unitary feminist agenda and recognizes the possibility that 'feminist theory seems to be dead'. Although the notion that feminist theory is dead or moribund is obviously rhetorical, we hold that the 1970s version of radical feminism is incontrovertibly in disarray. The cuts in British higher education funding during the Thatcher–Reagan years condemned the new generation of postfeminists to the margins, as casualized academic labour. In their eyes, it highlighted the privileged positions of older feminists who had gained tenure in the 1970s and 1980s.

Generalization here is dangerous. However, the underlying common theme of postmodern theory is, following Lyotard's analysis of the postmodern condition, that the notion of authoritative grand traditions of theory is no longer tenable. Further, the attribution of authority is often a mark of privilege over subjection, instead of veridical pre-eminence. There is a parallel here with decorative sociology. It borrowed from Foucault the idea that culture is constituted by the power/knowledge dichotomy. This had a dual effect. First, it problematized the distinction between the centre and the margins in social and political thought. Gitlin (1995) argues that the margins became the centre. The result is that cultural politics became obsessed with nomenclature and issues of positioning. This obsession reinforced the tendency to analyse all human life in terms of texts and intertextuality. The fascination with liminality and borders is an important identifying characteristic of decorative sociology, but the 'centre' becomes curiously amorphous and implausible in direct proportion to the expenditure of analysis on the excluded and the marginal. For example, the Orientalist debate turns on a conceptualization of the Occident which sets up a false conceptual dichotomy by skating over the split-subject distinctions in each polar category (Said, 1978; Spivak, 1990, 1993; Bhabba, 1994). Said in his later work (1993, 1994) has attempted to distance himself from the dichotomy by proposing that there is an indissoluble gap between representation and its putative object. So that, for example, in analysing 'Orientalism' it is not necessary to posit the existence of a concrete actual object. However, to allow for this much slippage between representation and its putative object is to introduce a degree of generosity into analytical propositions which makes judgement between positions impossible. As Young (1991) notes, if Said is saying that true representation is impossible, upon what basis is he criticizing the Orientalists? This dilemma was particularly acute in *Covering Islam* where Said criticized American journalists for their superficiality and lack of understanding, which distorted the complex nature of Islamic reality. The implication is that misrepresentation of politics in international journalism could be resolved by improvements in journalists' education (Turner, 1994c). In his defence, we should note that Said (1991: 5) rejected simple deconstructive strategies and affirmed

> the connection between texts and the existential actualities of human life, politics, societies and events. The realities of power and authority – as well as the resistances offered by men, women, and social movements to institutions, authorities and orthodoxies – are the realities that make texts possible, that deliver them to their readers, that solicit the attention of critics.

We would simply add that these connections between 'texts and the existential actualities of human life' are the stuff of empirical sociological research. They cannot be understood only and exclusively through the analysis of textuality.

## The University of postdisciplinarity

These changes in sociology as a discipline can only be understood against a larger background whose central feature is the changing nature of the relationship between the university and the national culture. The historic alliance between scientific knowledge and the state of the late seventeenth century has been partially eroded by globalization and the fragmentation of knowledge, with the result that universities can no longer articulate universalistic values. There is some justification therefore for believing that the postmodernization of knowledge has taken place, thereby intensifying traditional debates about the problem of the relativization of knowledge with the growth of multiculturalism. While this argument is convincing, we need to keep in mind the fact that the university has been, since its medieval foundations, fractured around a contradiction between nationalistic particularity and a commitment to more universalistic standards, and that this tension has if anything intensified with globalization.

In the medieval period, when the university typically worked in harness with the Church to articulate certain universalistic aspects of Western culture such as the use of Latin as the principal mode of academic and intellectual expression, the dominant elites shared a common culture that defined Western values. At the same time, the universities continued to provide a vehicle for regional, provincial and national values, languages and perspectives. The medieval corporate structure of universities recognized national communities of students, which had their own elections for leadership positions. The student bodies of the universities of Bologna and Padua, for example, were organized in terms of two national structures: *ultramontana* and *citramontana*. At Oxford, student 'nations' were organized in terms of northern (*boreales*) and southern (*australes*) students in which the river Trent was the borderline (Gieysztor, 1992).

This tension between national and cosmopolitan standards intensified with the rise of capitalism and the secular challenge to traditional Catholic belief and practice. The university came to serve as the main repository for national identity with the rise of the nation state and it came to provide the principal training ground for the bourgeois citizen and the new nationalistic basis for civil society. Although Latin continued to be taught and preserved within high culture, the university also functioned as a vehicle for establishing and defining specific national languages and national cultures. Traditional universalism declined in the eighteenth century. For example, professors were no longer selected from across Europe as the culture of *peregrinatio academica* was eroded. The professor who had been a member of the republic of letters 'became a *Nationalgelehrte*, the independent teacher became a civil servant [and] the teacher paid by fees became a salaried professor' (Vandermeersch, 1996: 252). One can see this development very clearly in smaller, more marginal European states such as the Netherlands, Sweden and Finland. Although universities in Scandinavia, for example, were articulated and shaped around the Humboldt reforms which had been successful in creating the modern national university in Germany, certain departments such as language and ethnographic studies were crucial in collecting, defining and specifying national standards of language and custom.

In the Netherlands universities were crucial in preserving the nation through the production of dictionaries and the creation of associations to maintain the language. The national language was fundamental in securing a cultural bond for the distinct and separate provinces (Brachin, 1985). Universities thus function within an international context to define local cultures through the maintenance of minority languages and the creation of national ('imaginary') communities. This issue was particularly important in Finland where ethnographic studies of poetry and the epics were crucial in consolidating the state around the nation. The Finnish Literature Society was founded in 1831 and the first volume of the *Studia Fennica* appeared in 1933. Such academic activities were crucial in preserving the ancient rune-singing traditions of the Finnish-Karelian culture and the recordings of the *Kalevala* poetry were significant in defining borders between Finland and its neighbours, partly because the *Kalevala* claim to record a culture that is pre-Christian and mythical (Siikala and Vakimo, 1994).

Of course, the university also had a key sociological function in producing and consolidating a national elite. It is well known that in the class structure certain universities have always been crucial in recruiting, training and cultivating the dominant elite of the nation and from this elite the principal personnel of the state bureaucracy, the Church and industry have been recruited. This sociological function, for example, has been particularly important in the case of Great Britain where traditionally the universities of Oxford and Cambridge have produced the entire upper echelons of the civil service and have been the principal recruiting grounds for government leaders and Church dignitaries (Kelsall, 1955). Even British spies have tended to have a degree from either Oxford or Cambridge! In modern Japan, despite the overtly competitive nature of the examinations system, membership of elite universities provides students with almost automatic entry into the upper rungs of the business, financial and administrative elites (Wolferen, 1990: 84–5).

The globalization of industrial and cultural production has challenged the traditional role and function of the university as the cradle of humanistic and universal values. We might note that in particular the global communication system has required a sudden and rapid growth in so-called 'symbolic analysts' (Reich, 1991) who are the key actors in the production of symbolic knowledge, information systems and the global technology which is the foundation of the new media cultures. We can assume that these symbolic analysts will be highly mobile within the global system and that their commitment to particular nation states or corporations will be minimal because their social and geographical mobility precludes emotional or rational commitment to any particular corporation. In one sense, it is in their interests to be disloyal in the long term. The production of such symbolic analysts may not require the traditional patterns of university training. Indeed, the recent emphasis in universities on the idea of lifelong learning, mid-career development, reaccreditation and professional studies is closely associated with this sector of the labour market. The much discussed 'crisis in the humanities' and the commercialization of the arts curriculum (Duncan, 1995) appears to be intimately related to these significant changes in the labour market and the production of knowledge. Whereas the nineteenth-century university operating within the nation state produced individuals to function as national citizens, the new global universities, which may operate heavily via the world wide web, have no such particularistic location in national cultures or even within particular national corporations. One assumes that the new global university will not be committed, even implicitly, to such national formations.

Globalization has also recast traditional notions of fellowship and colla-boration. The first universities were monkish institutions in which strong collective ties of participating in the disinterested quest for knowledge and truth were prosecuted. The privilege of research often carried over into an intense sense of common identity and shared purpose. Very few depart-ments in the humanities and social sciences now offer this. As universities move into virtual forms of service delivery, using the internet to provide on-line lectures and seminars, the sense of the university as a haven for critical culture is likely to dissipate. Already, the net means that academics have closer relationships with colleagues in different continents than colleagues in their own corridors. The reason why the metaphor of the 'nomad' figures so prominently in discussions of contemporary intellectual life, is that global communication systems have largely freed many academics from the campus (Braidotti, 1994). Indeed, it is not unreasonable to propose that an informal division has emerged between research-active staff, who enjoy high levels of flexibility in work attendance, and non-research-active staff, who carry out the bulk of the teaching and administrative affairs in under-graduate programmes. This division has occurred because the modern university requires high profile academics to enhance the institution's cul-tural capital. In the marketization of knowledge and the decentralization of service delivery, the symbolic status of institutions in the academic pecking order is crucial. Institutions with big-name professors are likely to attract fee-paying students from around the world and to give vice-chancellors the sense that their institutions operate on a world scale of reputation and activity.

This globalization of culture appears to be associated with the separation of the nation state from high culture, a development that gives some credibility to the argument presented by Zygmunt Bauman (1987), namely that whereas intellectuals were the legislators of culture in the national university system, in the new market place they are merely interpreters of culture. Culture for Bauman is inextricably connected with power (hence his interest in the work of Michel Foucault). He regards intellectuals as important in guarding this power relationship. Culture in Bauman's soci-ology is the capacity to order, to separate and create boundaries. Power and culture are always endemic to all human situations in this structuring capacity. The crisis in the role of the public intellectual is associated with the growth of mass cultural markets which are somewhat disconnected from the university and thus from high culture (Ross, 1989). The post-modernization of culture is closely related to this hybrid culture where high, low and popular cultural forms become mixed in a cultural mélange within the media system. High culture, which at one time was firmly rooted in the national university system, is now challenged by a variety of cultural fragmentations, of which postmodernity is probably the most prominent. Following J.-F. Lyotard (1984), we can define postmodernism as simply a scepticism about 'grand narratives'. The university as the vehicle of the high culture of particular nations is now the target of such scepticism because in rhetorical terms it continues to defend grand narratives which have become partially dislocated from their national foundations.

In summary, the university appears to be caught within a well established contradiction between national cultures and cosmopolitanism, and between localism and globalism. These tensions in the political system have structured the debate between particularism and universalism. The contemporary globalization of culture has merely pushed these historic contradictions to a higher level, but within the modern global system we can see continuing struggles between national and cosmopolitan elites. One can already see, with the globalization of the university through the world wide web, the creation of a new type of intellectual who will be global and mobile, and thus not necessarily committed to any particular national system. This reinforces the importance of corporate culture. Transnational corporations have been adept at inspiring brand loyalty throughout the world. Their success has left many intellectuals sceptical about the possibility of intervention, let alone change, in the postmodern world. Postmodern irony, scepticism and distance may well come adequately to describe the mental outlook or worldview of such global intellectuals.

A defence of the idea of the university perhaps inevitably has a conservative flavour. A university involves a hierarchical principle of knowledge and a typically exclusive character. Its values of scholarship, of which discipline is essential, are not easily reconciled with popular democracy. Of course, the growth of a mass tertiary educational system in Europe after 1945 undermined much of the power of the traditional system of university hierarchies and the control of professors over that system was also undermined. Nevertheless, principles of selectivity and hierarchy remain. The move to widen accessibility still obeys limits defined by the universities themselves.


## Conclusion


As every schoolchild knows, sociology is the study of society. Its vitality suffers when the government defines social and cultural life in pluralistic terms. The absence of a state-directed welfare system with a strong commitment to social policy, privileges decorative tendencies because it rewards work which focuses on concrete group-related interests, and penalizes work driven by strong collectivist assumptions. Third way politics, which we shall examine in a later chapter, extols widescale social inclusion and super-reflexivity in politics, but severely underplays the disparity in wealth and power in society today. Its championing of liberty and equality recalls the inconsistencies in Crosland's (1958) articulation of democratic socialism. It is by no means clear that third-wayism has transcended them. Even so, Giddens (1998) is useful, because he has tried to break free from social theorizing to examine concrete, practical questions about what is necessary and feasible in social reorganization. In a later chapter we will discuss and compare Giddens's solutions with the work of Castells (1996, 1997, 1998).

For the moment, we wish to set out some reasons for praising disciplinarity. We argue that reviving disciplinary boundaries is one strategy for combating decorative tendencies. We identify four strengths of disciplinarity. First, it provides a common agenda to inform theory and research. Secondly, it generates a stable and cumulative programme of research. Thirdly, it refines a professional lexicon, whereas the decorative tendency has proliferated lexicons, often in contradictory and unhelpful ways. Fourthly, it creates a professional presence for sociology, which is important in ensuring that sociological work reaches government and business levels.

The greatest weakness of constructing disciplinary boundaries is that it may create an ostrich tendency in research and theory. This is, indeed, what we believe happened in the late 1960s and 1970s. Abstract theory and theory-free empiricism cut off sociologists from their natural constituency – that is, the people who make up society. We agree with Mills (1959), that sociology must be popular without being populist. By implication, we believe that ostrich-like tendencies did indeed develop in the discipline of sociology between the 1970s and mid 1990s. Sociology lost touch with the public. The recent interest in 'risk society' and citizenship has somewhat alleviated these tendencies. However, it has not eliminated them. If sociology is to survive it must establish a position of disciplinary boundaries which is both defensible and practical. We hold that the principles of scarcity and solidarity must be the foundation of such a position.

# 2

# ORGANISMS

Organisms, especially the human body, have historically provided a rich source of metaphors for describing and understanding social relations and social processes. Within Western cultures, this metaphorical use of organism as a description of social structures derived considerable analytical and ideological strength from the centrality of the notion of Christ's body as a description of the Church as the body of the faithful. The Eucharistic festival provided the means of entry into the body of Christ as the fabric and foundation of the Church in both this world and the next. The notion of a sacrificial meal provided Christian theology with a language of membership, authority and association. Indeed the very notion of an institution as a corporation demonstrates the robustness of the idea of the human organism as a theory of social relations. With the expansion of European trade and the growth of trading associations, this notion of the Church as the body of Christ was transferred to the secular business world, from which we have derived our understanding of the role and constitution of secular business corporations as functional associations of human beings for the purposes of trade and exchange. One problem for ecclesiastical discourse is that the orthodox metaphors of the Church as an organism were developed within a pastoral economy and it is difficult to translate these metaphors of authority (such as the Lamb of God) into a post-industrial civilization.

It is hardly surprising that the emerging discipline of sociology in the nineteenth century should have adopted much of this metaphorical language of social groups from the human body as a metaphor of membership. For example, sociology, especially under the influence of Social Darwinism, developed a robust organic analogy of social relations in the work of writers like Auguste Comte. The organistic school of sociology produced a complex theory of social organization in terms of structure and function, whereby the existence of an institution was explained by reference to its functional contribution to the survival of the whole.

This early formulation of functionalism was directly derived from nineteenth-century biological discussions of the evolutionary processes of the natural world. The structure of society was a systematic organization of institutions and roles that contributed to the survival value of the social organism through their functional interrelationships. The organic analogy sought to understand society in terms of the structure and function of living organisms.

The organic analogy was often contrasted with a mechanistic view of society, because the former treated society as a natural phenomenon existing independently of human intervention and planning, while the latter view conceived of society as a project of human construction. In turn the organic analogy was associated with conservatism, because it suggested that society could not be changed by political intervention. The so-called organic school of sociology was associated initially with the work of Herbert Spencer (1820–1895), but it has also been connected with more recent developments in American functionalism (Peel, 1971). This trend in social theory found its nineteenth-century fulfilment in the sociological works of Spencer, who laid the foundation for the view that societies as collective organisms develop or evolve through the evolutionary differentiation of their system parts, which contributes to their capacity for survival. With this sociological model, Spencer attempted to unite utilitarian individualism with an organic model of the development of social systems. Thus social systems, like other organisms, adapt to their environment by an evolutionary process of internal differentiation and integration. By applying this principle of the survival of the fittest to social systems, Spencer developed a historical model of social change that conceptualized human history as an evolutionary process from militant to industrial society. Herbert Spencer was one of the most influential British sociologists of the nineteenth century, but his work also had a strong attraction for American political ideologies, where it was used to defend both individualism and racial inequality. In turn, these views were closely associated with racial ideologies in the work of writers like Ludwig Gumplowicz and with Social Darwinism.

While in England and North America Spencer's evolutionary sociology became popular as a justification for social struggle and for racial inequality on the basis of the principle of the survival of the fittest, in France sociologists like Emile Durkheim also borrowed extensively from contemporary medical theory to formulate an understanding of social relations which embraced a medical version of the evolutionary organic analogy. Durkheim was particularly concerned with the nature of social solidarity and its maintenance in a society characterized by individualistic struggle and urban anomie. He developed a powerful view of the autonomy and independence of social systems conceptualized as organic entities which exist over and above the lives of the individuals who happen to comprise that collectivity. Despite this significant influence of medical theory, this aspect of Durkheim's sociological development has been somewhat neglected by commentaries. His contribution to the sociology of anomie was developed in his work on suicide and later in his contribution to sociology of religion.

Durkheim became famous for his distinction between mechanical solidarity – the forms of social solidarity found in primitive societies, where there exists a common set of beliefs and a consensus about social issues, and which is subsequently embedded in the *conscience collective* – and organic solidarity in advanced industrial societies, where social relations

depend increasingly on an extensive division of labour and the differentiation of social roles. Durkheim believed that the newly emerging industrial
society would require a set of institutions to mediate between the individual
and the state, if social chaos or anomie were to be avoided, or at least
contained. This work on social solidarity and anomie provided the basis
for his later writing on the negative consequences of social change as
manifested in such phenomena as suicide. Durkheim went on to conclude
his sociological investigations by drawing inspiration from the study of
Australian Aboriginal communities to provide a sophisticated understanding of religious belief and practice in the evolution of human societies.

In Germany we find an alternative form of this basic approach to social
relations in the work of Ferdinand Tönnies who established the now
famous distinction between community and association (*Gemeinschaft* and
*Gesellschaft*). This distinction continues to provide much of the core
sociological understanding of social organization. Societies characterized by
communal relations are thought to be based upon homogeneity, which is in
turn founded on kinship, organic ties and moral cohesion. By contrast
*Geselleschaft*, or association, refers to social relations which are based upon
individualism, heterogeneity, competitiveness and an extensive division of
labour. This distinction in the work of Tönnies was developed by Max
Weber in his general analysis of the sociology of social action to provide the
foundation for a division between traditional, emotional and rational
patterns of interaction. In turn this paradigm for the sociology of action
was further developed in America in the work of Talcott Parsons, who
established the notion of the 'pattern variables' to provide a synthetic view
of the relationship between emotions, rationality and individualism in social
relationships. These notions of association and community were fundamental to the work of Ferdinand Tönnies (1957), first published in 1887,
and were also fundamental to Max Weber's theory of social action, for
example in *Economy and Society* (1968), and in the subsequent work of
Parsons on the pattern variables (Robertson and Turner, 1991).

This historical sketch of the development of sociology in the nineteenth
and early twentieth centuries is hardly original. However, it does pinpoint
the importance of an underlying organic analogy of society and show how
the organic metaphor has been adapted and developed through a period of
a century of sociological theory and research. Against this conventional
account of the development of sociology as a discipline, we can observe that
the human body has remained a submerged dimension of sociological
theorizing and it is only recently that a genuine sociology of the body has
gained some level of acceptance in mainstream sociology. Instead prominence has been given to cognitive processes in the understanding of social
action and interaction, especially rational cognition in the understanding of
human action. The effect has been to negate the significance of embodiment
in the understanding of social relations.

In addition the organic analogy has obscured an important distinction in
the understanding of social institutions and social relations. We can

distinguish two notions of the organic analogy. The first is direct and obvious and involves a theoretical process of reification in which the metaphor of organ is transformed into the understanding of society as a concrete thing. Reification as a theoretic strategy denies the presence of a metaphor by treating society as a genuine organism. However, there is a more indirect and lesser use of metaphor in the notion of organizing as a necessary foundation.

In this chapter we wish to compare and contrast the notion of society as an organization and the idea of society as a collection of organizing principles. Both of these perceptions (organization and organizing) have an epistemological root in the notion of an organ but they have very different implications for social theory as versions of an organic metaphor. To treat society as an organization is somewhat to reify the notion of social relations. In contrast the notion of society as a collection of organizing principles is more solidly grounded in the idea of social action and inter-action as a fundamental basis of sociological theory. Finally, we wish to suggest that in order to understand organization and organizing as theor-etical approaches to social relations we should attempt to understand these two aspects of social theory in relation to a sociology of the body.

## Sociology as the study of companionship

Nineteenth-century social theory was profoundly motivated by the question: how is social solidarity possible, that is, how can the organic nature of social relations be preserved in an environment of competition and individualism? In short, sociology was concerned with the nature of social solidarity in an urban industrial capitalist environment. The term 'sociology' in its modern sense dates from the correspondence of Auguste Comte in 1824 and became more generally used in his *Cours de philosophie positive*. There is some agreement that sociology as a discipline should be seen as an intellectual response to the social changes brought about by the French revolution and the industrial revolution. It drew its intellectual inspiration from a limited number of fundamental concepts (sacredness, authority, ethics, power, community, and so forth) and so was influenced by both liberalism and conservatism (Nisbet, 1966).

Sociology can be said to have a profoundly nostalgic theme as a backward-looking reflection upon the basis of solidarity within traditional societies in a historical context of rapid industrialization and social change. The quest for community expressed this traditionalism in sociological thought that sought the roots of organic solidarity in the density of recipro-city within primitive or traditional society. The fascination with the primitive in early anthropology was likewise a nostalgic reflection upon the roots of human solidarity in premodern civilizations and primitive systems.

Within this paradigm, the human body and the organic analogy are clearly present. The term 'sociology' is itself intrinsically interesting, being composed of two stems: *socius* and *logos*. As we noted earlier, sociology is literally the scientific study of friendship or companionship and it should be recalled that the notion of companionship is derived from the Latin *panis* or bread. Companionship is the consequence of a shared meal of a reciprocity around a table where food is exchanged between people who trust each other because of shared involvement in a ritualistic community. This notion of the sacrificial meal as the foundation of society played an important part in the origins of the sociology of religion. Thus, writers like William Robertson Smith attempted to derive the meaning of religious beliefs and symbols from their social and cultural foundations in a primitive meal. Smith argued that in primitive societies there was no development of a professional stratum of priests and hence there was no systematic theology, but that religion was embedded in beliefs surrounding rituals and rights. Smith drew particular attention to the importance of the rituals of sacrifice because one of the most fundamental religious acts involved an exchange of goods between human beings and their gods, an exchange which took the form of a ritual meal. Within this totemic meal, the collective consumption of the sacred totem created a social bond between the individual and the divinity. These totemic meals illustrated the obligatory nature of religious rituals and social relations which served to bind the group together. Indeed the word *religio* itself indicated the function of binding together into a social group. Smith's analysis of religion in 1889 in his *Lectures on the Religion of the Semites* gave rise of course to the possibility that the central liturgical practice of Christianity, namely the Eucharistic meal, was itself the legacy of primitive totemic festivals wherein the 'savages ate their own God'. Smith's work drew attention nevertheless to the sociological functions of communion as a version of totemic integration. Here again we conceive the background assumptions about meals and sacrifices as the framework for an organic pattern of solidarity. This approach to the anthropology and sociology of primitive societies gave rise eventually to a debate about the importance of gift relations and exchange in the formation of social solidarity.

Against this development of an analysis of companionship and gift giving, sociology emerged as the study of the conditions that make social relations possible, or more fully, the study of the (affective) bonding of individuals into social relationships. Sociology can be technically defined thus as a science which attempts to comprehend and explain the formation and maintenance of patterns of social solidarity and consensus. Broadly speaking there are two approaches to this notion of social solidarity. First, there is exchange theory, which conceptualizes solidarity as a consequence of the endless exchanges or reciprocities between individuals seeking to satisfy their needs in a competitive environment. Secondly, there is an approach which gives greater emphasis to the shared values or culture which sustain such institutions as the family and the Church as pivotal agencies of the socialization of individuals into collective life. The notion that social solidarity depends upon shared values has given rise to the idea of a relationship between the individual and the social whereby the two processes of socialization and internalization guarantee some agreement between individuals in the maintenance of social order. Now the giving of gifts shows these two dimensions of social solidarity effectively, because an exchange of gifts illustrates the role of exchange relations in society as the foundation of social order, but the exchange of such gifts presupposes the existence of shared values in underpinning the notions of exchange and contract. One aspect of Durkheim's contribution to the development of sociological theory was to identify the so-called non-contractual element of the contract, that is the assumptions and values which lie behind a contract and which guarantee its authority and force.

## Scarcity

One dimension of this notion of exchange as the foundation of social solidarity is that exchange relations typically take place in a context of scarcity, that is, individuals seek solidarity and exchange in an environment where their needs cannot be immediately or wholly satisfied. Scarcity and solidarity emerge in sociology as the two dimensions of social stratification which have moulded and determined the development of social theory. We need therefore to complicate the definition of sociology as a science of solidarity by introducing more carefully the principle of scarcity into our account on the origins of sociology. We can note, as an opening obser- vation, that sociology is concerned with the idea of how solidarity is achieved (if at all) in a context of scarcity. 'Scarcity' is, from a common- sense point of view, an economic term. This commonsense notion suits our purpose rather well, because we can see sociology as a discipline which has an intrinsic rather than an accidental relation to economics.

If sociology has been traditionally concerned with the analysis of social solidarity, we can assert that economics is a science of scarcity. Economics is concerned with economizing behaviour in a context of scarcity brought about by the competitive struggle of individuals in markets over the allocation of limited resources. It is this scarcity in the market place which is the ultimate origin of inequality, hierarchy and social class in society, namely the origin of those dimensions of social structure which appear to stand in opposition to the principle of solidarity as mutuality, affective relations and social bonding. Thus sociology is that social science which seeks to analyse the tensions and contradictions between two fundamental principles of social formations: between behaviour directed towards scarcity and behaviour directed towards solidarity. In short, sociology is concerned to understand the relationship between markets (which primarily involve the conflict between social classes) and society (which primarily involves communal forms of organization). Typically sociology treats citizenship as a form of political solidarity and studies the processes by which social rights, in providing a crucial link between markets and communities, reduce the negative impact of scarcity on solidarity.

We should note, parenthetically, that the polar opposite of scarcity, namely surplus, has not featured prominently in the sociological tradition.

Veblen (1899) discussed the surplus time and conspicuous consumption of the American ruling class, while Sombart (1913) examined the connections between luxury and the development of capitalism. However, in general, the question of the surplus has been undertheorized. This observation points to the limitations of the concept of organism which has been deployed in the classical tradition. Organisms do not just produce equilibrium or scarcity, they also produce excess.

The question of excess has not interested sociologists, although it has been a central theme in criminology. Nietzschean-minded criminologists like Jack Katz (1988) have analysed many aspects of deviance as an attempt to generate pleasure through transgression. Solidarity can certainly be organized around excess. The counter-culture movements of the 1960s were examples of transgressive cultures which emerged precisely from the ability of postwar capitalism to generate year-in, year-out surplus. Although in this study we focus on the centrality of scarcity in establishing earthly solidarity, we note the importance of the metaphor of the surplus in explaining several features of utopian and religious forms of life. But the subject is so vast that it requires another book.

Within the organization of the academic disciplines, economics is the science of scarcity; sociology, the science of solidarity and politics, the science of violence within a framework of citizenship participation. In a more philosophical language, sociology has been generally interested in how strangers (competitive actors within the market place) can live together without perpetual conflict, that is how strangers can come to form social relations of friendship and companionship.

From this brief account of the historical origins of sociology, and in particular from the sociological studies of the origins of religion in the sacrificial meal, we can now see that sociology emerged as a critique of classical economics, especially as a critique of the conventional notion of utility as a universal criterion of rational action. Rationalist economic notions of action defined utility with reference to scarcity. Thus, rationality is simply the application of scarce resources to the achievement of ends in order to satisfy wants in an individualistically competitive market context. The value of a good is determined by the amount of expenditure individuals are prepared to allocate to its achievement in order to satisfy their desire for such a good. Marginal utility is the rational allocation of an extra unit of effort to the satisfaction of a want via scarce means. Gossen's First Law stipulates that as one consumes more of a given product, the marginal utility (the addition to aggregate utility) declines. From an economic point of view, social relations stabilize around the point at which individual wants are satisfied within a market place. Marginal utility theories have been applied to social relations to suggest that, for example, the marginal utility of friendship will decline with each additional interaction.

Classical sociology emerged as a critique of these dominant assumptions of marginal utility theory as a universal criterion of rational action. For example, sociologists like Max Weber argued that it was important to distinguish between traditional and affective social actions which are not in fact determined by 'instrumental rationality'. He also distinguished between value rationality (*Wertrationalität*) which is consistent with a dominant value or moral system and instrumental or purposive rationality (*Zweckrationalität*) which is simply the utilitarian principle. In short, people can rationally follow a moral system in terms of being consistent and coherent. Such value rationality is quite distinct from instrumental or utilitarian economic behaviour. Sociologists also argue that one cannot explain moral or religious belief and commitment in terms of an economic framework, because religious commitment is neither rational nor irrational but simply non-rational. Sociologists subsequently also came to criticize the conventional notions of consumer rationality, the free flow of information within a market and the market as an effective means of distribution. Sociologists pointed out that, while fraud and force may be perfectly reasonable and rational means of action to satisfy wants, they are incompatible with social solidarity and social consensus. There is therefore often a profound tension between market rationality and social integration. One of the sustained criticisms of rationality in contemporary sociology was presented by Talcott Parsons in *The Structure of Social Action* (1937).

Social anthropologists also challenged marginal utility theory as a universal model for the understanding of society and social action. For example, some anthropologists believe that primitive and modern societies operate on very different economic principles. While classical economics assumes that, through the principle of utility, the modern market economy was based upon the idea of conservation, the ancient economy typically worked upon the criterion of loss, that is of unconditional expenditure, regardless of how contrary it might appear to the economic principle of balanced accounts, namely expenditure regularly compensated for by acquisition. Exchange systems based on loss can be regarded as rational only in the very narrow sense of the word. Georges Bataille developed many of Durkheim's ideas about ritual and sacrifice in his analysis of the practice of potlatch, where North American natives destroyed their wealth in order to gain social dominance (Bataille, 1985). This principle of loss was illustrated particularly in the cults which were associated historically with religious sacrifice.

From this commentary on the origins of the debate about economics and sociology, it is possible to claim that the underlying issues concern the problematic relationships between scarcity and solidarity, with the proviso that the subject of surplus is undertheorized. Classical economics emerged as a modern science in the eighteenth century as a result of the growth of consumer society. Conspicuous consumption, the creation of possessional goods, the emergence of possessive individualism, the psychology of the narcissistic self and the representational self, and finally the growth of the leisure class committed to conspicious luxury and under-employment were social developments which identified the growth of a new social order within industrial, competitive capitalism. The eighteenth-century consumer society produced a paradox: the rise of scarcity as an outcome of economic abundance. Infinite elasticity of demand meant that social scarcity became a condition of economic surplus and rising individual expectations. In a society of elastic desire, economic affluence produced a world of scarcity with modernization, and the competition for symbols and cultural goods resulted in a society of distinction with its endless status gradations and differences of taste. The study of symbolic goods, positional status and cultural capital is to be found in the work of Pierre Bourdieu (1984).

## Scarcity and risk

The notion of scarcity raises traditional analytical problems in the social sciences about the relative nature of need. What is scarcity for one individual may be abundance for another, because human wants appear to be both finite and elastic. There are the usual problems of cross-cultural comparisons and historical differences. The growth of prosperity in the West has often been at the cost of third world underdevelopment so that prosperity paradoxically produces scarcity. Although in commonsense terms, we think about modern societies as based upon abundance, there are strong anthropological reasons for believing that in fact traditional societies were the first leisure societies based upon a surplus. While the work on primitive abundance has been inspired by Marshall Sahlins's *Stoneage Economics* (1974), the analysis of scarcity in the process of modernization has been influenced by Nicholas Zenos's *Scarcity and Modernity* (1989).

We can deal with the issue of scarcity at a number of levels. We might for example start with a notion of ontological scarcity or fundamental scarcity. The German sociologist Arnold Gehlen has described human beings as 'not yet finished animals' in the sense that they live in a condition of world-openness where their instinctual apparatus is not specific to any given environment. Human beings do not have a determinate instinctual structure and so they have to create their own environment through institution building. The principal feature of human societies is the importance of building cultural institutions in order to complete their unfinished ontological characteristics, thereby providing themselves as it were with a canopy which is a canopy of security. Arnold Gehlen's view of ontology was directly influenced by the philosophy of Nietzsche, who profoundly criticized conventional forms of rationalism through his exploration of the idea of the will to power. Gehlen's major work has been translated into English as *Man. His Nature and Place in the World* (1988).

Human beings must try to satisfy their basic needs (for food, shelter and security) in a competitive context of natural scarcity. This type of ontological insecurity has been most commonly and profoundly expressed within a political tradition which derives from the work of Thomas Hobbes wherein life is 'nasty, brutish and short'. This notion of natural scarcity is the major assumption of economic science, because generally speaking when economics talks about scarcity it has in mind the primitive needs for shelter, food and rest. This ontological security derives directly from the notion that human beings are organisms operating within an environment of scarcity, where they have to satisfy their needs for survival through collective means. Hobbes's theory of the state therefore has to presuppose a particular set of circumstances determining the life of the human being as an organism in a natural environment characterized by wants and needs. The embodiment of human beings as precarious organisms in a frail natural environment is the main covert assumption of economics as a science.

From a sociological point of view this notion of ontological scarcity has been relatively unsatisfactory, because for sociologists human beings are not so much creatures of need as creatures of desire. Both sociology and psychoanalysis have speculated extensively on the nature of human fantasy, imagination and fiction. Because human beings are creatures of desire, it is assumed not only that scarcity is a permanent feature of all human existence, but that desire will expand with the promotion of commodities under capitalist conditions, where advertising cultivates and promotes our desire (which sociologists regard as artificially produced) for commodities. In short, while we may have a need for food, our desire for chocolate assumes an infinitely elastic characteristic. Furthermore, an obsession with chocolate does not satisfy a particular need but it is directly related to an elastic desire. The craving for chocolate is treated by so-called critical theorists as an inauthentic and hence false desire because it results from a distortion of nature. Although this distinction between need and desire is central to much of the sociology of cultural consumption, an economist might still object that chocolate has a marginal utility in the sense that there will be a point where the supply of chocolate exceeds demand, and where an additional unit of chocolate does not satisfy the desire of an individual who is already satiated by the consumption of chocolate. Against this argument, a sociologist might reply that obsessional behaviour does not correspond to the criteria of marginal utility theory and that in a society characterized by the fetishism of commodities, rational calculation is an irrelevant model of consumer behaviour. Karl Marx's economic analysis of the problems of business stability in capitalism was of course dependent on a metaphor of religious fetishism as applied to commodities. The fetishism of commodities was an important aspect of his analysis of the reification of consciousness in capitalism. Exchange relations in contemporary society are therefore comparable to a form of neurosis (Abercrombie, 1980).

This comment on the difference between (biological) need and (culturally specific) desires leads us to the conclusion that scarcity is culturally relative or at least that scarcity is socially produced and organized. Paradoxically therefore it appears that modernization and industrialization have in these terms increased scarcity rather than reduced it by the production of prosperity. Rising individual and social expectations have expanded and increased demand, because advertising and commodification increase and multiply demands by bringing about a democratization of consumption.

With these developments we have the continuing, possibly increasing, state of social inequality or scarcity in the very midst of abundance.

Behind this distinction between need and desire there may also be a historical notion about the evolution of organisms in society, namely that with the growing sophistication of a consumer culture, the needs and desires of human beings are multiplying, expanding and becoming deterritorialized. Both commercial and scientific developments have increased the elasticity of demand for goods and services in an advanced civilization, thereby making the relationship to scarcity and solidarity more problematic. They have also contributed to deterritorialization of value, whereby scarcity becomes virtually neutralized through the mobility of high income sections in society. Strata who occupy the highest echelons of society, the rich, can develop dual nationalities and pay their taxes in the most cost-effective setting, in order to minimize personal liability. The classical tradition's interest in velocity never made the proposition that increased mobility insulates the self from problems of value. However, postmodernism makes the links between velocity and the transparency of embodiment (Baudrillard, 1986; Virilio, 1986).

While scarcities have multiplied with consumerism, the process of modernization has increased the risk in the nature of society, while also changing the nature of risk. Within a contemporary environment, risk is typically general not specific, democratic rather than hierarchic and global rather than local. With modernization the risks of the environment have been diffused through the entire population. It therefore becomes possible to argue that whilst prosperity is hierarchic, pollution of the environment is democratic in the sense that it is experienced by all members of a society who are exposed to such hazards as the hole in the ozone layer, pollution in the environment and the decline in the quality of the food supply and food chain. With globalization, the risk of disease is no longer confined to geographical or social niches, but is distributed globally throughout society. The incidence of AIDS, HIV, CJD and Mad Cow Disease is the perfect illustration of a risk society. The idea behind the notion of risk society is that the traditional social patterns which organize individual lives are now uncertain, insecure and risky. Further, some risks are so great that insurance companies refuse to cover them. Existentially speaking, we experience life in legal-rational authority without a safety net. This is a significant development since Max Weber's day. There is less stability in the individual life course and life pattern because the labour market is fragmented and flexible. Stability within the domestic and private arena has declined with the erosion of the traditional nuclear family and the differentiation and fragmentation of the domestic sphere. We have a heightened awareness of the precariousness of the environmental canopy under which we live.

The organism within its natural environment is exposed to an increasing level of hazard and uncertainty because industrialization has had profoundly negative consequences for the quality and diversity of the environment. The human organism within its social context is also exposed to social risk and cultural uncertainty as a consequence of the modernization of the social system, and the social organism is itself precariously located within a historical trajectory of the risk society.

We can see the growth of the risk society as the context within which over the last decade there has been a robust growth of a new sociology of the body. This new branch of sociology is specifically concerned with the notion that the human organism is not a natural phenomenon but a socially and culturally produced form of existence which is shaped by nurture rather than by nature. This view of the socially constructed character of the organism has been produced partly by gay and feminist politics which seek to deny the notion that anatomy is destiny, that is, to assert by contrast that the body has a history and this history is a cultural and social product. In addition to the growth of sexual politics, the technological development of medicine has also had a profound impact on how we think about the human body because in a literal sense the body can be constructed through cosmetic surgery, organ transplants, hormone replacement therapy and other forms of medical intervention. The impact of prosperity and medicine has contributed to the decline of morbidity and mortality, producing an ageing population, which also raises profound questions about the nature of the body in modern societies.

In addition, as we have noted, the commercialization of everyday life has identified the human body as the place, site and target of commodities where appetizing typically takes the human form as the principal vehicle for the promotion of the sales of commodities. This commercialized culture is often described as a postmodern environment because it is closely attached to the new information technologies which, to some extent, have gone beyond traditional patterns of rational organization and management. The post-modern body in this respect is seen to be a fragmented and fluid body where the boundaries and borderlines between machines and bodies are blurred and confused. The rise of the cyborg and cybernetics, as in such popular films as *Terminator* and *Robocop*, illustrates the notion of the fluidity and flexibility of the body as an organ subject to infinite transformation. As a result the traditional divisions between gender and sex have been eroded and trans-formed not only by political movements but by technological interventions, making possible successful transsexual surgery for an expanding middle-class audience. Postmodernism has questioned the organic nature of the human organism and has brought into prominence the traditional issues of the metaphorcality of the human organism. There is therefore a complex inter-play between the organ, the organizing of human action and the organization of society in a risk environment where traditional solutions to scarcity and solidarity are increasingly complex and problematic.

### Conclusion: organizing actions

This chapter has been a reflection upon the nature of the social sciences with special reference to economics and sociology, which we have identified with the twin problems of scarcity and solidarity. In addition we have explored the notion of society as an organization and society as a collection or process of organizing actions. This distinction between organization and organizing is yet another way of expressing the traditional philosophical and sociological issues about action and determinism in terms of a contrast between action and structure. The organic analogy encourages us to reify the concept of organism into the notion of a thing-like organization which exists over and above and separate from the actions of individuals. The life of the individual organism is thus taken over by, and incorporated within, the organization.

However, both economics and sociology tend to regard themselves as disciplines primarily concerned with actions rather than with reified institutions, that is, economics is concerned with economizing actions and sociology with actions which lead to, or are a product of, patterns of solidarity. We might extend this notion to include other disciplines. Clearly politics as part of the social science disciplines is concerned with the organizing of political actions in terms of the distribution of power and authority. We might argue that politics is concerned with those actions which produce and sustain governmentality, namely the regime of power which regulates the relationship between the collectivity and the individual through disciplines and practices. In these terms we could argue that societies are organizing practices which are concerned through economics with the distribution of goods, through politics with the distribution of power and through sociology with the distribution of actions that produce and support solidarity.

What then would we make of the various disciplines which in one way or another are concerned with cultural production (such as anthropology, theology, philosophy and aesthetics)? We might argue, again following the work of Max Weber, that these cultural disciplines are concerned with the production and distribution of meaning within social systems, that is they are concerned with the organizing activities of significance or signification. Cultural anthropology has been historically concerned with the rights and practices whereby culture is diffused through time and space through meaningful actions such as rituals and sacrificial activities. Cultural sciences are concerned with hermeneutics, that is with the production and explanation of the interpretation of meaningful actions in society.

It is possible from this scheme then to generate a general theory of society as the ensemble of organizing practices for the production and maintenance of economic, political, social and cultural phenomena through the endless structured activities of individual organisms. In terms of the social system we can now recognize this as in fact a traditional scheme whereby within a social system economics and politics are concerned with the management of an external environment and solidarity (integration), and meaningful behaviour (latency) is concerned with the individual concerned with motivation and organization of individuals with respect to cultural phenomena. The social organism is therefore divided into an external and internal environment where these four patterns or organizing behaviour are located along a dichotomy of internal and external system requirements.

This social organism is changing because with modernization we can argue that meaning systems become more uncertain. With secularization there is in fact a decline in meaning and value: that is, with modernization and secularization, meaning acquires an increasing scarcity. With the recognition of multiculturalism and difference, we might even postulate a diminishing margin of collective meaning as 'real values' are concentrated in ethnicity, sexual preference, religious conviction. Increasing abundance also multiplies taste cultures and conspicuous consumption, thus enabling individuals to avoid commitment to the social organism. Indeed, commitments are tending to be defined as liabilities, since fiscal policy requires the individual to contribute to the social organism, whereas consumption enables the individual to escape from these commitments into a world of unregulated desire and fantasy.

Actions relating to solidarity and meaning therefore require greater effort in securing cultural significance. Yet the velocity of modernization and globalization is weakening the power of institutions to play an integrating role. The nation state is experiencing a drainage of power to transnational corporations and organizations. This, together with the challenges of multiculturalism, places the question of who 'we' really are as a standing item on the agenda of everyday life. The recognition of hybridity underlines the fact that scarcity is intrinsic to the very categories of communication we use to make policy. The development of solidarity derives from a sense of common belonging. It is precisely this sense of belonging which is compromised by risk society. As Bauman's sociology makes plain, men and women today must live first of all, and above all, with contingency. Contingency is a precarious foundation upon which to build a new sense of belonging, because it is always changing, often in unpredictable ways.

Contemporary men and women may therefore be said to live in a condition of over-determined scarcity. Their desires expand at an exponential rate; their capacity to consume is finite; and their environment is uncertain, both in its capacity to sustain itself and in the means of representation they use to understand it.

# 3
# DISORDER

Classical sociology was born from an attempt to elucidate principles of gravity in collective life in the midst of seemingly exponential and destabilizing increases in the mass of populations and the velocity of industrial and economic change. Industrialization and modernization did not simply uproot traditional practices, communities and formations of identity. Rather, they uprooted them without allowing new forms of social integration to gain a footing. That is why the problem of social order was identified as such an urgent issue in the classical tradition. The fusillade fired against traditional religious and aristocratic forms of authority left the *philosophes* without a prayer book, but clutching a lantern of flickering, 'objective' insights into the nature of truth and social change.

The Enlightenment legacy has famously been criticized for engendering a dubious sense of complacency about the direction of these developments. In some hands, the Enlightenment lantern did not so much flicker as dazzle with irresistible, refulgent light about the future direction of social development. For example, classical economics promised to reveal and explain the real principles of economic life. It posited the 'hidden hand' of the market behind the countless reciprocal relationships generated through industrial and economic expansion (Smith, 1776). The foundation of classical economics lay in the quest to construct a scientific understanding of the operations of the market. Since classical economics held that men were rational actors, it was assumed that the trend of economic development would, in the long run, maintain a rational direction.

Classical sociology developed a similar cast of mind in exploring the expanding social realm. Comte's (1830–42) law of the three stages, and Spencer's (1893) Social Darwinism which predicted increasing differentiation and integration in the social structure, both taught that progress is essentially orderly. Indeed, both conflated social development with progress so that conflict and anomie were presented as temporary epiphenomena in an epic and overwhelming positive transformation in human affairs.

It is now fashionable to dismiss the *philosophes* and Social Darwinists as theorists who looked at society through rose-tinted spectacles. Comte and Spencer's view that progress is inevitable is hard to justify in the age of 'risk society' (Beck, 1992). Without doubt, the faith of the Enlightenment and of Social Darwinists in the integrity of orderly progress was a type of power. They identified a civilizing mission in the economic and territorial expansionism of the West which permitted a wide variety of horrors, including genocide and environmental destruction. Sociologists need no reminding of this in the wake of Bauman's (1989) great work on the connections between rationality and the Holocaust, and the growing body of postcolonial literature on the pulverizing effects on ethnic cultures of the Western mission to civilize (Said, 1978; Spivak, 1988; Bhabba, 1994).

It has become a veritable convention in the field for sociologists to regard the Enlightenment as a poisoned chalice. However, Adorno and Horkheimer (1944), who perhaps first made this case in relation to the perverted rationality of National Socialism in Germany, were careful to emphasize that there is a *dialectic* of Enlightenment. Arguably, the point is glossed over in the postcolonial and postmodern literature with its excoriating attack on the colonial formation and its legacy and the postmodern celebration of the end of rationality. For white, male, social scientists residing in the West, it is now difficult to write about the Enlightenment without adopting an apologetic, hang-dog mien. However, those who deplore the Enlightenment for its authoritarian roll-call of apparently universal truths must also acknowledge that the *philosophes* were quite capable of self-criticism. Universalism, empiricism and science were key values of the Enlightenment; but so were a profound scepticism about *a priori* truths, a respect for individualism and a belief in the value of tolerance. These divisions carried over into the scientific and political arena associated with the Enlightenment. The culture which eventually produced Samuel Smiles and Cecil Rhodes also produced Karl Marx and Rosa Luxemburg.

We formulate the point not to atone for the obvious and egregious sins of the Enlightenment. These have been well documented in the postcolonial literature, and we are only too conscious of the shadow they cast over the whole subject of modernity. Rather we wish to reclaim an understanding of the Enlightenment as an intrinsically dialectical process, comprising both positive and negative elements. We acknowledge that there are hazards in making this claim. In the current climate in sociology, merely invoking the name of rationality invites the canard that the discredited concepts of cultural universalism and Western imperialism might be smuggled back into the building. Naturally, we have no interest in doing that. We concur with MacIntyre's (1987) account of rational justification, namely that rational justification is not independent of social and cultural particularities. MacIntyre concludes that we should replace the Enlightenment concept of universal rationality with that of *rationalities*. Since we hold that comparative and historical analysis is indispensable for sociological understanding, we have no quarrel with MacIntyre's general proposition.

MacIntyre's case is usually interpreted as justifying cultural relativism in the social sciences. The main objection to cultural relativism is that it often blurs into moral relativism. A good example is Hall et al.'s (1978) analysis of mugging in *Policing the Crisis*. Hall et al. argue that mugging can only be properly understood by situating it in the appropriate historical and cultural context. They interpret the rise of mugging in 1970s Britain to be the response of the culturally marginalized to a society which systematically excludes or marginalizes them. Mugging, they submit, is a rational choice made by individuals who know that the system is stacked against them.

The argument attracted considerable attention at the time, because it appears to legitimize violence on the grounds of the blatant social and economic inequality produced by the system. Hall and his colleagues' response was that they were not interested in defending the morality of mugging. However, the arguments they offered to elucidate why mugging occurred were popularly interpreted to propose that the mugger was also a victim of injustice. We do not wish to become embroiled in the question of whether Hall and his associates were right or wrong. In any case, Hall has now moved away from the Althusserian 'moment' and would doubtless wish to qualify his argument in various ways. The example is relevant for our purposes only because it demonstrates how cultural relativism (the system supports an inequitable allocation of resources) operates to disable a commonsense moral principle (violence against others is wrong).

We argue that cultural relativism vitiates the proposition that we inhabit a moral universe embodied in the codes of the law. Since Greek and Roman times, this proposition has been the foundation of social order. Law imposes conventions on social behaviour in the Weberian sense that it extends 'the probability that unusual behaviour will be met by physical or psychic sanctions aimed at compelling conformity or punishing disobedience and administered by a group of men especially charged with the authority for that purpose' (Weber, 1962: 75).

An important consequence of the cultural turn over the last twenty years is that many social scientists take it for granted that the law is pre-eminently the expression of cultural, not moral, power. Once this is allowed to be generally the case, it damages the gravity of morality, for it corrodes the principle of impartial justice upon which this gravity is founded. Of course, we would be among the first to acknowledge that there are often good reasons to question the impartiality of the law. In particular, where the law is applied to construct a climate of terror it might be submitted that it is the moral duty of the citizen to resist. At the same time, generalized cultural relativism has a strong tendency to create a blame culture in which persons are deemed to be victims merely by reason of the social position they occupy. Because the law is seen as skewed in favour of the interests of the powerful, no independent recourse to justice is conceivable.

We submit that this line of thinking is objectionable because it eliminates moral responsibility as an attribute of individual citizenship. The interest in aesthetics and difference, which has been such a prominent feature of recent work in the area of culture, reinforces this tendency, because it dwells on matters of symbolic capital and difference at the cost of interrogating questions of moral mutuality and commonality. Mutuality and commonality are not questions of structural determination, they are the often unacknowledged consequences of maintaining and advancing life with others. In other words, consciousness of individual responsibility is bound up with the state of being with others. We propose that the emphasis in some forms of multiculturalism on acknowledging that different groups have fundamentally different views of the world, is not a basis for inferring that the quest for agreement is fruitless.

One of the noteworthy achievements of Beck's (1992) argument is to lift the quest for agreement from the cultural plane and to relocate it in the realm of physical necessity. In highlighting the global character of environmental risk, Beck produces a cogent basis for attempting to move beyond cultural boundaries and ethnic, religious and sexual particularity. His book raises the possibility of imminent global disorder caused by the industrial attrition of the environment. It is unusual in appealing to universal reason as the most hopeful defence against the risk of global collapse. The burden of Beck's case is that the potential impending environmental disintegration of the biosphere requires a universal strategy of collective action.

Interestingly, Beck's argument has tasted a better fate than Habermas's (1970) defence of universalism through his formulation of a 'universal pragmatics' in human communication and the 'ideal speech situation'. This is because Beck's thesis ultimately works by positing a commonality of bodily risk. He submits that if we refuse to use reason to combat the universal environmental risks facing us we jeopardize the future of life on the planet. Ultimately, it is a materialist rather than an idealist interpretation of disorder. Habermas's universal pragmatics is a contribution to cultural and political sociology which also made use of concepts of commonality, mutuality and, to be sure, universalism. He strives to outline principles of adjudication between competing knowledge systems, but his view of disorder does not have the inclusiveness or urgency of Beck's. Indeed, Habermas suggests that the central problems facing humanity arise not from impending disorder but from the over-determination of order through the irreconcilable character of competing validity claims. Universal pragmatics is presented as the solution to crises of legitimacy. However, it is premised on the proposition that validity claims are multifarious and therefore the experience of legitimacy crises is multiform and incommensurate. Habermas appeals to an idealist concept to transcend this state of affairs. His advocacy of the ideal speech situation is not so far removed from Popper's (1945) defence of the 'open society'. Both have recourse to the Enlightenment tradition in restating the political necessity of tolerance, anti-essentialism, anti-ideology and open debate. Yet this argument is perhaps deficient in failing to fully represent inequality and material difference. Not surprisingly, Habermas and Popper were ferociously attacked by cultural critics.

## Sociology and disorder

Sociology never developed strong traditions of studying genocide, famine, plague or environmental catastrophe. Empirical data on social disorder and disintegration are hard to find in the achievements of sociological work in the nineteenth and twentieth centuries. Despite this, we maintain that collapse and disorder have always composed the dark, velvet backdrop in the mirror that sociology holds up to the world. Beck's (1992) work provides a powerful metaphor of this through his concept of 'risk society'. However, for us, risk anxiety in sociology preceded the debate on environmental scares. It was, for example, the primary stimulus behind Hobbesian contract theory. Thus, Hobbes was not offering a solution to the actual war of all against all, but a pre-emptive strategy to avoid the outbreak of conflict. He focused on an imaginary, not an empirical state of affairs.

Risk anxiety is a characteristic of Enlightenment thought, because only in the Enlightenment did a secular, humanistic view of action become predominant. The Renaissance was a moment of liberation, but it was clad with vestiges of religious and metaphysical belief systems. In contrast, the Enlightenment nailed its faith to the mast of science. Essential to scientific method is an assessment of risk probability, because science seeks to classify and identify causal chains and consequences. If it is right to see sociology as the child of the Enlightenment, it follows that risk anxiety and risk probability are coterminus with the subject.

Abercombie et al. (1980) demonstrated the exaggerated and overblown character of risk anxiety in institutionalized sociology through their critical analysis of the dominant ideology thesis. They showed that the thesis that a dominant stratum controls the means and ends of power is commonly expressed in sociology. Every sociologist is familiar with the various arguments that society is controlled by a ruling class, male power or white interests, and that these agents, allegedly, seek to imprint universal order on everyday life. Abercombie et al. (1980) argued cogently that the dominant ideology thesis seriously exaggerated the integration of the protagonists in social control and accentuated the passivity of actors who were assigned subordination. They concluded that dominant ideology is a misplaced metaphor to describe the operation of power in human collectivities. In stating this we do not mean to cast doubt on the proposition that gross imbalances of power are part and parcel of human collectivities. Bauman's (1989) study of the Holocaust demonstrated how the Nazi oligarchy successfully ruled Germany from the 1930s through to the mid-1940s via a reign of terror. It is unusual in being one of the very few full-length sociological studies devoted to the subject of social disorder. Central to Bauman's argument is that bureaucracy's tendency to seek the optimal solution for problems laid the foundations for Nazi party politics to launch a programme of genocide. The Holocaust was the product of the disjunction between technical means and moral ends. For Bauman (1989: 160), bureaucracy is driven by a twin impulse to neutralize the moral significance of non-technical issues and to moralize the technical purity of bureaucracy. At the same time, of course, Bauman is careful to emphasize that bureaucracy is a cornerstone of Modernity. The logic that produced Auschwitz is an extension of the Ford assembly line.

In terms of the question of the relation between sociology and disorder, the significance of Bauman's study is that it demonstrates the ill effects of the over-determination of order. Bureaucracy tends to deny complexity and favour standardization. The result is that the technical means designed to create order carry within them the sparks of a moral inferno. Of course, whether these sparks ignite or not is a matter of a specific concatenation of socio-economic circumstances. The point to emphasize is that Bauman insists that bureaucracy carries within itself the potential to make people prioritize obedience over moral responsibility.

So far, over-determined regimes of order have shown themselves to be highly defective in denying complexity indefinitely. After all, in the end, the Nazi order collapsed in ignominy. However, this is no reason for complacence. Bauman's analysis demonstrates that the normalization of what was hitherto morally unacceptable behaviour is a repetitive theme in Modernity. For example, in the postwar period, Stalin, Pol Pot, Idi Amin, General Pinochet and Saddam Hussein, to name but a few, committed human rights violations and mass executions. What matters, for Bauman, is that the disjunction between technical means and moral ends, which figured so prominently in Nazi power, continues to be latent in contemporary bureaucractic systems of control. This is why Bauman (1989: 183) concludes that 'responsibility is the essential, primary and fundamental structure of subjectivity'; and also why his later work endeavours to achieve the reconstruction of ethics for postmodern times.

We do not seek to deny the validity of risk anxiety *per se*. Professional and popular worries about ontological insecurity are entirely appropriate responses in the age of bureaucracy, nuclear power and genetic engineering. Our concern is more prosaic. We propose that it is wrong to regard risk anxiety as a novel identifying characteristic of sociology in the 1980s and 1990s. We argue that the long-standing infatuation in sociology with the problem of social order was, from the first, pregnant with anxieties about the risks of collapse and disorder. To some extent the issue is obscured by highlighting the evangelical side of Enlightenment rhetoric. Bauman's (1992) insistence that contemporary conditions require us to develop strategies of living with contingency is a useful reminder that social institutions are fragile. However, we submit that risk/contingency-consciousness was an original and continuous feature of the Enlightenment. Behind the outward confidence of the *philosophes* lurked the realization that the new industrial order was highly provisional. Indeed, we submit that this was inevitably the case since industrial development was founded in the constant revolutionizing of the forces and relations of production. When Marx and Engels (1848) wrote that a 'spectre is haunting Europe', they had in mind not merely the revolution of the proletariat, but also the disintegration of the bourgeois industrial order.

This sense of spectres overshadowing social order was not confined to the Marxist tradition. Durkheim's sociology described the negative consequences of egoism, anomie and the abnormal division of labour. It called upon the state to effect remedial action. Weber's analysis of bureaucracy and the unintended consequences of social action pointed to the long night of disenchantment gathering over Western society. These traditions grew out of the Enlightenment and they certainly do not confirm, in any direct and simple way, that the Enlightenment operated merely to repress ambiguity and difference. Indeed, it might be proposed that modern consciousness was split between one strand of opinion that regarded the growth of progress and order as inevitable, and another strand that regarded order and progress as conditional and uncertain. This is the proposition advanced by Adorno and Horkheimer (1944) in their thesis of the dialectic of Enlightenment.

### Postmodernism, ethnomethodology and disorder

Sociology could not avoid being influenced by this division. In the postwar period, after the collapse of structural functionalism as a putative all-encompassing approach, sociology drifted into a condition of multiparadigmatic belligerence. Looking back, the tensions between conflict theory, symbolic interactionism, ethnomethodology, Marxism, feminism, structuralism, figurational sociology, poststructuralism and cultural theory can be interpreted as category disputes about the nature of normative order. Postwar sociology has been profoundly sceptical that a shared concept of normative order is universally acceptable. This is one reason why the Foucauldian argument about discourse and knowledge as power proved to be so influential in the 1970s and 1980s. By transposing questions of normative order to the plane of communication and power, Foucault dissolved the salience of Goffman's (1967) old and, by then, increasingly *passé* question: 'what is really going on' in social situations? From now on, the answer to Goffman simply depended on the social position and discursive field of the analyst *vis-à-vis* the object of enquiry. The stage was set for postmodernism to overturn the entire debate with the explosive argument that none of the category disputes of the postwar period carried water any longer. Reality has disappeared. There are no certainties left.

   The quicksilver logic of postmodernism was intoxicating and exasperating in equal measure. Those who occupied venerable traditions of sociological enquiry rightly objected to the flip, often woefully raw, rejection of paradigms of research by postmodernist savants. Who were the postmodernists to reject years of Marxist, feminist and even structural-functional analysis with a mere shrug of the shoulders and sniff of disapproval? There was always something both seigneurial and *arriviste* about the postmodernist rejection of postwar sociology.

   At the same time, the sheer effrontery of postmodern assertions of the disappearance of the real and the implosion of the masses (Baudrillard, 1983a and b) seriously challenged dogmatic assumptions about the operation of power which had been undisturbed for decades. Two senses of disorder must be distinguished here. First, postmodernism rejected mainstream sociology for failing to produce relevant theories. Sociologists were depicted as contemplating their own navels and squandering resources on second order disputes. Secondly, and by extension, postmodernists held that social, economic and cultural conditions really had changed and that the accumulated changes required new types of theory. In particular, the notion of social identity as a stable, evolving category was rejected in favour of a conception of the social which emphasized division, difference, fragmentation and ambiguity. This, in turn, raised profound doubts about the validity of the concept of social totality as the bedrock of sociological enquiry.

Within sociological circles there was a distinct sense of *déjà vu* about the postmodern palace coup. For sociologists were familiar with the predicament of having their favourite concepts and shared assumptions denigrated by tribal parvenus. In the 1960s, ethnomethodology took upon itself the task of shredding the pretensions of structural functionalism. Like postmodernism it cast dominant forms of sociological activity in the demeaning role of second order investigations which led to the proliferation of vacuous abstractions about social life. Garfinkel (1967) and his followers insisted on ploughing ever deeper into the microscopic substrate of interaction and meaning. One result was that sociology's umbilical cord connecting it with national and global politics and social transformation was cut. For the concepts of nation and global relations were now seen as inherently problematic. In the context of the Vietnam crisis, Garfinkel was urging his students to act as lodgers in the homes of their parents in order to disrupt and expose the tacit assumptions that regulate life. This observation is designed to take nothing away from Garfinkel, who is unquestionably one of the great sociologists of the postwar period, or to cast a slur on his adherents. His analysis of how order is reproduced and why sociology gets so much wrong about ordinary interaction was seminal. Notwithstanding this, the capacity of ethnomethodology to reorientate enquiry in the subject appears to have been very modest. Ethnomethdology played a significant critical role in exposing the conceits of macro-level sociology, but it was unable to go beyond this role. Moreover, it contrived to suggest that there is a sort of pathetic futility in attempting to operate theoretically or politically at the macro level.

Ethnomethodology dramatically revived the importance of the social competence and tacit knowledge of the subject in sociological analysis. However, it proved unable to connect with the larger problems of normative order and power that bound classical and contemporary sociology together. The interest in indexicality and tacit knowledge logically pointed to wider questions of power and transformation, but these were never fully pursued. Garfinkel and his followers deliberately refrained from engaging in category disputes about the character of normative order, because they regarded mainstream pontifications about this subject to be the main defect of sociology. What this underestimated is the force of the generalizing and nomothetic tendencies in sociological practice. Sociologists did not cease to make generalizations simply because ethnomethdologists lectured them that generalizations would always be invalid. Ironically, Giddens (1978, 1984) generalized many key ethnomethodological insights, especially relating to the tacit knowledge and social competence of members, in his attempt to bridge the micro–macro divide through structuration theory. By a tangential route therefore, many of the most important aspects of ethnomethodology were restored to the macro level of sociological debate. Garfinkel's work certainly touched some tender spots. It reawakened the sociological imagination to the complexity of the social universe and reminded sociologists of the potential arrogance and misuses of professional power. The re-emergence of reflexivity as a central issue in sociology in the 1990s owes much to the criticism of over-confident macro-sociology by Garfinkel and his associates in the 1960s (Beck et al., 1994). Although Garfinkel gave the debate about ordinary knowledge and members' accounting practices a Californian twist, much of the preliminary work had been done by Dilthey, Windelband and Rickert in the famous *Methodenstreit* dispute in German sociology in the late nineteenth century, and of course, by the phenomenological sociology of Scheler and Schutz.

However, a crucial difference in the reflexivity debate in the 1990s is that it occurred in the aftershock of postmodernism. Postmodernism was modern sociology's Waterloo. It might be said that the central domain assumptions of modern sociology were order, identity, meaning and action. Postmodernism sought to replace them with flexibility, difference, contingency and hybridity. Modern sociology appealed to scientific solidarity to transform shared social conditions in cases where these conditions are assessed to be insupportable or intolerable. For postmodernists, this was like being equipped with a battalion of wooden soldiers in the age of the smart bomb. They pronounced that politics must henceforward set its course for difference rather than follow the quest for solidarity. All hierarchical authority was subject to scepticism. Meaning and life with others were redefined as inherently contingent and endlessly ambivalent. Knowledge is not only power, it is also perspectival, approximate, multi-accented and disposable. Modern sociology operated with a relatively stable research agenda. It recognized the new in life with others but interpreted it in quasi-organic terms. When postmodernism came along, the proposition of progress through evolution had long been a discarded element in the sociological worldview. Yet most sociologists still believed in the growth of knowledge and the necessity of the historical and comparative frameworks. Postmodernism declared an end to all of this. No longer could assumptions be made. The multiplicity of perspectives, the internal division and contradictory desires of the subject, the erasure of received forms of power, the intertwining of absence with presence in the chain of interaction, the politics of difference, and the effervescent unpredictability of 'new times', now buttonholed debate.

Postmodernism had an enormous impact on sociology. In a decade in which most sociologists swapped the typewriter, or in some cases the ballpoint pen, for the desktop and laptop computer, the argument that we were in the throes of fundamental change was, naturally, compelling. But postmodernism also overstated many things and mixed up several distinct tendencies. Technological revolution is not in any simple sense equivalent to a transformation in social values. The miniaturization of information tools, and the flexibility achieved by the microchip and fibre transmission, does not automatically assign a prehistoric significance to notions of established communities or ways of thinking, feeling and acting. These communities and forms of being in the world are obviously influenced by radical technological innovation. At the same time they are sensuous connections of place and belonging which have grown up over many years and along many pathways.

There is an apocalyptic quality to much postmodernist writing which grates with readers. This was reinforced by a fondness for using examples from technology to underline the postmodernist case. The revolutionary significance of the microchip, the internet and fibre communications engineering intelligence reeked of the old-fashioned techno-fix. Undoubtedly, the new technologies which flooded popular culture in the closing decades of the twentieth century gave added impact to postmodernism. But similar claims were being made one hundred years ago, in respect of the imagined consequences of the telephone and the automobile (Kern, 1976; Gartman, 1994).

However, postmodernism amounted to more than the reprise of 1960s-style theories of technological determinism and post-industrial society painted with a new gloss. Its most trenchant form rejected all of the central tenets of Enlightenment epistemology. Specifically, cumulative, rational, organic models of knowledge accumulation were cast aside as modernist myths. Now the emphasis was on cultural particularism, fragmentation and difference. Universalism, progressivism and the quest for objectively adequate theory were consigned to the dustbin of history. The humanist revolution ends in the inhuman culture of the present day. There is no solidarity left, save for a sort of generalized, negative scepticism and a belief in the abounding ambiguity of communication and identity. What made postmodernism so exasperating to a postwar generation raised on radical criticism and reconstruction was that it took seriously the proposition that there is nowhere else to go. Ultimately the radical and critical theory of the postwar period is seen to be as delusional as the mainstream currents of social thought and practice which its seeks to oppose. The quest for socio-cultural and economic transcendence ended when 'the presently existing alternative' to capitalism collapsed.

In a sense, postmodernism was the realization of the state of disordered rationality that had been feared ever since the Enlightenment raised the banner of progress and rational control. What could be more disturbing to rational thought than a movement in society and culture which proclaimed an end to universal meaning, objective truth and grand narratives *in toto*? Doubtless, Comte would have recommended the practice of 'cerebral hygiene' to deal with this barbarism. However, this option assumed a status distinction in favour of the sociological priesthood who, Comte predicted, would be ascendant in society, and of one mind on the crucial issues of the day. Cerebral hygiene was not a serious option when the rejection of grand narratives and the criterion of objective truth was being declared by colleagues in one's own departmental corridor.

Of course, few of the significant writers associated with postmodernism seriously proposed the end of everything. Baudrillard (1983a and b, 1988) came closest to doing so, and his attack perhaps derived as much from his disillusion, and the bitterness of his generation, with postwar Marxism, as from a conviction that things had finally fallen apart. Postmodernism would never have built up the head of steam it achieved in the late 1980s and 1990s had it not been for the exhaustion of traditional radical traditions of dissent and reconstruction. Marxists who argued for class action, feminists who repeated attacks on the male order of power, and black activists who sought to mobilize black consciousness against white domination, simply seemed *passé* and beside the point, in the new world of *différance*, ambiguity, hybridity, split subjectivity and contingency, unveiled by postmodernists. But postmodernists were unable to offer new foundations for belonging and solidarity. Indeed, the whole point of postmodernism was to emphatically identify such foundations as the exhausted shibboleths of Modernity. The espousal of multiculturalism and identity politics was therefore a suspect attempt to retain vestiges of collectivist agency in cultural theory and politics (Hall, 1988). For on what basis can collectivist agency subsist if life with others has genuinely moved into a condition in which the signifier is detached from the signified and where identities are multiform, split, protean and continuously slide over one another?

Postmodernism sometimes appears to be the operation of a particular strain of poststructuralist philosophy mobilized, in part, to take revenge on both the bland certainties of functionalist sociology and the conceits of critical structuralist and agency theory. Derrida, Lyotard, Deleuze and, to a lesser extent, Bataille and Foucault, were the primary philosophical influences. Added to them were Lacanian psychoanalysis, with its pronounced readings of split subjectivity, imaginary unity and symbolic difference; and Barthesian cultural criticism, which proclaimed 'the death of the author' and the end of linear narrative in favour of the intertextual, heterodox play of meaning. Poststructuralism radically recast the notion of the subject by asserting that subjectivity is discursively constituted. Strictly speaking, this did not lead to the erasure of the subject, since subjectivism was recognized as an effect of discursive power. However, traditional notions of identity, linear history in personal biography and collectivist evolution were deeply problematized. Poststructuralism argued that identity and culture are structured like a language. The linguistic turn emphasized the productivity of 'signifying practice' and the 'deferral' of meaning. The desire was to liberate interpretation from essentialist rhetoric and the fallacy of misplaced concreteness. This would have been a welcome development had it not entailed the over-extension of linguistic method. The signifier and signified became the boundaries of a new analytical universalism which refused to acknowledge concrete reality. To some extent this is unavoidable. Thus, for example, the relation of a body to a place is necessarily mediated through language. We cannot understand or communicate our feelings about where we come from unless we put them into words. However, the poststructuralist equation that feelings are *only* words, and the corollary, that meaning is fundamentally arbitrary, since it derives from the unarticulated relations of difference with other terms in the signifying chain, is a false liberation, because it denies concrete reality. Ironically, the result of this is that interpretation becomes confined by a new form of universalism defined by the couplet of signifier and signified. Granted, the permutations of this couplet are infinite, but the method behind them provides no means of transcending the sign economy.

We propose that this is unsatisfactory because it erases bodily concreteness and interdependence from the sphere of interpretation. We argue that bodily concreteness and interdependence are the preconditions of meaningful life with others. Further, the relations between body and place, and body and others, are profoundly sensual. Although some contemporary sociologists, notably Paul Willis (1978, 2000), have recognized the importance of sensuality in meaningful life with others, the discipline as a whole has tended to reproduce a Cartesian view of the actor, in which reason is presented as the pre-eminent force in agency. We reject this view and seek to replace it with an approach which posits bodily concreteness and sensuality as the basis of human *recognition*. This recognition does not derive from metaphysical or theological origins. Rather we maintain that recognition is a demonstrable matter of human sentiment. Why do people donate to charities charged with the task of looking after people whom they have never met or will never know? What makes us offer hospitality to strangers? Bauman (1993, 1999), via Levinas, has advocated care for the other as a principle of postmodern ethics. It is a proposition that brings to mind a question debated *ad nauseam* in classical social science, yet cast aside in recent years: the question of the human condition.

## Labour, work and action

Not so long ago, Arendt (1958) argued that the *vita activa* consists of three activities: labour, work and action. She (1958: 9) regarded labour as referring to the necessities of life associated with the reproduction of the human body. Work consists of the human transformation of the external world through the use of tools. Action is the expression of individual will and common contract. Arendt wrote, that the human condition is a useful concept in pursuing the subject of life with others. In her view, labour is dictated by the human metabolism, work by the requirements of the economy, and action by the realms of culture and politics. Of course, she recognized historical and comparative variations in the *vita activa*, but she asserted that the three components constituted the human condition on the basis that they amounted to 'the basic conditions under which life on earth has been given to man'.

Arendt's perspective logically entailed the now unfashionable precept that use value underpins recognition and belonging. Several generations of critics of capitalist commodity aesthetics have argued the opposite: that the aestheticization of the capitalist commodity world has buried use value under the surface of superficial exchange value (Haug, 1986; Ewen, 1988; Fiske, 1989a, 1989b). According to this view, the tawdry modern tragedy of individual and community life is that exchange value sets the horizon of the lifeworld. In Beck's (1992) study, the attachment to exchange value is presented as the engine of chronic risk development in the global economy. As nations compete to maximize surplus value they degrade the biosphere which is the ultimate source of use at the disposal of mankind. One way of reading Beck's argument is that the unregulated pursuit of exchange value marginalizes use value from the common course of human endeavour. Use therefore becomes an alienable quality in human experience. The largest and most compelling example of this in Beck's work is the risk posed to the earth through pollution of the environment.

Cultural studies and the sociology of culture also recognize the pre-eminence of exchange value in the conduct of life with others. These traditions further suggest that use value has been made alienable from the common course of human experience. Identity, association and practice are theorized as the articulation of the capitalist sign economy. Baudrillard's (1983a and b) nightmare of living in a world of simulation, and finding no recourse to authenticity or truth, is the ultimate expression of this line of thought.

What it obscures is that exchange value has social use for consumers as well as economic attraction for the capitalists. People who buy Armani or Versace suits, Apple Mac computers or BMW automobiles cannot be satisfactorily regarded as the mere dupes of capitalist advertising strategies. Their purchases are, in part, calculated status-placing strategies, which are intended to symbolize both cultural and economic value to others. The same holds for lower range purchases such as Nike sportswear, Camel cigarettes or Lynx hair gel. In the anonymous, episodic conditions of advanced urban-industrial existence, brand names perform a communicative function which presents instant recognition and a sense of belonging. In this sense the Marxian concept of commodity fetishism needs to be revised. For it wrongly implies that manipulation is a one-way process and therefore conceals the strategic, reflexive evaluation in the ordinary processes of consumption. Moreover, the disapproval of commodity culture that one finds in much of the cultural studies and cultural sociology traditions requires critical revaluation.

Some encouraging signs exist to suggest that this is already happening. For example, Willis's (1978, 2000) work proposes that commodity culture generates socio-symbolic homologies between material objects and the human meanings associated with or invested in them. His (1978) famous analysis of the meaning of the motorbike in biker culture is a good example. Leaving aside for a moment the problem of temporal change, Willis maintains that the range of meanings that arise from interaction with the concrete material object is finite. He proposes a homology between the physical processes of the motorbike and the *techne* and symbols of biker culture. This applies at both the local and global levels. Thus, given commodities support homologies of behaviour on a cross-cultural basis. For Willis, the mechanical operation and design of the bike is enmeshed with non-linguistic communicative codes designed to express masculinity within the group. His approach discounts the poststructuralist emphasis on the arbitrariness of meaning and replaces it with an accentuated insistence on the creativity and interpretive skills of the actor. Meaning stems from the interpretation of the concrete forms in which the actor is materially located.

There are parallels here with Bourdieu's (1984) sociology. Bourdieu's investigation of *habitus* and distinction identifies taste cultures which produce and confirm identity. He recognizes that *habitus* is embodied and, therefore, that *habitus* predisposes individual choice. At the same time, the reader is left in no doubt that Bourdieu regards human actors as reflexive and interpretive agents in the cultural remaking of everyday life. Bourdieu's social actors not only have the theroetical capacity to make a difference, they apply this capacity in reproducing and developing the social worlds which they inhabit. Both Willis and Bourdieu highlight the sensuous, interpretive capacities of the body in sustaining and extending a sense of collective order. Both analyse social actors as beings located in a real world of material and cultural restraints and opportunities.

Interestingly, their work is weakest when they raise political questions. It is when they seek to tackle questions of material inequality or gross imbalances in power relations that the limitations of their ethnographic approach become most evident. This is because they operate with a weak version of social totality. An approach based in *habitus* or group homologies can provide a remarkably rich understanding of the dynamics of cultural capital and creative action. But it reduces the concept of society to a collage of taste cultures.

## The relevance of disorder

This is perhaps a good point both to summarize the argument made so far in this chapter, and to indicate some of the most important implications. From its origins, sociology placed the question of social order at the centre of enquiry. The Comtian equation of 'order through progress' accentuated the positive aspects of cultural-scientific change. However, the post-Enlightenment conventional wisdom, namely that the *philosophes* were naïve positivists who believed only in the primacy of reason and Western domination, is a *faux cri de coeur*. From the beginning, the Enlightenment was a contradictory system of beliefs in which instrumental reason was at odds with critical reason, and universal edicts and propositions were always in tension with the peculiarities of particularism. Towards the end of the nineteenth century the *Methodenstreit* debate in German sociology focused on the methodological deficiencies of unalloyed positivism and empiricism. Similarly, Marx's sociology can be interpreted as a sustained attack upon bourgeois political economy for presenting an essentially imaginary perspective on social order; and Weber's action sociology produced a striking and durable critique of the unintended consequences of Enlightenment theorems, maxims and procedures. It is stretching the point to present these criticisms as a break with Enlightenment traditions, for criticism of Enlightenment theory, method and procedure was the corollary of the Enlightenment respect for tolerance and scepticism. In a nutshell, the Enlightenment legitimized self-criticism as a counterpoint to all forms of *a priori* reasoning.

These criticisms raised both the question of the defects of Enlightenment positivism and the larger possibility that the Enlightenment revolution constructed myths in the attribution of empiricism, universalism, individualism, science and freedom. However, they did so from within the Enlightenment camp. Sociology's deep-rooted anxieties about value-neutrality, ideology, inequality, social friction and injustice point to the limitations of the positivist approach. Critical classical sociology was predicated on the proposition that traditions of study were themselves disordered inasmuch as they failed to faithfully represent social reality. In this sense, the problem of disorder is partly expressed in the criticism of orthodox positivist traditions and categories of thought. It suggested that mainstream sociology is incapable of embracing social reality or, at the very least, is seriously out of joint with the times.

By the 1960s, much institutionalized sociology was impugned for imposing categories of social totality upon society rather than describing a true state of affairs. On this account, the question of social order is regarded to be a matter of attribution driven by the professional need of sociologists to exercise fiat over commonsense, humanistic or other 'non-scientific' approaches to social life. As the 1960s drew to a close, the emergence of feminism in universities added another significant critical front against the so-called orthodoxy. Ethnomethodology and the qualitative research tradition also played an important part in destabilizing nomothetic tendencies.

The net effect of these various critical reactions to institutionalized sociology is to seriously weaken the concept of social totality as a meaningful foundation for sociological study. Today, the construct of social totality is routinely rejected. Of course, intersubjective action suggests some sort of context, otherwise it is vulnerable to the charges of solipsism or metaphysics. Social totality has been eclipsed by the much vaguer concept of 'globalization'. Sociologists now regularly refer to global 'networks' and 'flows' to challenge established notions of social structure. Theories of globalization challenge the Weberian precept that the nation state must be the primary unit of sociological analysis. Furthermore, they argue that established notions of society are redundant because governmentality and economic management have been eclipsed by the multiple displacement of power from the nation state to international chains of flexible accumulation. These arguments connect up with the linguistic turn taken by poststructuralism and postmodernism which assigns latent authoritarianism and ethnocentricity to nomothetic analysis.

### Ernest Gellner: rational fundamentalism regained?

Not long before his death in 1995, Ernest Gellner (1997) confronted the rise of globalization as a central explanatory concept in sociology and concluded that it is premature to discard notions of nationalism and the nation state. He implied that many of the claims made by theorists of globalization are portentous and overblown. In particular, he held that they do not advance beyond the more commonplace arguments of linkage and interdependence made by mainstream postwar political sociology. Gellner was suspicious that a new lexicon would be mistaken for genuinely new developments in human relations. As with his (1992) earlier attack on postmodernism, he recommended that sociologists must not desert first principles just yet. By this he meant, among other things, that the notions of endogenous social structures, endogenous social reproduction and culture-free knowledge are still relevant in sociological argument and explanation. The history of the nation state has not come to an end; those who believe in the quest for objective knowledge in the social sciences should not pack up their bags just yet.

Arguably, Gellner's (1992, 1997) attempted refutation of globalization and postmodernism was too irascible and liverish. He saw globalization as the recrudescence of idealism, and postmodernism as the revival of relativism. Neither, he believed, was capable of coming to terms with the universal and perennial features of culture and social organization. Gellner (1992: 80) declared himself to be an adherent of what he called rationalist fundamentalism. He defined this as:

> a position which, like that of religious fundamentalism, is firmly committed to the denial of relativism. It is committed to the view that there *is* external, objective, culture-transcending knowledge: there *is* indeed 'knowledge beyond culture'. All knowledge must indeed be articulated in some idiom, but there are idioms capable of formulating questions in a way such that answers are no longer dictated by the internal characteristics of the idiom or the culture carrying it but, on the contrary, by an independent reality. The ability of cognition to reach beyond the bounds of any one cultural cocoon, and attain forms of knowledge valid for *all* – and, incidentally, an understanding of nature leading to an exceedingly powerful technology – constitutes *the* central fact about our shared social conditions. (1992: 75; emphasis in the original)

We do not completely agree with Gellner's conjoining of globalization with idealism or postmodernism with relativism. We hold that governmentality has been significantly displaced from the social structure of the nation, and that postmodernism accurately conveys exhaustion with grand narratives, and holistic, cumulative traditions, in ways which go beyond a mere revival of relativist spirit. Nonetheless, faced with what we might term the thrilling nullity of Baudrillard's denunciation of social reality, and Lyotard's withering philosophy of the *differénd*, we consider Gellner to be a more relevant and useful guide for understanding the conditions of the present (Rojek and Turner, 1993, 1998). He is more relevant and useful, we contend, because his work:

1   Identifies cumulative, stable research traditions which transcend the contexts of culture, class, gender and religion.
2   Repudiates the conviction that there are *a priori*, substantive truths.
3   Submits that analysis must be permanently *attentiste* rather than relativist in its approach to social enquiry.
4   Indicates that academic research has an obligation to treat all evidence impartially, and all moments in time as conditional and unfinished.
5   Confirms the proposition that societies constitute systems of real restraints, as opposed to coded orders of linguistic nuance or lexical difference.
6   Counsels wariness in the face of claims of the universal revelation of meaning or transcendence.

The Enlightenment banked on the progress of rational order, but it held, in reserve, the possibility of contradiction, disorder and chaos. Because it was a reserve judgement, it was understated in the regnant optimism of Comtian faith in the future. But its symptoms are evident in sociology from the very beginning, in the anxieties about social friction, disharmony, deviance, irrationality and the limits of governmentality.

Gellner knew that his argument was unfashionable. He went ahead for two reasons. First, he genuinely regretted the ground gained by post-structuralism and postmodernism in the 1980s and 1990s. He saw it as the unwelcome recurrence of irresponsible idealism. He judged that the supreme task of culture and politics is to ease the recognition of mutuality and commonality. Cultural relativism aestheticizes politics by emphasizing the external appearance of difference. He held that it militates against the notion of common interests and common pursuits by making a fetish of particularism.

Secondly, and paradoxically, he recognized that ethnic and nationalist conflicts were cries against the train of globalization, leaving standardization and the levelling of culture in its slipstream. Gellner recognized that a sense of place is the prerequisite of a sense of identity. Split identity does not have much of a place in Gellner's work. He is struck by both the conviction of immanent, identity between blood and soil and the immemorial belief in national and ethnic destiny. He regarded both as irrational passions. His defence of rationalist fundamentalism follows from the conviction that overcoming cultural and political.

We have argued that the problem of disorder in classical sociology is logically and historically twinned with the problem of order. If the latter has been overstated in the sociological tradition it is probably because sociologists have absorbed the Enlightenment habit of optimism and the respect for instrumental knowledge. Disorder, then, has led a tacit existence in the classical tradition; it has been displaced and refracted by the wider debates around disharmony, conflict and inequality.

Despite this, there is one area of social enquiry in which the question of disorder is paramount: criminology. Criminology began as a branch of general sociology devoted to the study of social friction and deviance. It is legitimate to describe the forms of life studied by criminologists as 'disorderly', because despite their often highly structured indeed regimented character, they are ways of being which are regarded as deviant from, or threatening to, official order. One can argue about the validity of 'official order'. For example, Goffman's (1967) injunction to study 'what is really going on' in society has sometimes been misinterpreted as a licence to focus on underground behaviour and deviant conduct, as if the normative order of monotony, predictability and restraint is nothing but an illusion. This is a misinterpretation because Goffman's sociology held fast to an, admittedly undertheorized, notion of 'paramount reality' (Goffman, 1974). By this term, Goffman appears to have meant the collection of values, beliefs and restraints which constitute the popular understanding of normative order. That the character of this order is contentious is not in doubt. For example, Marxist and feminist traditions in criminology recognized the notion of paramount reality, but they interpret it as ideology. Poststructuralist approaches go further, and dismiss notions of paramount reality and ideology as subject to the principle of the endless deferral of meaning. We have already had occasion to deplore the use of the linguistic metaphor as an appropriate device to picture or study culture. We insist on the centrality of bodily concreteness and the multiple sensuous pathways that make life with others meaningful. Rather than cover this ground again, we prefer to turn to the lineage of criminology in order to reveal how the notion of paramount reality has been deployed.

## Criminology and the crowd

Consider the early sociology of urban life. We are thinking, in particular, of the work of Gabriel Tarde (1895) and Gustave Le Bon (1901). It is caught up in the positivist urge to assemble a science of the new forms of collective life emerging in the industrial revolution. These writers are half-amazed by the Promethean power of capitalism to found nations, destroy kings, create entire cities, build transcontinental transport links, solve what were perceived, hitherto, as insoluble conundrums in medicine, public health and the mobility of people and ideas. Yet they are also half-aghast at the ferment of energy unleashed by urban-industrial growth. What troubles them above all? The collective, the crowd, the citizens whose very mass symbolizes unruliness. The crowd symbolizes the surplus power of concentrated mass existence that is beyond the reach of the various principles of normative governmentality. The analysis of this mass now reads as a symptomatology of nineteenth century power hierarchies. It reveals the projection of fears and fantasies (class/gender/race/health) onto the expanding urban-industrial populations.

Le Bon is the theorist of crowd control, *par excellence*. He fully grasped that the French revolution demonstrated the exhaustion of the absolutist power of the monarchy and signalled the power of the collective. For Le Bon, the crowd is the unstable expression of all of the unwieldy, volatile, turbulent powers of the uneducated, seething mass. It embodies the dark side of collective life.

Fears of contagion and pollution recur regularly in the medicalization of society in the nineteenth century. Although health reformers like Kay-Shuttleworth, Edward Chadwick and, later, William Beveridge, primarily addressed the physical dangers of the multitude, there is an unmistakable moral dimension to their policy. Poverty and immorality were twinned in the minds of these reformers, and this logic carried over into the nineteenth- and twentieth-century programmes of moral normalization forced through by schooling, public health legislation, law and order concerns and the rational recreation movement.

Le Bon certainly shared this logic. He interpreted the surplus energies of the crowd as a threat to social stability. The uncontrolled multitude represent moral disorder and contagion at the gates of civilization. This is not to say that he denied that crowds can act in heroic ways. Rather it is to insist that the balance of his discussion concentrates on the irrational or primitive aspects of crowd behaviour. Le Bon advocated the science of crowd control as a requisite of civilized government because he believed that there is a spontaneous tendency for mere assembly to revert to animal type. At the very least, the crowd is situated on the border of civilized and primitive conduct. For this reason, he argued (1912: 55–6), the crowd is a magnet for criminals, degenerates and demagogues. Naturally, Le Bon understood that the crowd predated industrial society. After all, the Ancient Romans and Greeks invented public spaces and thus comprehended well enough the seditious power of the crowd. However, because of the relatively simple division of labour and limited communication networks that prevailed in these societies, crowd disturbance was, for the most part, a phenomenon of the periphery.

Similarly, the long rule of the Church, in complicity with the monarchical-baronial class, which was the hallmark of the Middle Ages, boxed the prospect of insurrection from below. If the perditions of hell did not dissuade the potential revolutionary from rising to arms, the obstacles of communication were sufficient reason to give pause for thought. Yet as Arendt notes (1958: 188–92), order in human affairs in all times is notoriously frail. For example, in 1381, Wat Tyler, an obscure labourer from Essex, emerged as the leader of the Peasants' Revolt. The rebels seized Canterbury and marched on London, forcing the King, Richard II, to flee to the safety of the Tower of London. Tyler's men – ordinary, uneducated, rudely armed – ransacked John of Gaunt's palace. For a brief moment, feudal England teetered on the brink of peasant control. Tyler's demands were radical: the abolition of serfdom, the limitation of rents, and the execution of Chancellor Sudbury, Treasurer Hales, John of Gaunt and others. Another England bloomed in that dawn, one which the nineteenth-century Diggers and Levellers would resurrect, and which also scented the antinomian traditon of the eighteenth and nineteenth centuries and, we would argue, the decorative revolt into style of the twentieth century (Rojek, 1998). As for Tyler, at a meeting with Richard and his noblemen in Smithfield, he was tricked and suppressed, then murdered by Mayor Walworth.

Disturbances like the Peasants' Revolt and the protests of the Diggers, Levellers and Ranters in the seventeenth century exposed the limits of ruling ontologies and epistemologies. They hinted at new ways of being and more egalitarian, liberal forms of social organization. However, they were also generally contained by the governing political machine (Hill, 1975; Underdown, 1985). The transport and communication system capable of supporting national armed insurrection was not in place until the eighteenth century. This, together with the exponential growth of populations and their concentration in urban-industrial centres, led Le Bon to describe the modern age as 'the era of crowds' rather than the era of revolutions. For Le Bon and Tarde the crowd has a 'mental unity' and a latent anti-social character. If social commentators are searching for a representation of social dislocation and chaos, they will find it in the potential for disturbance and pollution located in the crowd.

Later writers, notably Rudé (1985: 237), criticized Tarde and Le Bon for failing to situate the crowd in the appropriate social and historical contexts. The chaotic capability of the crowd, and the unconscious aggressive mental unity of assembly, are presented as historical universals. Against this, Rudé presents assembly as a conduit for social protest and transformation. The crowd, he argues, is one of the main fronts of popular resistance. The cloacal images which Tarde and Le Bon use to describe crowd behaviour are therefore deemed inappropriate. He concludes that they reflect the political prejudices of the writers, not historical reality.

Be that as it may, Tarde and Le Bon's fear of the crowd as a disruptive agent in public life has clear historical roots. Overshadowing their approach is the stereotype of the unruly, rampaging mob in the French revolution. Le Bon equated the mob with the lower classes (Rudé, 1985: 9). He regarded them as relishing the revolutionary moment as an orgy of unabashed aggression and crimes against property. Rudé (1985) again points to the stereotypical qualities of this reading.

Yet the image of the frenzied, amoral revolutionary mob also haunted English political economy in the nineteenth century. Stedman Jones (1971) has demonstrated that social policy in health, education and law and order was partly formulated in response to the category of 'the residuum'. That is, the category of unemployed and seasonally employed labourers who were regarded as the home of pestilence, primitive values and social unrest. English political economy partly defined the values of respectable society in reaction to the residuum. One of the main thrusts of public policy after the 1840s was the elimination of this class, through the various means of colonial exportation, and eventually through urban rehabilitation schemes and the expansion of the public education and health systems. Pearson's (1983) research broadly supports this analysis, but it adds two new important elements to a critical understanding of the chimera of disorder in modern capitalist society. First, he demonstrates that in the mid-twentieth century respectable fears about the cloacal mass were supplemented with anxieties concerning youth culture and the ethnic diaspora. To be sure, these were always themes in the modern body politic, but after the 1950s the growth in real income of youth groups raised them as a 'threat' on the social landscape. Cohen's (1972) classic study of moral panics demonstrated how the various processes of media amplification operated to heighten worries about juvenile delinquency. The work of Hall (1988) shows how these worries extended to the ethnic diaspora. Secondly, Pearson (1983: 236) illuminates the immense cultural capital of the law, and its associated institutions, in presenting itself as the *locus classicus* of reason and tolerance. As such, unrest and protest are usually presented, in the first instance at least, as 'irrational' or 'debased' acts.

## The specialization of criminology

The study of social disorder became a specialized branch of sociology early in the nineteenth century. Beccaria's *Essay on Crimes and Punishments* (1804) is generally held to be the foundational work of classical criminology. Beccaria follows Hobbes, Montesquieu and Rousseau in broadly confirming a social contract perspective on the law. Thus, he holds that men agree to formulate binding laws which restrain personal desire because they wish to avoid a continual state of war in civil society. Classical criminology presents the state as the legitimate agent of law enforcement. Citizens are portrayed as rational beings who are responsible for their own actions. The purpose of the law is to deter individuals from violating the interests of others.

Classical criminology was evidently infused with the spirit of positivism. It held that criminal behaviour can be scientifically classified and controlled. The great weakness of this approach was that it concentrated on the criminal act rather than the motivations and situations of the criminal. Neo-classical revisionism became significant in the 1880s. It was primarily associated with the writings of Rossi, Garaud and Joly (Radzinowicz, 1966). Revisonism introduced two important amendments into the hegemonic perspective on crime and criminiality. First, it pioneered the notion of mitigating circumstances in the aetiology of criminal acts. Social and environmental factors were allowed a role in explaining the motivation behind crime. Secondly, the failure of classical criminology to allow for physical or mental factors in criminal behaviour was dismissed as unsatisfactory. Neo-classical revisionism established the notion that the offender's record of past behaviour, and physical, mental and social background, is germane in explaining crime. These two amendments effectively encouraged jurists to situate criminal behaviour in relevant biographical, historical and social contexts. Whereas classical criminology imposed choice and responsibility for action entirely on the shoulders of the citizen, neo-classical revisionism recognized structural influences behind actions. Instead of attributing the undifferentiated condition of evil to disorderly acts, the emphasis was now upon classifying behaviour and formulating causal explanations of deviance.

Until well into the twentieth century, criminology is notable for pursuing independence from the central concerns of social theory. With one or two exceptions, notably the Chicago School's attempt to locate social pathology in urban-industrial conditions and Merton's (1957, 1968) neo-Durkheimian work on crime and the American dream, criminology was dominated by the positivist objective of eliminating crime through scientific analysis and policy. Deviance was therefore theorized as an epiphenomenon which could be brought to book by the concerted application of scientific rigour. Ferri (1895, 1901) was a leading figure in the quantification of criminal behaviour. He enjoined that statistical analysis of criminal behaviour in relation to social environment and defined physical conditions of the offender would produce general laws of crime. These would become the cornerstones of scientific criminology in the twentieth century.

Interestingly, scientific criminology developed a focus on the body long before mainstream sociology. One aspect of the positivist interest in criminal statistics was aggregating data on criminal types. This data fell into environmental and cultural sub-classifications, but the physical and mental appearance of criminal types was also an issue. Social Darwinism posited unmistakable trajectories of evolution from 'primitive' to 'advanced' species and 'low' to 'high' cultures. It was but a short step for criminology to posit biological determinism in criminal and deviant behaviour. The most notorious example is Lombroso's (1911) theory that much criminal behaviour can be explained by the biological principle of atavism. According to this, the criminal is not simply a law-breaker, but a throwback to an earlier type in human evolution. Lombroso supported his theory by a statistical analysis of the physical characteristics of criminals. On this basis, he proposed that criminal types can be identified by transparent physical stigmata. Among the stigmata he listed were large ears, eye defects, prominent superciliary arches, tattooing, sensile ears and abnormal dentition.

Lombroso recognized that environmental factors, such as poverty, poor education or political ideals, are relevant in explaining the aetiology of criminal behaviour. However, the *succès de scandale* of his theory resided in the proposition that there is a demonstrable link between biological characteristics and criminal conduct.

Lombroso's theory has been discredited on the grounds of faulty methodology. In particular, his statistical analysis is now regarded as over-selective and his specification of physical stigmata confused social conditions with biological necessity. For example, physical abnormalities such as abnormal dentition, eye defects and tattooing can more adequately be explained by the social conditions of the offender's life.

## Criminology and Modernity

As exponents of the 'new criminology' advocated in the 1970s, the classical and neo-classical traditions in criminology adopted a managerial stance in commenting on crime (Taylor et al., 1973). Although the revisionist tradition gave greater scope to social and environmental factors in the aetiology of criminal behaviour, it failed to provide satisfactory accounts of criminal *experience*. The classical and neo-classical traditions saw the proper role of criminology as consisting in understanding the causes of crime and determining tenable policies of social control to diminish crime rates and rehabilitate offenders. This tacitly discounted a number of propositions about the relationship between crime and society as merely speculative and therefore not worth addressing scientifically. In particular, the phenomenology of criminal experience became a category neglected by the classical literature. For example, Leyton's (1986, 1995) work on murderers and serial killers reveals the extent to which explanations of murder are typically medicalized without integrating cultural and social conditions into the causal chain.

Durkheim's studies of suicide and abnormal forms of labour, Weber's theory of the rationalization process, Simmel's work on the blasé and neurasthenic personalities and the destabilizing consequences of social change, and Veblen's work on the enlargement of conspicuous consumption, implied that crime and deviance are endemic in modern life. They run counter to the notion that deviance can be eradicated, although admittedly Durkheim's recommendations for dealing with egoism, anomie and the abnormal division of labour imply that acceptable containment was certainly a realistic goal of the scientific management of society. The 'juggernaut of modernity', to use a term later popularized by Giddens (1990), guaranteed that social rules cannot be binding. The classical tradition adduces two reasons for this.

First, the velocity and differentiation of modern social change is such, that some conservative moral positions in respectable society are bound to be outflanked by social progress. For example, the decriminalization of homosexuality and the relaxation of laws against pornography in the 1960s overturned precepts about the limits of decent behaviour that respectable society had cherished for generations. Similarly, the bio-genetic engineering movement of the present day is opposed by many sections of respectable society on the grounds that it tampers with God's work. We believe that these opponents will suffer the same fate as 1960s campaigners who pitted themselves against the law on liberalizing homosexuality and the rise of the permissive society. The accumulation of critical mass in some trajectories of social and technological change regularly outstrips the capacity of social groups to morally rationalize or contain the process.

The second reason why rules cannot be binding under Modernity is that technical innovation ordinarily requires a degree of rule-infraction. Bending the rules which other people live by often carries competitive advantage. Surplus wealth is generated by taking society in new directions. Allied to the heroic ethic of corporate culture, which requires business leaders and critics of business to be risk-takers, this endows modern life with a continuous anomic quality: Durkheim (1897) well understood this, as his thesis on the immanent character of social friction in urban-industrial life shows.

Lyng (1988) has produced an impressive cartography of 'edgework'. He demonstrates the forms of pleasure generated from pushing behaviour over the edge of legal or habitual practice. He concentrates on examples of physical risk-taking, such as bungee jumping, sky diving and joy riding. Computer hacking and illegal drug use are also examples of edgework. Yet the point we wish to emphasize here is that edgework should not be polarized as an aspect of deviant culture. Risk-taking is built into the mundane processes of capitalist accumulation. It is an orthodox component of successful business culture. There is indeed a thin line between many forms of business success and breaking the law.

Weber's (1922) distinction between formal and substantive rationality fully anticipated this and confirmed his thesis on the irrationalism of modern life. In his view, formal rationality consists of the quantitative accounting and calculation of social action. Substantive rationality is a criterion of choice and action which is affixed to an ultimate value of some kind. As Weber recognized, substantive rationality cannot be conceptually systematized in any exhaustive sense, because it involves an infinite number of possible value-scales. The necessity of success in the modern business corporation, and the pressure and opportunities provided by global competition, mean that businesspeople wrestle with the ambiguities of the formal-substantive dichotomy in their ordinary business decisions.

What is interesting about this observation is that it suggests that layerings of moral chaos or quasi-chaos are compatible with the apparent order of formal rationality in modern social organization. Again, this is anticipated in classical social theory. For example, Durkheim's (1895) distinction between the normal and pathological in social life recognized that deviance is normal, providing it does not exceed the level appropriate for each social type. Durkheim (1895: 55) defined the normal as the 'social conditions that are most generally distributed'. The pathological is a residual category, pertaining to social forms and practices which are not generally distributed. Durkheim reasoned that the normal forms of life, at least in their aggregate, were those that were the most advantageous to the social organism.

There are, of course, significant sociological objections to this. Most importantly, the discussion does not allow for differences in power which enable the powerful to impose frameworks of normality on the less powerful. For example, the Marxist attack on dominant ideology and the feminist criticism of patriarchy concentrate precisely on the inequality of power in society. These criticisms have some purchase, although there are also grounds for suggesting that the dominant ideology thesis and the conceptualization of patriarchy have exaggerated the uniformity and pre-eminence of some forms of power (Abercrombie et al., 1980). Moreover, in Durkheim's defence, his standpoint on moral individualism recognized that the social organism consists of individuals who are not uniform in their hereditary origins, physical milieux or cultural outlook. Moral individualism presupposes diversified consciousness. On this basis he (1895: 70) insists on the normality of crime, providing, of course, that it remains within a certain level for the concomitant social type. Durkheim, then, believed that the division of labour and the moral preconditions of organic solidarity rendered deviance unavoidable.

A similar conclusion is reached by Jack Katz (1988) although he reaches it by a separate, and perhaps more interesting, analytical route. If the classical and neo-classical traditions are guilty of dividing criminology from social theory, Katz is outstanding in fusing the two together. Katz twins the subject of the experience of crime with the experience of modernity. He acknowledges that his approach owes a debt to the interactionist perspective of Becker (1963) and Matza (1969). The work of both queried the classical and neo-classical belief that crime can be scientifically controlled. But neither theorist went as far as Katz in conceptualizing crime and deviance as integral to modernity.

Katz's view of crime and deviance takes a Nietzschean turn. He focuses on the experience of crime as sensual gratification. In contrast with the materialist versions of crime found in the work of Merton (1957, 1968) or Cloward and Ohlin (1960), Katz interprets crime and deviance in terms of the pleasure gained by going beyond the rules of 'normal' society. His interpretation reinforces a reading of social life which emphasizes sensuality and bodily connectivity. By breaking these rules and flaunting rule infraction, the offender signals personal opposition to conventional, 'straight' morality and the system of mundane authority. Like Durkheim, Katz considers deviance to be a normal feature of contemporary society, but unlike Durkheim, he regards the law as reflecting inequality in the distribution of power rather than constituting a tangible expression of the *collective conscience*. By extension, Katz dismisses the positivist argument that crime can be scientifically controlled. His work suggests that deviance and infraction inhere in the interstices of society. The various support structures that make modern life possible also make fiddling, blackmail, embezzlement, violence towards others and ancillary forms of crime unavoidable. On this reading the dichotomy between order and chaos in classical sociology and criminology is far-fetched. Deviant subcultures, which hold values and practise lifestyles that are antithetical to the formal rationality of liberal democracy, are institutionalized layers in organic society. Yablonsky's (1997) study of the ordinary character of sociopathic tendencies in the metropolis supports this interpretation.

In asserting that deviance is unavoidable in modern society, we are not issuing a tacit message of social approval for agents of disorder and violence. We are as fearful of muggers, con-men, burglars, pickpockets, terrorists, tricksters and sociopaths, as anyone else. Instead, we seek to challenge the supposition that deviance is external to normal social order. We argue that deviance is latent in every social relationship. The ethical ambivalence of Modernity requires strategic interventions in relations with others (Bauman, 1991; Smart, 1999). The student who buys model assignment essays from the internet, or the professor who fails to declare earned income on his tax return, are ethically equivalent to the company that includes undeclared, addictive additives in its food products or the democratic state that sells arms to dictators. From face-to-face interaction to foreign policy initiatives, strategic imperatives chronically override ethical considerations of right and wrong. In general, sociology has supported the view that deviant behaviour is divorced from ordinary life. By avowing the latent character of deviance in ordinary facework and everyday social relations we maintain that the dichotomy between order and disorder is false. The development of criminology as the specialized study of disorder and deviance obscures the pertinence of these issues for mainstream sociology.

### Conclusion: disorder in the new capitalism

Postmodernism, poststructuralism and the various other critical positions that became prominent during the 1970s and continue to be so up to the present day, have produced a volte-face in sociological concerns. Given our preoccupation in this chapter, the most significant result is that the problem of social disorder has replaced the problem of social order as the focus of sociological debate. In Parsonian (1951) sociology, social order is presented as a functional prerequisite of society. Parsons argues that order is engendered through the internalization of shared values and norms. The critical and radical rebuttal of structural functionalism dwells on two arguments. First, the Parsonian view of order is ideologically impregnated. Structural functionalism is vitiated for tacitly supporting a particular order of *power*. Secondly, Parsonian sociology is attacked for failing to sufficiently recognize that norms and values are under-internalized in society. Strata that are relatively marginalized in society exploit and develop retreatist and oppositional systems of norms and values. Yet even those who outwardly claim inclusive membership, regularly demonstrate a calculating attitude in Katz's (1988) sense, of seeking to gain personal advantage by unethical means if opportunity dictates. The order that Parsons sets such store by turns out to be more murky and ambivalent than he imagined.

These criticisms were instrumental in elevating, Gellner's *bête noire*, cultural relativism, as the sociological orthodoxy of the post-1970s. The weak version of cultural relativism states that cultural norms and values are variable and that all cultures have a moral duty to respect the difference of others. The strong version of cultural relativism asserts that difference is an attribution of power, and that all cultures have a moral responsibility to dismantle structures of power which are identified as supporting hierarchy. Neither the weak nor the strong version of cultural relativism has proved very successful in addressing the problem of social disorder. The weak version confines ethical questions to matters of procedure. Since difference is predefined as sacrosanct, the political and ethical task boils down to ensuring that the category claims of difference and mutual tolerance are honoured. The strong version of cultural relativism also concentrates on procedure as a method to ensure, for example, justice in the allocation of resources. Yet ethically, the goal is to bring marginal cultures from the periphery into the core. In this regard, a common rhetorical technique is to seek to unravel claims of status hierarchy between cultures, by assigning hybridity as a cultural universal. What basis can there be for proclaiming European culture superior to non-white culture if all cultures are understood as mixtures of ethnic and cultural influence?

Gitlin (1995) has criticized the strong version of cultural relativism on the grounds that it affirms rights of diversity without articulating equivalent principles of mutual reliance or common moral obligations. Concentration on procedural issues in the constitution of citizenship rights has dominated debate since the 1970s. What this neglects is the substantive distribution of power in society which is the real foundation of the unequal allocation of economic and cultural resources. Identity politics may raise the consciousness and unleash energies of the margins, but it has left the centres of power largely unscathed and under-theorized. In the late 1980s commentators used to refer to global economic deregulation, delayering, downsizing and flexible accumulation as symptoms of 'disorganized capitalism' (Lash and Urry, 1987). They speculated that the cultural consequences would include the decline of the work ethic, chronic anomie, the deindustrialization of once prosperous cities and urban unrest, as workers realized that the practices of training and deferred gratification which had served generations intent on upward mobility in the past, no longer held good. Those on the left looked forward to an inevitable confrontation between the oppressed and the system.

Nowadays, commentators speak routinely of 'the new capitalism' in which flexible accumulation and instability contribute to generalized ontological insecurity (Sennett, 1998). The difference is that few any longer predict a looming historical clash between forces and relations in the new capitalism. Capitalism has not become more philanthropic. Workers still experience inequality, control and deskilling in the workplace. What has changed is that flexible accumulation has disembedded control from the immediate point of production. Flexible accumulation depends upon the liberalization of the labour market because investment follows the best rate of return on fixed and variable capital. Precisely for this reason, it disempowers collectivism. Workers in a company manufacturing micro-chips in Britain for parts of a computer system co-assembled in Germany, Ireland and Poland, do not know who to complain to when the company regional headquarters is located in Brussels, the executive board reside in New Jersey and the shareholders are dispersed throughout North America, Western Europe and South East Asia. Managers and shop-floor workers are in the same boat if New Jersey decides to switch investment to Thailand or South Korea. Thus, the tracks of capitalist power are much less legible than they were, even twenty years ago.

Confronted with a system that reproduces indifference to individuals by making them redundant, inadequately educated for the jobs available today, under-pensioned and without effective health cover, individuals no longer know who to blame. National governments are at the mercy of the whims of transnational corporations, just like workers at the place of work. True, they have more leverage through legislation and fiscal machinery. Even so, ultimately, they cannot effectively regulate investment flow and resource allocation in the new capitalism.

A notable feature of Sennett's argument is the presupposition that the disruptive transformation in the capitalist world order between the 1960s and the 1990s has culminated in the reintegration of the system. The 'new capitalism' may work upon different principles to the preceding system. For example, it is more global in real time, more mobile in switching resources from one source of accumulation to another, more data-based than person-based, less concerned with performance, and more concerned with inno-vation. Nonetheless, it is far from the disorderly state of affairs depicted in poststructuralist and postmodernist accounts. It is perhaps obligatory to add that Sennett's analysis does not erase the presence of disorder in the new capitalism. On the contrary, the proposition that many people still experience the reordering of capitalism as personally disruptive and emo-tionally annihilating, is central to his argument.

Giddens's (1991, 1998) writings on the fundamental issues in the new 'life politics', and Bauman's (1993) concern to elucidate the ethical content of life in postmodernity, broadly confirm the argument that reordering, not disorder, is now the urgent focus for critical enquiry. What is being reordered? In essence, it is argued that the personality structure is being reconfigured with the socio-economic system. It would be too crude to say simply that flexible accumulation requires flexible personalities, because other factors are involved; but this provides as least an initial orientation. Modernity constructed performative culture as the normative order.

Performative culture may be characterized as ways of behaviour, thinking and feeling that prioritized action. Classical political economy regarded business as the precondition for utility. Veblen's (1899) sociology may be thought of as a repudiation of performative culture for fetishizing conspicuous consumption. Veblen's leisure class are busy doing nothing which adds to the wealth of society. By immersing themselves in cultural practices which symbolize renunciation of the commitment to wage labour, they represent aloof status. Veblen notes that the leisure class represent social *éclat* by cultivating dead languages like Latin and Greek, indulging in hunting and horsemanship and throwing lavish parties. None of these activities are necessary in the industrial age. On the contrary, they persist precisely because they demonstrate to others that this class is free from the submission to wage labour.

Goffman's (1967, 1971, 1974) sociology is perhaps the most complete critical inventory of the regime of performative culture. Goffman's analysis of the mechanics of trust and tact shows how the individual negotiates appropriate behaviour in interaction settings and adjusts the presentation of the self in accordance with the requirements of different social situations. Goffman's (1971: 252) work shows how performance exploits and develops the shared conception of paramount reality. Goffman's social actor emerges as a skilled performer in the maintenance of normative order. However, central to Goffman's approach is the proposition that social actors are bound by ritual, ceremony and scripts. Performative culture may be pliable, but its heart is programmatic.

It is this arrangement of Modernity which Giddens (1990, 1991), Bauman (1992, 1993) and other writers suggest has now come to an end. For Giddens (1991: 209–31) critical politics under Modernity has typically been concerned with emancipation from aspects of normative order which are experienced or perceived as inhibiting, unequal or unjust. He contends that emancipatory politics is now being supplanted by life politics. Emancipatory politics is primarily concerned with transcending tradition and equitable resource distribution. In contrast, life politics focuses on self-actualization, choice and the ethical foundations of responsible co-existence. The conceit underlying Giddens's account is that the goals of emancipatory politics have been accomplished. To be sure, women's struggle for freedom and justice, ethnic resistance to white power and the traditional class objective of equality have not been wholly successful. Indeed, the essence of emancipatory politics is that the goals constantly shift. Giddens accepts that there is much still to do in working for freedom, equality and justice. Yet emancipatory politics and economic growth have combined to create the cultural and economic space in which many more individuals focus their energies on questions of self-realization and reflexivity.

Bauman's (1992, 1993, 1998) attempt to delineate ethical principles for postmodern times also accepts that the traditional goals of emancipatory politics have transformed social conditions. Notably, he (1998a, 1998b) is more sceptical than Giddens that the traditional goals of emancipatory politics have been accomplished. His work is more sensitive to the plight of the excluded, even to the point of positing the emergence of new strata of vagabonds and welfare claimants. Bauman argues à la Levinas that the decisive ethical principle of postmodern times must be care for the other. There are good sociological as well as philosophical reasons for arguing thus. Individuals are always and already interdependent and personal utility is pursued through relations of reciprocity. Moreover, humans are group animals. So the principle of caring for each other has an intuitive appeal. Yet the mere facts that we are born, live and die, interdependent with others, and that involvement is the precondition of viable selfhood, are no basis, in themselves, for presenting care for the other as a workable ethical principle. Bauman (1993: 74) himself expresses the tension, in his observation that the reader is entitled to be 'incredulous' about his suggestion. For the ethical principle of care for the other must, for the moment, subsist in a world of racial, class, gender and status division.

Bauman, of course, knows this. There is an 'ideal-typical' quality to his advocacy of 'care for the other' as a principle of ethical reorientation. It is intended to crystallize issues and provoke debate. As such, it is part of a reaction to cultural relativism which became more pronounced after poststructuralism and postmodernism. We do not discount civic virtue or the challenges to performative culture presented by the cultural turn. Nonetheless, we hold that the accounts by Giddens and Bauman suggest a largesse of virtu in civil society which is not confirmed by the observable facts. The gap between the rich and poor has grown under the new capitalism. Sennett (1998: 54) reports that the weekly wages, adjusted for inflation, for the bottom 80 per cent in America fell by 18 per cent between 1973 and 1995; while the income of the coporate elite rose by 19 per cent before taxes and 66 per cent after the audits of their accountants. In the UK the top 20 per cent of the working population earn seven times as much as the bottom 20 per cent, while in the 1970s the wealth gap was only four times. Social exclusion and marginalization remain realities for millions, for whom 'life politics' is a somewhat rarefied concept. Beyond the question of the persistence of poverty and inequality, we would also emphasize the transgressive quality of contemporary life. People of good will abound in society; but even they participate in rule-infracting behaviour from time to time. The ordinary state of disorder identified by Katz (1988) and other writers, may be a sociological cliché, but it bears repeating in the face of exaggerated claims for the achievements of redistributive justice and the emergence of a post-nationalist, world government.

# 4

# SOLIDARITY

The problem of social order is constitutive of sociology as such. That is, the question concerning the nature of social order is a question which sociological theory cannot ignore. Any sociological statement about social reality must carry with it, whether overtly or covertly, some set of assumptions about the very possibility of social order. The issue may be expressed in various ways, but ultimately this debate is best summarized by the title of a famous essay by Georg Simmel (1971): how is society possible? In these introductory comments, our approach is obviously influenced by what we take to be the principal twentieth-century analytical location of this debate, the work of Talcott Parsons (1937).

For Parsons, this question had its roots in Thomas Hobbes's theory of social contract and the state in *Leviathan*, so he referred to this issue as the Hobbesian problem of order. In Parsons's version of this classical statement of contract theory, if *homo economicus* follows egoistic ends by rational means within a utilitarian framework, then fraud and force are appropriate and common means for securing these individualistic goals. In short, Parsons argued that any positivistic theory of action, which took instrumental rationality as the only standard of meaningful action, would be incapable of producing a consistent theory of social order. Such utilitarianism could only solve the problem of order by 'residual categories' which were ad hoc solutions, incompatible with the rational assumptions of the theory. For Parsons, the 'hidden hand' in classical economics was an ad hoc solution of the fundamental sociological problem of social order. This criticism of the classical economic explanation of both rational action and social order provided an abiding attack on marginal utility theory.

A sociological theory of social order would have to examine (what Emile Durkheim regarded as) the non-contractual element of contract (that is common values, collective sentiments) which underpins everyday reciprocities and relations. Although Parsons's version of the history of sociological theory has been heavily criticized, it can reasonably be argued (Holton and Turner, 1986; Turner, 1989; Robertson and Turner, 1990; Turner, 1991) that Parsons's defence of sociological explanations of social order is still a coherent alternative to, for example, rational choice explanations of social order (Hechter, 1989; Coleman, 1990). In following Parsons in the introduction to this chapter, we take it for granted that any sociological enquiry into the nature of social order will be concerned with this fundamental question (how is society possible?). That is, it will be an enquiry into what set of conditions are necessary for social action to occur at all in a context of relatively stable expectations.

A discussion of social order necessarily outlines a set of conditions of existence of recurring patterns of social action. Furthermore, at least one element of these conditions will be a set of mores or normative standards, namely the common values, beliefs and norms which are shared by social actors. In more detail, a sociology of social order will examine the mixture of consent and constraint which structure these social relationships.

Turning to the historical development of sociology, the issue of social order was especially important in the evolution of classical sociology in the period from 1890 to 1920. The rapid urbanization of societies such as Germany, the crisis of the Austro-Habsburg empire, the growth of anti-Semitism, the Dreyfus affair in France and the violent devastation of the First World War produced a cultural crisis which was expressed in the idea of a *fin-de-siècle* catastrophe, which included the decline of the West, nihilism and decadence (Hughes, 1959). Vienna came to be seen eventually as a key epicentre of these changes, which were in turn understood as a frontal attack on the rational values of the liberal bourgeois world. The philosophical and artistic worlds of Freud, Klimt, Mahler (Beller, 1989) were indicative of the depth of the crisis. Vienna was the *Wertvakuum* (value-vacuum) of Europe which produced a culture of feeling (*Gefühlskultur*). We might say that our current concern for the nature of social order in the context of a postmodernist critique of modernism parallels (perhaps parodies) the *fin-de-siècle* crisis of the 1890, which 'produced' classical sociology.

This general sense of social crisis appeared in classical sociology in terms of a series of debates and questions about legitimacy, order and cohesion. There are grounds for believing that Durkheim's attempt to produce a science of morals was a response to what he saw as the inadequacy of traditional Kantian rationalism. Furthermore, there is a certain similarity between Arthur Schopenhauer's emphasis on compassion and Durkheim's rejection of the idea that ethical life is based ultimately on sanction (Meštrović, 1991). Although Durkheim's concept of 'anomie' perhaps best summarizes this sense of social disorder, at the time Ferdinand Tönnies's distinction (Tönnies, 1957) between *Gemeinschaft* and *Gesellschaft* was particularly influential in the development of European sociology. In Tönnies's original theory, which was published in 1887, this dichotomy expressed a contrast between different types of will, but it was gradually transformed into a dichotomous view of society. The contrast between community and association in later sociology came to lose much of its original philosophical connotation. In sociological terminology, *gemeinschaftlich* arrangements were characteristic of primary groups in which direct, ascriptive and affective relations were dominant. *Gesellschaftlich* institutions were based on competition, anonymity, individualism and neutrality. Durkheim's contrast between mechanical and organic societies, and Max Weber's contrast between traditional and rational-instrumental social relations might be regarded as a parallel contrast; more specifically, in *Economy and Society*, his discussion of open-associational and closed-communal relationships directly incorporated Tönnies's legacy into mainstream sociological terminology. It became an essential distinction in the evaluation of the negative impact of industrialization on the quality of social relationships.

In general, classical sociology was a reflection on a dichotomy, which was made famous in legal theory by Sir Henry Maine, between status and contract: namely that the emergence of a modern, industrial civilization involved a transition from societies which were based on traditional status hierarchies to those based on market-oriented, contractual, associational relations between strangers (Turner, 1988). For Maine, the rise of contractualism tore the individual from the all-embracing network of family and community, and ushered in a society based on individualistic contracts between strangers.

These issues of market and fellowship were brilliantly analysed by the historian Otto von Gierke (1990) in his study of the social functions of premodern fellowships (*Genossenschaft*), a notion which has subsequently become important in contemporary debates about citizenship and associative democracies. Independent associations are crucial links between individuals and the modern state, because it is through participation in this associative life that individuals can express public virtues. Classical sociology took the position that social order under *gesellschaftlich* arrangements was inherently unstable, and most mainstream sociologists (but especially Durkheimian sociologists) attempted to locate some new factor of coherence which would guarantee minimal social integration if industrial civilization was to survive. Traditional conditions of social order, such as a shared worldview or a common religion or communal propinquity, were undermined by the division of labour, the secularization of religious values, the urbanization of society, and the fragmentation and pluralism of culture (Nisbet, 1966). Few classical sociologists, apart from Simmel, thought that the metropolis, while a threat to conventional values, also offered new possibilities for individuality, creativity and social change.

## Three traditions of sociological explanation

Before turning to this classical sociological tradition in more detail, we first want to outline, in a very general way, three traditional analytical frameworks which have provided explanations of social order. These perspectives were developed before the classical period of sociology, and they obviously provided, as it were, the background to the evolution of sociological approaches to the explanation of social order. In conventional social theory there were basically three major approaches to the explanation of social order.

## Machiavellian (power as politics)

The first approach emphasizes constraint and coercion as basic dimensions of society. Societies are held together and social conflict is contained by the fact that there are powerful means of constraint, regulation and coercion to subordinate opposition, to regulate dissent and to intimidate the population with the threat of superior force. In general terms, it is the state which has enjoyed this monopoly of violence, which is exercised in the interests of the dominant class or elite. For the sake of argument, we may conveniently regard this tradition as the legacy of Machiavelli's *The Prince*. It was Machiavelli who recommended to the Prince that he should either destroy or embrace his enemies. Although this view of social order is ancient, the notion that an element of coercion is an essential prerequisite of order continues to inform modern social theory, for example Louis Althusser's discussion of the coercive apparatus of the state (Althusser, 1977), or Gramsci's view that hegemony was a mixture of moral leadership and coercion. We might add that the notion of coercion can take a strong or weak form. In its strong form in *The Prince*, coercion is understood to be conscious, directive and overt: it is a conscious manipulation of social actors. However, it is equally appropriate to think of social institutions as such in terms of their coercive and constraining effects on action. This weak version of the notion of constraint blends invariably into some assumption of shared values, whereby coercion is rendered legitimate. It is assumed that naked force is ultimately an ineffective, expensive and unstable basis for social order. There are relatively few historical examples, for example in wartime conditions, were social relations are based upon totalitarian power or systematic violence. Some degree of consent is typical of all social relationships, even in slavery or concentration camps or in what Erving Goffman called 'total institutions' (Goffman, 1961).

Secondly, there is a sociologically more convincing tradition which suggests that social order rests on a common set of agreements or rules or conventions which bind people together into a community. In traditional societies, it is generally thought, following Durkheim, that it was religion which provided this social cement (Turner, 1994c). There are many versions of this theory. Some comparative approaches to religion argued that it was the sharing of common rituals (such as sacrifice) which created solidarity. In his study of the ancient city, Fustel de Coulanges (1956) argued that social unity in the classical world emerged out of the rituals which had their primary location in the symbolism of the hearth. In classical sociology, this interpretation of social order has been closely identified with Durkheim and Parsons (Holton and Turner, 1986). For the sake of convenience, one may call this tradition the Parsonian contribution, because Parsons's emphasis on education, training and culture in the theory of internalization, which he derived from Charles Horton Cooley, suggests that harmony in society will require an agreement on basic values, and in particular on the meaning of the constitutive rules of society. This explanation of social order has been criticized for its lack of historical understanding of the changing nature of values in society and the claim that religion forms an important basis of social cohesion and fails to address the implications of secularization in contemporary societies. The notion that values in modern society are fragmented and diversified by postmodern consumerism also represents a challenge to this tradition.

Thirdly, there is the notion of social reciprocity. There are two versions of this tradition. In the social contract version, rational men (we use this gendered noun deliberately) exchange their individual freedom for public order by giving authority to a third party (the state) to ensure that the conditions of social contract are secure. This social contract provides a framework for competitive relationships in the market place, but ensures a minimal degree of social co-operation because there are definite benefits to individuals from these collective arrangements. Sociologists, such as Parsons, have understood this traditional approach as a primitive theory of social order. It is a minimal theory of society and social contract theory is not, in its traditional version, especially interesting for sociology, because it lacks an understanding of the symbolic reality of social order. In any case, Hobbesian social contract theory is probably better regarded as a theory of the origins of the state rather than as a theory of social order. It is an influential approach to society and has been partly incorporated into versions of rational choice theory.

### Parsonian (power as shared culture)

The second version of reciprocity theory is far more important for the present discussion. This theory suggests that social order emerges as an unintended consequence of the endless process of exchange (of goods, services and symbols) which creates a dense network of infinite obligations, duties, claims and expectations rather than as an outcome of deliberate rational choice. Social actors are both integrated into, and constrained by, the facticity of the social order as a consequence of social exchange obligations and claims. Because human beings generally cannot satisfy their wants without exchange, the social division of labour creates an endless chain of claims and counter-claims, which hold individuals in a timeless linkage (typically across generations and thus also including the dead) of mutual obligation. In fact society could not survive without the emergence of a sense of intergenerational obligation. When these networks are in some rough balance, we have a condition of justice (as fairness) where these mutual dependencies are reciprocated. Where they are systematically distorted, we have a situation of exploitation. Much work has been done in anthropology on sacrifice, potlatch and the gift (Mauss, 1954) as forms of reciprocity. We may therefore designate this approach to social order the Maussian legacy. Anthropological research on exchange has made us aware of the complexity of exchange relations with respect to obligations and duties which cannot be easily ignored, and which are not based on precise notions of utility. Thus any theory of social order is a theory of society.

## Maussian (power as economics)

The division of theories of social order into three traditions is somewhat artificial, but for the purposes of this chapter it is heuristically useful. Continuing with this formal, metatheoretical approach, the Machiavellian tradition puts the issue of power at the heart of any explanation of social order. Power is the causally most significant factor in sociological orientations to the question of order. By contrast, the Parsonian legacy points to culture as the critical issue in understanding social stability because without a set of shared cultural values, no social order can survive. Finally, employing the term in a rather broad fashion, the Maussian approach offers an economic explanation of social order. In reciprocity or exchange theory, social order (specifically the social coherence of social groups) requires a general balance of exchange. Where these conditions are not maintained, individuals feel a sense of relative deprivation and they are unlikely to regard existing arrangements as fair and legitimate; they will be inclined to leave the group (Blau, 1964). This 'indigenous' sense of fairness arises out of the infinite stream of human exchange, and it is here that we should locate the social roots (or 'elementary forms' in Durkheim's sense) of the general notion of equality (Turner, 1986). This 'primitive' notion of injustice, which emerges when there is felt to be a rough imbalance of ongoing reciprocity, can be regarded as universal (Moore, 1970: 52). This is probably the only case of a universalistic principle of normative action emerging from the empirical substratum of social relations which has been identified by a relativizing sociology.

Theories of social order have, therefore, traditionally depended on explanations which examine the contribution of power (the political), values (the cultural) and exchange (the economic) to social integration. It might be objected that this formulation has the peculiar consequence of not having a specifically 'social' variable in the explanation of social order. One further consequence of this absence is that sociology as a discipline appears to have been marginalized in relation to political science, cultural theory and economics. In fact in this formulation of the problem, the 'social' refers to the ensemble of institutions and practices which connect the political, the cultural and the economic into a social system, and hence sociology is indeed the study of 'the social', but this 'social' is the totality of institutions, practices, beliefs and symbols which in everyday language constitute a 'society'.

This is certainly a controversial strategy for defining the 'social' (Frisby and Sayer, 1986), and an equally problematic approach to sociology. There could be other objections, which we will have to consider later, but one problem with this approach is that it treats 'culture' as an alternative expression for 'values', and thereby ignores the idea that culture is the ensemble of symbols by which a society represents itself to itself. We have adopted this strategy to bypass problems about ideology and knowledge, because a secular society is one in which the traditional 'grand narrative' of symbols has been profoundly challenged by social differentiation.

Our task in this chapter is to examine theories of social order, not to provide an explanation of sociology, but clearly these two issues are interrelated. There are three ways of defining sociology. It is either a special way of examining the world – an aesthetic or, in the language of C. Wright Mills (1959), a type of imagination; or it is the analysis of the 'social' so that social science disciplines are defined by reference to their object (Durkheim); or sociology is a discipline which provides a synthesis of the various disciplines within the humanities (such as history and linguistics), and the social sciences (politics and economics in particular) (Comte). In this sense, sociology is the core of social science interdisciplinarity. This idea of sociology would be roughly equivalent to Hegel's view of philosophy.

These three perspectives are not exclusive, and most sociologies will contain unstable and uneven aspects of all three approaches. For example, Parsons appears to define sociology as a special discipline which concentrates on the analysis of the integration subsystem. That is, sociology provides an analysis of value integration, but Parsons also appears to regard sociology as that discipline which stands as the crown of the general theory of action, whose task is to analyse the allocative and integrative problems of the social system as a whole (that is to provide an analysis of scarcity and solidarity). In this respect, sociology studies the various political, economic, cultural and psychological media of exchange between the four subsystems of the social system (Alexander, 1984). In adopting this final stance in this chapter we argue that sociology is that general, synthetic discipline which considers the multiple conditions (cultural, political and economic) which are, as it were, the infrastructure of social order.

## Preliminary specification of a theory

It is clearly the case that, while one can identify at least three major traditions in the explanation of social order, any particular theory is likely to include all three elements (political aspects of order, cultural conditions and finally economic circumstances of exchange and exploitation). To take one obvious example, Marxist theories tend to combine all three aspects in a general account of how capitalist societies operate. Thus, Gramsci's influential theory of hegemony specifically develops the idea that, although state power is important in regulating the working class, authority depends on the capacity of dominant classes to exercise some form of moral leadership, or to mobilize cultural orders (the Church) to legitimize their power (Femia, 1975). One reason for this tendency to merge these alternative approaches is that each separate tradition carries quite distinctive analytical or empirical problems. Taken separately, these three approaches do not provide a satisfactory account of social order. As we have briefly indicated, the Machiavellian notion that, for example, one might explain social order via the effectiveness of institutions of violence is not convincing. It appears from historical evidence that regimes that depend on violence cannot mobilize sufficient public support to stay in office indefinitely. The utility of violence may well decline with use, so naked coercion is best used sparingly. It is almost impossible to imagine any society or social group that has rested *only* on force. The concept of 'oriental despotism' as a system of total power (Wittfogel, 1957) is at best misleading as an analysis of Oriental political systems (Turner, 1978), and at worst is part of a persistent Occidental myth (Said, 1978). There appear to be definite limits to imperial power, which makes the use of force and violence increasingly ineffective.

Explanations of social order which rest on some assumption of shared values are equally problematic. We shall explore this issue in some depth shortly, because it relates directly to the idea of a 'dominant ideology' (Abercrombie et al., 1980, 1983, 1990). At this point, three rather critical difficulties with the Parsonian tradition may be noted. First, in advanced industrial societies, where there is a potent legacy of conflict, there will tend to be several class-based cultural traditions which are in opposition. In other words, there is no such thing as *the* dominant culture, and where there are many competing systems of ideology and culture, the consciousness of subordinate groups in society will be structured by many contradictory elements. In the literature, this situation is often referred to as the existence of 'split consciousness' (Mann, 1973), where elements of dominant and subordinate ideologies are held simultaneously (Parkin, 1972). Secondly, the historical evidence suggests that, in addition to the presence of diverse and competing cultures and ideologies, the apparatus of transmission by which dominant values, beliefs and symbols are conveyed is never sufficiently effective to deliver successfully the dominant culture to subordinate groups and classes. Thirdly, the notion that there are general, dominant and effective social values fails to take notice of the many different *ways* in which values might be held and received. For example, the dominant beliefs might be held cynically, ironically or pragmatically (Mann, 1970). Some aspects of this problem are covered in sociology by so-called 'reception theory', which examines the effects of messages through the study of reading practices of social actors. The work of M. de Certeau (1984) shows how everyday practices mediate, co-opt and transform the culture and commodities of consumerism.

Although one can argue theoretically against the idea that there is 'a dominant ideology' or 'a dominant culture', this should remain an empirical question which requires research into what values are characteristic of industrial societies and how these values are actually held. *The Dominant Ideology Thesis* argued that, on analytical grounds, a dominant ideology was not 'a condition of existence' of a capitalist order; this position would not be refuted by the empirical discovery that some capitalist societies appear to have a dominant ideology.

There are also problems with explanations of social order in terms of theories of reciprocity, or social contract theory, or rational choice theories or exchange theories. Social contract theories have been a topic of dispute for at least three hundred years. Are they hypothetical, heuristic devices to suggest that it is 'as if' society is based on a contract? In general terms there are no historical examples of societies based on an actual contract. Are social contract theories based on a dubious assumption about 'possessive individualism' (Macpherson, 1962), and are they formulated around some culturally specific version of the notion of a 'sovereign individual' (Abercrombie et al., 1986)? Can such theories explain the relationship between women and society, since contract theory appears to exclude women from the public domain of contract formation (Pateman, 1988)? Rational choice theory has yet to produce a coherent and consistent explanation of individual interest, group interest and participation (Margolis, 1982). Having made these criticisms, it is obvious that both rational choice theory and exchange theory have made significant contributions to social theory and to the understanding of everyday life (Abell, 1996).

Thus, while it may be analytically instructive to consider separately various traditions which emphasize power, culture or economics in the explanation of social order, in practice any specific theory will tend to combine all three elements. As a preliminary observation, any general theory of social order must examine the interrelationships of political, cultural and economic components of social cohesion. The connections between these three structures produce the social basis of order.

The next important analytical issue is to ask: at what level is the explanation of social order located? It is conventional in sociology, although the parameters of this dichotomy remain obscure, to distinguish micro and macro levels of analysis, and the interrelations of these levels. We can, for example, contrast Weber's macro analysis of the prospects of social cohesion in Germany in terms of class relations and state formation (Mommsen, 1984) with Goffman's studies of the micro problems of managing embarrassment, engagement and role-distance in everyday interactions (Goffman, 1959). In social science generally, it is in fact difficult to specify in analytical terms what the distinction between macro and micro entails, apart from some commonsense notion that 'macro' refers to large societal processsses and structures, while 'micro' refers to small, interpersonal, everyday encounters. However, for the purpose of our subsequent argument with respect to intergenerational exchanges it is important to suggest that 'micro' should include the idea of the life cycle of the individual, while 'macro' would refer to generational or cohort effects. Thus, the question of social order at the micro level would be related to individual processes of reciprocity over time through life cycle patterns. Micro research in these terms might for example consider patterns of teenage violence or deviance in individuals as a feature of life cycle maturation and intergenerational obligations and duties. Such research might consider violence against the elderly in modern societies, where familial obligations of middle aged persons might include several generations, as a consequence of social strains on the household created by 'unproductive' grandparents. By contrast, macro questions of life-style patterns of social order would consider generational differences. For example, it is commonly assumed that the 1960s generation was especially troublesome and deviant. Macro research would consider the impact on society as a whole of student generations and their conflicts with authorities (Feuer, 1969). These comments are partly inspired by the fact that age and ageing are issues which have been somewhat neglected by sociologists who, in the analysis of social stratification, have concentrated primarily on class, race and gender. Sociologists have only rarely taken 'the generation' as a significant social variable (Mannheim, 1952), whereas there are important historical and sociological reasons for believing that the unique historical experience of generational cohorts may have profound implications for social order. While the postwar baby boom was often blamed for subsequent social disorder – such as the middle-class cohort of the 1960s causing university disruption (Parsons and Platt, 1972) – the social impact of warfare on the life histories of combatants in major wars in relation to social order has been likewise neglected. One exception is the controversial, but brilliant, analysis of the life histories of the German youth of the *Freikorps* in relation to the formation of National Socialism, by Klaus Theweleit in his *Male Fantasies* (1987). In this chapter we want to argue that in general terms sociologists have also neglected the crucial importance of *experiences* of legitimacy and involvement at the micro level (Heller, 1990). Thus, a theory of social order would have to consider the nature of social order in terms of political, cultural and economic relationships at both the macro and the micro levels in terms of actual experiences of order and disorder. While sociologists might successfully construct an index of social dislocation (by reference to homicides, rape, family violence, divorce and so forth), it does not follow that individuals or social groups would necessarily or automatically experience the everyday world as disorderly. The round of daily activities – sleeping, eating, talking and cleaning the house – *may* remain relatively normal and stable despite considerable macro dislocation. Social groups appear to be highly resilient under social stress, and can undertake ongoing 'repair' work to normalize social relations. In the middle of revolutions or wars, the everyday round of eating and sleeping must be attended to, because the embodiment of human agents imposes certain necessities on their interactional patterns. Here again, although theoretical work is essential, it is obvious that in empirical terms the relationship between the micro and macro order is not stable and uniform; it will vary over time and between societies. How macro social disorder (such as violent revolutions) impinges on micro social relations in terms of everyday interaction can only be understood through historical analysis and empirical cross-cultural research. Explanations of social order inevitably raise questions about what Weber called value-relevance. At one stage in the development of postwar sociology, it was fashionable to contrast consensus and conflict sociology (Rex, 1981). Thus, so-called Parsonian structural functionalism was criticized because it was assumed to be inevitably ideologically conservative (Black, 1971). By asking the question, how is social order possible?, consensus theories neglected two equally significant questions: how is social conflict possible and how do societies change? Parsonian sociology, because it appeared to concentrate exclusively on aspects of social order, was regarded as an ideological defence of capitalist society (Gouldner, 1971). This battle between consensus and conflict theories preoccupied many (English) sociologists through the 1970s as a debate between the 'two sociologies' (Dawe, 1970). The battle lines between these positions have been drawn and redrawn on many occasions, giving rise in recent years, for example, to significant reformulations of functionalism with the rise of neo-functionalism and with various attempts to reconceptualize the central problematic of Parsonian sociology (Robertson and Turner, 1991).

The outcome of this debate is both complex and unclear. However, we can summarize the issues in the following manner. Theories of order and change are in fact complementary, because to identify the conditions of change is to identify the conditions of order (but in reverse) (Lockwood, 1992). Secondly, many of the critical readings of writers like Parsons were both biased and unidimensional (Alexander, 1984, 1985; Holton and Turner, 1986). Thirdly, Marxist theories of ideology as explanations of the absence of social revolution make *analytical* assumptions which are parallel to theories of cultural integration; it may be difficult in analytical terms to distinguish between the idea of a dominant culture and a dominant ideology (Abercrombie et al., 1980).

The debate between so-called conflict theory and Parsonian sociology is no longer productive, and in this chapter we shall simply assume that any debate about social order will automatically include an analysis of the coercive and constraining aspects of social structure, and will seek to understand social change in terms of continuous processes of transformation. Anticipating subsequent arguments about social order, we shall place considerable emphasis on Marx's idea of 'the dull compulsion' of everyday (economic) relationships in producing social order (Marx, 1970, vol.1: 737), because, regardless of their beliefs, social actors have to produce and reproduce in order to exist. They are constrained through embodiment to engage in endless, everyday reciprocities.

Perhaps the important issue between consensus and conflict theories is whether the conditions that produce social order are regarded in positive or negative terms. Conflict theory has regarded social order as the consequence of negative constraints, coercive relationships, political force or ideological incorporation. Marxist theory in particular has assumed that, since it is not in the real interests of the working class to support or comply with capitalist relations of exploitation, there have to be special reasons which explain working-class compliance. By contrast, Parsonian consensus theory assumed that social order exists because the rewards of membership are sufficiently positive for the majority of a society to find the existing system beneficial and acceptable. The reward of individual conformity to social norms is psychological satisfaction, and hence there is a 'double contingency' between social norms and individual rewards in the processes of socialization and internalization (Parsons, 1968). Parsons has been criticized for the fact that deviance occurs merely because there is inadequate or incomplete socialization. In this interpretation of Parsonian sociology, it is assumed that individuals enjoy conformity because deviance is, by definition, not socially rewarded (Wrong, 1961). This difference is especially important in the sociological analysis of power. Conflict theory has generally treated power in the negative sense of a capacity to control the behaviour of other individuals or social groups in ways contrary to their desires or interests. 'Power' means the capacity to constrain, control and regulate the behaviour of others, if necessary without their consent. Although Parsons has often been criticized for overlooking the importance in the control of social action (Giddens, 1968), he made one crucial point against conflict theories of power. That is, they typically ignore the positive aspects of power, namely that power also entails the capacity to bring about things that are commonly desirable. In short, power should also involve the notion of 'empowerment' (Parsons, 1963). It is interesting that Michel Foucault, arriving at a debate about power via Nietzsche, came to a similar position, although for very different reasons (Clegg, 1989). In Foucault, the exercise of power/knowledge produces effects such as sexuality. Foucault's studies of disciplines demonstrated how individuals are produced through a 'micro-physics of power' as a consequence of routines and disciplines of everyday relationships (Simons, 1995: 31).

In treating power as negative constraint, conflict theory, and more generally neo-Marxist theory, has treated social order as the effect of the constraint or suppression of opposition and dissent which results from the exercise of power by dominant classes or elites. By contrast, we will argue later that citizenship represents what we might call the positive dimension of power, because citizenship involves the empowerment of members of a society to achieve desirable goals as a consequence of their enjoyment of important entitlements (Bell, 1976; Turner, 1986). At the same time, citizenship excludes strangers and rewards membership through processes of inclusion which normalize and standardize behaviour in the interests of conformity. Similar contrasts also exist in terms of culture and social reciprocity as features of the social structure. In treating culture often as ideology, Marxism and critical theory until very recently had a negative view of, for example, mass culture as part of the 'culture industry'. Mass culture was part of the ideological system of a society, which had the consequence of incorporating the working class into the dominant cultural system. It was this culture industry which created the conditions for the cultivation of 'false' needs through advertising, the norms of consumerism and the institutions of the 'throw-away society'. Culture is part of the unidimensional, hollow reality of industrial capitalism; it is part of the inauthenticity of modernity.

Capitalism, and the capitalist social order, has survived because, through credit and hire purchase arrangements, promotional techniques and advertising, the creation of mass markets in consumer goods, and the extension of radio and television to the masses, the working class has been partly incorporated into 'the leisure society' and the 'promotional culture' (Wernick, 1991). The paradox here is that in its critique of mass culture, critical theory was often forced to defend some version of high culture as a genuine alternative to the culture industry of mass society (Stauth and Turner, 1988; Ray, 1993). One problem with the Frankfurt School critique was that it translated the experience of the Fascist use of film in Germany directly into the experience of North American mass culture. More importantly, this negative view of mass culture failed to recognize the democratization of culture which was made possible by the extension of education to a wider cross-section of the population of the industrial societies in the period of postwar construction. This was also facilitated by the mass availability of modern communication systems, not only radio, cinema and television, but also hi-fi, video, cassette recorders and so forth. Cultural democratization represents an extension of citizenship rights into the cultural field, typically at the expense of the exclusionary claims of high culture and its intellectual guardians.

This negative view of mass culture has been challenged by postmodernism, which undermines the conventional division between high and low culture, but also offers a critique of Marxism and its offspring as theories which give a priority to ascetic labour over hedonistic consumption. If economic exploitation is the negative side of the economic reciprocities of industrial society, consumption is the positive feature. Commitment to capitalism is not simply the effect of the negative constraint of employment, that is of the need to labour to live; a key feature of the social order of late capitalism is the postwar boom in consumerism. Against the defenders of high culture and authenticity, one might reasonably contemplate the proposition that 'a washing machine is a washing machine, is a washing machine'. While critiques of modern consumerism (whether from neo-Marxism, poststructuralism or feminism) are sophisticated explorations of the symbolic order of capitalism, a washing machine saves time as well as human energy. Against the argument that washing machines save time for women only to intensify their exploitation in their 'spare time', women in contemporary societies live longer than their grandmothers, because they have fewer children, more leisure, more education and a higher status in society. There has been a general rise in the standard of living, which is partly reflected in improvements in infantile mortality rates, an increase in life expectancy and a decrease in morbidity. Although radical critics (Phillipson, 1982) have suggested that illness is to be explained by capitalist exploitation of the working class, workers live longer in capitalism than they do in state socialist systems (Turner, 1995b). It is simply not true that 'capitalism makes you sick'. The fact that in the postwar period large sections of the population have enjoyed higher standards of living and better health is a major feature of the legitimacy and stability of a type of society (capitalism) which is fundamentally unequal.

However, where there is an expectation that rising standards of living and high levels of personal consumption are, as it were, 'natural', then social order is undermined, or at least severely disrupted by economic recession. The business cycle of capitalism becomes a problem for the maintenance of social order only when there are citizenship expectations about certain levels of employment, retirement benefit, housing, education and consumption. Once expectations about welfare benefits have become entrenched, it is extremely difficult for governments to persuade citizens that it is economically necessary to reduce expenditure on health care or retirement benefits. In the UK, the Thatcher decade did not successfully undermine the general assumption that maintaining existing levels of expenditure on health care was desirable.

There is a general contradiction between state expenditure on welfare and the conditions for profitability of the private sector, which a number of writers believe is one source of 'legitimation crisis' (Habermas, 1976). Governments cannot simultaneously maintain the support of voters by heavy expenditure on 'social investment' and the support of private industry which requires low taxation, high profits and control of public expenditure. Although this contradiction is thought to be an inevitable feature of Keynesian economic policies, the problem of 'government overload' has become more acute with the development of 'globalization' (Robertson, 1991). It is no longer possible for any government to regulate autonomously its 'own' economy, because with the development of a world economic system, the interconnections of economies and the penetration of national economies by global corporations means that 'economic policy' is now largely determined by global economic institutions and processes. It is difficult for national governments to respond to Keynesian pressures from the local electorate (for lower personal taxation, more expenditure on welfare, a lower retirement age, and so forth) without the threat of inflation producing a sharp depreciation of the currency and rising interest rates. This situation is not peculiar to economies which are somewhat marginal to the world market such as Australia and New Zealand. Britain was caught in this dilemma for most of the 1970s and 1980s. These tensions between the local and the global economy are reproduced in nationalist outbursts against the gnomes of Zurich, the German Bundesbank or the European Community's currency policies. The inability of national governments to resolve these dilemmas is one source of considerable social and political instability.

In summary, a sociological explanation of social order should first consider the primary components of the social structure, namely culture (shared values), power relations and economic reciprocities. The 'social' is the ensemble of these three structures. Of course, this formulation has certain problems. For example, where is law? Although positive theories of law as command might want to regard it as part of the system of power, our own preference would be to regard law as part of the value system of society, because, unless law is regarded as legitimate, it is very difficult to enforce through the courts. Law may be regarded as normative constraint. We are adopting from Durkheim (1957) the argument that law is a system of moral constraint.

Secondly, sociological explanations of social order would examine these relations at both macro and micro levels, but we are specifically concerned to put some emphasis on the everyday experience of the 'facticity' social order. This experience of social order should be seen in the context of life-cycle and generational processes. We have taken this emphasis on the facticity of social order from Peter Berger's dicussion of the sociological problem of theodicy in modern societies (Berger, 1969). The 'sacred canopy' of social reality is secured ultimately because individuals cannot live with the threat of chaos; they are involved in a constant round of repairing threats to social reality by clothing its precarious nature in the garment of factual normality. Although in our view Berger's approach depends too heavily on Arnold Gehlen's philosophical anthropology (Gehlen, 1988), this idea of the importance of the humdrum nature of everyday social reality is a valuable contribution to the debate about social order.

Thirdly, the structuring of the everyday world by culture, power and economic arrangements has to be seen as a dynamic tension between their negative and positive potential. Power, we have argued, involves both constraint and empowerment. Power both prevents and makes possible the achievement of the ends of action. In this respect, the development of citizenship in Western societies since 1789 is a critical aspect of the empowerment of individuals as active members of society. We cannot simply regard culture as a hegemonic regulation of human beings. Giddens's insistence on the knowledgeability of the social actor (Giddens, 1984) is a key aspect of the notion of 'structuration' which has attempted to resolve some problems in the traditional dichotomy of agency and structure. A theory of social order must avoid producing a model of the social actor as a 'cultural dope'; we have to avoid conflating a voluntaristic theory of action and a theory of social order (Alexander, 1988).

Finally, sociology has to develop very general ideas and categories about social action, but, having specified a set of theoretical relations, sociologists then undertake comparative and historical research in order to see if these relations actually exist and how they change over time. For example, it now appears that social order in East European socialist societies depended more on the exercise of power to bring about constraint than on the existence of general agreements about common values (Pakulski, 1990). By contrast, the economic relations of the housing market and the political management of dissent have been critical ingredients of social order in Singapore in the postwar period. Our understanding of exactly how cultural values, political power and economic reciprocities produce social order in different societies over time has to be based on historical and empirical research.

Before attempting to develop a more elaborate and detailed version of this argument, we want to examine, briefly, the contribution of classical sociology to the debate about the possibility of society. We seek here to provide the background to 'the dominant ideology thesis' debate, because our main conclusion depends on a sequence of prior theoretical positions. There are aspects of debate and critical evaluations of it which permit us to elaborate a more sophisticated and general position on the importance of citizenship as an approach to the production of social stability in contemporary societies.

## Conclusion: classical sociology and social order

In postwar critical theory and Marxism, it was common to explain social order in capitalism, partly or wholly, in terms of the existence of a dominant ideology, which had the consequence of masking the real interests of the working class (which is the overthrow of capitalism), or of making capitalist reality appear 'natural', or of excluding alternative views of social reality by making them appear illegitimate. Much research in the sociology of the media, for example, attempted to show how television news was biased in the interests of the dominant class (McQuail, 1977; Cohen and Young, 1973). The press has been influenced by the need to raise revenue through advertising to appeal to the values of the professional and managerial middle class. Research in educational sociology has suggested that the curriculum prepared working-class children for working-class jobs (Willis, 1977). The absence of a revolutionary tradition of working-class opposition to capitalism in Britain was partly explained by the success of the dominant ideology of individualism. However, for some writers, this ideological hegemony was not entirely complete, and capitalist societies are periodically punctured by a 'legitimation crisis' (Habermas, 1976). In general, however, Western industrial capitalist societies could be classified under the heading 'ruling class, ruling culture' (Connell, 1977).

The empirical evidence for these arguments was not convincing, because sociological research (Moorhouse, 1973; Moorhouse and Chamberlain, 1974; Chamberlain, 1983) on the working class suggested that working-class communities held many values which were oppositional and collectivist. Working-class cultures in Western capitalism developed their own oppositional and autonomous cultures, which constituted them as distinctive communities (Guttsman, 1990). The historical evidence also suggested that in medieval societies the religious worldview of the Church was not necessarily shared by peasants, or in general by the rural hinterland which was peripheral to the urban centres of literate Christianity (Hepworth and Turner, 1972). Community studies in many parts of the Western world indicated that the working class experienced the world in terms of 'us' and 'them' (Hoggart, 1957). We do not, however, want to challenge the idea of a 'dominant ideology' at this empirical level; our aim is rather to suggest that this thesis cannot be adequately derived from Marx. The peculiarity of neo-Marxist arguments was that they gave so much emphasis to ideological incorporation as an explanation of social order that they neglected what appears to be the core of Marxism as a theory of society – the economy. If anything defines Marx's theory of society, then it must be the idea that economic relations ultimately determine the general character of a society – its legal codes, religious practices, dominant ideas, scientific innovations, the relationship between men and women, and so forth. Any attempt to weaken or modify this statement by, for example, raising questions about the meaning of 'ultimately' or 'determine' also weakens the notion that Marx made a unique contribution to social science. Any attempt to move too far away from the notion that 'the base determines the superstructure' undermines the view that Marxism is a coherent theory of society. Thus, while historical materialism is problematic as a general theory of history, at least such a position made Marxism both distinctive and coherent.

In *The Dominant Ideology Thesis* an explanation of social order in capitalism was developed which was compatible with Marxist economism. The essence of this 'Marxist' explanation of social order was as follows:

1  The social order of capitalism does not depend on the ability of a dominant ideology to incorporate the working class.
2  The continuity of a specific capitalist society probably depends more on the internal (moral) cohesion of the dominant class than it does on the ideological incorporation of the working class.
3  Working-class acceptance of capitalism occurs at the level of everyday life where the routine necessity to secure full employment, to maintain a household, feed children, cope with illness, secure savings for future needs (in retirement, for example) and provide for elderly parents produces a 'dull compulsion' of economic relationships. Success in achieving these mundane goals results in an enormous sense of pride and satisfaction in the working class. These practical necessities reduce any proclivity for strike behaviour or absenteeism, and make sustained revolutionary activity unlikely.
4  The dull complusion of everyday life also gives such routine activities a facticity (Berger and Luckmann, 1967) which, according to classical theories from Lukács onwards, makes everyday existence in capitalism appear supremely natural, and therefore unquestionable.
5  While it may be empirically the case that some capitalist societies *do* have a dominant ideology, such a condition is not a necessary requirement for the capitalist order.
6  A dominant ideology also requires an effective apparatus of transmission, and the concentration of ownership of the massive system of

communication in modern society will generally be inadequate to secure such a circumstance, because media messages are always selectively received.

It is only when there is some massive disruption to this everyday world – either a natural catastrophe such as earthquakes, plagues or droughts, or an economic catastrophe such as hyper-inflation which destroys the international value of the local currency, or a political crisis such as a revolution or foreign occupation – that this facticity is challenged. To take a historical illustration, Boccaccio's description of the bodies of victims of the Black Death of 1348 (with their painful buboes emerging from armpits and groins) gives some idea of the dramatic shaking of this facticity in medieval society when the merciful nature of a personal God was brought into question (Herzlich and Pierret, 1987). Because it is this everyday social reality which determines consciousness (or to put it in a modified form of Marx's words, it is this everyday being which determines consciousness, not consciousness which determines the facticity of mundane existence), aspects of consciousness which, as it were, fall outside this everyday world may be easily manipulated by the media. Thus, in the area of foreign policy, it is much easier to understand how a dominant ideological construction of 'other nations' could operate without challenge. If there were dominant ideologies in the postwar world, we would expect them to have been more typical of state socialist societies than of capitalism, because it was in the former that the means of communication were centralized by the state and because the Party had largely destroyed or colonized the network of voluntary associations (trade unions, churches, leisure associations, political clubs and so forth) which constitute 'civil society'. However, even in these circumstances, it appears that the legitimization of the communist system by ideological means was ineffective (Pakulski, 1990; Turner, 1990c).

If Marx's economic theory of society has been diluted by the twentieth-century emphasis on culture, Durkheim's normative view of social order has been overstated in the literature. The conventional view (Parsons, 1974, 1981) of Durkheim suggests that he emphasized the importance of the *conscience collective* in the stability of societies, thought that public rituals were essential for maintaining a living, emotive commitment to society, criticized utilitarian individualism as a major corrosive of social order, and that the concept of 'anomie' was his major contribution to the development of sociological theory. This interpretation of Durkheim is often associated with the idea that Durkheim was in both political and cultural terms a conservative (Nisbet, 1966). More recent interpretations of Durkheim have rejected such a view by, for example, taking Durkheim's political sociology more seriously (Giddens, 1986), or by noting Durkheim's sympathy for Saint-Simonian versions of socialism (Gouldner, 1962). In *The Dominant Ideology Thesis* (Abercrombie et al., 1980), it was argued that Durkheim's original argument in *The Division of Labour in Society* had been neglected.

In his work on the consequences of the division of labour in modern societies, Durkheim claimed that the traditional basis of social order in simple societies was indeed the *conscience collective*, but modern societies would depend on the density of social reciprocity between individuals in a highly developed division of labour. This idea was the basis of the famous distinction between mechanical and organic solidarity. The core of Durkheim's view of social order was the notion that in the division of labour the dependencies and reciprocities between individuals create a social bond (an organic solidarity). What Marx called the dull compulsion of economic relationships, Durkheim called the moral restraint of organic, social reciprocities.

In retrospect, we are no longer entirely satisfied with this interpretation, which gives too little weight to Durkheim's concern for 'the science of morals and rights' (Durkheim, 1957). In the series of lectures which he gave in the years 1890 and 1900 and which we know as *Professional Ethics and Civic Morals* (Durkheim, 1992), Durkheim expressed his perennial concern that economic life was not adequately regulated by moral standards. He hoped that a system of professional ethics would emerge which would contribute some element of moral regulation to the economy. Without such moral regulation, 'individual appetites [which] . . . are by nature boundless and insatiable' (Durkheim, 1957: 11) would be out of control. Durkheim appears to have adopted a position rather close to Schopenhauer in treating compassion not reason as the basis of ethical commitment (Meštrović, 1991). As one aspect of the regulation of appetites, it was necessary to oppose the kind of utilitarian individualism represented in Durkheim's eyes by the writing of Herbert Spencer. In the same lectures, Durkheim looked towards the state to provide some general regulation of society as a whole. Durkheim saw the state as the ultimate moral 'organ' which protected the individual and guaranteed individual rights. The role of the state 'consists in calling the individual to a moral way of life' (Durkheim, 1957: 69).

Durkheim may have anticipated some aspect of the modern debate about globalization (Featherstone, 1990). It is patriotism which binds the individual to the state, but Durkheim could also imagine that individuals might have loyalties to more universal social entities such as humanity itself (Durkheim, 1957: 74). For Durkheim, there was a definite contradiction between the emergence of cosmopolitanism and traditional sources of political commitment such as patriotism.

Finally, Durkheim's political sociology appears to follow a set of ideas which were crucial to Alexis de Tocqueville's theory of democracy (1968), namely that social order depends on the existence of a set of effective associations linking the individual to the state. This idea that the mediation of social power in a democracy by voluntary associations is an essential safeguard against dictatorship has continued to be a central feature of democractic theory (Lefort, 1988). This problem of power is primarily about the proper relationship between the state and the individual. Thus, for Durkheim, 'our political malaise is due to the same cause as our social malaise; that is, to the lack of secondary cadres to interpose between the individual and the State. We have seen that these secondary groups are essential if the State is not to oppress the individual: they are also necessary if the State is to be sufficiently free of the individual' (Durkheim, 1957: 96). It is a common mistake to neglect Durkheim's theory of the state. His emphasis on associations linking the individual to the state has remained a vital component of contemporary democratic theory with its emphasis on communitarian values, voluntary associations, and subsidiarity in civil society (Hirst, 1994). These issues will play an important role in this study of citizenship as a basis for understanding the connection between the public and the private realms.

Durkheim continues to be significant as a basis for conceptualizing modern citizenship. One aspect of citizenship, in relation to the problem of order in Marshall's theory of citizenship and class, is concerned with solidarity in secular societies. Citizenship is a form of civil religion which does for modern societies what organized religion did for premodern societies – create a web of solidarity based upon common beliefs and practices. In the early form of citizenship which expressed membership of a nation state, it was the nation which was the sacred and affective foundation of national citizenship. Durkheim's sociology provides a critique of the individualistic and rationalist model of citizenship which derives ultimately from Kant. Against the individualist notion of obligation in Kant, Durkheim, following Schopenhauer, offers a science of morals, where obligation has its roots in affective commitment to society. Without these affective bonds of social membership, social commitment would be shallow, egoistic and utilitarian. This Durkheimian problem of the affective foundations of collective commitment to society and the state has become increasingly relevant to the new global order which depends on the information superhighway in order to function economically and politically. The new question facing us is: where will the affective ties to the public arena be generated in a global community which is held together by electronic networks? This hyperreal communication system is increasingly described in a scientific language which is derived primarily from postmodernism. It is however interesting to consider this electronic social reality as a 'thin' Kantian community of rational egoists, which lacks any significant 'thick' Durkheimian sentiments by which to cohere as a viable social system.

# 5

# SCARCITY

The analytical relationship between economics and sociology was fundamental to the development of classical sociology, particularly in the work of
Marx, Weber and Simmel, but it was also crucial to the evolution of the
sociological theories of Talcott Parsons (Holton and Turner, 1986). In this
chapter, in order to develop an interpretation of *The Structure of Social
Action* (Parsons, 1937) we make, following Parsons's notion of 'the economic element', a primary dichotomy between economics as a science of
scarcity and sociology as a science of social solidarity, based on 'common-
value integration'. In Parsons's early treatment of the means–ends schema,
sociology was understood to be concerned with the ends of action which are
determined by values, and economics was classified as a science of means to
the efficient achievement of ends in the satisfaction of wants. These disciplinary issues emerged early in Parsons's Amherst essays, in his articles on
German sociology (Parsons, 1929) and of course in *The Structure of Social
Action* (Parsons, 1937). Parsons regarded economics as clearly the most
advanced of the social sciences in its conceptual parsimony, its relevance to
policy formation, its quantification of variables and its institutional power
within the academy. Nevertheless, classical economics was flawed as a
general theory of action in what Parsons called 'the utilitarian dilemma'. In
his treatment of the social sciences, sociology emerged as a critical commentary on the limitations of marginal utility theory as an explanation of
voluntary action. The aim of *Structure* was twofold, namely to criticize
various positivistic forms of utilitarianism and to establish the claims of
sociology to a separate status within general action-systems theory.

To be more precise, there were several stages in this intellectual development. In *Structure*, there is the notion of 'the economic element' in which
economizing behaviour is concerned with the rational selection of scarce
means to satisfy needs, where the goals of action are multiple. In the
Marshall Lectures at Cambridge (Swedberg, 1986), Parsons attempted a
more systematic integration of the instrumental features of economic action
and the normative elements of choice. Here, he sought to establish the
argument that economics is a special case of a more comprehensive social
theory which is concerned to develop a general analytical approach to
social systems – a theory which will be genuinely interdisciplinary, inclusive
and general. In *Structure* Parsons criticized classical economics in terms of
the utilitarian dilemma where the ends of action are random and an
explanation of order is impossible, or ends are reduced to the environment,

in which case the sovereignty of the autonomous actor is compromised. In *The Social System* (Parsons, 1951), Parsons had moved on from classical economics to develop an action-systems schema based on the famous AGIL property-space. Whereas *Structure* was based on Alfred Marshall, his later economic sociology embraced Keynes's *General Theory*, which encouraged Parsons to believe that micro- and macro-economic theory could be integrated with sociology (Parsons and Smelser, 1956).

We might note immediately that this schema appears to elide sociology and anthropology, to marginalize social psychology and to leave unresolved some questions about history. In addition, Parsons's sociology does not concern itself, generally speaking, with spatial questions and hence geography as a discipline does not find a place in AGIL. While spatial issues do not become theorized, time (as a scarce resource) is central to the unit act where there is some 'delay' between need and its resolution. Action which economizes on time is a crucial feature of the 'economic element' in general theories of the social system.

Parsons's attempt to produce a general theory based primarily on a reconciliation of economics and sociology was probably an analytical failure (Holton, 1991). Economics as a discipline is in many respects indifferent to the findings of sociology; it is, in terms of institutional power, far more successful than sociology, and it is typically housed in university faculties separately from sociology. Sociologists have retained an interest in some aspects of rational choice theory, but continue to believe that, generally speaking, economics offers few solutions to mainstream sociological problems and issues (Abell, 1996).

However, the contrast between scarcity and solidarity provides a useful overview of action-systems theory. If social existence is characterized by an irreducible scarcity, then there are profound problems with economic allocation of resources and the political management of conflicting interests in terms of decisions about (re)distribution. Economics and politics are thus fundamental social sciences. But the conflict around scarce resources has to be resolved, or at least managed, if the Marxian class war and the Malthusian famine are to be avoided. For Parsons, common or shared values are crucial to the creation of social solidarity, and individuals have to be motivated to co-operate in a social environment which they regard as legitimate. Parsons was clearly interested in racial inequality in American society, and he followed T.H. Marshall in the development of a theory of citizenship as an institution in liberal democracy which contributes to social solidarity through a redistribution of resources. This interest in citizenship can also be regarded as an 'outcrop' of the preoccupation with the allocative-integrative dilemma.

The integrative problems of society also require commitment and loyalty from social actors for the performance of collective tasks. In his mature work, Parsons came to integrate psychological studies of human commitment and loyalty into his earlier studies of economics, politics and sociology as an expression of the relationship between individual and society (Parsons et al., 1955). The allocative/integrative and scarcity/ solidarity themes remained fundamental to his view of the social sciences and the empirical problems of social systems.

### The utilitarian dilemma in social theory

Parsons's economic sociology was overtly a critique of utilitarian theories of economic action, and an attempt to lay the foundation for an auto- nomous discipline of sociology, interconnected closely with economics and politics. For Parsons, classical economic theory has to assume the random nature of the goals of action because it remains largely silent about values. Furthermore, its notion of instrumental rationality cannot preclude the use of force and fraud in human societies as rational solutions to scarcity, and thus the instrumental assumptions about action cannot provide a satis- factory account of social order.

There is therefore a crisis in classical utilitarianism that was resolved by an appeal to a set of assumptions which are not explicable within the original rationalist assumptions. This analysis provides a clear illustration of the use of the 'residual category' as a critical device of deconstruction: Marshall's questioning of the hedonistic assumptions of the notion of need in his discussion of real and artificial wants; Pareto's difficulties in managing 'non-rational' action in the distinction between residues and ideology; Durkheim's difficulties with the theory of happiness with respect to the division of labour and the problem associated with values as social facts; or the inherent problems of defining rational and irrational action in Weber in relation to behaviour versus action. In general, classical eco- nomics solved the problem of order by ad hoc and random theoretical solutions which involved appeals to the 'hidden hand of history', shared 'sentiments' and common wants.

The crisis in utilitarianism was resolved by various forms of radical positivism which explained action either by reference to environmental features or as hereditary. In fact utilitarianism had great difficulty in explaining rationality at all. If rational men[1] are driven by hedonistic desires to satisfy their wants in an environment of scarcity, how and why do they act irrationally? Given inadequate means, why will men allocate scarce resources to luxuries? Some aspects of these problems of irrationality are outlined in the section on 'taste' towards the conclusion of *The Structure of Social Action* where Parsons provides a discussion of the problem of habitual action. Irrationality within a paradigm of radical positivism has to be explained either in terms of faulty psychology, or lack of sovereignty, or inadequate information about the market. Some set of circumstances has to inhibit the 'natural' exercise of egoistic reason to explain why interest does not rationally determine the selection of means. There is a parallel problem in Marxism where the working class, following its own collective interests, should overthrow the ruling class and embrace socialism. Proletarian irrationality has to be explained by faulty knowledge which is produced by the existence of a dominant ideology (Abercrombie et al., 1982).

The Hobbesian problem of order is therefore the theme which provides coherence to Parsons's early sociology. In Hobbes's political theory, rational actors are driven to agree to a social contract to end the state of nature in order to bring about stability and order, but fraud and force still remain viable and indeed rational options. A social contract is in the collective interest of society as a whole, but individuals or social groups may well turn to criminal behaviour to achieve personal advantage, which erodes wider social benefits. Parsons's use of the fraud/force couple is a powerful criticism of radical positivistic utilitarianism in the 1930s but also raises important problems for contemporary economic rationalism, because Mafia-type organizations are effective means of social redistribution in societies where state organizations are corrupt and ineffectual. Mafia-type organizations are, in some sense, voluntary and local, and they are organized around a principle of subsidiarity. In Parsons's terms, they present a traditional pattern of exchange where values of loyalty and honour are dominant. But we also know that Mafia-type organizations represent a 'mischief of faction' (to quote the language of the Madison papers in the American debate on the Constitution) and ultimately destroy society, because violent means are necessary to guarantee its operations.

For Parsons, the Hobbesian problem of order has to be resolved by reference to shared values which control the fraud/force problem by regulating contracts in a normative fashion. Thus for Parsons one of the critical tests for sociology was the explanation of religious values. In fact the sociology of religion, as a special field of sociology, remained an ongoing preoccupation of Parsons throughout his academic career. The complex place of religion in the process of modernization could not be resolved by some simple theory of (one-way) secularization, which meant that Parsons embraced neither a naïve notion of disenchantment nor a nostalgic view of value-harmony in traditional societies (Robertson and Turner, 1991). Parsons's rejection of nostalgia allowed him to see the United States as a society within which Protestantism had shaped the values of individualism and activism in a manner that made secular, liberal capitalism the fulfilment not the denial of the Reformation.

Questions about the validity of sociological or economic explanations of religion play a dominant role in Parsons's view of what constitutes a sociological theory. These aspects of Parsons's account of the failure of classical sociology to provide an understanding of religion which was not individualistic, reductionist, positivist or rationalist, are well known. There is the commentary on Durkheim's attempt to treat religion as a social fact within the positivistic paradigm and the alleged idealism of Durkheim. Parsons believed of course that eventually Durkheim's sociology of religion lurched towards idealism in the notion that it is not society that produces religion, but religion which produces society. Durkheim looked for an elementary form of religion in the Arunta tribes, where ritualistic festivals brought these hunter-gatherer Aboriginals together to celebrate God/society. We know that religion was central to the historicism problem in Weber and that his work can be interpreted through his studies of the economic ethics of the world religions. Both Durkheim and Weber turned, for very different reasons, away from the reductionist tradition of Feuerbach, Marx and Engels to establish a deeper analysis of religion in relation to human values.

The argument so far has been that the emerging AGIL scheme in *The Structure of Social Action* provides a map of the interdisciplinary nature of the social sciences and a justification of sociology as a critique of the limitations of the utilitarian dilemma. The social science disciplines are structured around the scarcity/solidarity couple or in more technical terms the allocative (political-economy) question and the integrative (psychosociological) problem. The Hobbesian problem of scarcity can, for Parsons, not be resolved by marginal utility theory but only by a deeper understanding of the role of values in human society. This exegesis of Parsons's sociology now deals with two questions – what produces scarcity and what produces solidarity, or more simply how does economics relate to sociology?

### Scarcity as a residual category

Employing Parsons's deconstructive strategy, we could argue that 'scarcity' itself is a residual category in *The Structure of Social Action*; or that it is at least an assumption of classical utilitarianism. Scarcity can in classical political and economic theory be located in 'nature'. In the pessimistic version of utilitarianism, scarcity exists because nature is niggardly. While utilitarianism and liberalism are often presented as the optimistic ideologies of bourgeois capitalism, they often obscured a profound uncertainty about the social world. In Hobbes, the state of nature is not one of abundance, and thus rational men struggle over limited resources to satisfy their bodily needs. The solution to this dilemma is the establishment of monopoly powers over the means of legislation and the legitimate use of violence in the body of the state. In Malthus, the unrestrained sexual drives of men produce scarcity through overcrowding and thus the demographic equilibrium is restored by periods of famine and pestilence. The Malthusian population problem requires sexual restraint and contraception to avoid plague and war. In Durkheim, again we have the classical psychological model of *homo duplex*. Men are rational in terms of their grasp of 'interests', but their irrational and egoistic drives (especially their 'sexual' drives) lead to excessive individualism and unhappiness – the result of which is suicide and social anomie. The Durkheimian problem of order requires religious restraint or parallel mechanisms such as nationalism, or professional ethics and civic morals (intermediary institutions).

In Weber, in the Freiburg lecture there is a Nietzschean view of the political and economic needs of the German state for 'elbow-room' in Eastern Europe. The scarcity which faces the nation requires a strong bureaucracy, a plebiscitary democracy and an imperialist strategy. Nietzsche's notions of resentment and the will to power played a significant role in shaping Weber's views on politics, and Weber's view of culture probably followed Nietzsche's distinction between Apollo and Dionysus, in which the erotic forces have to be reconciled with the rational powers if society is to achieve a 'healthy' condition. This notion of scarcity is related to the struggle over the limited resource of power. But there is a second form of scarcity in Weber, namely a scarcity of (religious) meaning. With the disenchantment of the world, secularization brings about a crisis of meaningfulness, as Weber argued in the lectures on science and politics as vocations. The old gods are dead, and the new ones are yet to be born. This we might call the second Nietzschean problem of values – God is dead, and the revaluation of values has yet to be achieved. This secularism is the famous issue of German historicism which runs through Dilthey, Troeltsch and Weber. In Freud, about whom Parsons was eventually to write much in the work on socialization and the family, scarcity is expressed in the struggle between the id and the superego. The ego is trapped between the endless play of libidinous desire and the needs of civilized society – a struggle which often leads to neurosis. Society has to impose limits on sexuality in the interests of the social order. Human beings experience desire in the form of a lack.

## Scarcity in *The Structure of Social Action*

Scarcity is seen to be fundamental to what Parsons called 'the economic element' (Parsons, 1937: 89). Scarcity in Hobbes's theory of the state of nature is related to the fact that men are guided by 'a plurality of passions', but these cannot be fully satisfied, because passions are infinite and nature is niggardly (Parsons, 1937: 93). In Hobbes the precarious state of order rests on the scarcity of means: 'on the existence of classes of things which are scarce, relative to the demand for them, which as Hobbes says "two or more men desire" but "which nevertheless they cannot both enjoy"' (ibid.). The scarcity rests in the shortage of means to satisfy commonly held ends – hence the potential for war.

Parsons went on to observe: 'This problem is that of the allocation of scarce means as between their various potential uses. This is what may most usefully be referred to as the specifically economic element of logical action' (Parsons, 1937: 233).[2] These regulations of resources are achieved by pricing, which 'is society's principal instrument of economizing, of insuring that scarce resources will not be applied wholesale to the least important uses' (Parsons, 1937: 234). In conclusion and with reference to Weber, Parsons argued that 'the fundamental economic facts are scarcity, adaptation of means to alternative ends and cost. The economic element involves the weighing of the relative urgency of different uses of a given scarce means, which the technology does not' (Parsons, 1937: 655).

In summary, Parsons identified two crucial elements of the theory of action in Pareto, Marshall, Durkheim and Weber. First, the economic element involves economizing – the selection of scarce means to ends. Secondly, there is the need for decision-making and 'the element of coercive power may be called the "political"' (Parsons, 1937: 240). The spheres of economics and politics as disciplines are defined by these two features of action.

His own theory of *voluntaristic* action recognized that the political economy of action in utilitarianism could not solve the problem of order without recognizing the existence of an independent and autonomous realm of values without which ends would be random and action would be deterministic. Hence, a voluntaristic theory of action requires a social component and we might reasonably argue that 'the social element' involves the creation and maintenance of the cultural system wherein lies ultimate values which in turn provide norms for the selection of means.

**The place of sociology**

Towards the end of *The Structure of Social Action* Parsons offered a definition of sociology (or the social element) as a solution to the power question. The solution was both anticipated by his earlier interest in 'institutional economics' and came to preoccupy him in his later work on 'action-systems theory', especially in the collaborative work with Smelser. The solution to the power problem (Hobbesian rationalist in an environment of scarcity) 'involves a common reference to the fact of integration of individuals with reference to a common value system, manifested in the legitimacy of institutional norms, in the common ultimate ends of action, in ritual and in various modes of expression' (Parsons, 1937: 768). This social element, which he calls 'common value integration', is an emergent property of action. He thus defined sociology unambiguously as 'the science which attempts to develop an analytical theory of social action systems in so far as these systems can be understood in terms of the property of common value integration' (ibid.).

He identified social, political and economic disciplines of the social sciences of action, and then recognized that the actor is not wholly explained by these three elements. At best they account for what he calls the 'social component of personality' (Parsons, 1937: 769). He then suggested that psychology, which deals with 'the hereditary basis' of personality and psychology could enter the voluntaristic theory of action as 'the analytical science concerned with the variable properties of action systems derived from their reference to the hereditary basis of personality' (Parsons, 1937: 770).

This discussion of sociology therefore begins to outline systematically the AGIL scheme of later works. Economics (the supply and demand schema) is concerned with the adaptation of social systems to scarce resources;

politics (power relationships between individual and group) is about deci-sion making with respect to setting goals; sociology deals with the integ-ration questions around common values; and psychology (the hereditary element of personality) comprehends the actor's motivational relations with the group (latency). In short, action-social systems have to resolve both allocative and integrative problems in solving both scarcity and solidarity issues. In this respect, the task of *The Structure of Social Action* was analytically to secure the place of sociology in the social sciences alongside economics, politics and psychology. Parsons also had some important comments to make about the role of history in helping us to understand economic history, political and social history, and biography, but he does not want to place history at the core of the analytical theory of action-systems research. This issue may be (indirectly) related to later conflicts with historical sociology such as the work of Norbert Elias and with the criticism that Parsonian functionalism could not explain social change.

## Sex and love

We have seen that the notion of the 'residual category' helped Parsons to identify certain recurrent analytical problems in utilitarianism and on the basis of a critique of positivism to construct his own voluntaristic theory of action (as a solution to the determinism and reductionism of the Benthamite view of the actor in terms of the so-called felicific calculus, or measure of happiness), the analysis of the emergent property of values (as a solution to the randomness of ends in economic theory) and the idea of common values as a solution to the Hobbesian war of all against all. In conclusion we wish to argue that we should use the notion of 'residual category' to probe some undertheorized aspects of *The Structure of Social Action*. Parsons's main concern was first to establish the notion of common values as an emergent property of action and secondly to establish sociology, the science of 'the social element' in voluntaristic action, as an independent discipline in the social science academy. He could therefore take 'scarcity' (the core of 'the eceonomic element') and power (the core of 'the political element') for granted, because his main concern was for common values (the core of 'the social element'). Parsons's sociology theory after 1937 was largely devoted to the content of common values, their place in the social system and how they are internalized by social actors.

He defined scarcity in the context of delineating 'the economic element' as arising because of the plurality of goals, which forces human beings to choose between alternative causes of action. We nevertheless find the minimalistic discussion of scarcity in the economic sciences as outlined in the early Parsons somewhat unsatisfactory.

There are a number of logical possibilities:

First, scarcity exists because nature is niggardly; it is not strictly speaking a sociological problem, because it exists in nature. But this is not convincing: 'nature' can only be scarce in relation to human wants. What is 'natural' cannot merely be taken for granted;

Secondly, scarcity exists because human desire is infinite, elastic and rapacious. Scarcity exists at the level of the individual in the theory of the hedonistic actor. This fact was recognized first in Parsons's discussion of Durkheim's theory of anomie, where he wrote that 'since individual wants are in principle unlimited, it is an essential condition of both social stability and individual happiness that they should be regulated in terms of norms' (Parsons, 1937: 382). Now these norms can only achieve this end not if they merely act externally but if 'they enter directly into the constitution of the actors' ends themselves' (ibid.), that is if they become constitutive of the social nature of the actors.

Parsons gives some time to the discussion of Marshall's classification of wants in terms of: biological needs which humans share with animals (food and sleep); there are wants 'adjusted to activities' (Marshall), the satisfaction of which 'affords strength', that is, increases the efficiency of labour; and there are 'artificial wants' in relation to the 'standard of comfort'.

Parsons argued that Marshall did not dwell on the problems of wants because he sought to define economics as a science of activities. Therefore the nature of wants and consumption remained somewhat outside the Marshallian view of economics.

Thirdly, scarcity exists at the socio-cultural level, because it is produced by the social construction of wants, especially so-called artificial rights. Modern theories of scarcity have tended to follow Marshall Sahlins in suggesting that scarcity is relative and historical, depending on the cultural production of the desire to consume. To provide an example, critical theorists of the Frankfurt School assumed that it was capitalism through the advertising industry which created an artificially high level of individual needs to consume.

This overview of the problem suggests that the notion of scarcity floats around nature or the hedonistic individual or artificially induced consumer needs. We want to suggest that in the authors whom Parsons had studied in *The Structure of Social Action* (Hobbes, Locke, Malthus, Marshall, Pareto, Weber and Durkheim) and those who entered his later work such as Freud, it is the hedonistic nature of man which causes scarcity rather than the plurality of ends. Hobbesian man is driven by hedonistic wants that are infinite, elastic and evolving. Man is an animal whose wants can never be fully satisfied; there is no possibility that human need can be finally satiated. Man is dangerous, reckless, and anti-social – hence the need for social contracts, states, religion and the accoutrements of civilization.

This view of the hedonistic man results in the famous *homo duplex* notion characteristic of Hobbes, Durkheim and Freud. Human beings have an animal side (hedonism) and a rational side (a capacity to calculate interests and to work co-operatively to satisfy wants through collective action). Man is an irrational animal with a rational mind. *Homo duplex* is thus Cartesian Man – divided neatly between a body as a desiring machine and a mind which is robustly rational. Desire can never be subordinated or finally controlled, but the rational mind also realizes that individual interests can be satisfied through fraud and force. Society is thus an unstable mixture of contradictory forces which Parsons wanted to stabilize around emergent common value patterns, as the glue which holds or promises to hold the social contract together.

What, however, is the real essence of the hedonistic character of desiring man? We wish to argue that sexual appetite is the underlying reality of the notion of hedonism. It is human sexuality which is infinite, unsatisfied, excessive, vicious and uncontrolled. Because human sexuality is 'plastic' in the sense of having no particular target, it is not easily regulated. In the language of Arnold Gehlen, human sexuality is world-open and not instinctually specific and it is hedonistic sexuality which produces wants in the form of an absence or lack with the result that man appears as a perpetually unsatisfied animal. In the language of Nietzsche, man is a not-yet-finished animal, who is yet to be formed.

Male sexuality in the state of nature brings men into conflict with other men over the ownership of women. Human sexuality is violent, subordinating women to male desires and fantasies, and producing violent confrontations between men over the possession of women. In Malthus, human sexuality threatens to create a situation where population growth (as a consequence of uncontrolled sexuality) destroys men through famine and pestilence. Men will not only use force and fraud, but their sexual desires are driven by fantasies – the equivalent of the notion of 'artificial wants'. The social contract attempts to solve this problem in two ways: either the Hobbesian tradition of individualistic contracts to regulate interests through a contractual state or the patriarchal tradition of Sir Robert Filmer who sought a paternalistic theory of the state in which the King is God's representative and in the family men must have patriarchal authority.

This theme of sexuality and power runs throughout the Western tradition of social and political philosophy. The *homo duplex* theory was characteristic not only of Durkheim but we have already seen it outlined clearly in Nietzsche's contrast between the two gods Apollo and Dionysus where Apollo is the rational force and Dionysus the ecstatic and violent principle. For Nietzsche these forces have to be resolved in a recreation of culture if human society is to be restored to health. This Dionysus–Apollo theme runs throughout Weber, Freud, Klages, Adorno and Marcuse. The core of the tradition is the contrast between sexual violence (which men share with animals) and the prospect of civilization, or in Parsonian sociology the Hobbesian war versus shared values.

### Conclusion: *agape* versus *eros*

This tradition concentrates on the negative and destructive features of human sexuality or what Deleuze calls the negative theory of the will to power. The Christian tradition, upon which this vision of animal sexuality is based, also identified love (as charity and caring) as the antidote to sexuality, producing a theology of social relationships whereby the sexuality of men could be resolved through a collection of institutions (primarily celibacy, monasticism, dietary management and the family) that recognized sex as a necessary evil. However, the Church also elaborated a view of human nature which distinguished between *eros* (the violent, negative and egoistic drive) and *agape* (the caring, forgiving and sharing principle of divine love). Parsons argued (often rather by implication than directly) that utilitarianism could not provide a satisfactory account of religious values because, for example, charity could not be understood within the paradigm of the hedonistic actor. The notion that charity is ultimately self-serving negates the essence of charity. Similarly, religion cannot be reduced to the environment or to biology; it was an emergent principle of action.

We hold that love has the same 'place' (so to speak) in the action schema. If love is reduced to biology, then love is equated with sex, but love is by definition not an egoistic, individualistic or necessarily individualistic drive. Love is not about scarcity but about abundance. Furthermore, true love is not economizing but giving. It cannot be explained or understood within the utilitarian paradigm, unless that is love is reduced to the hedonistic/animalistic schema of drives and wants.

Finally, the Cartesian assumptions about individualistic rationality and the mind/body split as the basis of seventeenth-century social contract theories was challenged profoundly by Spinoza, who provided an alternative to the transcendentalist assumptions of Christianity with its opposition between man and nature, and to the mind/body dichotomy of Descartes. For Spinoza, body is not merely an extension of mind but mind and body are related in a dialogic parallelism, and hedonistic man is not separated from nature in a relationship of competition. Spinoza had a vision of human beings as co-operatively and necessarily part of nature. His philosophy of connectedness was close to the spirit of John Donne's vision ('Send not to know for whom the bell tolls, it tolls for thee'). Spinoza's theological-political treatise on the social contract provided an alternative framework for the Hobbesian action-system schema with its vision of endless violence by presenting what Deleuze has called an affirmative will to power.

Now there is no reference to Spinoza in *The Structure of Social Action* and at least in the 1930s Parsons appears to adhere to a Cartesian view of the relationship between mind and body, because biology is merely a condition of action. The biological sciences stand outside the voluntaristic theory of action. Parsons's social actor in *The Structure of Social Action* is not an embodied actor as such, because Parsons adopted a view of action which emphasized the biological character of actors as an environmental condition or heredity as the 'natural' element of personality. Parsons's view of body and mind/biology and sociology became more complicated and more sophisticated as he absorbed more of Freudianism into the analytics of the action-system schema but it is fair to argue that in Parsonian sociology the status of the body in relation to action and the possibility of a non-Cartesian understanding of embodiment were not adequately resolved (Turner, 1992). Of course, now we are all much more aware of the environmental crisis, the centrality of risk to human existence and the importance of a 'social contract' with other species, if our world is to survive. As a result the problem of biology in relation to the action-system schema is much more pressing than when Parsons was a young man in Heidelberg. The Spinozan ethic of responsibility and interrelatedness presents a more persuasive vision of man-in-nature than the Hobbesian wasteland and hence the politics of interdisciplinarity is somewhat different from the way that Parsons framed the problem in 1937. However, the idea of emergent common-value integration is still relevant to modern social science and to the green politics of the late twentieth century.

## Notes

1 Throughout this chapter the terms 'men' and 'man' are used deliberately to recognize the gendered nature of classical sociology and political economy. Furthermore, political economy was literally about men engaging in economic conflict in the public sphere.

2 Parsons's footnote here draws attention to his paper, 'Some Reflections on the Nature and Significance of Economics', *Quarterly Journal of Economics*, May 1934.

# 6

# NORMS

In this chapter we want to comment on the influence of the work of Foucault and Beck in exploring the institutions of normative coercion as a perspective for the continuing growth of sociology. In particular, this chapter attempts to make links between Foucault's analysis of power/knowledge/discipline (namely 'governmentality') and the notion of 'risk society' (Beck, 1992). These two frameworks may be analysed as paradigms for understanding the new epidemiology of disease in late modern or postmodern society and elucidating the modalities of normative coercion today. The philosophical choice between these two paradigms also indicates real tensions in contemporary society between the deregulation of the macro-global level (so-called 'risk society') and the micro-local requirement for a continuing micropolitics of surveillance and control (so-called 'carceral society').

## Foucault and the theory of power

Foucault's academic reception within the English-speaking world was initially based upon his work on the history of psychiatry and the problem of madness in Western civilization. Because Foucault was associated politically with the interests of minority groups such as the mentally ill, prisoners and homosexuals, his contribution to sociology was seen in oversimple terms as an exercise in the study of social control. Foucault's critical work on psychiatry appeared in the context of the anti-psychiatry movement. Shortly after the English publication of *Madness and Civilisation*, Thomas Szasz published *The Manufacture of Madness* (1971). R.D. Laing's important *Sanity, Madness and the Family* had been published in 1964. In sociology (especially in North America) the dominant paradigm of deviance and mental illness was labelling theory, which leaned heavily on the work of Becker (1963) and Goffman's (1960) work on asylums.

Although this work did much to illuminate how power operates between the established and the outsiders, it was generally ahistorical and cross-cultural comparisons were eschewed. The intellectual and political context within which Foucault's work was launched guaranteed that his original philosophical and historical studies were misinterpreted as a contribution to social control theory. In this perspective, the mentally ill were a socially deviant group who challenged the basic norms and values of society and who as a consequence of being labelled deviant were forced into careers of secondary deviance.

This interpretation of Foucault was probably reinforced by the appearance in English translation of *The Birth of the Clinic* (1973) and *Discipline and Punish* (1977). The complexity of Foucault's interest in 'technologies of the self' (Martin et al., 1988) only became apparent with the volumes on sexuality he published in the 1980s. Indeed the subtle relationships between Foucault's notion of the self and discipline were not adequately noted until the importance of his treatment of 'governmentality' (Foucault, 1991) was recognized within the secondary literature. Foucault was of course interested in the issue of social control, but this interest has to be situated within his theory of power, where governmentality can be seen as the bridge between the early historical interest in regimes of discipline and the later work on the production of the self, which began with his investigations into the ancient world and early Christianity. This intellectual evolution is now fully supported by the biographical studies of Foucault's life and work by Didier Eribon (1991) and David Macey (1993). In retrospect, the single most important thread or theme in Foucault's diverse and complex work is the study of power (Simons, 1995).

It is now clear that Foucault made three major contributions to contemporary social science: (1) an analysis of power/knowledge; (2) a contribution to the understanding of the emergence of the modern self through disciplinary technologies, and (3) an analysis of governmentality, which integrated these two dimensions into a single theory of power. Partly for the sake of economy of presentation and interpretation, we shall leave to one side Foucault's work on the philosophy of social science and methodology (Foucault, 1970). However, in a more elaborate presentation of his work it would be difficult to separate these dimensions of his research. Foucault's analysis of power has been particularly useful in understanding the functions of the medical profession and the related sphere of psychiatry, for example, in locating the historical functions of the clinic as a site of bio-power (Foucault, 1973). Foucault's theory of power can be seen as a critical reaction against both French Marxism and the existentialism of Sartre. Recent biographies (Eribon, 1991 have shown that Foucault's preoccupation with his own sexuality, his critique of Marxism and his involvement in the politics of the French academy did much to shape his theory of power. Foucault attempted to challenge the Marxist conceptualization of power as a macro structure such as the state which functioned to support industrial capitalism and which was displayed through major public institutions such as the police, the law and the Church. Such a view of power was central to the work of Louis Althusser, the dominant Marxist theoretician of the state and the ideological state apparatus in the 1960s.

By contrast, Foucault saw power as a relationship which was localized, dispersed, diffused, mobile and typically disguised by the social system, operating at a micro, local and covert level through sets of specific practices. Power is embodied in the day to day practices of the medical profession within the clinic through the activities of social workers, the mundane decision making of legal officers, and the religious practices of the

Church, as they operate via such rituals as the confessional and the class-room practice of schoolteachers. In this sense, governmentality may be considered as the mundane management of normative order. But in Foucault's sociology, the capillaries of power linking the micro to wider levels of normative coercion are not unidirectional. Somewhat like Elias (1978a and c, 1982), it is perhaps most accurate to conceive of his view of power in terms of 'tension-balance'. That is, for both Elias and Foucault, power is conditional, contingent and ever-unfinished.

It is Foucault's emphasis on the mundane character of power, and his insistence on examining it as a *historical process*, which makes his contri-bution between the 1960s and his death in 1984 so singular. Other writers, notably Elias (1978a, 1982), and Lukes (1973), were highly critical of ahistorical and zero-sum views of power. Yet their writing was apolitical and so it was often difficult for students to see how their criticisms applied to everyday life. In Foucault's work, politics is central. The effect of power in inhibiting desire, enabling change and organizing subjectivity is constant. It provides a useful contrast with contemporaneous feminist readings which emphasized that the 'personal is political' and that male power has a history, but explicitly posited transcendence in the form of standards of equality and respect. Foucault's work does not discount equality and respect as laudable goals. To the contrary, much of his political life was dedicated to securing these aims. However, he also insists that the project of transcendence, and the negotiation of new forms of equality and respect between actors, produces new forms of compulsion and control. It is the inexhaustible character of power, that emerges most clearly from his work.

This approach to politics had a particular message for radical Marxism. It suggests that the attempt to seize the state through political action would not destroy power, because power is rather like a dye diffused through the entire social structure and saturated in daily practices, so that it becomes transparent. This view of power is very closely associated with Foucault's fascination with discipline, namely that power exists through the discip-linary practices which produce particular individuals, institutions and cultural arrangements. The disciplinary management of society results in a carceral system that is a form of society in which the principles of Bentham's panopticon are institutionalized. In retropsect the metaphor of the panopticon, although compelling, was probably misleading, for it suggested a centralization of power in a column or nexus, as with Marx's metaphor of the bourgeoisie as the 'ruling executive class' of capitalism. Foucault's concept of power is that it is distributed through the interstices of body and society. Implicitly, his position is anti-utopian because it posits reflexivity without transcendence.

Foucault's originality as a theorist and historian was to see how the ethical systems of ancient civilizations and early Christianity produced the self through practices of self-subjection. Power is strongest when individuals voluntarily apply it through self-regulation for the sake of, among other things, moral improvement, religious purification or self-advancement. These ethical systems involved the identification of an ethical substance (such as desire) which is to be shaped through moral activity. Secondly they require subjection in which moral obligation is recognized (to subject oneself to God, for example). This subjection leads to the objectification of moral obligations into codes or discourses of ethics, such as the discourses of sexuality which Foucault studied under the notions of the 'care of the self' (Foucault, 1986) and the 'use of pleasure' (Foucault, 1985). These discourses of subjectivity then produce identities, codes or roles such as the hysterical woman or the masturbatory child. It is these identities which then become the object and focus of medicalization and normalization. In the modern period, the medicalization of the menopausal woman in North America and the export of those discourses and identities to other societies such as Japan are clear illustrations of these processes (Lock, 1993). These practices of subjection and self-formation also involve the emergence of complex pedagogies of self-transformation and education. The medieval confessional has now been elaborated and refined by modern forms of 'talking therapy' in psychoanalysis and, at another level of society, manuals of self-help (Giddens, 1992). Finally, subjection requires the production of a moral telos towards which these practices are directed. In contemporary society, these goals typically include not only the ideology of self-fulfilment through self-knowledge, but a range of preventive health policies and measures which can be seen as an extension of these self-regulatory activities.

These ideas about power were further elaborated through Foucault's interest in 'governmentality', a system of power which articulated the triangular relationship between sovereignty, discipline and government. Governmentality (Foucault, 1991), which emerged in the eighteenth century, is a mechanism for regulating and controlling populations using an apparatus of security. This governmental apparatus required a whole series of specific *savoirs* and was the foundation for the rise of the administrative state (Gutting, 1989). A further important feature of Foucault's work was the analysis of the relationship between power and knowledge. Whereas liberal theory tended to separate power and knowledge on the grounds that truth is always corrupted by the exercise of power, Foucault saw that they were always inevitably and inextricably interconnected. Thus, any extension of power involved an increase in knowledge and every elaboration of knowledge involved an increase in power. Foucault approached this question typically through a consideration of populations and bodies. For example, the growth of penology and criminology was closely associated with the development of panoptic principles of surveillance and control. In a similar fashion the whole development of psychology and psychiatry was seen in terms of forms of knowledge, related to an extension of power over the subordinate populations of urban Europe. Foucault normally spoke about knowledge in the plural (*savoirs*) in order to illustrate the notion that specific forms of power required highly specific and detailed formations of knowledge.

This conceptual apparatus which Foucault built up around the study of the history of ideas, the analysis of power, and the explication of forms of discipline proved enormously useful for medical sociologists in their attempt to understand the forms of power assumed by medical practices. Foucault's work permitted sociologists to think about the medicalization of society within a new framework, where the exercise of medical power was seen in terms of local diffuse practices. The medical sociology inspired by Foucault is typically understood to be a distinctive break with the past. It was heavily informed by theoretical and philosophical analysis; it was highly critical of established medicine, seeking to provide alternative ways of examining mental illness and disease; it placed power and knowledge at the centre of the sociological understanding of medical institutions; and it showed how medical ideas of the moral character of disease operated at an everyday level.

As Foucault's work evolved, and as more of Foucault's studies were translated into English, such as *The Use of Pleasure* (1985) and *The Care of the Self* (1986), it also became clear that his view of medicine was part of a larger programme which examined the evolution of sexuality in European societies from classical Greece onwards, and how that evolution was intimately bound up with the transformation of medicine. In his final publications Foucault appeared to turn more and more to an analysis of the self in the context of medical history and the development of sexuality. His interest in how the self in Western societies was an effect of discourse of the self became increasingly obvious in his studies of 'technologies of the self' (Martin et al., 1988). Medical sociology and the sociology of health and illness were now seen to be both far broader in their terms of reference and also more central to the mainstream concerns of sociology as a whole.

Foucault provided a description of the institutions of normative coercion, such as the law, religion, schooling and medicine (Turner, 1992). These institutions are coercive in the sense that they discipline individuals and exercise forms of surveillance over everyday life in such a way that actions are both produced and constrained by them. However, such institutions as the medical clinic are not coercive in the violent or authoritarian sense because they are readily accepted as legitimate and normative at the everyday level. These institutions of normative coercion exercise a moral authority over the individual by explaining individual 'problems' and providing solutions for them. They impose shape upon what otherwise might be regarded as the shapeless anxiety of patients. By these means they both liberate and curtail options. In this sense we could say that medicine and religion exercise a hegemonic authority because their coercive character is often disguised and masked by their normative involvement in the troubles and problems of individuals. They are coercive, normative and also voluntary.

## Foucault and the sociology of the body

Although there was significant change in the intellectual evolution of Foucault's social philosophy, it is also clear that the body and populations played a continuous role in the analytic structure of his work. The body was the focus of military discipline, but it was also subject to the monastic regulation of medieval Catholicism. The body is the target of the medical gaze and governmentality. Generally speaking, health is a form of policing which is specifically concerned with the quality of the labour force. This view was clearly expressed by Foucault (1980a) in an article on 'The Politics of Health in the Eighteenth Century', where he suggested that the trans-formation of population

> arguably concerns the economic-political effects of the accumulation of men. The great eighteenth-century demographic upswing in Western Europe, the necessity for co-ordinating and integrating it into the apparatus of production and the urgency of controlling it with finer and more adequate power mechanisms caused 'population', with its numerical variables of space and chronology, longevity and health, to emerge not only as a problem but as an object of surveillance, analysis, intervention, modification etc. (Foucault, 1980a: 171)

The nexus of knowledge/power was thus initially an effect of demographic changes, particularly the pressure of populations on systems of government and regulation from the eighteenth century. This demographic transforma-tion has been taken to be, in fact, the major societal context for the emergence of modern forms of management, discipline and government (Turner, 1987a, 1992). It is the principal context for governmentality, as a regime which links self-subjection with societal regulation.

The body was of major significance in *Discipline and Punish*. It also continued to play a crucial role in the larger project of *The History of Sexuality* where Foucault was concerned with the body in relation to medicine and the body in relation to the development of the self within a Christian paradigm. Briefly, Foucault was interested in the production of bodies, the regulation of bodies and the representation of bodies within a context of disciplinary surveillance (Turner, 1984). The integration of legal and medical controls over the body and identity was a theme in the study of hermaphrodites in *Herculine Barbin* (Foucault, 1980b). Foucault's work on the production of sexual identity played a major part subsequently in the historical analysis of gender and sexuality (Laqueur, 1990) and in the relationship between women and medicine (Martin, 1987). In later years the sociology of the body emerged as a major theme in medical sociology because it provided a powerful perspective upon, *inter alia*, the socially constructed nature of disease categories and the role of medicine in regu-lating individuals through regulating their bodies, and also contributed to new perspectives on the question of sexuality and medicine. Having been neglected as a theoretical topic for many decades the question of the human body has recently become a critical issue in the social sciences. There have been a number of major publications in this area, resulting virtually in a new sub-field of sociology (O'Neill, 1989; Leder, 1990; Featherstone et al., 1991; Shilling, 1993; Synnott, 1993).

The causes and nature of this interest in the cultural aspects of the human body are both divergent and complex. However, this new interest in the body is related to the growing problems of human identity brought about by legal and social changes which in turn are a consequence of technical transformations in medicine, specifically in the area of human reproduction. There is also widespread public anxiety about the nature of contemporary epidemics such as HIV and AIDS which have drawn attention to the complexities of sexuality in modern society. These medical changes are associated with various movements in modern society which seek to change social attitudes towards the body, particularly the gay and feminist movements. These anxieties about the body are part of a broader concern about the demographic revolution of the last century, the process of ageing and the ecological deterioration of the environment. Within the context of capitalism, the body has emerged as a significant feature in consumption advertising and consumer culture (Falk, 1994). Cultural postmodernization has underlined the idea that the human body is simply a fabric or social product which has no ontological fixity. These postmodern questions about the body have brought a number of writers to speculate about the interaction between information systems, computer technology and the body.

Through these studies of the self, discipline and the body, medical sociology evolved more fully and effectively into the sociology of health and illness. At the same time, it became part of the mainstream interest of sociology, because the sociological study of health was perceived more openly as a sophisticated contribution to the study of power, where micro-practices of power were interpreted from Foucault's perspective of governmentality. These changes in the intellectual climate of the social sciences were direct consequences of the adoption of Foucault's perspective on bio-politics.

## Risk society and contemporary politics: evaluating Foucault

We have argued that to see Foucault's work as a contribution to the sociology of social control and deviance is, if not mistaken, at least an oversimplification. Nevertheless, Foucault's focus on discipline, power and governmentality does have an intellectual proximity to Max Weber's study of instrumental rationality and bureaucracy, and to Theodor Adorno's contributions to the notion of an administered society. It also suggests a parallel to Erving Goffman's notion of the total organization. The carceral society indicates a regime of micro regulations and disciplines which operate through a complex web of self-subjection. In short, we can see Foucault as part of a sociological tradition that emphasizes the importance of regulation and administration as key features of 'modern society'. Like Weber, Foucault provided a profound insight into the bureaucratic mentality of a society dominated by the logic of instrumental rationality. How relevant then is Foucault to a social environment which is seen to be postmodern, deregulated and risky?

Throughout the 1980s there were major changes in the structure of the economy and government, which in retrospect we can see as part of the new right revolution in the marketization of social relations, including the marketization of the provision of social services. Managerialism, privatization and deregulation were dimensions of a profound globalization of the world economy, including services, tourism, consumerism and labour markets. We can see the current enthusiasm for the concept of 'risk society' as a response to this general sense that the modern world has become more uncertain, contingent, flexible and risky. It appears to be in structure and ethos very far removed from the carceral society with its dependable and recognizable processes and procedures.

In the health field these changes have been profound. The traditions of centralized mechanisms for the provision of social security and welfare have been replaced by a logic of internal markets, competitive tendering and devolved budgets. The very notion of 'security' sits oddly with the contemporary enthusiasm for a discourse of entrepreneurish, just-in-time management systems and the culture of risk. These changes in bureaucratic structures have occurred alongside major epidemiological changes which in a sinister fashion appear to mimic the contingency of the market place. We have in mind here the spread of AIDs and other infectious diseases, the deterioration of the food supply, the danger of inter-species disease such as 'mad cows' disease' and the associated risks of CJD. These changes are not encapsulated easily within Foucault's language of discipline and control. It is true that Foucault was aware of changes in the provision of welfare (Foucault, 1988) and his notion of governmentality can be extended to analyse some aspects of a risk environment. However, there is a profound tension between the metaphors which lie behind risk society and governmentality (Turner, 1995b: 218–27).

How might we, at least in theoretical terms, resolve some of these tensions? There are a number of possibilities. To some extent we might argue that financial deregulation in the 1980s produced a global environment of political and economic uncertainty between nation states, but within each industrial society the need for micro-surveillance and discipline continued with greater intensity. Indeed the importance of a carceral society has increased with the growth of externalized macro-risk. As the global economy develops into a culture of risk, the nation state is forced to invest more and more in internal systems of governmentality. Secondly, a risk society, based on deregulation and devolution, often requires more subtle and systematic forms of control. For example, the state is forced to create regulatory systems of quality control, where public utilities have been privatized. Thirdly, financial deregulation increases the scale of economic risk. Where major companies and public institutions fall into debt and bankruptcy, governments typically intervene, despite their ideological commitment to privatization and deregulation, to save such institutions. Fourthly, we can argue that modern societies are structured by two apparently contradictory processes: the growth of risk cultures and the McDonaldization of society (Ritzer, 1993).

McDonaldization is the application of Fordist production methods and rational managerialism to the fast-food industry, and this is then extended

to all sectors of society. McDonaldization reduces uncertainty and unpredictability; it is, in short, a response to risk and uncertainty. McDonaldization removes surprises from everyday life by an extension of instrumental
rationality to production, distribution and consumption. After the
McDonaldization of the fast-food industry, these principles have been
applied to universities and medicine. McDentists and McDoctors extends the
principles of cheapness, standardization and reliability to the health industry:
the welfare and health system is now a complex mixture of risk culture and
McDonaldization of services. Finally, the notion of generalized risk in the
environment may lead to greater surveillance and control through the promotion of preventive medicine (Lupton, 1965). The AIDs 'epidemic' creates a
political climate within which intervention and control are seen to be both
necessary and benign. Individuals need, especially in the area of sexual
etiquette, to become self-regulating and self-forming.

If Foucault's theories of sexuality and governmentality are to continue to
inspire and shape the development of the sociology of health and illness,
followers of Foucault will be compelled to address the new environment of
risk cultures, political contingencies and deregulated welfare systems. The
burden of dependency, with the ageing of Western societies, is being
answered increasingly with the privatization of medicine and a doctrine of
obligation. The traditional notions of citizen rights (to health and social
welfare) are being questioned by a liberal ideology of individual obligation
(to save and to create personal bases of security). The cost of mental health
to the community is being resolved, not with greater surveillance, but with
deinstitutionalization. In America, the number of residents in state mental
hospitals fell from 513,000 in 1950 to 111,000 in 1986 as a consequence of
such a policy. The economic cost of state intervention in health care has in
most advanced societies resulted in new policies of privatization, 'out-
sourcing', downsizing, internal markets, managerialism and deinstitutionalization. Such economic and social processes are not easily described or
explained by Foucault's paradigm of the disciplinary society, panopticism
and governmentality. The intellectual challenge is to comprehend the
structures and institutions of postmodern society within the conceptual
apparatus of Foucault's understanding of governmentality.

# 7

# RIGHTS

In this chapter, the sociology of the body is employed as a basis for defending a universalistic theory of human rights. Such a proposal immediately runs into at least two formidable obstacles. First, notions about universalism have been radically attacked by a variety of traditions in social philosophy with the result that there is a broad consensus that universalistic arguments are likely to be sociologically naïve. For example, Max Weber's sociology of law was an overt criticism of the idea that natural law could provide an authoritative and convincing basis for rights. The second obstacle is that the body in sociological theory is typically seen to be socially constructed and as such could not act as a general foundation for human rights. For example, Michel Foucault's analysis of the human body was an attempt to show that the 'body' was a contingent effect of power. In his *Technologies of the Self*, Foucault (in Martin et al., 1988) wrote: 'All of my analyses are against the idea of universal necessities in human existence. They show the arbitrariness of institutions'. In order to clear the ground for a discussion of the sociology of human rights, a long detour is required to consider cultural relativism and social constructionism.

Arguments about cultural relativism can be, and have been, manipulated and abused by authoritarian governments to justify various forms of state violence under the banner of cultural authenticity. It is all too easy to justify abuses against children and women or devastation of the natural environment by an appeal to ethnic privilege or moral superiority. In the postwar years figures like Pol Pot, General Pinochet, Saddam Hussein and Milosevic have all used appeals to moral superiority or ethnic privilege for the purposes of genocide.

Philosophical and sociological arguments against relativism are an important part of the political programme to protect and defend human rights traditions in the public arena. But they need a metatheory if they are to avoid being a desultory, disaggregated contribution to the field. We argue that the body provides the foundations for such a metatheory, even if it cannot function as the basis for a universal system of human rights. All bodies are frail and the vulnerability to ageing and disease is the common human condition. All bodies have the capacity and desire to experience pleasure and recognize pain. All bodies live in environments which are precarious. These twin conditions are universal, although, on the individual existential level, they are mediated in different forms according to economic, political and cultural factors. The frailty, sensuousness and vulnerability of the body and the precariousness of the physical and social environment compel human groups to devise protective strategies to maintain life. While not all rights are attached to the goal of achieving protective security, a large part of the human rights legal tradition is dedicated to providing common security for human beings.

Talk about human rights is often difficult in sociological and anthropological theory because these traditions are committed to the notion of cultural relativism. Since cultures obviously differ in quite fundamental ways in their values, the notion of universal standards is difficult to defend intellectually. The tortuous efforts of the Protestants and the Catholics to achieve a peace settlement in Northern Ireland shows, with tragic clarity, the difficulties that human groups have in forging common agreements.

We do not discount these difficulties. We seek to employ the sociology of the body as a strategy for exploring the moral basis of a universalistic doctrine of human rights. We do fully recognize that universalism is an unpopular approach in social theory. It is often associated with claims about the privileged status of Western thought, or with patriarchal fantasies of dominance. In any event, universalism as a basis for epistemology and political philosophy is seen to be problematic and difficult to defend. Universalistic claims about truth or justice have been challenged by various forms of postmodernism and pragmatism, and the general mood of social science and the humanities has been more sympathetic to relativism and to the notion that 'grand narratives' cannot be easily sustained (Lyotard, 1980). If the tone of univeralism suggests a triumphalist attitude, contemporary thought has been generally anxious about bold claims to general, let alone universal, relevance and validity.

Cultural relativism is a popular, and often exciting, position. But there is a danger of making a fetish of difference and diversity. We live in a capitalist-dominated world. Our economy, culture and politics are dominated by capitalist values. Capitalism imposes common disciplines on bodies and environments: it produces risks which place everybody at risk. Genetically engineered crop production, the destruction of the ozone layer, industrial and chemical pollution, the commodification of everyday life are just some of the risks to the physical and cultural environment which capitalism causes. A politics organized around identity is unlikely to achieve success in tackling these risks, because it ultimately privileges identity over collectivism. People today may see themselves first and foremost as homosexual, feminist, disabled or ecologically aware. In a condition in which various global tendencies are combining to weaken the nation state, these orientations to identity may be much stronger than ties of nationality, or region. Nevertheless, to combat some of the negative effects of ICI, British Petroleum, General Motors or Microsoft, a collective approach beyond identity is required. By emphasizing the universality of sensuousness, frailty, vulnerability and precariousness, we seek to underline that communities throughout the world, whatever their material circumstances, face similar circumstances. By emphasizing the material level of univeralism we hope to avoid some of the problems that idealistic readings of universalism have produced. The body and the environment are the concrete foundations of life with others. This is why we privilege them here.

Moreover, although postmodernism has done much to foment relativism, it does not follow that postmodern thought has been, so to speak, 'ethics-proof'. On the contrary, postmodernism, influenced by Martin Heidegger, has been specifically interested in the ideas of 'care' as an ethic that does not involve grand claims about universalism. Following Heidegger on forgetfulness versus concern for otherness, we can detect a postmodern ethical stance in the idea of care for marginal or powerless groups, and commitment to the recognition of difference and otherness. Similarly, cruelty is, for Richard Rorty, the most serious human crime. For example cruelty, in the form of torture, is a denial of the humanity of the victim, involving a forgetfulness about the human status of victims. Similarly, not even Baudrillard (1983a and b), in his exultant celebration of the explosion of community, advocates that the disabled, the sick and infants should be abandoned.

These authors seek a grounding for concern, not in the universal characteristics of human nature, but in the practical requirements for active care and affective sympathy. While such an approach has considerable merit, we argue that human vulnerability provides the basis for a universalistic ethic of concern which goes beyond the apparent complacency of Rorty's pragmatism. In his defence of Western liberalism, Rorty comes close to a Leibnizian view that we (bourgeois Westerners) live in the best of all possible worlds (White, 1991: 93). The notion that the vulnerability of the body provides a foundation for rights is in fact highly compatible with Heidegger's account of the vulnerability of human beings as bound to death through the inexorable passage of time. Heidegger's views on the 'throwness' of being as a state which is permanently precarious provide an account which is highly compatible with an emphasis on human frailty and vulnerability as a starting point for an analysis of rights. We would add that human frailty and vulnerability must be understood in physical and psychological terms: we see them as the adjunct of sensuality. In as much as physical and social necessity combine to express sensual desire, albeit in regulated ways, they entail making connections with others. Humans live in the constant knowledge not only that bodies decay, but that relationships can go wrong. Relativist accounts use this type of argument to refute universalism. However, the problem with relativism in political theory is that it cannot simultaneously develop an ethic of care and satisfy questions about justice or produce a theory of desire and satisfy issues of ethical decency. The recognition of difference does not easily feed into a theory that can give a good account of the conditions of justice or ethics. There is therefore an ongoing question about the universality of the treatment of human beings as human beings. In this chapter, we attempt to develop a view of human rights as protective social mechanisms which address issues of human vulnerability, sensuousness, frailty and precariousness. We return to these issues in the final chapter, in the discussion of cosmopolitan virtue.

A perennial problem of modern social theory has been to identify a basis, however minimalist, for some universalistic criterion of justice in relation to separate and particular social groups and communities. The core of this issue is to reconcile the aspiration for political equality with the stubborn fact of social differences (in class, ethnicity and gender). Traditional accounts of the principle of equality of opportunity have been appropriately challenged for example by postmodern feminism for their blindess to difference (Williams, 1995). However, if we regard justice as an issue about fairness (Rawls, 1971), then there has to be some foundation of a universalistic character in order for such discussions about justice to take place. Otherwise, we are left with a mere talking shop of difference. Some implicit commitment to universalism, typically as a residual category, is embraced by theorists who want overtly to adopt a resolutely anti-foundationalist or contextualist position. Post-modern relativist epistemologies are often combined with the implicit search for a common vocabulary with which to talk about politics and ethics. Is care for others a universal imperative in a context of apparently chronic cultural diversity?

While these questions have become increasingly salient with the growth of multiculturalism and postmodern diversity, the problem of relativism in the sociology of knowledge was a prominent issue in social theory during the last century. In part, this was a consequence of the development of the sociology of knowledge from the perspective of Karl Mannheim (Turner, 1991). The idea then that beliefs have an 'existential basis' is hardly new, but in recent decades the notion of universalism has come under attack from a variety of intellectual sources: feminist theory, postmodernism, 'subaltern studies' and decolonization theory.

In an earlier period the relativistic thrust of the sociology of knowledge was challenged and rejected by the Frankfurt School, because critical theory wanted to do more than merely describe ideology as a perspective on the world. The ambition of critical theory was to go beyond traditional forms of theory, and the relativism of the sociology of knowledge, to produce critical insights into the exploitation and alienation of capitalist society. Critical theorists disliked Mannheimian relativism, because Mannheim had argued in *Ideology and Utopia* (1960) that radical forms of socialist utopianism were the product of social groups which had no stake in present society. The goal of critical theory was to combine theory and practice in order to avoid the apparent neutrality and factual limitations of traditional sociology of knowledge, at least as it was practised by Mannheim. In the work of Habermas (1981), there is the quest for a communicative basis to belief and knowledge which will overcome the limitations of the relativism of sociology. The ideal speech situation offers a basis for transcendence, albeit a flawed one, since Habermas offers no convincing account of how the unconscious can be elucidated in everyday life encounters. Freud's point that the unconscious structures much of the ordinary interactions that take place in everyday life has never really been appreciated by critics seeking social transcendence. With respect to Habermas's model of the ideal speech situation, the question is, how can the role of the unconscious be externalized and monitored to ensure clarity and justice? Within contemporary critical social science, the battle lines have consequently been drawn between the critical legacy of Adorno and Horkheimer in the work of Habermas on communicative theory, and postmodern theory which has embraced a more particularistic or deconstructed approach to reason and truth.

Although relativism is by no means a recent development in social theory, it has acquired a certain urgency as a consequence of the growth of the politics of identity and difference. In this chapter we want to articulate a sense that particularism and contextualism are inadequate as orientations to problems of justice and equality. One conventional criticism has been that postmodern theory does not lend itself to any particular political theory or perspective on contemporary society, and therefore it is rather difficult to move from the deconstructionism of postmodern epistemology to genuine political commitment and action (Habermas, 1988). We want to challenge this conventional view by claiming that most postmodern con-textualists in practice want to adopt a political theory of society, especially one which embraces some notion of justice as a central concept of political discourse. While equality, as a principle, is not easily reconciled with a postmodern emphasis on difference, justice as a concept has become part of the vocabulary of postmodernism (Lyotard and Thebaud, 1985). Stephen White (1988, 1991) has illuminated this interpretive question by showing that there is an underlying political theory in contemporary postmodern-ism, namely a willingness to listen to difference rather than to command equality.

In White's view Derrida, Lyotard, Walzer and Rorty attempt to come to terms with the problem of justice, while also taking on board a whole legacy of postmodern thinking about contextualism. Walzer (1983) has been particularly influential in contemporary views of justice. Lyotard and Walzer share a common hostility to the metanarratives of modernism (Lyotard, 1984). Lyotard claims that the metanarratives of dominance in modernity will be eroded by 'thousands of uncomfortable little stories' (Lyotard, 1989: 127). Because modernity requires a systematic storage system (a grand memory), Lyotard's political theory advocates forgetful-ness as a strategy. Postmodernism does not necessarily assume an apolitical orientation towards society; its main political position has been tolerance for the voice of marginal and forgotten social groups, but such a political theory cannot easily deal with the conflicting claims of a variety of groups for justice (Rojek and Turner, 1998).

One could argue that traditional liberal political theory, for example in the philosophy of J.S. Mill, was also concerned to protect the voice of minority dissent against the tyranny of mass democratic opinion (Turner, 1990a). How then is the postmodern emphasis on heterogeneity different from late nineteenth-century liberalism? White notes that there are two new dimen-sions to the pluralist approach to justice in postmodern theory. First, postmodern pluralism unlike traditional liberal thought rejects the emphasis on the sovereign individual and individualism, and postmodern pluralism is thought to be more sensitive to the social and political dimensions of private and public goods. Secondly, because postmodernism is particularly influenced by language theory, it tends to regard the question of justice not of doing political acts leading to just outcomes but of 'listening', that is listening to the differences and heterogenity of the social world. Postmodern politics involves attentive listening, especially to inarticulate minority groups (Williams, 1995: 82). Lyotard, for example, was strongly committed to the promotion of a notion of justice that is more sensitive to questions of otherness and difference.

But what are the common assumptions upon which listening to others might be possible? For many political theorists, the quest for a communal understanding of political life is still desirable and feasible. It is for this reason that writers like Walzer are often associated with the communitarian defence of liberalism (Cladis, 1992). Although Walzer promotes and celebrates the idea of moral pluralism and cultural diversity, he nevertheless believes that the political community is based upon a shared understanding of common values and sensibilities. In a similar fashion, Rorty is concerned to discover a common solidarity that will underpin and shape contemporary societies (Rorty, 1989). Again, Rorty attempts to discover solidarity within a new sensibility, driven by an openness to literature, poetry and art. It is a solidarity based upon a common aesthetic experience of great literature, especially the novels of Dickens and Kundera, from whom we can learn a sensitivity to suffering. Reading Dickens on the mundane nature of human misery makes an attitude of forgetfulness unlikely or at least difficult to sustain. But not everyone wants to read Dickens, and part of Rorty's problem is that he adduces a philosophy which is incapable of embracing a culture in which McDonaldization and episodic, glancing interrelations are becoming more pronounced.

While new postmodern pluralism differs from strong-minded liberalism in this emphasis on communitarianism, perhaps the major division between traditional liberalism and postmodern thought is around rationality, in particular around what Weber (1978: 24) referred to as actions which are instrumentally rational (*zweckrational*). Weber's sociology of action attempted to identify an ethic of responsibility whereby social and political action involved a compromise between alternative courses of action. The ethic of responsibility forced reasonable people to make practical decisions about appropriate means to ends. Weber's sociology as a whole was based upon an ethic of world mastery whereby, through the Protestant Ethic, human beings were driven to the need to control themselves in their environment in a context of uncertainty and risk. This ethic of responsibility was Weber's transformation of the idea of the will to power in Nietzsche. Within Weberian sociology, power and knowledge were combined to produce an ethic of world control, self-mastery and sovereignty in which the men of calling would subordinate reality to their own needs. Nietzsche's will to power therefore resulted in a sociology of callings and vocations in Weber's view of heroic instrumental reason. Postmodernism explicitly rejects this form of ethical orientation by stressing instead an openness to difference and otherness, namely as an ethic of care and concern.

If Weber's sociology is based upon a responsibility to act, postmodern morality is based upon a responsibility to listen to otherness and to care for difference. This ethical view within postmodernism is not only based upon a rejection of the ethic of responsibility and its underlying commitment to a doctrine of world mastery, but the postmodern ethic of concern also flows from its particular view of language, and the postmodern commitment to the idea that the world is ultimately humanly constructed. World mastery is rejected not only because it is incompatible with a concern for otherness, but also because the foundational view of reality which lies behind instrumental reason and technology is rejected in favour of anti-foundationalism, contextualism and constructionism. Thus 'following Nietzsche, the post-structuralists would say that all the normality within a world is ultimately sustained by nothing more than fictions whose fictionality has been forgotten. This forgetting has the effect of denying the otherness that is spurned by any human construct' (White, 1991: 26). For Nietzsche, the heroic values of Western civilization – the soul, man, truth and beauty – were only metaphors pulled together and constructed by a will to know and a will to power. By recognizing the fictions behind such moral constructs, postmodernism delegitimizes the responsibility to act in favour of a more passive orientation towards accepting existence in a mode of care and concern.

## Bodies and power

Our purpose is to make the body, or more specifically embodiment, central or foundational to a theory of human rights and to use embodiment as a critique of the tendency of sociologists and anthropologists to accept relativism as taken for granted in contemporary social science. In making this argument, we have to simultaneously reject the social constructionist view of the body and abandon the professional assumption in sociology about the fact/value distinction.

In order to develop this foundationalist theory of the body, we must distinguish our position from that of Foucault. It is obvious that recent analysis of the body in relation to power has depended heavily on the work of Foucault, particularly in terms of the themes of discipline and punish, the self and sexuality, and the general topic of governmentality. Foucault's analysis of 'the bio-politics of populations and the anatomo-politics of the body' can be summarized in the following arguments. Disciplinary power – such as panopticism – functions to produce servile, disciplined and effective bodies through a micro-politics of disciplinary regimes, practices and regulations. Docile bodies are functional for the modern state, as part of a general apparatus of control which can be termed 'governmentality'. The modern self arises from these bio-regimes which control the body to produce 'truths' such as the truth of the self which is a consequence of both torture and the confessional. Power which is typically local, diffuse, practical and normative means ultimately the power to produce different types of bodies, that is power over life.

These issues about the body are widely dispersed through Foucault's work. They arise in a simple and direct fashion in *Discipline and Punish* which, as a history of the prison, traces rational management practices from Bentham to modern times. The multiple-volume study, *The History of Sexuality* examines how the control of sexuality produces truth and, through the confessional practices of Western rationality, how in a system of 'technologies of the self' the modern self is produced. All of these studies could be seen as a complex history of the production of sexuality in Western systems of thought and practice as the foundation of the modern self. The body in Foucault's work was the historical site upon which this apparatus of the self was constructed. More recent interpretations of Foucault have argued that his entire position on power can be summarized under the notion of 'governmentality', the idea that the need to control population was the driving force behind seventeenth-century bureaucratic processes in the state's quest to control space. Throughout his work, however, the control of the body is a primary task of power.

Foucault's work has been subject to a large and systematic body of criticism. There is a common argument that Foucault never developed a satisfactory account of how resistance to power occurs. For example, he failed to describe how panoptic and regulative powers might be counter-posed by various social struggles. At the same time, he also regarded all forms of state intervention as resulting in normalization. There are similarities here between Foucault's view of the operation of power as normalization and Weber's analysis of the effects of instrumental rationality and asceticism on the regulation of social life – a regulation summarized in his metaphor of 'the iron cage'. One problem with such a view of power is that it cannot give an account of social co-operation and trust that does not assimilate social solidarity to the negative processes of normalization and governmentality. It is obvious that social relations are, in Hobbesian terms, characterized by systemic conflict, struggle and violence, but in common-sense terms there is also co-operation, trust and common purpose. This contradiction provides the traditional foundation in sociology for the conventional conflict and consensus approaches in social theory, or the alleged differences between functionalism and Marxism.

### Allocation and integration problems

In more sophisticated terms, we can say that social systems are faced by two fundamental problems, the allocative and the integrative problems. In any social group there has to be an allocation of (scarce) resources, which inevitably produces inequality and conflict, but there also has to be the orchestration of solidarity for common objectives to be achieved. The problem of power at a societal level is to reconcile the conflicts produced by allocative inequality in a context of scarcity (the classical problems of economics) and to mobilize trust and co-operation to achieve collective goals (the classical problem of sociology, namely the Hobbesian problem of order). It is the lack of an account of trust and co-operation in Foucault's pessimistic *Weltanschauung* which illustrates his primary dependence on Nietzsche, for whom the will to power explained both morality and truth. The will to power is the will to impose a body, namely my body. Nietzsche's vision of the *Ubermensch* did not allow much scope for illness, disease and ageing, despite his own chronic hypochondria, his persistent headaches, stomach disorders, and final insanity. Because he violently dismissed Christianity as a slave morality which had sublimated the drive for power into control over the self, Nietzsche's view of social relations was antagonistic to notions about empathy, sympathy or agape. Foucault, taking the will to power as the model of power/knowledge, also treats power as either power of disciplinary regimes over bodies or resistance of bodies (through deviance) to governmentality. Such a theory can only see co-operation of bodies for survival as a cunning defeat. The possibility of empowerment of vulnerable bodies through collective resources is necessarily denied in the Nietzsche/Foucault paradigm. The theory is defective because it cannot give a satisfactory account of reciprocity in everyday life or about functional collective arrangements in the public domain. For Foucault, citizenship is only a further means of (negative) governmentality.

There is one final and important critical observation to be made about the account of the body in Foucault's history of sexuality. The more Foucault deconstructs the body and the more he shows that there are no 'universal necessities in human existence', the more the human body in its phenomenal facticity disappears from view. The more the body is a product of discursive strategies, the more the human body of the everyday world of interaction and reciprocity evaporates. This disappearance is a problem for all forms of deconstructive techniques from Foucault to feminism. Because Foucault, for political reasons, wanted to demonstrate that heterosexuality was the classic example of what he called 'the arbitrariness of institutions', he needed to show that the taken-for-granted bodies of the everyday world were phantasms. The more social science pushes the idea of the constructed and arbitrary nature of the body, the more difficult it becomes to give a sociologically and ultimately morally satisfactory account of the suffering, pain and ordinary misery of the human body in its phenomenological condition.

This observation serves to remind us that the recent sociology of the body has been divided by two contrasting and competing epistemologies, one associated with Foucault and the other with Maurice Merleau-Ponty. Foucauldian poststructuralism has examined the enormous variety of discourses by which 'bodies' have been produced, classified, normalized and regulated. At the same time, the Foucauldian denies the sensuous materiality of the body in favour of an 'anti-humanist' analysis of the discursive ordering of bodily regimes. He examines the various 'governments of the body' rather than the phenomenology of embodiment. It rejects the commonsense assumption that the body (in the singular) can have any unitary coherence or significance. By contrast, the phenomenology of the body uncovers the ways in which the everyday world is organized from the perspective of the embodiment of human beings.

We can illustrate these issues by commenting on a recent treatment of dentistry (Jones and Porter, 1998). From an orthodox Foucauldian perspective, mouths as such do not exist; as a site of professional practice, the mouth is a late invention of dental science. Such a critical poststructuralist reading of the mouth expunges any interest in what one might call oral phenomenology. We can contrast this poststructuralist argument with a study of disability, that is attentive to both the normalization of the disabled body and its phenomenological presence. Wendy Seymour's moving account of the experience and consequences of spinal cord injury represents a markedly different approach to the injured body. *Remaking the Body* (1998) is a welcome sequel to her *Bodily Alterations* (1989); her two studies of trauma are indicative of the new directions in the study of disability. Employing qualitative data from interviews, she examines the social construction of the body in a literal sense, namely how bodies are remade following trauma, whether by accident or disease. The post-traumatic rebuilding of the body also involves a 'second chance' at refashioning the self. This remaking is not merely a discursive process; it involves, following Merleau-Ponty, the reconstruction of the lived, sensual body. However, it takes place within the gaze of habilitation which holds out the (false) promise of a normal body – young, athletic and sexual. It is not enough to return to society via rehabilitation; the rehabilitated body has to be discursively normal.

There is a parallel between Foucault's desire to deconstruct the body in the interests of a politics of sexual identity and the desire to deconstruct the 'disabled body' in the interests of a political critique of 'able-ist' ideology. With these political objectives, we have no debate. However, the consequence of these political strategies is paradoxically to dismiss the body once more from theoretical inspection. However, the choice between either poststructuralism or phenomenology may be an artificial option in the sense that they were developed to answer different types of theoretical problem. On the one hand, one can accept the spirit of Foucault's work as a critical inspection of 'the arbitrariness of institutions'. The arbitrary history of medical institutions is a case in point. The dental mouth, surrounded by the professional institutions of dental care, can be constructed otherwise; in that sense, it is arbitrary. However, it is also important to recognize another reality (of universal necessities) of the lived body in the mundane world of such practical activities as living, breeding and dying, where the mouth, tortured by cancer or by dental decay, may have something different to say. The pain of dental decay is also arbitrary from the victim's point of view – why me now? But this pain is not simply the effect of discursive professional practices. It has a phenomenological reality and presence that demands urgent action. It is a practical problem of the everyday world. No amount of philosophical talk about its constructed character will convince us otherwise: a pain is a pain is a pain.

## Max Weber, value neutrality and the sociological tradition

We wish now to open up a discussion of the relationship between a foundational account of human embodiment and human rights by reference to a previous publication (Turner, 1993). The problem with sociology's reluctance to talk about human rights is that human rights have become a powerful institution and play a major role in political mediation of social conflict. In the post-communist global order, local ethnic and inter-faith violence has escalated with a corresponding demand for the protection of human life through human rights legislation and action. In this context it is urgent, if sociologists want to enter the debate about justice in an inter-national relations context, that sociological theory should develop an approach to human rights. The point of the 'Outline of a General Theory of Human Rights' (Turner, 1993) was to establish the theoretical basis for a sociological approach to human rights and to new social movements which embrace human rights discourse. Although sociology has made a major contribution to citizenship studies and thereby to social rights research and analysis, it lacks a genuine approach to human rights for reasons which are related to the essential relativism of classical sociology. We largely accept Leo Strauss's critique (1950) of Max Weber's attack on the legacy of natural law in which Weber rejected any possibility of establishing, for example, a hierarchy of values.

Of course any attempt to defend human rights through a foundationalist theory of the body will come up against a social constructionist objection (Waters, 1996). The core assumption of social constructionism is 'that the institutionalization of rights is a product of the balance of power between political interests' (Waters, 1996: 595). One problem with this criticism is that contrasting research on the sociology of the body (Turner, 1992) has been based upon the argument that the dichotomy between foundation-alism and constructionism is false and misleading as an epistemology for the social sciences. By contrast, our approach to the vulnerability of the human body as a foundation for human rights research attempts to go beyond these conventional dichotomies. For example, in Marcel Mauss's 1934 essay on 'Techniques of the Body' (1973), this epistemological oppo-sition is rejected in favour of the view that human beings are equipped with foundational capacities, which can nevertheless be developed, modulated and constructed by cultural processes. Mauss gives the illustration of the human capacity to walk as a foundational characteristic of human embodiment, but the ways in which we walk (goose-step, slow march, ramble or waltz) are products of cultural variation and socialization. The goose-step is not a 'natural' mode of movement; it is constructed by the requirements of military organization and military display.

Another example can be taken from the influential work of Peter L. Berger and Thomas Luckmann (1966) who develop much of the groundwork for the social constructionist. While Berger and Luckmann are typically associated with the social constructionist position, the fact that their thesis was based upon a foundational ontology is often neglected. Berger and Luckmann followed the philosophical anthropology of Arnold Gehlen (1980) in arguing that human biology was 'unfinished' and therefore the social canopy of knowledge was a necessary construct in order to provide human beings with basic security. Culture was constructed as a shield against anomie, which was the outcome of the peculiarities of human embodiment. This philosophical anthropology of Gehlen (1988) was ultimately derived from Nietzsche's proposition that human beings were not-yet finished animals. Therefore in classical sociology there was no artificial division between a foundationalist ontology and a social constructionist epistemology.

It is perfectly consistent to argue, as a consequence, that human rights can have a foundationalist ontology in the notion that human beings are frail, vulnerable and sensuous. From this follows the argument that human rights will be constructed, in a contingent and variable way, according to the specific characteristics of the societies within which they are developed and as a particular outcome of political struggles over interests. The point of the foundationalist ontology was to provide a universal basis for normative evaluation of rights abuse.

Attempts to spell out a foundationalist theory of rights had two prongs. First there is the argument about the biological nature of human frailty where human rights emerged as a protective canopy, and secondly there is the argument that social institutions are precarious. Given frailty and precariousness, human beings need a universalistic legal framework in which to seek protection. Both of these arguments (frailty and precariousness) are an attempt to develop a contemporary version of Hobbes's theory of the state based upon the notion of a social contract. Hobbes argued in *Leviathan* that rational human beings with conflicting interests in a state of nature would be in a condition of perpetual war. In order to protect themselves from mutual, endless slaughter, humans create a state through a social contract, which organizes social space in the collective interests of rational but antagonistic human beings. To say that human beings are frail and live in a state of precarious social arrangements is merely a restatement of the notion that life is 'nasty, brutish and short'.

Furthermore, the state institutions, which humans create as protective or defensive mechanisms, have to be sufficiently powerful to regulate social space and as a consequence come unintentionally to present a threat to the human beings who institute state through a social contract. The state is a guarantor of social security but also necessarily an instrument of violence. In this respect the argument follows Weber's definition of the state as that institution which holds a monopoly of legitimate violence within a given territory. One final comment on Hobbes is that the precise character of the state cannot be derived from the common existential problem of inter-personal violence. The state could either take the form of a despotic monarchy (Charles I) or authoritarian militarism (Oliver Cromwell).

In taking Hobbes's basic position as a starting point, we have adopted Gehlen's philosophical anthropology to argue that human beings are rational, but they are also embodied, sensuous and they have a capacity for sympathy towards their fellow human beings. The capacity for suffering and affection is an important feature of membership of a moral community (Morris, 1996). The notion that sympathy is the social glue of a society characterized by precariousness can also be seen as a contemporary restatement of Adam Smith's theory of sentiments. The point of this neo-Hobbesian theory of rights is to provide a theoretical structure which will connect individual human rights as protective arrangements, the organization of the state as an institution which guarantees rights but also threatens them, and the notion that sympathy is a major requirement of all social relations along with more traditional categories such as trust.

## Towards a sociology of human rights

We are no longer entirely satisfied with this existing account of rights in relation to embodiment, for three reasons. First, it fails to give a sufficiently detailed and systematic account of vulnerability to be convincing; secondly to give an ontological account of frailty is not in itself a sociological account; and finally in attempting to outline a theory of human rights we should also consider what would constitute a system of human obligations. We attempt to address these three critical observations through a discussion of Gideon Sjoberg and Ted Vaughan's similar efforts to develop a sociology of rights in their critique of contemporary American sociology (Sjoberg and Vaughan, 1993). Following a critical review of the impact of the principle of value neutrality, ethical relativism and utilitarianism on sociology as a professional discipline, Sjoberg and Vaughan argue there is an underlying and largely implicit commitment in the sociological tradition to the nation state. Their principal examples are Max Weber, Talcott Parsons, and Rheinhard Bendix. This covert assumption of the centrality of the nation state in the analysis of society has combined with a narrow set of assumptions about ethical neutrality to prevent sociologists from making any satisfactory contribution to the analysis of crimes against humanity. We need to develop an under-standing of rights and humanity in a global context. It follows that any 'adequate theory of human rights must be grounded in a conception of human nature that recognizes the interdependence of human beings' (Sjoberg and Vaughan, 1993: 134). This interdependence is underpinned by the existence of what they call 'the social mind', the central defining feature of which is 'reflectivity'. This argument allows them to distinguish human beings from other creatures and to define humanity in terms of a common characteristic, namely reflexivity. Thus, 'human agents stand apart from other species because they think about thinking' (Sjoberg and Vaughan, 1993: 135).

But how is this 'social mind' that defines humanity connected with human rights? It is because humans are characterized by reflexivity that they are able to take the role of the other and to understand the humanity of the other. In our terms, reflexivity is a precondition for sympathy. Secondly, the attainment of human rights rests on the ability of humans to reflect critically on their situation and to communicate their critical reflections to other humans. It is through this critical capacity that they can reflect on both the limitations of their entitlements and their opportunities for enhancing their rights. Sjoberg and Vaughan conclude by arguing that the repressive role of large corporate bureaucracies in the modern world is a central constraint upon and threat to human rights. The role of sociology is to provide a critical reflection upon these corporate constraints to human rights. Sjoberg and Vaughan's approach is attractive but like earlier attempts to develop a theory of human rights it fails to provide a sufficiently detailed account of the humanity of humans, the sociological causes producing human rights talk and the parallel existence of human obligations.

Our attempt to elaborate the idea of ontological insecurity has the following components. First, we hold that the human condition is vulnerable, involving sensuous openness to the world. Engagement with the physical and social world is the source of delight and the cause of anxiety. The joy of discovery that accompanies every meaningful human relationship is always tainted with the foreboding that relationships can decay, and commitments can atrophy. The discomfort that we feel at the state of being in the world is the result of the knowledge that pleasures gained may not be repeated. The conditional nature of being requires engagement with life, since self-satisfaction, like self-reliance, is a chimera.

Secondly, there is the argument that we are biologically frail. Ageing is an important illustration of this argument. While of course age and ageing are culturally defined, we are necessarily subject to an ageing process. This process is individually variable, but our immune systems tend to decline with age and we are more exposed to physical dangers as we age. There is also a potential conflict between generations over scarce resources with the ageing of populations. Because there is scarcity, there is conflict over resources. In our version of Hobbesian contract theory, embodiment for human beings creates insecurity, because we are all prone to illness, ageing and death.

## Vulnerability and belonging

It is possible to derive the need for (protective) human rights from the (Hobbesian) notion that human beings are biologically frail and their lives are precarious. Human beings as embodied creatures are subject to death, illness and disease, ageing, disability, suffering and mental decay (through dementia, Alzheimer's, Parkinson's Disease and so forth); they have what Anthony Giddens, following R.D. Laing, calls 'ontological insecurity' and what we would prefer to call 'chronic ontological frailty' as individuals, which creates a range of dependencies on social arrangements. Frailty also involves vulnerability, namely a sensuous openness to experience and to the pleasures of the experiences of the everyday world.

Of course, the notion that humans are frail could produce an argument, not about collective arrangements for protection, but a Darwinistic account of the survival of the fittest. Our argument against this option involves two steps. First, fitness is temporary, because in the political discourse of disability the apparently able bodied are TAPs (Temporarily Able Bodied Persons). As Bourdieu pithily observes, 'old age is also a social decline'. Secondly, vulnerability opens us to social interaction with and dependency upon other social agents. There are social processes of interaction which produce countervailing forces (emotions) of trust, sympathy and empathy which lead, following Richard Rorty's account, to solidarity. Of course, human rights violations are everyday regular occurrences which lend ample credibility to a Darwinistic pessimism about human nature, but human rights interventions should not therefore be dismissed as either idealistic or of no interest to social science.

In addition to being biologically frail, we are at a social level also vulnerable. Once more the ageing process provides a clear illustration of the issue. As we age in biological terms, we are exposed to social vulnerability because old age is, particularly in modern society, a period of loneliness. We cannot provide for our own wants and needs, and we become dependent on family and kinship networks. With increasing longevity in societies where traditional family systems have broken down, the elderly become increasingly dependent and exposed to social abuse. Biological frailty and social vulnerability tend to reinforce the problems of marginality and isolation that the sick, disabled and elderly experience. These are always matters of degree in the sense that we are all TAPs. In this context, one could attempt a preliminary definition of power from the perspective of the sociology of the body which self-consciously takes Weber's action theory as a model of power relations. We may define power as the probability that a body will act (or not act) in such a way as to maximize its well-being in relationship to other embodied social actors. A more powerful body lives longer and with fewer ailments than a less powerful body. The etymological root of 'ail' is, through the Old English *eglian*, the Gothic *agls* or disgraceful. A weak body is without power or grace; it lacks charismatic vitality. However, the main assumption of our argument is that human beings are ontologically insecure and relatively powerless without the social support they require to compensate for their biological frailty.

In addition to the human body being fragile and frail, we live in a societal environment that is essentially precarious and this precariousness is an inevitable consequence of the nature of power and its investment in the state. This argument is a variation on the theme in social contract theory derived from the work of Hobbes. Powerful institutions such as the state, which are set up according to social contract theory to protect the interests of rational actors, can of course function to terrorize and dominate civil society. While strong states may protect society from civil wars, they can, for that very reason, be a danger to the very existence of citizens. By precariousness we also mean that institutions which are rationally designed to serve certain specific purposes may evolve in ways which contradict these original charters. Social life is essentially contingent and risky; individuals, even when they collect together for concerted action, cannot necessarily protect themselves against the vagaries of social reality. Following through with the theme of ageing, we are precarious at the societal level because we cannot wholly control macro-policy decisions about such issues as compulsory retirement, mandatory superannuation contributions, inheritance taxation, health cover and so forth.

While social theorists might grant that social reality is precarious, the argument that human beings are universally frail may appear to be controversial and contentious. There are a number of problems here. If human beings are frail by definition, then frailty is variable and our argument could easily be converted into a theory of the survival of the fittest. Those who are least frail may combine to dominate and subordinate the vulnerable and fragile. The disposition of the strong to support and protect the weak must be based upon some collectively shared sympathy or empathy for human beings in their collective frailty and weakness. That is, a recognition of a surplus or underlying humanity, which exceeds claims to 'difference'.

Like Rorty, we derive a theory of human rights from certain aspects of feminist theory, from a critical view of the limitations of utilitarian accounts of reason and from an interest in notions of sympathy, sentiment and emotionality. In so far as the strong protect the weak, it is through a recognition of likeness which is itself a product of affective attachment and sentiment. People will want their rights to be recognized because they see in the plight of other human beings their own (potential) unhappiness and misery. Their vulnerability is a precondition of social relationships. Because individual ageing is an inevitable biological process, we can all anticipate, in principle, our own vulnerability and frailty. More importantly, sympathy is crucial in deciding to whom our moral concern might be directed. Sympathy derives from the fundamental experiences of reciprocity in everyday life, particularly from the relationship between mother and child. However, if the argument is to prevail it needs to elaborate the notions of human frailty and sensuousness. For example, the argument could be made more sophisticated by developing a distinction between pain and suffering. Human beings can suffer without an experience of pain and conversely they can have an experience of pain without suffering. Suffering is essentially a situation where the self is threatened or destroyed from outside, for example through humiliation. We can suffer the loss of a loved one without physical pain whereas toothache may give us extreme physical pain without a sense of loss of self or the humiliation of self. While suffering is variable, pain might be regarded as universal. This is closely related to a position adopted by Rorty, who argues that

> the idea that we have an overriding obligation to diminish cruelty, to make human beings equal in respect of their liability to suffering, seems to take for granted that there is something within human beings which deserves respect and protection, quite independently of the language they speak. It suggests that a non-linguistic ability, the ability to feel pain is what is important, and the differences in the vocabulary are much less important. (Rorty, 1989: 88)

While we accept Rorty's argument, we do not believe that it falsifies a universalistic foundation for human rights. In short, it is possible to argue that frailty is a universal condition of the human species because pain is a fundamental experience of all organic life. While Rorty argues that suffering is local and variable, the concept of the frailty of the human body is defensible using concepts of human pain (and pleasure). It would be possible to adopt all of Rorty's philosophical arguments about irony, cultural variation, the absence of authoritative justification and so forth, while also adhering to a universalistic view of human nature and human embodiment as the underlying criterion of humanity. Indeed, this is the foundation of any social theory of human rights. One could therefore embrace postmodern irony while also advocating a universalistic notion of human rights as a protective screen to limit the vagaries and contingencies of embodiment and social relations. Metaphysicians and ironists could both happily come to the agreement that there is a universalistic foundation to the discourse of human rights without too much intellectual discomfort. From a sociological point of view however, Rorty's notion of frailty needs to be supplemented by an idea of the precariousness of all human institutionalization. Some recent studies of the historical development of rational policy formation prior to the Holocaust provide additional evidence of institutional precariousness (Bauman, 1989).

The notion of sympathy is parallel to the idea of reflectivity in Sjoberg and Vaughan, but both positions are open to the simple empirical observation that sympathy appears to be in short supply in places like Bosnia, Northern Ireland, Rwanda, East Timor and other places of civil conflict. A more potent argument would be that ontological insecurity (frailty, vulnerability and precariousness) creates interdependences and interconnectedness.

**Conclusion: how relative is moral relativism?**

This theory of rights may appear, from a sociological point of view, historically static. In our historical interpretation of human rights, we claim that there has been an intensification of human rights debate as a consequence of globalization processes in the second half of the twentieth century. However, one can also argue that human rights discourse had its origins in the world religions which, so to speak, provided a precursor or model of the cultural globalism which is a persistent theme of contemporary theory. Indeed the rise of the nation state as the framework for national citizenship undermined much of the universalistic thrust of natural law, with its conception of a foundationalist groundwork for human rights as part of the legacy of world religions, particularly Christianity and Islam. The Universal Church and the Islamic *ummah* created global communities within which in principle ethnic or regional divisions were irrelevant to the notion of a person's worth *qua* human being. It was precisely the collapse of the natural law theory of rights which led Weber in his sociology of law to promote a relativistic view of legitimacy. Citizenship rights do not extend beyond the legal boundaries of the nation state; in this sense, they are particularistic, local rights.

United Nations legislative enactments of human rights can be seen as a feature of the globalization of the political community, but this does not assume an evolutionary or unlinear model of history. As we have argued, much of the cosmopolitanism of medieval society under the auspices of the Latin Church was indeed destroyed by the rise of bourgeois civil society and later by the nation state. Here again, the shaping and content of human rights vary considerably because of the different legacies of the world religions and as a consequence of variations in political struggles over rights. Finally, this global thrust of human rights is developed and promoted by new social movements, particularly those responding to the ecological crisis where the issue of protection and rights is especially prominent (Newby, 1996). This sociological view of the historical growth of human rights can be associated with the modern development of risk society (Beck, 1992) where the issue of environment, hazard and pollution is a major focus of sociological enquiry. Human rights legislation via ecological movements is a protective response to risk society, in which pollution is a global threat to embodied human beings.

Finally, our foundationalist account of rights attempts to provide sociology with a moral discourse by which inter-societal comparisons could be made with respect to either the implementation or the abuse of rights. Waters notes that his version of a social constructionist position would permit scientific sociology to engage in moral discussion, because it recognizes that human beings are ultimately responsible for their own social constructions (Waters, 1996: 598). However, social constructionism plays into the hands of naïve relativism which would suggest that the human rights claims of any particular group have an authority within their own cultural framework. In this respect, Ernest Gellner's argument (1970) against anthropological functionalism (in which all forms of irrational belief can be justified by reference to a specific context) could be directed against social constructionism (in which any human rights violation can be justified once it is understood or explained). The abuse of the human rights of Kurds in northern Iraq is obviously the consequence of the failure of the institutionalization of rights in a context of regional and global struggles between Iraq, Iran and the United States. However, this descriptive political sociology of rights does not allow us to make any moral observations on this abuse. Waters's position is wide open to the criticism which Strauss made of Weber's attempt to combine the principle of value freedom with Nietzsche's doctrine of perpetual struggle in the will to power. The result of Weber's fascination with power politics that 'If peace is incompatible with human life or with a truly human life, the moral problem would seem to allow of a clear solution: the nature of things requires a warrior ethics as the basis of "power politics" that is guided exclusively by considerations of the national interest' (Strauss, 1950: 65). This solution was explicitly embraced by Weber in his Freiburg inaugural address of 1895 where he framed German foreign policy in terms of the need for 'elbow room' in eastern Europe. Weber's perspectivism (read 'social constructionism') was based on precisely the assumption that rights are simply outcomes of power politics. It is difficult to understand how Waters's descriptive account of human rights as merely the outcome of political struggles could form the basis of moral analysis. By contrast, following the work of writers like Elaine Scarry (1985), we attempt to resolve the dilemma of value neutrality and ethical evaluation through a philosophical anthropology of the body as a foundation for a sociology of rights which is not 'orientalist' or individualist (Howard, 1995), namely a sociology which recognizes the common ontology of human beings regardless of the contingencies of culture or the vicissitudes of politics.

Human rights are causally driven simultaneously by the motors of globalization and by technological changes to the biological basis of human existence – biological warfare. New reproductive technologies, cloning, and GM foods create what we might call an existential crisis. Human rights form one of the principal substantive illustrations of legal globalization, namely the creation of a global system of commonly agreed standards of procedures for protecting human rights. Although they are often criticized for their Western bias, they do in fact enjoy largely universal consent. The growth in human rights as a feature of national legal proceedings is a major sociological fact about our national legal systems. One interesting feature of this development is the tension and frequent conflict between national systems of social rights and human rights: the tensions around Aboriginal land rights is one crucial illustration.

Secondly, human rights issues have come to the foreground because of the anxieties that surround the risks associated with the new biology. These scientific developments are an almost perfect illustration of the arguments contained in Beck's notion of risk society. We argue that issues of biological security are an outcrop of the underlying instrumental rationalism that has followed from Cartesian rationalism. Our obligations towards the environment are a parallel to the obligations of cosmopolitan virtue that we go on to outline at the end of the book. The obligation that sits alongside human rights is an obligation of cosmopolitan responsibility to human diversity.

Finally, as a critique of taken-for-granted relativism, we have questioned whether postmodern deconstructive techniques can do away with talk of common political foundations by enlisting a version of Heidegger's concept of 'care' (*Sorge*). Postmodern versions of relativism seek a common basis for ethical talk in such notions as the right to communication. The problem with philosophical schemes that emphasize difference is that they find it difficult to give a convincing account of justice or ethics. The strong version of relativism has, however, come from anthropological fieldwork rather than from postmodernism. Radical anthropological ethnography claims that the world is constituted by the incommensurability of cultures. One argument against such a radical scepticism is that the world is no longer incommensurable, because, to the extent that globalization has occurred, the world is increasingy interconnected. Now globalism does not necessarily mean standardization or Americanization. But it does question whether there are any anthropological sites of pure Aboriginality. If the world is a single place, then a single system of human rights is feasible. In any case we have questioned what we might call primitive anthropological incommensurability theory by arguing that, regardless of cultural diversity, there is an ontological universalism because there is a common ontological insecurity composed of frailty, vulnerability and precariousness. Such an ontological foundation can function as an argument that there is a common humanity to which rights could be attached.

Anthropological scepticism can also be challenged by historical arguments on the grounds that studies of small scale communities in Africa were used by British anthropologists to argue the case for relativism. Cultural relativism evolved through the study of the Little Traditions that had survived locally against acculturation. But what would have happened if anthropologists had studied the Big Traditions – classical Islam of the scholars rather than the Sufis, or the Sanskrit of the Hindu philosophers rather than lower caste practices in the villages, or the high tradition of Buddhism? Our argument is that cultural relativism emphasized the minor traditions of peasant culture. Common historical connections between for example the literate cultures of the Abrahamic religions have been neglected. Religious ecumenicalism and awareness of a shared tradition of prophetic monotheism is not an invention of the twentieth century. The anthropological emphasis on the ways in which local rituals embodied different cultural meanings that could only be understood hermeneutically within a specific context became an argument in favour of the notion that, since cultures remain obdurate in the face of translation, moral systems are incommensurate.

Our argument in favour of a common ontology and the possibility of a sociology of human rights forces one to take up a position on modernity. Like universalism in moral claims, the idea that human rights are feasible is a product of modernity. Postmodernism is not just 'after modernity' but often 'against modernity'. To defend a principle of the authority of human rights to coerce behaviour is to reject much of the romantic and nostalgic baggage of postmodernism. If citizenship has been predominantly the idiom of modern politics, then cosmopolitan virtue is the obligation that in the modern world must follow a commitment to human rights.

# 8

# INTIMACIES

The history of sociological theory can be written as a sustained criticism of utilitarian models of economic action as the exclusive and positivistic measure of rationality. This criticism of economic paradigms of rational action can be traced in classical sociology from Karl Marx's analysis of the limitations of the bourgeois economics of Bentham and Mill, through Emile Durkheim's commentary on the non-contractual element in social contract theory, to Max Weber's conceptualization of non-rational action in response to marginal utility theory and finally to Talcott Parsons's critique of the 'residual category' (of sentiments) in economic assumptions about the theory of social order (Holton and Turner, 1986). Many features of social life cannot be understood or explained within the paradigm of utilitarian economics, and religion in particular is a fundamental institution of human societies which cannot be interpreted appropriately within a narrow paradigm of instrumental rationality.

For Durkheim in *The Elementary Forms of the Religious Life* (1954), whereas profane actions in the everyday world are governed by mundane utilitarian concerns, the sacred is determined by notions of ritual purity, separateness, otherness and taboo. Attitudes towards the sacred are characterized by fear and trembling, by awe and reverence. Whereas economic selection of the means to scarce resources requires self-interested coolness and calculation, attitudes towards sacred entities are typically excessive, involving trance, effervescent joy, hysterical frenzy and violent involvement.

These Durkheimian ideas were developed in anthropological approaches to 'primitive economics' which appear to defy the logic of utilitarian economic theory. Anthropological fieldwork demonstrated that, for example, such institutions as sacrifice and potlatch do not follow a pattern of utilitarian exchange and individualistic interest. The dichotomy between the sacred and the profane can therefore be described in terms of a Nietzschean conflict between Dionysus and Apollo, which contrasted intoxication and rational order. Bataille's (1993) work also emphasizes the limitations of a political economy based in the notion of scarcity. He argues that the main problem that human groups face is not scarcity, but surplus. The tasks of accumulating, distributing and protecting surplus are the business of the central institutions of society. Bataille's theory is not fully satisfactory, because it omits to develop a convincing sociological model of power. His anthropology is naïvely universalistic. Yet in connecting political economy with libidinal economy, he offered an important, and largely neglected, set of issues for social science to pursue.

These contrasts should not suggest, however, that the sacred is irrational, thereby guaranteeing the validity of the economic paradigm. The sociology of religion demonstrates that religion (sacrifice, ritual behaviour and collective festivals) is to be understood as the non-rational, namely outside the paradigm of economic rationality altogether. Economic actions presume that interests and needs are immediately comprehensible to all parties, but religious meaning is often seen to be ineffable. Religious phenomena fall outside the simple rational/irrational paradigm of action, because they are concerned with the ineffable character of the sublime: religious experiences resolve or attempt to resolve the paradox of the communication of the incommunicable. Religious experiences belong to the world of *Erlebnis*, the unmediated inner experiences which are the foundation of all spirituality.

The Durkheimian tradition contrasted profane economic behaviour (individualistic, emotionally disinterested, utilitarian and contractual) and sacred behaviour (collectivist, emotionally committed and ritualistic). We might also note that whereas classical economics presumes scarcity (hence calculation and interest), religion often assumes abundance, plenitude, and an inexhaustible supply of grace. In the Judaeo-Christian and Islamic religions, divine love is described as overflowing and boundless in its generative powers. The loving God of Christian theology surrenders, for the salvation of humanity, his only Son, who has to be incarnate to experience the suffering of humanity. In the folk cults of Islam and Christianity, the motif of generative power is illustrated in collective healing rituals where charismatic love flows out of the bodies of saints through their blood, tears and sperm. The charismatic power of saints survived their death, because their capacity for healing, while not intelligible in rational terms, was an important counterweight to the dry legalism of official religion (Shoshan, 1993: 21). This theme of the suffering god has played an important role in the development of contemporary theories of love, including Julia Kristeva's studies of Mariolatry and Christology in the evolution of women's experiences of birth and love (Kristeva, 1986).

In contemporary social theory, this approach to social relations has been influential in the analysis of a 'general economy' by Georges Bataille who, following Durkheim, attempted to analyse such notions as abundance ('luxury' or 'excess'), the 'pure gift', and immediate consumption (Bataille, 1985, 1987). Bataille sought to understand the sacred in terms of an alternative and general economy of abundance, which is the opposite of the utilitarian economy of scarcity, an analysis which is based on anthropological fieldwork on the Australian Aboriginals and the potlatch of the American natives of north-Western America, and on the biblical and historical studies of the Eucharistic festival (Turner, 1991). Religious activity leads from abundance to social fusion via the collective effervescence of shared rituals and festivals; eroticism and orgy break down the neat and precise barriers between individuals. Such modes of action are entirely outside the field of economic exchanges where strangers buy and sell in the market place (Godbout, 1992). Bakhtin's (1968) analysis of the carnival provides another example. Bakhtin argued that the medieval carnival, which followed the intense labour of harvest and which lasted for a number of days, was a festival of plenitude. During Carnival, hierarchy was overturned and authority was subject to licensed abuse. Sexual prohibitions were relaxed and alcohol flowed more freely. The conceiving soil was the basis for a symbolic introversion of the moral and economic order. Bakhtin's account emphasized the close relationship between transgression and social order. Mundane reality is only possible if the world on the other side of reality can be glimpsed by the unfettered use of stimulants, sexuality or political carnival.

The anthropologist, Victor Turner (1973) argued that all cultures include 'antistructures' of behaviour in which the ruling standards and values of the day are subject to criticism and stretching. Turner saw these antistructures as creative, since from them emerged the critical initiatives in social development. Implicit in his account is the argument that the moral order is never capable of utilizing or containing human energy. Any moral order that we are capable of imagining will produce antistructures of behaviour in which surplus energy is explored. Utilitarian thought and rational choice theory are limited in being unable to account for this.

Now 'love' occupies similar analytical terrain to 'religion' in an economy of abundance, and further contradicts the utilitarian paradigm of economic exchange. As Balzac argued, 'L'amour qui économise n'est jamais le veritable amour'. Love is spoken of in terms of its overflowing, abundant and generous nature; romantic discourse understands love as an uncontrolled and involuntary flowing of affection and meaning. Any calculation of love counterfeits its very nature, because love is an aspect of the sublime which explodes conventional notions of appropriate behaviour. The metaphors of love are constructed around notions of bursting, falling and drowning – of violent superfluity. Love is a surplus condition of affective relationships; a luxurious state of social exchange.

We may define love as an abundance of affective attitudes and emotions between two individuals whose separate identities are (partially) merged in a relationship of desire, the consequence of which is to infuse their (separate) lives with a common meaning. The intention of this definition is deliberately to tie love to religion. If religion can be defined in the language of the theologian Paul Tillich as 'that which is our ultimate concern', then love, for those who are in love, is their ultimate, exclusive and exclusionary concern. Love stands on the awesome side of the sacred/profane dichotomy; it is set apart from everyday life, because it intervenes in the everyday world as a threat – something which is outside mundane routines.

Love in this respect may be associated with the meaning of existence for individuals. In fact one of the more interesting definitions of love in philosophy is offered in *The Pursuit of Love* by Irving Singer, who argues that for human beings 'love is the principal means by which creatures like us seek affective relations to persons, things, or ideals that have value and importance for us . . . meaning in life is the pursuit of love' (Singer, 1994: 2). Love is both the appraisal and bestowal of (uniquely important) meaning on another. In the question for meaningful social relationships, satisfaction is reached when the need to love and to be loved are in harmony. While love is in popular discourse often seen as an event (of falling in love), it is in fact an accomplishment, a successful and mutual attribution of significance, the consequence of which is to cause affect or an emotionally excited state.

Singer distinguishes several types of love (Singer, 1994: 44): sexual love, love of self, group or social love, and religious love. One obvious difficulty with many sociological approaches to love is the failure to distinguish successfully between types of love. A particular difficulty with any definition of love relates to the question of love of self or narcissism, which has dominated many influential approaches to the issue from Freud's original analysis of mourning and melancholy (Lear, 1990) to feminist theories (Kristeva, 1987) and to studies of romanticism (Schapiro, 1983; Hagstrum, 1989).

## The theoretical importance of love

Although passionate love and other erotic relationships have played a major part in shaping human society, there is no established literature which might constitute a sociology of love. In recent years there has been a number of major publications on love, emotions and erotic relationships, but this is a relatively new development.

It is interesting to note that William J. Goode, writing in 1959 on 'the theoretical importance of love', observed that 'serious sociological attention has only infrequently been given to love. Moreover, analysis of love generally has been confined to mate choice in the Western World, while the structural importance of love has been for the most part ignored' (Goode, 1959: 38). Goode's observations on the absence of a coherent sociology of love still remain largely accurate. Goode identified several different types of literature on love: poetic writing, marital counselling, a small literature on the functional significance of love in sociology and finally the cross-cultural work of anthropologists, most of whom argued that while there was evidence of violent passionate relations, there was no real tradition of romantic love in premodern or non-Western societies.

On the basis of this literature Goode argued that love, by which he meant 'a strong emotional attachment, a cathexis, between adolescence or adults of opposite sexes, with at least the components of sex desire and tenderness' (Goode, 1959: 41), should be controlled in society as a necessary prelude to marriage. For Goode, love was a pathway to mate selection and marriage which functions to distribute wealth and status within a system of stratification. Love had to be controlled because it was potentially disruptive of stable social relations and hence to the routine and regular allocation of wealth between generations. The irrational nature of passionate and adulterous love threatened the stability of normal marriage relationships. Although adultery is implicitly tolerated in most societies, it is not allowed to form a significant structural challenge to marriage itself (Lawson, 1988). While adulterous love (in the mythology of the relationship between Yseult and Tristan) has often been regarded as true love in societies where marriage was primarily an economic relationship between households, it cannot be allowed to disrupt normal patterns of exchange and power.

Goode concluded his analysis by noting that the degree to which love is a normal and expected prelude to marriage is correlated with the degree of free choice of mate permitted in the society and the degree to which husband–wife solidarity is the strategic solidarity of the kinship structure. Love is not disruptive therefore if it is merely a prelude to permanent mateship in marriage and where it can help to solidify the husband–wife relationship into a close bond.

One problem with Goode's analysis is that it assumes that romantic love is for the young or at least that love is a prelude to marriage. Much of the literature since Goode's article has emphasized the importance of love throughout the life course, including in old age. The contemporary debate about love has rejected the conventional notion that ageing necessarily brings about a termination of romantic attachment (Friedan, 1993). Secondly, Goode wanted to attach love to particular structural arrangements such as the connection between love and property in a system of stratification and hence in his analysis there is relatively little space for the notion of love for love's sake. He does not address the significance of romantic love as pure affection. Thirdly, he assumes that love is heterosexual, but much of the modern literature on love assumes that lesbian and homosexual relations can provide a model of companionship. Finally, there is little psychoanalytical complexity to Goode's sociology of love which, for example, has nothing to say about narcissism. Unfortunately, many of these limitations in Goode's article of 1959 are repeated in the contemporary literature.

While Goode's assumptions now appear limited, his article is important in so far as it identifies love with structural risk: love is seen to be an irrational threat to normal routines. We can consequently reconstitute Goode's approach in developing a Weberian contrast between charisma and tradition. If we treat love as cultural risk via Goode's modified functionalism, then romantic love can be described as a charismatic breakthrough into the routines of everyday life in which its disruptive force undermines customary or traditional patterns of activity. If pre-marital romantic love is a charismatic challenge to kinship structures, then marriage from a Weberian point of view might be described as a routinization of charisma.

Goode's article was also interesting in its discussion of the origins of contemporary romantic love in the American context, an argument which raised important questions about the universality of romantic love. In the 1960s there was a general view that America, with its popular emphasis on expressivity, youthfulness and personal authenticity, was an appropriate context for the evolution of love. Romantic themes in popular culture had been discussed in the sociology of Talcott Parsons, who argued that in contemporary society the nuclear family had become isolated from the rest of the kinship system, it was a small, emotionally intense unit and that its major function was the socialization of children in an environment of intimacy and affection. Courtship, mate selection and marriage occur in an open and competitive environment, where kin do not play a formal role in marriage arrangements. The 'romantic love complex' is important in the determination of partners and in sustaining marriage relationships (Parsons, 1949: 188). Mate selection is not overtly determined by a 'rational' choice of a partner; instead, sexual attraction or 'glamor' (Parsons, 1949: 308) determined the preference for a partner. In men there developed 'the cult of "compulsive masculinity"' (1949: 309) as part of this cultural system of sexual glamour, which Parsons described as 'an adolescent type of asssertively masculine behaviour which rejected more mature expressions of masculine responsibility and sobriety'. These social changes were aspects of a youth revolt which the postwar generation had cultivated.

Because the nuclear family is isolated, husband and wife became bonded together in a heightened emotional relationship. Parsons also noted that the values of the youth culture had spread to all age groups, putting a special emphasis on activism, emotion and subjectivity. Indeed contemporary society has gone through an 'expressive revolution' giving a particular legitimacy to emotionally intense relationships.

There was an interesting difference for Parsons between Germany and America. With the development of Nazi values, young women had become sentimentalized and idealized, but the ideal role for the woman was marriage and motherhood. Importantly, Hitler rejected Speer's request that women should be employed in industrial occupations when wartime Germany faced a chronic shortage of labour, especially in the armaments industry. This attitude to woman perfectly reflects the romantic view of woman as mother in Nazi ideology. As a result the 'romantic love pattern' (Parsons, 1949: 114) did not evolve, and instead relations between men as brothers achieved a romantic form in the traditional *Brüderschaft* arrangements.

Parsons has of course often been criticized for suggesting that there is a functional fit between family and stratification system, but in fact he argued that family life with its specialized emotive relationships put a special burden on the wife to offer emotional support for the husband and children. Parsons can therefore be defended as giving a significant insight into the emotional significance of family life (Holton and Turner, 1986: 15). Parsons noted that the role strain of the married wife produced a 'neurotic illness of compulsive domesticity' and he went on to argue that 'in all of these and other fields there are conspicuous signs of insecurity and ambivalence. Hence it may be concluded that the feminine role is the conspicuous focus of the strains inherent in our social structure, and not the least of these sources of these strains is to be found in the functional difficulties in the integration of our kinship system with the rest of the social structure' (Parsons, 1954: 194).

Following Parsons, one might argue that in contemporary society love has become a more significant and prominent feature of popular culture, precisely because of this relative isolation of the nuclear family. Love, falling in love, romance and marriage are the principal ingredients of popular film and television with their ritualistic coverage of the love affairs of celebrities and royalty (Sarsby, 1983). Songs about sexual encounters and passionate love have come to shape the imagination of generations and to define attitudes towards self and society. The 1960s in particular were shaped by Rolling Stones' songs like 'Satisfaction', 'Lady Jane' and 'Let's Spend the Night Together', which defined youthful rebellion. For some commentators, 'Satisfaction' was 'the anthem for an era' (Andersen, 1993: 111).

In Parsons's terms, the rise of modern love is clearly associated with the changing functions of the family, with rising expectations of marital satisfaction in emotional terms, a greater emphasis on affective socialization and parenting of a limited number of children, and the spread of youth values with its strong emphasis on eroticism. Indeed, in *The Social System* (1951) Parsons attempted to develop a theory of 'expressive symbolism'. Expressive symbols for Parsons are concerned with the communication of affect and thus with aspects of gratification in action and interaction. While these symbols are important and part of the basic paradigm of Parsons's functionalism (in relation for example to cognitive and evaluative systems) Parsons noted that this aspect of the sociology of the social system was the least clearly worked out part of the broad pattern of analysis. Parsons noted that these expressive aspects of action were important in terms of attachment and loyalty to social relationships and in his classification love is an illustration of diffuse affectivity in interactional terms.

Love, unlike instrumental actions (economic behaviour), is diffuse and affective, where the affectivity involves mutually rewarding erotic gratification and this in turn involves bodily stimulation and somatic processes. The expressive symbolism of these erotic encounters is organized around the genital level of erotic contact (Parsons, 1951: 390). Sexual intercourse in romantic attachments requires privacy and appropriate surroundings which contribute to the aesthetic enjoyments of eroticism. The rise of Western romantic love is also closely connected with certain architectural changes in domestic space, where the privacy and comfort of the 'home' become important for the enjoyment of love relations between couples. These changes apparently occurred originally in the Netherlands in the seventeenth century where traditional patterns of domestic life (sharing bedrooms and beds between parents and children) became segregated and specialized; the result was the development of spaces for children, including sleeping and playing areas Domestic architecture reflected changes in the importance of intimacy, the socialization of children and affection in family life (Rybczynski, 1986: 59–66).

## Contemporary sociological analysis

Contemporary sociological interest in love has been significantly influenced by Nickolas Luhmann's *Love as Passion* (1986), by the work of Ulrich Beck (1995), Ulrich Beck and Elisabeth Beck-Gernsheim in their analysis of *Das ganz normale Chaos der Liebe* (1990) and finally by Anthony Giddens's *The Transformation of Intimacy* (1992). Although these texts approach the issue of love and intimacy in modern society from somewhat different perspectives, they nevertheless reflect common questions of modernity, including the issue of identity in modern society, the changing nature of marriage in the social structure and the new emphasis in ideological terms on gender equality.

Luhmann's study, which is concerned with the changing historical nature of the semantics of love, is a further elaboration of his general theory of communication and social differentiation. Thus for Luhmann, love is part of the generalized symbolic medium of communication in society. Luhmann followed Parsons in his analysis of the symbolically generalized media of interchange in social systems. For example, money is a generalized medium of exchange which produces a differentiation of the economy. For Luhmann these symbolic media of communication 'are primarily semantic devices which enable essentially improbable communications nevertheless to be made successfully' (Luhmann, 1986: 18). For example, in Western society romantic love was conceived in terms of the ineffable. True passionate and romantic love cannot be adequately or fully expressed, yet it must be communicated if the fact of romantic attachment is to take place at all. Hence the semantics of romantic love make such communication a realizable event through the emergence of a generalized medium of communication.

In Beck and Beck-Gernsheim's treatment of love as 'normal chaos' in their *Das ganz normale Chaos de Liebe*, the sociology of love is organized as a special component of 'individualization theory'. In a post-Fordist economy, there is an expansion of indeterminate and contingent relations in society within which highly individualized social actors are forced to operate. Life patterns are more fragmented, complex and differentiated, resulting in the erosion of conventionalized life careers and life patterns (Turner, 1994a). Family life follows the increasing differentiation and cultural contingency of the economy.

This individualization theory has been expressed by Beck in terms of his analysis of risk society (Beck, 1992) as a 'new modernity'. Whereas risk in traditional society was individual, hierarchical and specific, risk in contemporary society is, in general, democratic and no longer palpable. Beck's clearest illustration of the growth of risk in modernity is presented in the analysis of environmental pollution and degradation. Beck attempts to transfer this analysis into the cultural and social sphere, arguing by analogy that contemporary social relations are also characterized by high risk and uncertainty. Within the family this dynamic of individualization undermines many of the traditional constraints and structures of class, age and gender. There is growing confusion over the nature and extent of the expectations of married life. These contradictions lead Beck and Beck-Gernsheim to argue that modernization is now characterized by a growing sense of reflexivity and self-reflexivity. As the contradictions of society increase so there is correspondingly a greater need for self-monitoring and self-analysis. As a process of individual detraditionalization, modernity requires greater understanding of and reflexivity about the self.

Anthony Giddens's *The Transformation of Intimacy* (1992) is an exploration of sexuality, love and eroticism in modern societies. This study of intimacy provides an elaboration of the ideas about self-identity in his *Modernity and Self-Identity* (Giddens, 1991). In many respects Giddens's book reproduces many of the arguments of contemporary sociology reflecting on the growing importance of intimacy and emotional satisfaction in marriage. Giddens in particular stresses the way in which the family has been transformed by the democratic values and assumptions of the polity. As a result of the women's movement and other social changes in the labour market and legal system, women now demand equality alongside men within the family, including equality in the enjoyment of satisfactory sexual relations and intimacy. Within this democratic context, the modern self is for everyone 'a reflexive project – a more or less continuous integration of past, present and future. It is a project carried on amid a profusion of reflexive resources: theory and self-help manuals of all kinds, television programmes and magazine articles' (Giddens, 1992: 30). Whereas in earlier societies the romantic love complex was associated with the individuality of the upper classes, in modern society popular culture has embraced the idea of romantic love as an opportunity for intimacy for everybody. The ideal of modern society is thus the 'pure relationship' in which considerations of economic benefit or social advancement are irrelevant in the choice of marriage partner and where the expectation of sexual satisfaction and intimacy determines all aspects of the love/marital relationship. Sexual satisfaction now defines personal happiness.

Giddens goes on to note that in modern societies romantic love is no longer exclusively associated with heterosexual relationships. There is a general recognition that romanticism embraces both heterosexual and homosexual couples, and there are significant demands for legislative change which would permit homosexual marriage and child adoption in homosexual partnerships. Indeed Giddens argues that heterosexual men generally speaking are still locked into a traditional notion of patriarchal hierarchy and dominance, and as a result they have been unable to adjust adequately to the new norms of mutuality and intimacy which have been embraced and developed by lesbian analysis of love relationships. Giddens implicitly follows Parsons's critical commentary on the 'cult' of adolescent male aggressiveness in societies where the youth revolt has been diffused through the stratification system. In general terms men are unable to establish extensive long-term friendships, relations of intimacy and tenderness, and the continuity of patriarchal values means that men still approach women, implicitly or explicitly, in terms of conquest and domination. These traditional male attitudes and patterns of behaviour are, according to Giddens, incompatible with the growing prevalence of the values of the pure relationship.

## Critical commentary

These sociological studies are useful contributions to the growing literature on love, friendship and intimacy in modern society. They reflect a social trend in popular culture which gives a special emphasis to intimate relations, romantic love and romantic alliances. A group of young women writers reflecting on love summarized many of the themes of popular romantic culture by asserting: 'Today's women must find ways to create love relationships, intimacy and romantic images that fit our needs' (Abraham et al., 1993: 7).

The emergence of these contemporary attitudes to love is a consequence of complex historical changes in the family, gender relationships and mentalities. Romantic attitudes in this sense assume that sensibility is an affective orientation to social reality which is available to all members of modern society. Whereas the notion of sentiment had been confined to the aristocracy, not only did the revolutionary settlement in England in the late seventeenth century produce Locke's liberal analysis of social contract, but the popularization of the virtue of sensibility in the eighteenth century took place alongside a growing concern for child-care, parental responsibility for the emotional nurturing of children, and an interest in the emotional well-being of the mother. Hume's philosophy regarded sympathy as the principal moral motivation which resulted in care for strangers. In fact the main thrust of British philosophy (especially Hume and Smith) was to anchor morality in sentimental feeling. The sentimental aesthetic (which included the Gothic novel, Gray's *Elegy*, and the sculptures of Antonio Canova) was, by the end of the eighteenth century, seen as a 'democratic' threat to classicism, the hierarchy of status and taste, and the authority of the Church and universities over popular sentiment. In the poetry of Gray, anxieties, trembling and melancholy reflected his sensibilities towards nature, sexuality and death (Hagstrum, 1989: 158). Writers like Sheridan, Johnson and Gibbon worked to protect an objective hierarchy of literary taste from democratic sentiment (Todd, 1986: 133). Luhmann, Beck and Giddens adopt an appropriately historical approach to the sociology of love, tracing the complex relationships between marriage, family and love.

We can see these sociologies of love as a contribution to the current debate about individualism and identity. However, romantic love and reflexive modernity have to be seen in a deeper and broader historical context. The notions of romantic love as romantic adventure and sexuality as risk are not a product of the twentieth-century isolation of the nuclear family; they are constitutive of Judaeo-Christian culture as such. Conceptualizing love in this broader context raises important sociological questions about the nature of modern identity. For Christian theology, passionate love is an expression of the sinfulness of human nature and therefore marriage was seen as a necessary evil to guard against the dangers of unrestrained sexual attraction. As a result, writers like St Augustine celebrated *agape* (selfless, caring concern) against the dangers and distractions of *eros* (passionate and violent sexuality) (Arendt, 1996).

This relationship between love and identity is particularly prominent in Giddens's approach. He observes a relationship between the idea of reflexive modernity and identity by arguing that identity in modern societies is constituted as a personal narrative within which love and intimacy form importance sequences in the construction of the self. For Giddens the self is a reflexive identity in modernity shaped and structured by the personal history of intimacies. Who we are is shaped by a history of interpersonal encounters with others where significant moments of love and intimacy provide the events of history as the foundational chronology of these identities. Identity is thus a peculiarly subjective set of experiences of the self that constitute a narrative discourse of autobiographical encounters. Sexuality in modern society is a product of this emphasis on identity as narrative where the narrative of intimacy is no longer significantly connected with kinship or marriage. Giddens refers to 'plastic sexuality', namely a sexuality which is disconnected from its traditional mooring in reproduction, household formation, property kinship and generation. We might argue that this plastic sexuality has become a free-floating component of the narrative structure of personal identity.

In Giddens's account of sexual identity, the body plays a role. Sexuality operates as a feature of the self which connects the body, self-identity and social norms. Who we are in modern society increasingly becomes associated with how we present and develop our bodies. As Chris Shilling (1993) argues, the project of the self has become the project of the body, that is, self-identity in late modernity is closely connected with maintaining a satisfactory body-image. The cult of slimness, fitness and personal health is an expression of this merging of self, self-identity and body image. Modern culture is itself anorexic, where fat indicates loss of self-esteem and self-control (Heywood, 1996). Self-identity is intimately connected up with body image and therefore with lifestyle, life activities and consumerism. For example, dieting and nutrition in modern society are important for shaping the self, for shaping the body image and therefore for presenting self-identity through the body. According to Giddens (1992: 32): 'diet connects physical appearance, self identity and sexuality in the context of social changes with which individuals struggle to cope, emaciated bodies today no longer bear witness to ecstatic devotion but to the intensity of this secular battle'. Religious definitions of the 'government of the body' through the medium of dietary advice have been transferred into the field of medical discourse and control, resulting in the medicalization of techniques of the self (Turner, 1982).

Giddens's account of love and modern society can be criticized on the following grounds. First, although Giddens makes reference to the body in relation to the experience of love and the construction of self-identity, the body is largely absent from his actual account of love and intimacy in his recent studies. Giddens's lovers are strangely disembodied. They are not confronted by the problem of ageing, they do not suffer from disabilities, they do not have physical blemishes, they are ageless and free from the anxieties of AIDS or HIV. They do not appear to confront love as a situation of risk, in both the physical and cultural sense. We know that 'love and sex have always been risky for women because our attitudes about them are often a result of our culture's social inequality' (Abraham et al., 1993: 5). How can a youthful self-identity be sustained in a society characterized by activism and successful romances when the individual is confronted by the inevitability of ageing, physical impairments, disabilities and finally death? We know that in general terms the actors in romantic love mythology are idealized socal beings – 'They do not have bad breath. They do not burp or fart or sweat. They do not have bits of food caught between their perfect teeth. . . . They are, in short, not human' (Krance, 1993: 116).

The social actors in Giddens's sociology of intimacy appear to be able to experience eroticism without the inconvenience of embodiment. While contemporary surveys show that the elderly in modern society also experience the trials and tribulations of romantic love, they do so against a personal background of biological ageing and physical decline (Riggs and Turner, 1996). In particular, contemporary research shows that the elderly do not run out of libido or erotic attachment, they simply run out of partners (Minichiello et al., 1996). Ageing is a process of social contraction in which the pool of eligible partners is irreversibly reduced. Giddens provides no account of how real embodiment operates in relation to self-identity over time in a context of individual ageing and physical decline. Any account of love must set the opportunities and risks of romantic love in the context of the life course and the ageing body.

Secondly, while Giddens suggests that the (romantic) love theme of modern reflexivity is a contemporary consequence of the women's movement and other forms of sexual liberation, the history of the sociology of the family indicates that debates about companionate love, and the importance of intimacy and sexuality in marriage have been a continuous theme in sociology, certainly since the 1920s and 1930s. Writers like Groves and Ogburn (1928), Nimkoff and Ogburn (1934) and Burgess and Cottrell (1939) recognized that marriage was based on an ideal of romantic love, that family breakdown resulted from failure to achieve or maintain intimacy, and that much of the uncertainty of marriage was a product of rising expectations about intimacy. W.I. Thomas (1908) writing on the 'older and newer ideals of marriage' recognized the impact of the women's movement on assumptions about equality in marriage.

Giddens (1992: 43) suggests that (romantic) love is essentially feminized love and, prior to the late modern period, when love was referred to in relation to marriage, it was always understood in terms of companionate love which was associated with the development of the mutual responsibility of men and women for running the household. Yet it is interesting that in the historical development of the sociological discussion of the family the notion of 'the companionate relationship' was originally defined as the childless marriage. Writing about the development of love relations, sociologists noted that the flexibility and anonymous character of urban life promoted what they called 'hotel living', that is relationships based upon intimacy where the couple deliberately chose not to have children. The social transience of their relationships were somewhat critically compared with life in a hotel (Hayner, 1927).

### Conclusion: love, ageing and embodiment

These earlier accounts of the family in sociology suggest that the debate about love and intimacy has been a continuous aspect of the analysis of the family in the twentieth century. It is not specifically a consequence of late modernity or high modernity with its emphasis on reflexivity and subjectivity. Romanticism is in any case probably better regarded as a defining feature of the nineteenth not the twentieth century. The legacy of Freudianism involved a reductionism whereby the affective tie between the lovers was recast in terms of the interplay of libido and ego. Freudianism also saw the primary drive for recognition in terms of a powerful narcissism. Historical psychoanalysis has often treated the evolution of Western eroticism in terms of a perpetual tension between eroticism and narcisism (Hagstrum, 1989). Twentieth-century versions of romantic love have, as a result, focused on the erotic foundations of the expression of 'pure' love.

While one can criticize Giddens on these historical and sociological grounds, obviously his account of the individual and the self in relationship to the body is useful but he fails to follow through these opportunities for analysis with a genuine account of the embodied self. Self-identity, self-reflexivity and intimate relations have to be understood in a framework of ageing in which the embodied self has to be reflexively negotiated, not simply in the context of social interaction, but in a context of inevitable biological decay. Our self-image has to be sustained through the well-known processes of 'the looking-glass self' but also through the body-image. Body-image is sustained as a function of external social validation but also by the dialogue between the subjective sense of the body-for-me and the objective reality of the body-for-others (Turner, 1995a). Ageing bodies and constructed body-images do not appear in Giddens's account of self-identity in late modernity.

In the semantics, romantic or passionate love means essentially young love. Indeed much of the quantitative research of the twentieth century (the Kinsey Reports, Masters and Johnson's studies, and the Duke surveys) assume that male impotence increases with ageing and that women's lack of libido is a function of male decline. These surveys, as the critics have frequently observed, assumed a definition of sexuality which depended almost exclusively on the assumption of male penetration and operated with a 'double standard' of ageing in which female sexuality is defined by male capacity. The female is defined in terms of reproductive capacity. Such an approach allows little scope for intimacy and emotion, but also fails to recognize the possibility of generational differences in sexual attitude and capacity. As Friedan (1993: 261) observes, the problem of sexuality in ageing is to do with social not biological relationships – 'helplessness – being unable to control or affect one's own life – is the key to physical and psychological deterioration and decline. If intimacy is indeed crucial to the effective sense of self, then feelings of helplessness and lack of control should inevitably result from the sharp sexual paradoxes and forced denial detailed in the research'. The place of intimacy has to be understood within the parameters of infirmities in the life course.

The accounts of love and intimacy of Beck, Luhmann and Giddens typically presuppose that love is for the young, or at least for people who do not suffer from arthritis, flatulence, deafness, Type 2 diabetes, and dementia. But these are the real risks, threats and hazards of everyday life which ordinary people have to face with whatever resources, courage and good fortune they can command in their struggles to sustain intimacies against infirmities. Contemporary studies of intimacy have to be set within existing historical scholarship on love and romanticism (Rougemont, 1983) and within an analysis of generational changes in values relating to love and marriage, but they also have to understand romantic attachment within the life course of individuals coping with the frailties and sensuous possibilities of their embodiment.

# 9

# CHOICE

The tension between determinism and voluntarism is integral to sociological analysis. The Marxist doctrine of historical materialism proposed that men make their own history, but not under conditions of their own choosing. More generally, establishing causal adequacy, in the Weberian sense of the term, is an established feature of mainstream sociological analysis. The most extreme form of determinism posits that human mental states and acts are necessitated by preceding causes. Choice and will are therefore dismissed as chimeras, since aetiology is pre-subjective. Although elements of determinism figure in the structuralist analysis of Marx, Durkheim, Lévi-Strauss and Althusser, sociologists have generally been reluctant to embrace it as a doctrine. The origins of the subject in the Enlightenment made questions of freedom and liberty central to the sociological tradition. Because sociology is essentially concerned with the operation of power in human collectivities, the notion of barriers, and the possibility of transcending them, are at the heart of sociological activity.

Durkheim's (1952) study of suicide was an imaginative attempt to demonstrate how social factors influence personal behaviour. His differentiation between egoistic, anomic and altruistic types of suicide aimed to illustrate the benefits of sociological reasoning. Interestingly, given that Durkheim's sociology is often presented as a counterpoint to Marxian theory, the foundation of his analysis is resolutely materialistic. Durkheim explains suicide by recourse to the relations between an individual and occupation, religion and economic change. This is consistent with his methodological injunction that the proper subject of social study is social facts which have priority, externality and constraint over the individual. Durkheim was concerned to establish sociology as the science of moral life. Basic to this was the rejection of Rousseau's idealistic notion of the isolated individual free from the chains of society as the desired state of affairs for moral life. This was replaced with an anti-metaphysical approach which partly drew on Schaffle's work on social morphology. In particular, Durkheim borrowed Schaffle's organic analogy of social relations with the organs and tissues of the body.

This approach to sociological research has been highly influential. It is apparent in the functionalist, symbolic interactionist and figurational traditions. Durkheim reasserted the Comtian interest in the principles of social order and social change as the focus of sociological analysis. By considering society as an organism, he enjoined sociologists to concern themselves with the study of the causal and reciprocal relations between social elements. This perspective prioritized observation and classification as the preconditions of sociological research and understanding. Durkheim's sociology is both interpretive and managerialist. Applying knowledge to regulate moral life more efficently is one of the standards by which sociological work must be judged. Comte looked to sociology to produce the secular clergy who would maintain social order and manage the 'positive' stage of social progress. Durkheim was less sanguine about the prospects for social progress. His study of the abnormal forms of the division of labour and suicide clearly identify industrialism's negative as well as positive aspects. Nevertheless, he shared with Comte a high degree of optimism that sociologists can unravel the secrets of society and thus manage social change more effectively.

It is not a view replicated elsewhere in the classical tradition. Marx also wrestled with problems of determinism and freedom, but his scientific approach identified class conflict as the motor of social change. He had no truck with organic analogies because he believed that the system of capitalist domination should be overturned and replaced with socialism. This involved accentuating the class consciousness of the proletariat. The Marxist tradition calls upon the sociologist to become an agent of social change. Later, Gramsci coined the term 'organic intellectual', to refer to individuals who were both specialists in the most advanced ideas about social life and transmission belts of revolutionary knowledge and energy to the oppressed. The Marxist tradition demands political involvement from sociologists. Durkheim's sociology leads sociologists into the academy and state think-tanks; Marx's sociology leads them onto the streets and into the theatres of political transformation.

Marx's theory of alienation identified capitalism as a system which negatively determines identity, association and practice. He counterposes this with a model of communism which is presented as the self-government of associated producers. Marx does not regard communism as a wholly free system. He distinguishes between the realm of necessity and the realm of freedom. The realm of necessity refers to the labour necessary to reproduce social life. The need to clean, cook, grow plants, educate children, provide public services and produce surplus production, will not disappear with the rise of communism. However, because these activities are conducted by the associated producers for the benefit of all, the forced character of these activities will disappear. Labour will be donated voluntarily and because the profit motive will have disappeared with the end of the capitalist class, Marx envisages a much shorter working day and working life. Beyond the realm of necessity lies the realm of freedom. Marx was rather evasive about what the realm of freedom constituted, stating that the details of existence in this state of affairs could not be particularized until the economic, political and cultural preconditions to support them had been achieved. Even so, it is clear that he regarded the realm of freedom as permitting the free and full development of the creative capacities in labour which had been repressed under capitalism. Marx, then, does offer a transcendent view of freedom. The riches of communism will make human beings more free than at any previous point in history.

Weber's approach raises a contrasting set of questions for sociologists. His concern is with establishing an interpretive understanding of social action. For Weber, sociology must be steeped in a historical and comparative approach. The dual purpose of sociology is to produce impartial analysis of the causes of social action and to evaluate the consequences of such action for the future course of social life. His emphasis on the rationalization process and the bureaucratization of the world underlines the limits of sociological understanding. The pathos of Weber's sociology is that it concludes first, that the complexity of modern life constantly outflanks the comprehension of the sociologist; and secondly, that science is unable to provide any guidance to the ultimate questions of social life. His work eschews the organicism of Durkheim and the class-based perspective of Marx. Instead, it places the politics of rational calculation and the pluralism of differentiated power groupings at the centre of sociological analysis.

In Weber's view, freedom is always contingent. He offers no solace that industrial society can be positively transformed through revolutionary change, and no guarantee that a secular clergy of sociologists is capable of providing accurate solutions to social problems. His approach is generally regarded as supporting liberalism in scientific enquiry and social organization. In this respect it anticipates some of the particulars later developed by Karl Popper (1962) in his defence of the open society. On the other hand, the Nietzschean influence on Weber leaves him with an unmistakable sense of pessimism about the prospects for social harmony.

**Secondary traditions**

The efflorescence of these ideas in the English speaking world owes much to the interpretations of Talcott Parsons. Writing in the 1930s, Parsons (1937) presented the classical tradition, especially the writings of Durkheim and Weber, as a response to the problem of order set out by Thomas Hobbes in the seventeenth century. As we have seen, Hobbes argued that the unchecked pursuit of freedom would produce a sociological monstrosity: the famous 'war of all against all'. He concluded that social order is only possible if men agree to surrender part of their selfish drives to a central authority.

Parsons interprets the Hobbesian dilemma as a question of how social co-operation is possible. Since social order depends upon co-operation, the principles of social integration and the normative institutions of coercion are the crux of sociological enquiry. Parsons argues that the answers that Durkheim and Weber gave to these questions are more profound and fruitful than Hobbes's emphasis on self-interest. Above all they recognize that social action is shaped by normative institutions and values which originate from the social structure rather than the logic of self-interest. Hobbes's contract solution to social order misses the place of self-sacrifice in everyday life, the tendency to spurn one's own interests in favour of the interests of family, religion, occupation or state. For Parsons, the classical tradition corrects this by revealing the roots of individualism and morality in the social structure. His theory of structural functionalism is designed to integrate the needs of society and the individual into a cohesive whole. It follows Durkheim in identifying a managerialist role for sociology in the conduct of everyday life. Parsons himself was employed by the Amercian government to offer advice on postwar reconstruction in Japan. His view of professionalism envisaged the sociologist as playing an active role in policy formation and government.

Nisbet (1966) argued that the classical tradition was a reaction to the Enlightenment. It opposed utilitarianism and rational individualism and it challenged the proposition of a revolutionary turn in human affairs. Nisbet believed that the proper domain of sociology was a concern with continuities – community, authority, tradition and the sacred. This restates Parsons's belief that the problem of social order is at the heart of sociological enquiry. The question of freedom is interpreted as secondary to establishing the necessary preconditions of social order. Parsons and Nisbet are usually regarded as conservative thinkers, because their primary concern lies in analysing the functional limits to self-interest and desire that society requires in order to persist and grow.

Giddens (1971) launched a famous counter-charge against this influential conservative tradition. He submitted that it is wrong to portray the classical tradition as dominated by the problem of social order. Rather, classical sociology was preoccupied with the question of what is distinctive about capitalism, industrialization and the modern nation state. For example, Durkheim was influenced as much by Kantian idealism as Hobbesian utilitarianism, because he was concerned to elucidate the distinctive character of moral life. He sought to evolve a system of moral individualism that would satisfy French conservative Catholics, landowners and peasants.

Giddens also argues that the interpretations of Parsons and Nisbet fail to situate the classical tradition in the context of history. Thus, Durkheim's sociology does not simply draw on French conservativism as Nisbet alleges. The republican and socialist traditions associated with Saint Simon and Rousseau, and the German socialist thought of Wagner and Schmoller which looked to the active transformation of society also influenced him. Durkheim and Weber developed their sociological work in response to the concrete political clashes between conservatives, liberals and socialists in France and Germany. Nor is it satisfactory to regard Durkheim's theory of moral individualism as an attempt to posit limits to human behaviour. On the contrary, Giddens maintains that Durkheim clearly regarded the cult of the individual as a liberating dependence. Submission to the moral life of society does not deprive the individual of freedom; rather it supplies the individual with freedoms that are greater than under absolutist forms of rule.

Giddens also made the case for regarding Marx as a key figure in the classical tradition. Parsons prioritizes the contributions of Durkheim and Weber in his account of the roots of classical theory. He sidelines Marx and the Marxist tradition. For his part, Nisbet gave pride of place to Durkheim. Against all of this, Giddens emphasizes the relevance and importance of Marx. Marx, Durkheim and Weber all recognized that industrial society is discontinuous with traditional society. In Polanyi's (1944) famous phrase, industrial society constitutes 'the great transformation'. One of Giddens's important contributions to the sociology of knowledge is his insistence that the classical tradition cannot be interpreted in abstract terms. The work of Marx, Durkheim and Weber must be situated in the context of the scene-changing developments in economics, politics and culture that overran nineteenth-century society in Britain, France and Germany. This combats Parsons's idea that core themes can be detected in the classical tradition, especially in the work of Weber and Durkheim. In contrast, Giddens argues for the historical and cultural specificity of the core contributions to classical social theory. This is evident in the shortcomings he detects in the three central traditions. He argues that Marx exaggerates the prospects for social progress and the centrality of class conflict. Giddens calls for a more nuanced reading of the division of labour and the social conflicts concomitant with it. He also sees Marx as a typical nineteenth-century thinker in underestimating the consequences of environmental degradation. Marx's view of nature is instrumental. That is, he regards it as a productive resource. This neglects the destabilizing social consequences of unregulated productive activity. Turning to Durkheim, Giddens argues that his emphasis on moral life and moral individualism underplays the place of power in social life. In particular, Durkheim fails to develop a satisfactory view of the significance of political power in the regulation of wants, interests and desires. A strong view of the importance of power is one of the assets of Weber's sociology. But, Giddens argues, his melancholy view of the rationalization process produces a misleading view of the political possibilities in the great transformation. Weber is unable to frame the question of solidarity beyond a tepid version of bourgeois order. Weber praises the rectitude and rational justice of individualism, but his roots in Nietzsche cause him to lament the restraint imposed on affect. Hence the metaphors of the 'iron cage' and 'the disenchantment of the world' which resonate so powerfully through his work.

Giddens's assessment constitutes a break with the American version of classical social theory. He, as it were, re-imports the classical tradition into Europe from the USA and offers an account of its continuing relevance. However, he stops well short of proposing that classical ideas can be simply reapplied to make sense of contemporary experience and conditions. For Giddens, the main analytical weakness of classical social theory is a tendency towards reductionism. This is evident in Marx's concentration on the economic substructure, Durkheim's emphasis on the importance of the *conscience collective*, and Weber's thought on rationalization. Giddens argues against theoretical closure. He submits that classical theory fails to take account of the rise of administrative power, the significance of war, the growth of the nation state and the importance of culture. History is not unilinear, but a contingent process involving actors who possess and exercise the capacity for reflexive understanding.

Giddens's critique can itself be criticized for being too partial. In particular, his account of the classical tradition finds no place for the 'sociological impressionism' of Simmel or Benjamin (Frisby, 1985), the cultural sociology of Veblen (1899), the attempt by Freud to introduce the role of the psyche in social theory; and it is too dismissive of the Enlightenment contribution made by Comte and Saint Simon. A regular criticism of Giddens is that he darts too quickly over the origins of his own ideas so that, for example, the influence of Elias, Winch, Wittgenstein and, later, Bourdieu, is not adequately elucidated in his writing. Against this, one might observe that Giddens is motivated above all by the relevance and utility of ideas in the development of structuration theory. Despite the learned and penetrating account of the classical tradition in *Capitalism and Modern Social Theory* (1971), the origins of ideas generally hold less interest for him.

The emphasis on reflexivity, knowledgeability and action in Giddens's critique partly derives from his assimilation of the ethnomethodological tradition in American sociology. Giddens agreed with Garfinkel that mainstream social theory tended to produce an over-deterministic account of human action. Ambiguity, reflexivity and choice, which became so central in Giddens's analysis of social life in the 1980s and 1990s, are already present in his early critique.

A contrasting view of the classical tradition can be found in the work of Jeffrey Alexander (1982, 1987). Alexander casts the classical tradition in terms of the duality between freedom and determination. According to Alexander, Marx and Durkheim fail to provide an integrated synthesis of the dimensions of freedom and determination. Rather they oscillate between presenting action as voluntarily motivated and structurally determined. In contrast, Alexander argues that Weber and Parsons attempt this synthesis but their solutions are unsatisfactory. In particular, they fail to incorporate an adequate view of multidimensionality into their analysis.

Alexander develops his argument by an attack on positivism. The positivist tradition, he argues, is defective for several reasons. First, it falsely separates metaphysics from science. Metaphysical beliefs are often contained in empirical observation and positivists overstate the capacity of scientific method to overcome metaphysics. Secondly, positivism fetishizes the methods of natural science as the role model for the social sciences to follow. For Alexander, this creates an oversimplistic split between theory and empirical observation and contributes to the belief that scientific knowledge is cumulative and progressive.

Drawing partly on the work of Thomas Kuhn (1957, 1962) Alexander calls for a 'post-positivist' revolution. The cornerstones of this are the propositions that empirical analysis is always shaped by theoretical constructs; scientific establishments act as gatekeepers of knowledge and do not spontaneously combust if empirical analysis demonstrates that their theorems are wrong; scientific communities are frequently closed and dogmatic rather than open and reflexive; and scientific research is not necessarily cumulative and progressive.

Alexander's approach seeks to underline the central role of theory in shaping scientific discourse and empirical work. In social science debate does not simply revolve around the question of whether empirical findings fit theoretical propositions. In addition, debates in social science continuously raise questions of value relevance, logical coherence, the contexts in which knowledge is created, and historical and comparative dimensions. The classical tradition is important to Alexander because it acts as the sheet anchor of these debates. It offers a common research agenda and set of discursive resources. Alexander's view assigns more coherence to the classical tradition than is found in Giddens's account. Although Alexander does not posit a grand narrative, he recognizes continuities which ultimately revolve around questions of the motivation behind action and the reproduction of order. Alexander therefore seems to reiterate that the tension between freedom and determination is the central theatre for sociological exploration.

## Structuration theory

Structuration theory, which is perhaps Giddens's most significant contribution to social analysis, is an attempt to overcome the dualism of the individual/society model. Structuration theory is an attempt to defend the reflexivity and choice of the actor without dissolving the signficance of constraint. It begins with a restatement of the importance of the commonsense knowledge of social actors. The relationship between agency and structure is redefined in terms of a duality of structure in which actors are presented as reflexively making and remaking their social life. Giddens (1984: 374) introduces the concept of the 'double hermeneutic' to refer to 'the meaningful social world as constituted by lay actors and the meta-languages invented by social scientists'. He claims a 'constant slippage' between the two in the practice of social theory and research. The concept owes much to the phenomenological and ethnomethodological critiques of structural functionalism. Parsons, and his followers, were attacked for attributing goals to social systems and, *ipso facto*, producing passive readings of the intentions of social actors. Structuration theory follows suit. It is motivated by a twin desire to make ordinary, everyday, commonsense consciousness the centre of social theory, and to retain a notion of overarching structural influence.

The work of Turner (1984) draws on the classical sociological tradition and the tradition of phenomenology to propose that the body is the foundation of social theory. In contrast, Giddens's theory of structuration holds that time and space are of foundational importance. By conceiving agency as irremediably located in time and space, the historical and comparative dimensions of social structure are prioritized. Action is therefore always constituted around structural resources. For example, following Wittgenstein, Giddens holds that rules are basic to social life. Rules are not external to the individual, as the Durkheimian reading of social facts implied. On the contrary, they are already and always constituted through social action. Further, individuals already and always have the capacity for reasoning and monitoring rules and behaviour, unless they suffer physical or mental impairment. Reasoning and knowledge rather than will and the emotions are at the forefront of Giddens's theory of structuration.

While Giddens is concerned to demonstrate that social action is constituted through rules, he also seeks to situate power in his social analysis. Rules and other social resources are differentially allocated in society. The principles of allocation reflect the operation of power. Giddens follows Weber in regarding power as the capacity to achieve one's objectives, even against the wishes of other actors. He is careful to describe power both as the practical consciousness of the individual and the cultural and as material assets embodied in action.

A legitimate criticism of this view of power is that it fails to develop an adequate account of the place of the unconscious in everyday life. The emphasis on reflexivity and monitoring overshadows the role of unconscious energy. Giddens partly answers this criticism by drawing on R.D. Laing's concept of ontological security. Laing argued that a basic human need is the requirement to feel secure with others. Giddens agrees and adds that a notion of the continuity of self-identity over space and time, and the predictability of social life, are basic requirements. Trust relations bestow ontological security on actors. Trust is built through the infant socialization process and involves an emotional rather than cognitive commitment, which is ultimately rooted in the unconscious. It is actively made and remade through interaction with others. Basic to this argument is the proposition that tolerance and emotional space must be meted out to others as an ordinary accomplishment of stable social life. Respect for others is a condition of respect for oneself.

Giddens is concerned to avoid the polarity of agency/structure approaches. His thought on rules, resources, reflexivity and action is plainly influenced by French poststructuralist philosophy. Although once again, a legitimate criticism of Giddens is that he often fails to elucidate these influences in his analysis.

Tucker (1998) notes that the concept of *social practices* is crucial to Giddens's attempt to overcome the agency/structure duality. According to Giddens, writes Tucker (1998: 84), 'social practices are the behavioural and institutional dimensions of the practical consciousness of reflexive people, who draw on shared cultural beliefs and stocks of knowledge'. Basic to this is the presupposition that social practices have accumulated through deep processes of layering across space and time. Social practices can be thought of as habits of behaviour which motivate individual choices in social action. This has the virtue of emphasizing the historical, situated character of social action. It also locates social monitoring in the psyche of the actor, for it argues that memory traces of social practice mould individual choice.

Giddens is intent on avoiding the trap of attributing a thing-like status to social structures. His emphasis on deep processes of layering across time and space in social practice is designed as a strategy of anti-reductionism. In answer to the agency/structure dichotomy which has traditionally polarized sociological research, Giddens (1984) offers the concept of the 'duality of structure'. He (1984: 374) holds that structure must be reconceptualized as 'the medium and outcome of the conduct it recursively organizes; the structural properties of social systems do not exist outside of action but are chronically implicated in its production and reproduction.' To some extent, this concept revisits Saussure's distinction between *langue* and *parole*. Saussure sought to demonstrate that communication is the result of a complex system of presences and absences. *Langue* is the entire system of nuanced signs and symbols which makes comprehension possible. *Parole* is, so to speak, the concrete individual performance of communication. The individual communicative act necessarily utilizes some elements of *langue*, but the meaning of these elements is both a matter of the presented elements in communicative exchange and those remaining elements of *langue* which are absent.

Giddens takes over the idea of meaning as the result of a complex chain of presences and absences and applies it to the realm of social action. Individual behaviour is the result of reflexive choices, but these choices draw on layers of practice across time and space which, as it were, buoy up possibilities of interaction. Concrete action is the instantiation of social practices through the habit and memory traces of the actor. Through concrete action, these practices are themselves remade and altered. The result is a more fluid and flexible comprehension of structure. Limits to conduct are, of course, recognized. For example, resources are unequally distributed through the operation of power; social practices are layered across time and space, but individuals are situated in the concrete, local context which means that their knowledge is restricted; unintended actions have unintended consequences. In some ways Giddens's distinction between presence and absence continues the distinction made by Lockwood (1964) in his remarks on system integration. Face-to-face interaction is the requirement of social integration, since outright solipsism or the Hobbesian dystopia of the war of all against all makes social order impossible; but interaction with actors and practices that are not physically present is also the requirement of system integration, since the meaning and quality of concrete interaction derives from more expansive rules and resources.

Structuration theory aims to build time and space into the core categories of theory. Giddens (1984: 110) is critical of mainstream social theory for neglecting the centrality of time and space in social relations. He distinguishes three time-spans: the time of everyday life, the life cycle of the organism and the *longue durée* of social processes over centuries. Further, on the spatial level, he distinguishes between *locale*, which is the concrete setting and context of social interaction, and *regionalization*, which he (1984: 376) defines as 'the temporal, spatial or time space differentiation of regions either within or between locales'. The boundaries of face-to-face interaction are set by these time–space distinctions.

Tucker (1998: 89–90) postulates four major achievements for structuration theory. First, it emblazons questions of time and space as the focal points of sociological enquiry. Secondly, it produces a more satisfactory explanation of how people reflexively set goals in the bounded contexts of time and space. Thirdly, the notion of the double hermeneutic universalizes the issue of the sociology of knowledge in sociological analysis. Fourthly, the concept of the duality of structure transcends the agency/structure dichotomy which has traditionally restricted social research.

## Criticism of structuration theory

Structuration theory is a formidable contribution to social thought. It is better protected than the Trojan wooden horse, in that it uses categories of thought that are correctly calculated to be acceptable to the most, *prima facie*, hostile sociologists. This is no accident. Gouldner (1971), a strangely forgotten sociologist these days, identified paradigm wars in sociology during the 1950s and 1960s which, he contended, threatened the sustainability of the discipline. Seen from his standpoint, structuration theory came along at just the right time. It does not please everyone, but it offers an enormous canvas on which no sociologist can avoid finding a degree of recognition.

This is also, perhaps, the main problem with the theory. As the canvas has expanded in detail, the focus of enquiry has grown more oblique. Structuration theory offers something for everyone. It is actually a consensual form of theory, because it makes a virtue of eclecticism in framing the agency/structure problematic. Giddens even invents a new lexicon of richly bejewelled concepts – 'double hermeneutic', 'duality of structure', 'homeostatic loops', 'locale', 'time–space distanciation'. Leaving aside the question of whether it is legitimate to maintain that these concepts say anything new, they certainly give the impression of profundity.

We recognize that Giddens attempts to restore the grand ambition of social theory that animated the classical tradition. *Contra* the criticism of Lyotard (1980) and other anti-grand-narrative theorists, we believe that this is a laudable aim. That is, we believe that there are some issues, notably those pertaining to embodiment and environmental sustainability, which are the legitimate subject of, if not universal sociological theory, at the very least, universal sociological metadiscourse. We support the tacit criticism in structuration theory, that some forms of postwar sociology have become too 'localized' and 'particularistic' for their own good; just as we agree that many forms of grand theory – from Parsonian structural functionalism to structuralist feminism and Marxism – are too abstract. We are in agreement with Giddens in holding that theory is central to sociological enquiry. Indeed, we believe that the questions raised in the classical tradition remain central, and that sociologists must treat it as a living, evolving resource.

At the same time, we do not believe that structuration theory offers an adequate theory of embodiment. Indeed, we think it odd that a theory which sets such store by incorporating the common sense of ordinary actors into the centre of sociological enquiry, seems to neglect questions of bodily frailty, ageing and the emotions. While we would be the first to agree that these attempts are not beyond criticism, we contend that this work offers a more fruitful way of handling the agency/structure problematic. Most importantly, it places the body at the heart of sociological enquiry. By doing so it highlights the mutual interdependence of body and environment; the normalizing of bodily functions and relations, and the conflicts thereof; the processual character of human life which is perhaps symbolized most poignantly by the ageing body; the comparative differences between bodily normalization and learnt forms of action. Above all, we believe that the body is the foundational material reality in social life. At both intuitive and more sophisticated levels, we can understand social processes more accurately if we start with the body.

Moving on, we note the validity of Giddens's complaint that power has been inadequately theorized in much postwar sociology. As Giddens (1971) demonstrated, the concept of power in the structural-functionalist tradition dissolved subjective intentionality and reflexivity. Again, we would emphasize the influence of the American traditions of ethnomethodology and symbolic interactionism on Giddens's criticism. The chief weakness of these traditions is that they exaggerate the freedom of the individual. Garfinkel, Becker and Goffman may write from contrasting positions, but common to them is a relatively ahistorical approach to sociological enquiry. The result is that their analysis produces the paradox of actors who have values, exercise choice, resist power, but who apparently lack a biography. Interestingly, Giddens has also been attacked for presenting an ahistorical view of the individual (Bryant and Jary, 1991; Craib, 1992). Bauman (1989: 46) takes a leaf from the same book, by arguing that Giddens pays insufficient attention to the questions of which concrete individuals exercise power, and who is at their mercy and influence. When Giddens confronts the subject of social integration, he tends to slide into the more abstract issue of system integration, leaving an unresolved quality to his political sociology. The tacit criticism is that Giddens provides no satisfactory basis for strategies of social action, notably in the political sphere. As we shall see presently, Giddens's arguments about social reconstruction are criticized for vacillating between liberalism and socialism. The same quality of wanting to please everyone that is apparent in structuration theory, is present in his meditations on the 'third way'.

Another weakness of structuration theory is its excessive formalism. This is ironic, since Giddens clearly wants to get away from what he sees as the harmful abstractions and conservatism of Parsons. Yet what structuration theory shows, above all, is the orderly mechanics of social reproduction in advanced urban-industrial society. True, he (1984: 310–19) explicitly proposes that capitalism is a contradictory society because, à la Marx, the relations of production ultimately constrain the forces of production. However, in both structuration theory and his thought on 'third way' politics, the accent is upon living with contradiction. Where he recognizes 'structural perversity' in the shape of inequality or repression (1984: 317), his response is to develop policies which meliorate conflict, usually by widening the sphere of social inclusivism. What is missing is an engagement with the utopian tradition which looks forward to a transcendent social order. Giddens tends to imply that this debate ceased to be relevant when the experiment with 'presently existing socialism' collapsed in 1989, with the disintegration of the statist societies of Eastern Europe. This both falsely equates the only meaningful search for transcendence with Marxist politics, and turns a blind eye to the development of alternative lifestyles and forms of body politics that have emerged and flourished within advanced urban-industrial capitalism.

## Conclusion

Freedom and determination are clearly compatible in a number of permutations. No one is, or has been, absolutely free; and no one is wholly determined. This is of course, a platitudinous observation. Then again, as de Swaan (1990) noted accurately, sociology has rarely risen above platitudes in its conclusions about social life. Rather engagingly, de Swaan defends the value of sociological platitudes. When a free-marketeer like Margaret Thatcher spends a decade working on the assumption that 'there is no such thing as society', or a blinkered nationalist like Milosevic commits genocide in the Balkans, sociological platitudes show their worth in accurately framing social problems.

We believe that the twin tasks of sociology are to expose myths and humanize the self and life with others. In this we claim kinship with the Enlightenment heritage of the subject. Following the post-structuralist, anti-humanist, postmodern moments in social theory between the late 1960s and early 1990s, it is perhaps important to remember that the Enlightenment heritage is more than a poisoned chalice. Anti-humanist theorists are right to argue that the logic which invented the railway system also invented the Holocaust. The Enlightenment faith in science, order and progress was indeed overstated and it directly produced ethnic, religious, sexual, subcultural, economic and political subjugations of various kinds.

But the Enlightenment also promoted reflexivity and critical consciousness about the deformations of received ontologies and epistemologies. Sociology remains marked by this cultural revolution.

Yet sociologists are still at loggerheads about what the subject is for or about. Bauman (1987) coined the distinction between legislators and interpreters. It is a useful way to consider the web of contention in sociology. Legislators apply social knowledge to manage social affairs. They seek to steer society in particular directions – socialist, egalitarian, market or meritocratic. They are often passionate about the ends of sociology, regarding the privilege of social transformation to be the *sine qua non* of sociological enterprise. Interpreters explore the social world as a continuously unfolding universe of action, contexts and meanings. They regard the sociological task to be the achievement of detached understanding. In this perspective observation and theory are forever conditional. The ethic of ultimate values is regarded as a hobbled belief system because it minimizes the ambiguities and ambivalence in social relations.

The dichotomy is readily recognizable to anyone who is in the slightest involved with sociological work. Legislators and interpreters continue to slug it out in journals, conferences and books. This suggests a discipline which has grown removed from its subject of study – a condition in which the sociologist and 'ordinary people' live in two different worlds. Yet things are not so simple. In another work, Bauman (1990: 9–18) makes a passionate plea for regarding what sociologists do as reflections on the ordinary experiences of everyday life. He insists on the 'intimate' relationship between sociological knowledge and common sense. He asks us to regard sociology as a discourse which is 'wide open: no standing invitation to everybody to join, but no clearly marked borders or effective border guards either' (1990: 11). Yet he also insists that sociological knowledge is not equivalent to common sense. In four particulars, he claims decisive differences. In the first place, sociology is attached to an ethic of responsible speech. Sociologists seek to produce knowledge which is corroborated by evidence and/or which is commensurate with the rigours of theory. Secondly, sociological knowledge operates on a wider comparative and historical scale than the typical level of common sense. Thirdly, sociological knowledge strives to elucidate intentional human action and its unintended consequences. It does not seek to make sense from the narrow standpoint of self-interest, but rather from the wider historical and comparative perspective of social difference. Fourthly, sociological knowledge seeks to defamiliarize the familiar. The mores, rules and conventions which common sense typically takes for granted, are objects of scrutiny for sociology. This question of the 'intimacy' between common sense and sociology is moot. It parallels the tension between freedom and determination that, we argue, is integral to every known form of sociological reasoning. To some degree, our argument in this book is that the decorative tendency in sociology has developed a cocktail of philosophy, identity politics and aestheticized consciousness which divorces it from common sense. Anyone who attends the American Sociological Association, British Sociological Association or even more emphatically, the huge World Congress of Sociology organized by the International Sociological Association every four years, will be aware that these are meetings *for* sociologists. *Pace* Bauman, these are not colloquia in which the intimate connection between sociological knowledge and common sense is scrupulously observed. On the contrary, they are essentially retreats for academicians. Discussions revolve as much around threats of funding cuts and job opportunities, as the condition of moral individualism, methods of research and the soul of capitalism. In other words, what Bauman minimizes in what is, in fairness, merely an introductory discussion, is the academic professionalization of the subject.

Sociologists speaking only unto sociologists is a hackneyed criticism of the subject. Yet the extent to which the focal point of sociological knowledge production remains the university is remarkable. We maintain that the decorative tendency in sociology has been fuelled by the objective of widening accessibility. The attempt to jazz up the subject in the 1970s, by importing continental philosophy and cultural studies, was ultimately a numbers game. Declining enrolments on the traditional curriculum, made sociologists rethink ways of making the subject attractive to new generations of students. In Chapter 1 on the limits of interdisciplinarity we argued that there are now good reasons for a post-interdisciplinary reaction. In particular, we argued that the dilution of the classical tradition has weakened the persuasiveness of sociological perspectives. Hand in hand with this, we argue that we are entering the era of the post-university. The internet, the phone and computerized learning systems permit the domestic delivery of most pedagogic and research services now conducted in the university. Flexible forms of service delivery will replace the centralized, internally monitored systems of learning codified under the postwar expansion of higher education throughout the West. 'New times', indeed.

Can sociology survive? In the 1950s and 1960s studying sociology was almost like engaging in a moral crusade to change society. The subject was regarded as at the forefront of critical thought and activism. Doubtless, this was always an exaggerated state of affairs. What is indisputable is that by the late 1970s sociology had lost its fashionable sheen and become just another subject available to students in the university core curriculum. There are perhaps good reasons for suggesting that sociological knowledge, in Bauman's sense of the term, already flourishes more vigorously *outside* the academy. The sociological jargon of the 1960s, terms like 'alienation', 'bureaucracy', 'rationalization', 'ideology', 'deferred gratification', 'charisma', are now part of the lingua franca of journalism, politics and management. Unquestionably, sociology has contributed to changing the way we live now. Multiculturalism, difference, ethnic oppression, sexual oppression, deskilling at work, class influence are all now part and parcel of popular consciousness. Academic sociologists may still have to remind the public of how these and other social processes operate in contemporary life, but there is now a general acceptance of their significance.

In large measure, the main dilemma facing academic sociologists since the end of the 1970s has been the problem of preaching to the converted. It is because sociological knowledge about inequality, oppression and discursive domination became the homilies of popular culture in the 1970s that the space opened up for the decorative turn. The aestheticization of sociological theory and the interest in lifestyle and identity must be interpreted, at least in part, as an element in the survival strategy of the subject. But at what cost?

# 10

# SOLUTIONS

From Edmund Burke to the new right, the central dilemma in conservative thought has been to defend a moral economy based upon structured economic inequality, in the midst of the historical tendency for economic plenty to rise. The allocation of surplus through principles of redistributive justice has been one of the primary impulses in critical thought. Many influential commentators now view this debate as old hat. For these commentators, structural transformations in the global economy, in particular the rise of flexibility, interdependence and real time accumulation, signal a paradigm shift in social and economic conditions. According to Beck (1999: 2), 'a new kind of capitalism, a new kind of society and a new kind of personal life are coming into being, all of which differ from earlier phases of social development'.

Sennett (1998), working in a very different intellectual vein, in which the tradition of the American left is pre-eminent, nonetheless reaches the same conclusion. Drawing on the work of Coser (1977), Sennett argues that the recognition, articulation and negotiation of difference provides a discursive framework for the revival of community under the new capitalism. This assumes that the old class-based types of resistance and struggle, and the language that supports them, have had their day. Production is no longer a viable foundation for solidarity. This has far reaching consequences for the way in which politics is practised and how we conceive political institutions and action. Collectivism in the workplace was based in common experience and shared interests. The link between the town and the factory or mine was a vibrant source of community. Flexible capitalism recognizes no such link, as the closure of the pits in Britain and the growth of the rust belt in the USA in the last twenty years testifies. Capital pursues profit in the global market, and flees from local labour and legislative traditions that restrict its freedom of action. In addition, flexible capitalism has undermined the notion of common experience and interests in the work process by replacing the traditional expectation of work or career continuity with diversification. Today, workers must be prepared to retrain and relocate in order to maximize participation in the labour market. Moreover, the increasing sophistication of micro-communications and computing have reinforced the tendency for the home to emerge as a major site of paid employment. Together with the changes in work and career, medical innovation is profoundly changing long-established Cartesian notions of possessive

individualism, accumulation and social action. Some writers argue that
we have already moved into 'risk society' in which a new individualism
is emerging (Giddens, 1991; Beck, 1992). Later we will examine the
central features of this development when we discuss 'life politics'.
At this stage in the discussion it is enough to state that medical,
cultural, economic and biological developments have combined to
seriously erode traditional notions of identity, collectivity, social action
and accumulation.

Nowhere is this clearer that in relations of production. Marx argued
that production is the material base of society. Production may be thought
of as the cultural interaction with nature designed to generate surplus. In
Marxist sociology production is the chief patterning influence on the
distribution of resources. Although left and right have differed markedly
in their analysis of how surplus is generated and should be distributed,
both have assumed that labour is the foundation of identity and collectivity. This assumption is now openly refuted. For example, Gorz (1992,
1993) maintains that work-centred views of society and culture, which
present labour as a source of personal fulfilment, moral cohesion and
collective integration, have been untenable for some time. For Gorz, the
majority of the workforce holds an instrumental attitude to paid labour.
They seek financial reward and a measure of satisfaction with work
colleagues, but real life is concentrated in non-work spheres. It is in consumption, leisure and the emotional labour of family life that meaningful
experience resides. According to Gorz, paid labour is simply the means to
fulfil these ends. The argument reinforces the thesis advanced by Miller
(1987), Slater (1997), Ritzer (1998) and other writers, that consumption
has replaced production as the focal point of lifestyle. In short, there
appears to be widespread consensus among sociologists that a new type of
society is emerging. Castells (1998), who is generally regarded to have
produced the most complete analysis of this new formation, is reasonably
precise about the preconditions for determining macro-level structural
transformation. He argues that a new society emerges when a structural
transformation in relationships of production, power and experience can
be unequivocally detected (1998: 340). He argues that the new formation,
which he calls 'network society', started to emerge between the late 1960s
and mid-1970s.

Macro-level structural transformations present a specific set of challenges
for social actors. In a sense, one must conduct social life without a route-
map, because the contours of the new social, economic and cultural
conditions have not fully cohered. Later, we will examine in detail some
competing solutions to the problems and opportunities created by the new
formation. First it is necessary to consider how the social, economic and
cultural terrain is shifting. Although several contributions to this question
are now available none matches the three-volume study produced by
Castells (1996, 1997, 1998).

## Network society and the information age

Castells's work does not want for plaudits. Giddens (1996) and Webster (1997) rank his achievement with that of Max Weber in *Economy and Society*, and McGuigan (1999: 104) refers to the study as the '*Das Kapital* of our time'. Sociology is a notoriously fashion-prone and fickle subject, and its practitioners are peculiarly given to hyperbole. For example, who speaks of 'post-industrial society' or 'pluralistic industrialism' today? Yet these were seminal themes in the key debates about the trajectory of industrial society in the 1960s and 1970s (Kerr et al., 1962; Touraine, 1971; Bell, 1973). In these debates the propositions that the end of the nation state is in sight, that a global convergence of economic, social and political conditions is underway, and that information is altering the shape of identity and sociality, were already articulated. However, they were advanced in a world dominated by the bipolarity of command and market systems and in which real time accumulation and flexibility were, by today's standards, primitive. The gestation of Castells's *magnum opus* occurred during the collapse of the Soviet-type system and the rise of real time technologies of computerization and the internet. His work both comments on these developments, and provides a richly textured analysis of their relationship to the wider mechanics of global structural transformation. Castells maintains that several novel features of technology, economy, society and culture have combined to justify the proposition that we are living in the midst of a fundamentally new social formation. Among the features he identifies are:

1   The emergence of ubiquitous mobile telecommunications and computing links.
2   The emergence of genetic engineering.
3   The consolidation of electronically integrated, global financial markets operating in real time.
4   The expansion of an interlinked, cohesive capitalist economy over the whole planet, instead of specific regions.
5   The shift in the labour force, in the advanced economies, from primary and manufacturing activities to knowledge, information and communication industries.
6   The shift from a rural to an urban-based population on the planet.
7   The disappearance of what Bahro (1978) called 'the presently existing alternative' to capitalism.
8   The rise of the Asian Pacific as a major force in the world economy.
9   The widespread challenge to patriarchalism.
10  The expansion of green consciousness and environmental protectionism.
11  The emergence of 'real virtuality' (the hypertexting of cultural and economic relations.
12  The growth of social movements opposed to globalization.

The list is not exhaustive, but it does reveal the scope and importance of Castells's achievement. He integrates an analysis of these features of contemporary life into a cogent historical and comparative framework of the central processes of capitalism. Strictly speaking, the study does not demonstrate a novel structural transformation. In so far as Marx showed that the tendency of capitalism is to strive to break free of all constraints, Castells can be understood as continuing the Marxist project. However, as Castells (1997: 144–5) acknowledges, his is a highly revisionist form of Marxism, in which questions of materialism and transformation were initially filtered through problems of urbanism and post-industrialism. Castells did his PhD under the supervision of Alain Touraine. Although certain aspects of the analysis are prefigured in the post-industrial society and convergence theory debates of the 1960s and 1970s, Castells provides a canvas on which the cumulative, interlinking connections are more power- fully illustrated and explained. In particular, he provides a very persuasive analysis of the role of the multinational corporation in the globalization of power and the increasingly porous character of the nation state. Indeed, in Castells's approach, concepts of 'network' and 'flow' have replaced 'society' at the heart of sociological analysis. He may be said to have developed a fresh set of problematics and a new vocabulary for sociological work (see also Urry, 2000). His study is indeed a landmark work, for which claims of hyperbole are rash and mistaken.

Information and information technology form the centrepiece of Castells's account. Capitalism has become universal because the new information technologies are pervasive, flexible and permit levels of system integration unprecedented in human history (Castells, 1996: 61–2). Metaphors of 'circuits of power' and 'feedback loops' recur repeatedly throughout the analysis. It is the universal connecting up of nodes of activity achieved by the new information technologies that has allowed capitalism to dramatically enhance its capacity for real time accumulation. However, Castells protects himself from the charge of technological determinism, by insisting that the information technologies are themselves interlinked with a wider set of political, cultural and economic changes. Network society is the outcome of multidimensional and variegated processes. Unlike the convergence and post-industrial society theories of the 1960s and 1970s, Castells refuses to fall into the trap of positing a prime-mover, unilinear theory of development. His analysis of social change is multidimensional and cross-cultural. We believe that the question of Castells's relation to Marx is important, and we will examine this at greater length later in the chapter.

Castells follows other observers in rejecting the Weberian thesis that it is satisfactory to regard the nation state as the primary unit of sociological analysis. He argues (1996) that the power of transnational linkages of information, finance and communication flows requires new ways of con- ceptualizing collectivity. 'Networking' and 'network society' emerge as the presiding concepts that encapsulate his sense of the new developments. Castells regards networks as linkages of actors bound by common purpose.

This does not sound very different from orthodox sociological concepts of 'small group,' ' 'community', 'nation state' and 'society'. However, whereas the latter refer to exclusive and closed linkages, the concepts of networking and network society refer to inclusive and open connections. Networks are dynamic, open figurations in which innovation, adaptability and flexibility are privileged over tradition, routine and continuity. As an example, consider the network enterprise. Castells (1997: 8) defines this as

> the specific set of linkages between different firms or segments, organized *ad hoc*, for a specific project, and dissolving/reforming after the task is completed.

He argues that the network enterprise produces higher levels of flexibility, adaptability and innovation and is therefore most successful in the competitive struggle for the accumulation of value. Network enterprises have the characteristic of forming themselves into ephemeral units, because the communication and information codes in which they operate are universal and instantaneous. Thus, production webs in Microsoft, IBM, Siemens and Toshiba interweave with webs in other companies in pursuit of strategic, mutual objectives without necessarily resulting in continuous, consolidated units. One paradox of the new stage of 'information capitalism' (Castells, 1998: 341), is that capitalism achieves higher penetration while at the same time becoming more porous and open.

Networking is not confined to the domain of the business enterprise. On the contrary, Castells holds that networking arrangements now constitute the pattern of normative order. Thus, political movements, cultural phenomena and aesthetic trends utilize universal codes of information and communication to mobilize consciousness and action. Basic to the idea of networking is the proposition that actors now have the capacity to operate as a cohesive unit in real time and on a global scale. Co-ordination operates upon a much wider scale and reciprocity is more instantaneous. Yet mobilization does not necessarily entail the production and reproduction of concrete structures of power.

Bell (1973), in his account of post-industrial society, observed that social and economic conditions are moving in a direction in which 'knowledge is power'. Castells's analysis richly confirms this observation. However, he refines it by insisting that informational knowledge is now the seat of power and that education is the vessel for acquiring this knowledge. He identifies three fundamental social cleavages in the information age (1998: 346). First, the increasing importance of informational producers is counterbalanced by the declining power of generic labour. By 'generic labour' Castells means untrained, uncertified labour power. The 'haves' in society are increasingly defined by their trained capacity to participate in the information cultures, and the 'have nots' by their want of this capacity.

Secondly, generic labour is increasingly becoming discarded labour. That is, the generic labourer is becoming a replaceable category in the logic of the system. Replaceability, by mechanized or computerized systems, diminishes bargaining power and increases dependence upon, kinship networks, the welfare state or the voluntary sector. This is occurring at a time in which there are strong pressures to denude the welfare state of its powers of relief. Thirdly, the individualization of employment relationships for informational producers means that each worker receives a different deal. This connects up with Sennett's (1998) point about the diversification of labour considered in the opening pages of this chapter. Differentiated employment contracts undermine the principle of collective bargaining by rendering the collective a nebulous category. If one's personal terms and conditions of work differ from those of the team of colleagues with whom one works, there is no basis for asserting common experience, rights and responsibilities. The individualization of work is a tendency which applies to the category of informational producers. The generic labourer has no basis for negotiating an individualized employment contract. But since his/her employment experience conforms to the condition of casualization, there is no continuous means of collectivist opposition.

Nation states and societies operate with boundaries of legitimacy. Network society and networking recognize 'flow' as the conduit through which legitimacy is realized. By the term 'flow', Castells (1996: 412) means the

> purposeful, repetitive, programmable sequence of exchange and interaction between physically disjointed positions held by social actors in the economic, political, and symbolic structures of society.

The analysis of networking and network society identifies those who occupy the switchpoints of space and time flows as the key power brokers in informational capitalism. This dissociates power from hierarchy. While it achieves more effective market penetration, it decentralizes power to actors located at decisive points in the sequence of continuous activity. An instructive example is provided by the so-called 'rogue trader', Nick Leeson, a derivatives trader working on the Singapore International Monetary Exchange. In 1995 Leeson gained approval for the diversion of £700 million from Barings' Bank in London to engage in Japanese stock and bond speculation. The failure of the bet resulted in the bankruptcy of the 227-year-old bank. Leeson was a relatively junior employee who, by virtue of his control of a crucial switchpoint in the flow of capital, brought down the bank.

The Leeson episode is doubly instructive for Castells's general thesis, for it demonstrates that informational producers can no longer be analysed, *à la* Marx, as belonging to the ranks of the exploited. The individualization of work relations means that these workers possess a high degree of autonomy. The value of informational producers to those that employ them derives precisely from their innovative capacities, and these are necessarily unpredictable. Their unpredictability grants a degree of freedom and power to the activities of these workers. It is this independence that Nick Leeson exploited in his disastrous dealings on the derivatives market. What was formerly a source of profit became a source of catastrophic loss. But the steering power behind this speculation had long since left the headquarters of Baring's London office: it had fled to Singapore through the decentralizing, decentring processes of flow required by informational capitalism.

Castells's concept of flow radicalizes hierarchical models of power by denying that a ladder of power is any longer a satisfactory way of conceptualizing how will is exercised in contemporary society. There are two aspects to this point in Castells's argument. First, dialogic and linear models of power assume a personalized command chain between actors. In contrast, networking operates through data rather than people. Will is exercised by, so to speak, power nomads situated at decisive points in the flow of information, who operate instantaneously and relatively impersonally, over vast zones of time and space. An actor has a higher probability of realizing his or her will decisively over another in a social relationship if the other is present as 'data'. Data does not possess the identity to resist, it does not have a focus to oppose. This has far reaching implications for how we understand power and control. For one thing, it suggests that a disembodied view of power must be added to the orthodox embodied model for understanding social action. Power at a switchpoint in the informational flow, rather than power over an embodied other is decisive in many areas. Hence, the current interest among sociologists in Latour's (1995) concept of 'inhumanity'. By extension, this suggests that focusing on the will or determination of an actor to achieve his or her ends is now beside the point. It is the circumference of data at his/her disposal, and the capacity to react, that produces results. Although Castells (1996: 415) recognizes that dominant managerial elites claim notional control of informational flows, the logic of networking is that control cannot be concentrated for long at any single switchpoint in the system.

The second aspect is that social relationships under networking resemble a hypertext in which all cultural manifestations interact with each other. In a sense, network society delivers a prolific quality to cultural exchange. The will and meaning exercised between social actors is bounced down the flow of interaction and inflects and refracts in ways which no single actor can control. The concept of 'real virtuality' is partly designed to illustrate the prolific quality of cultural exchange under network society. By 'real virtuality' Castells (1996: 372–5) means a cultural system in which electronic representation establishes the symbolic and discursive parameters of social interaction. The concept has affinities with Baudrillard's (1983a and b, 1988) analysis of simulation and hyperreality. However, where Baudrillard uses the observation to posit the disappearance of reality, Castells proposes a change in the nature of experience. For Castells, the culture of real virtuality is technologically powerful, but economically and politically driven. It is a comprehensively integrated and interacting culture, which presents biased representations that privilege certain types of power. Once again, the notion that data replaces people under networking is proffered. This raises the question of the humanity of the system, and in particular, its redistributive potential. What then is Castells's position on inequality and social exclusion? The core point is easily stated:

Under the new system of production, a considerable number of humans, probably in a growing population, are irrelevant, both as producers and consumers,
from the perspective of the system's logic. (Castells, 1998: 344)

Castells (1998: 163) uses the metaphor of 'black holes of informational
capitalism' to refer to this phenomenon. He regards the proposition that
there are some populations which informational capitalism regards as
dispensable, as a moral outrage. These populations subsist in certain areas
of intense poverty in Africa, Asia and Latin America, but they are also
found among the homeless in the cities of the advanced core powers. In
many respects, informational capitalism is therefore analysed along lines
with which Marx would have felt at home. Thus, Castells believes that the
system entrenches inequality, dehumanizes social relations, immiserates
millions and degrades the environment.

Castells's analysis works at the level of massive, deep-seated global
processes which are beyond the capacity of any single individual or power
formation to control. At the same time, it fully recognizes that these
developments have triggered the emergence of critical and oppositional
movements. Volume 2 of the trilogy attempts a political economy of these
counter-forces, of which feminism and the green movement are singled out
as being particularly significant. Interestingly, Castells identifies the rash of
extreme left- and right-wing cults and movements that either sprang up or
crystallized in the 1980s and 1990s as, first and foremost, movements of
anti-globalization. He examines the belief systems of the Zapatistas, the
Militia and Patriot movement in the US and the Japanese Aum Shinrikyo
in this light. Of course, he is careful to emphasize that each of these
movements can only be finally comprehended in terms of its particularistic
circumstances and societal goals. Inasmuch as this is the case, there is little
underlying unity between them. Yet Castells argues that the momentum
behind them is resistance against the encroaching standardization and
routinization of globalization. His (1997: 328–33) analysis of populist
oppositional movements in Bolivia shows that radical leaders understand
the power of information technologies in resisting informational capitalism.

Events since the publication of Castells's *magnum opus* confirm his
suggestion that the central techniques of networking and accumulation
devised by informational capitalism can be turned against the system. For
example, in 1999, the J-18 and 'Reclaim the Streets' demonstration in the
city of London used the internet as a vital tool of organization. Similarly, the
radical anti-corporatist coalition, which was instrumental in the disruption
of the World Trade Organization meeting in Seattle and associated city riots
at the end of 1999, is known to have made extensive use of the internet.
Castells, then, is concerned to avoid a zero-sum reading of informational
capitalism, and to retain the traditional Marxist principle that 'men make
their own history' i.e. resistance and transformation remain viable options.

Notwithstanding this, his analysis, of both the dynamics of globalization
and resistance concludes that traditional Marxist models of social order
and change are no longer satsifactory. As he puts it:

The institutions and organizations of civil society that were constructed around the democratic state, and around the social contract between capital and labour, have become, by and large, empty shells, decreasingly able to relate to people's lives and values in most societies. . . . The dissolution of shared identities, which is tantamount to the dissolution of society as a meaningful social system, may well be the state of affairs of our times. (1997: 355)

What price solidarity in a world where markets, individuals, networks and strategic alliances predominate? The Cartesian world of rooted, bounded material identities and collectivities may well be currently transcended by fluid, virtual, imaginary identities and collectivities. The logic of networking predicts as much, since it allows that strategic opposition is as much an option in the new technologies of communication, as strategies of accumulation. This is a very different world from that which Marx, Engels, Luxemburg, Lenin, Trotsky, Stalin and Lukács once inhabited. However, in so far as the desire to transcend material inequality is shared, it is reasonable to suppose that movements of resistance will persevere, albeit in ways which few *communards* or Bolsheviks would have comprehended. To be sure, Castells avows that under network society various collectivist resistance identities have emerged:

The communes of resistance defend their space, their places, against the placeless logic of the space of flows characterizing social domination in the Information Age. They claim their historic memory, and/or affirm the permanence of their values, against the dissolution of history in timeless time, and the celebration of the ephemeral in the culture of real virtuality. They use informational technology for people's horizontal communication, and communal prayer, while rejecting the new idolatry of technology, and preserving transcendent values against the deconstructing logic of self-regulating computer networks. (1997: 358)

This is an admirable counter-blast to the maxim of the new right that 'there is no alternative' to the market. But can networks achieve anything more substantial than episodic, and basically romantic, skirmishes against overwhelming odds? Castells (1997: 359) urges that radical groups still have everything to play for. The new power in network society lies in control over information. For it is data and symbolic representations around which societies now organize their institutions and people orientate life choices and conduct. But there is an imaginary quality to resistance politics organized around information flows, which is simply more free-floating and ambiguous than in the classic factory and trade disputes between labour and capital in the nineteenth and twentieth centuries. Castells would abhor the thought, but perhaps his analysis of resistance politics in network society points to the return of social banditry, which Hobsbawm (1964) and other writers identified as the main front of resistance before nineteenth-century collectivist organization fully solidified.

To some extent, Castells (1997: 357) gives licence to this type of inference by vehemently rejecting the thesis that the new resistance politics draws any sustenance from the former identities and struggles of the industrial era. As with other aspects of his general argument, Castells leaves the reader in no doubt that the world of industrial civil society has gone. Network society may not adequately encapsulate the characteristics of the new social order, since the essence of Castells's case is that the new order is still emerging. On the other hand, it does contain enough to support the proposition that we already live in a new world, which has bypassed most of the concepts and theories minted in the old world of Cartesian, industrial, civil society.

The question remains of where this radical recasting of the condition of collectivity leaves Castells in relation to Marx.

As we have already indicated, Castells operates within the Marxist tradition. Yet he is the veritable St Thomas of Marxists. For example, he doubts whether class analysis is a meaningful way of reading contemporary social relations; he claims that there are no stable power elites left in the world; he views himself as adrift in a sea of submerged or leaky nation states; he posits that irremediable vertical and horizontal splits in the relationship to the employment contract divide labour; and he recants the thesis that the contradiction between the forces and relations of production will result in the disintegration of capitalism. On the contrary, Castells points to the reintegration of capitalism at unparalleled levels of global penetration and control. He challenges traditional Marxist models of class struggle by insisting that the key nexus of interaction in contemporary society is between the net and the self (1998: 352). There is little in Castells's analysis to suggest that we are on the brink of an efflorescence of collectivism against the power of capital. Rather, his analysis of resistance emphasizes the centrality of the imaginary in the debate about politics. He coins the concept of 'real virtuality' (1996: 329–30) to refer to the saturation of the symbolic capital of the media world into the interstices of political debate and action. The media produces an inclusive, flexible hypertext by means of which the discursive conventions of everyday life are navigated. This goes right to the heart of whether a *materialist* understanding of politics remains tenable. To be sure, a very great virtue of Castells's analysis is that it is abundantly supported throughout with hard facts, plucked from a historical and comparative framework, to support the general, central theorems and predictions. Yet what is one to make of a form of Marxism which acknowledges the state of 'real virtuality' and presents this state as beyond transcendence? If the texture of thinking, feeling and aching is so catastrophically saturated by the imaginary, what material bases for solidarity remain? Castells (1998: 346) concludes that the fundamental cleavages in informational capitalism are:

1   The division between informational workers and generic labour.
2   The social exclusion of large segments of the labour market who are consigned to casualized work or long-term unemployment.
3   The separation between the market logic of global network flows and the human experience of workers' lives.

Within each category there is substantial internal fragmentation, making it hard to believe in the possibility that a radicalized collective subject capable of revolutionizing capitalism will emerge. Indeed, the radical identities that Castells recognizes, which are capable of challenging the organizing principles of network society, seem to be defined by their singularity of goal specific purpose and incompatibility. It is in the umbrageous ensemble of the Zapatistas, the Militia-Patriots, the Aum Shinrikyo, the militant feminists and the radical ecologists, wherein the front line of radical collectivism is now dimly assayed. However, even if one were to fully embrace the values of any one of these particularistic groupings, there are, at the present time, no sociological reasons for proposing imminent, or indeed immanent, unity between them. There is no rainbow coalition here, nor a coat of many colours waiting to be woven and worn as a mantle against the more implacable and tenacious forces of informational capitalism.

The theme of internal fragmentation and cultural and political dissonance is continued in Castells's analysis of globalization. Instead of identifying with the 'one world' camp of globalization theory, Castells correctly emphasizes the emergence of geo-political global power blocs: North America, Europe, the Asian Pacific (centred on Japan and the 'Asian Tiger' economies, Singapore, Hong Kong, South Korea and Taiwan) and China. Much of Africa and Latin America is analysed as belonging to a veritable 'fourth world' in which the political economy of the black holes of informational capitalism applies. What is striking about the discussion is the painstaking description of the cultural, political and economic peculiarities that characterize each power bloc. Although each is a part of network society, immense historical, cultural and political differences divide them. For example, Japan's corporate paternalism is regarded as an impediment to the economic restructuring of the labour force, and the ability of the nation to exploit the new business opportunities available in informational capitalism. Similarly, the emergence of a covert international criminal economy in segments of the former Soviet Union and Latin America, centred on drugs, prostitution and money laundering, is an obstacle to full regional integration into network society. Castells shows a much higher appreciation of the internal divisions within the world other than rival theories of global capitalism. For example, by comparison, Wallerstein's (1974) core/periphery/semi-periphery model of the world system exaggerates regional integration and the development gap between the three levels of the system. Castells is more successful in showing that some areas of the Bronx, Manchester and Naples have more in common, in ontology and lifestyle, with peripheral economies in the former Soviet Union and Latin America, than with the rest of the USA, UK or Italy. This has implications for understanding the real dynamics of global accumulation and resistance. In particular, it suggests that the categories of core, periphery and semi-periphery differentiated by Wallerstein, obscure relations of horizontal integration between the excluded.

Castells has produced a great work, arguably the most outstanding contribution to political economy in the last twenty years. Yet its optimistic conclusion that people can change things finally strikes a hollow note. Informational capitalism is a social and economic formation more decisively invasive and regimenting than Marcuse's (1964) one-dimensional society. Castells's analysis confirms what Gorbachev and other advocates of *perestroika* throughout the world feared, or at least half suspected: capitalism has won, and although it has changed its spots, it will take no survivors. Ruthless, ceaseless accumulation, despite any cost and despite any risk, is the conducting rod of the entire system. These tendencies can be moderated through political, cultural and religious resistance, but it is unlikely that they can be overturned by these means.

## Life politics and post-work society

A good deal of the new thinking about flexible capitalism boils down to the question of the redistribution of time and the associated consequences. The logic runs something like this: new technologies deliver greater productivity, but require less human labour. In the nineteenth century, the reduction of human labour time was regarded as both the dream of organized labour and the dividend of collectivist transformation (Hunnicutt, 1988). However, for much of the twentieth century, and practically all of the postwar period, workers, faced with the choice of earning more money or having more free time, have elected to boost their take-home pay. The result is the phenomenon of the overworked worker. According to Schor (1992), many workers now do not merely elect to work more overtime, they take two or three more part-time jobs in order to achieve the living standards they desire. Overwork is associated with higher levels of stress, tension and illness, and the multiplication of dysfunctional relations in the family and society. In addition, the drive to accumulate poses a hazard to the environment. The attrition of the ozone layer, BSE (bovine spongiform encephalopathy), urban-industrial pollution and the decay of the green belt dramatically illustrate the horrific effects of overwork. The main incentive to transform free time into paid labour is no longer the desire to achieve subsistence. The welfare reforms of the twentieth century may have been eroded by the retrenchment of the new right in the 1980s and 1990s, but the welfare state has not been abolished.

For Schor (1992), people submit to overwork so as to maximize involvement with consumer culture. The argument echoes a wider thesis in sociology that lifestyle has passed from a production (work) centred regime to a consumption (leisure) centred regime (Slater, 1994; Ritzer, 1998). Be that as it may, Schor (1992), Aronowitz and Di Fazio (1994), Beck (1992, 1999) and other writers, now maintain that the marginal utility of intensifying the pursuit for accumulation, without regard to personal health, social well-being or environmental integrity, is no longer attractive. The quality of life is impaired by overwork, time famine and anxieties about the social and physical environment (Pahl, 1995; Hochschild, 1997).

André Gorz (1982, 1984) has long been associated with the proposition that the work ethic is redundant. He developed a new 'politics of time' as a strategy to increase the component of socially useful labour in society and to combat stress, tension and social dysfunctions. There is no need to detain ourselves here with the details (but see Rojek, 2000: 197–206). The point to emphasize is that many writers now share Gorz's view that the work ethic is no longer required by contemporary processes of production and, by extension, social and economic policy urgently needs to address the question of the redistribution of time.

Aronowitz and Cutler (1998) refer to the coming of 'post-work society'. Since this concept assumes the extirpation of the work ethic, it raises the question of the form of ethics in post-work conditions. By and large, Aronowitz and Cutler (1998) follow Gorz, in holding that post-work will augment socially useful labour. By this term is meant unpaid palliative and caring functions which contribute to environmental and physical integrity. Caring for children, the aged, those in ill-health, and tending to the ecological balance are all subsumed herein. The introduction of a minimum wage, and the expansion of public health, education and welfare services, will underwrite this redistribution of time, by liberating people from the necessity to work in paid employment. The cost of achieving this will be accomplished by the increased dividend produced through automation and the scaling down of the labour requirement in the public sector as paid labour is transferred to socially useful (voluntary) labour.

Gorz acknowledges that such a change in the fundamental mind-set in how people under capitalism conduct their lives may require external pressures, in the form of an enhanced state, or quasi-autonomous, regulatory agency. For their part, Aronowitz and Cutler honour the predilections of the young Marx, and point to the spontaneous transfer of the functions of labour to the commonweal.

Cautionary notes must surely resonate at this point. For it seems naïve to suggest that centuries of competitive individualism can be replaced by a sort of spontaneous humanism. Humans, who for generations have been schooled in the 'philosophy of money' (Simmel, 1978), are hardly likely to abandon lifestyles and values built around inequality and monetary status overnight. Gorz's suggestion, that some sort of external force will be required to ensure that labour complies with the new regime of unpaid socially useful work, probably requires a more pronounced place in his writing. Moreover, the evidence does not support the proposition that workers, trade unions or governments in the West are electing to reduce the salience of the work ethic and paid employment in society. The stigma of unemployment and poverty provides a measure of how central paid employment and participation in consumer culture remains in the construction of identity.

Setting these problems to one side, it is remarkable how much thinking on the ethical reformation of late capitalist, or informational capitalist, presupposes that these formations are either already in a 'post-work' condition or about to move into one. Traditional sociological concepts of social divisions are treated as a *passé* genre of analysis. Instead, new forms of universalism are asseverated as capturing the 'late modern' condition.

Consider Giddens's (1991: 214–31) concept of 'life politics', which he defines as:

> The politics of actualization, in the context of the dialectic of the local and the global and the emergence of the internally referential systems of modernity. (1991: 242)

Life politics suggests that most people, or at least a significant minority, have the time and resources to engage in systematic life-planning and life-monitoring exercises. The problem of time famine, identified by Hochschild (1997) and other writers, is not addressed. Instead 'life politics' implies that society has already, to a visible degree, liberated itself from traditional impediments of economic scarcity and routine. For in order to be self-actualizing and reflexive in the fullest sense of the terms, individuals must enjoy relative autonomy from the requirement to work for a paid income. Giddens (1991) links the formation of life politics with what he calls 'the pure relationship'. He defines the latter as a relationship

> in which external criteria have become dissolved: the relationship exists solely for whatever rewards that relationship as such can deliver. In the context of the pure relationship, trust can be mobilized only by a process of mutual disclosure. Trust, in other words, can by definition no longer be anchored in criteria outside the relationship itself – such as criteria of kinship, social duty or traditional obligation . . . the pure relationship has to be reflexively controlled over the long term, against the backdrop of external tensions, and transformations. (1991: 6)

Examples are romantic love or the absolute fidelity of close friendship. Since life politics is conceived as a systematic divesting of personal repressions, the implication is that pure relationships will flourish as life politics is extended. Life politics and pure relationships are fundamentally about self-discovery. They signify a stage in development in which people are no longer prepared to delegate decisions about nature, nation state, reproduction and lifestyle to government. Life politics signals a new intensity of social activism in the body politic. However, as we shall see more clearly below, Giddens regards this activism to be relayed and refined not only through the formal mechanisms of government, but also through new informal 'subpolitical' networks of pluralist interest groups.

There is much in this analysis that is refreshing. By posing the question of life politics and pure relationships, Giddens rightly submits that traditional sociological concepts deriving from enquiry into social divisions may not be adequate tools to study the flexible, mobile lifestyles and conditions of the present day. Traditionally, class, feminist and race analysis has emphasized the value of collectivism in resisting social divisions. Giddens's account problematizes many aspects of these traditional readings of social action, notably the proposition that collective subjects are agents of change. Although he is critical of the dichotomy between left and right, Giddens (1990, 1991) is justifiably wary of the conclusion that the age of emancipatory politics has come to an end. He argues that the goalposts of what emancipatory politics constitutes will always shift as the pattern of human development changes. Inasmuch as problems of scarcity universalize consciousness of limits to human existence, social movements will always spring up to try and overcome these limits, in whatever way problems of scarcity are defined.

Having noted this, there is a genuine sense in which the introduction of life politics assumes that many of the orthodox goals of emancipatory politics have been achieved. Beck (1999), who is a fellow traveller with Giddens in this respect, argues that life politics issues are intrinsic to capitalism. That is, their novelty must not be exaggerated. However, they became significant as a general political force in the expectations explosion of the 1960s and 1970s. It was at this time that questions of the environment, animal rights, gender, race and human rights around the world began to displace the concerns of traditional party politics from the political agenda. At this time also, a new set of questions emerged around issues relating to the transformation of tradition and nature. Globalization and new agendas of personal transformation developed from this structural condition.

On the whole, these questions were formulated, disseminated and refined through the system of 'subpolitics'. By 'subpolitics', Beck (1999: 91) means the range of 'activity, arguing, bargaining, deception, separating, uniting, loving and betrayal', which is conducted beyond the officially classified political sphere, and beyond the legitimate rules of formal politics. This is a somewhat imprecise formulation, for it suggests that subpolitics covers nothing less than the rest of life beyond the sphere of formal politics. In one sense, Beck's notion does little more than restate, in different terms, the critical maxim informing much writing, debate and protest throughout the 1960s, 1970s and 1980s, that 'the personal is political'. However, it also maintains that the agenda of formal politics has gradually been revised to address the concerns articulated and promoted by the counter-culture.

One implication of the thesis of the rise of subpolitics is that party politics has declined in significance. Subpolitics revolves around issues and choices which the officially prescribed, formal political system either marginalizes or treats negligibly. This is a huge question, but at its heart is the subject of identity. Life politics suggests a shift from donatory models of identity, in which the state lays down the parameters of behaviour, practice and personal values, to self-starting models in which individuals and groups creatively innovate and proselytize, as it were, 'from below'. Giddens (1991: 224–5) argues that existential and moral issues inevitably predominate here. Included among such issues are the dilemmas of pursuing a tenable ethical framework in interpersonal relations and relations with nature; devising personal and interpersonal methods of risk

management; developing non-instrumental life strategies in the conduct of
co-presence; and devising an ethically sustainable means for the scientific
manipulation of biology. Giddens and Beck hold that subpolitics is destined
to assume greater prominence in the general organization of everyday life.
The old political power blocs of left and right can no longer encapsulate the
most salient issues of everyday life. Social movements, single-issue groups,
non-government organizations and other associations of citizens, will
therefore play a more pronounced role in politics at both local and world
levels. The rationale behind this prediction is that subpolitics is a more
personal and compelling system through which to develop the issues and
strategies of life politics. It does not follow from this that subpolitics will
replace party politics. Traditional party politics and the nation state remain
significant in the present day world. But neither can accommodate to, or
adequately represent, the variegated identity and lifestyle issues represented
in the arena of subpolitics.

These arguments assume the magnification of discretionary time in
order to permit palliative, environmentally friendly and socially useful
labour functions. If that is not yet the generalized condition of labour, it is
the condition already attained by large segments in the information,
knowledge, communication and entertainment sectors. Flexible accumulation requires flexible workers, which in turn permits the extension of flexi
and 'modular' work time arrangements (Urry, 2000: 129). Workers in this
position are already preponderant in shaping the agendas of various non-
government organizations, such as the non-executive boards of national
and local charities, sports clubs, local government authorities and 'social
entrepreneur' projects. Now they are spreading into the field of formal
politics too.

Giddens (1997: 4) is understandably wary of the proposition that a
virtual class, consisting of designers, consultants, programmers and multimedia analysts, is now ascendant. He prefers to stress that telecommunications and computers cannot occur without social interaction, so that the
metaphor of 'virtual' class is misleading. Nevertheless, he argues that 'new
money' is qualitatively different from the established middle-class
formation. Specifically, their orientation to politics is global, not national;
they prioritize innovation and flexibility over routine and continuity; and
they reject both market- and state-based models of social and economic
management. For Giddens these conditions constitute a break with class
politics as it has traditionally been represented in the postwar struggle
between left and right. His discussion (1991: 224–7) of what life politics
concretely means for the organization of personality is somewhat nebulous.
He seeks to connect it to what one might call a fourfold transformation in
personality in late Modernity. The four fronts of transformation postulated
by Giddens are:

1   The transformation of the relationship between self and nature, caused
    by the emergence of risk society and the 'end of nature' debate.

2   The transformation of the relationship between self and biology, caused by bio-technology and new possibilities for the human programming of biological processes through bio-technology.
3   The transformation of the relationship between self and space, produced by globalization, the decline of the nation state and real time accumulation.
4   The transformation of the relationship between self and morality, caused by new strategies of self-actualization and the debate over the rights of persons.

This quartet of transformations is regarded to have disabled fixed and hierarchical constructs of identity and replaced them with more mobile, flexible lifestyle orientations and created fresh requirements of direct, personal involvement in politics. The political significance of this transformation is concentrated in the fields of nature, reproduction, global systems and citizenship. Thus, life politics demands a new political and ethical sensitivity to, and involvement with, the environment; the rights and principles in bio-genetic engineering; the transnational relations and institutions that globalization is calling forth; and human rights and responsibilities. Increased social activisim is, in one sense, not really a personal choice. The transformations between self, nature, reproduction, global systems and citizenship are so profound that contracting out is not an option. If industry threatens the global environment and science acquires control over human biology, the repercussions are all encompassing, and no one can ignore them. However, while there is a technical sense in which this is obviously true, the real question is the nature of the values that the personal confrontation with nature, reproduction, global systems and citizenship will articulate.

Giddens (1998) has tried to kick-start the debate by outlining the core values and political programme of what he calls 'third way politics' (see Figure 10.1).

Giddens regards the third way as the *renewal* of social democracy, so it is perhaps not surprising that there is little which is genuinely new in either list.

| Core values | Political programme |
|---|---|
| Equality | The radical centre |
| Freedom | New democratic state |
| Protection for the vulnerable | Active civil society |
| No rights without | Democratic family |
| responsibilities | New mixed economy |
| Democracy | The inclusive society |
| Cosmopolitan pluralism | Social investment state |
| Philosophic conservatism | Cosmopolitan nation |
|  | Cosmopolitan democracy |

Figure 10.1   *The third way*

The keystones of the third way are: open and accountable decision making, the qualified decentralization of power, recognition of multiculturalism and hybridity, global orientation, social inclusion and the revival of the family under the rubric of 'the democratic family'. One can readily see them as a direct reaction to the resurgence of neo-liberalism and market fundamentalism, during the Anglo-American turn to the right between 1979 and 1996. But one can also understand why many feminists, left-wing revisionists and neo-liberals feel that their ideas have been hijacked. Giddens (1998: 145–7), who is in favour of some form of global governance, submits that third way values can have an impact globally via bilateral and multilateral agreements. He asserts that 'there already is global governance and . . . global civil society' (1998: 140). As evidence he (ibid.) cites the growth of transnational government organizations. At the beginning of the twentieth century there were some 20 international government organizations and 180 transnational non-government organizations. By the end of the century there were 300 of the former and 5,000 of the latter. Beyond doubt, the boundaries of the nation state are becoming more permeable, and transnational forms of interdependence are solidifying. However, on the whole we side with Gellner (1997: 102–7) who insisted that the ideology of nationalism has contributed to a powerful fetishization of landscape and culture which reacts to deterritorialization as a pernicious tendency. The blossoming of multilateral trade agreements and agencies to control drugs, ecological disaster, poverty and the arms trade has been a laudable feature of statecraft in the last hundred years. But it has not produced the brotherhood of man. Nor, for Gellner, is this a likely outcome. He (1997) regarded nationalism as a deeply rooted feature of politics and culture. From at least the fifteenth century, nationalism was the motor force and principal means of legitimation behind the spurts toward imperialism pursued by the European nations. Similarly, with Barrington Moore (1970), he emphasized the significance of the ideology of nationalism in the industrialization programmes of the nineteenth and twentieth centuries. Gellner's (1997) study stresses the persistence and adaptability of nationalism in the face of the various tendencies towards globalization and information capitalism. To be fair, Giddens (1998: 31–2) recognizes a two-way effect of globalization on nationalism. Globalization operates to 'push away' from nationalism and the nation state by ceding power to transnational corporations and international government agencies. At the same time, he recognizes that it 'pushes down' on the consciousness of place and tradition and creates new opportunities for regenerating local identities. The resurgence of Scottish nationalism in the UK, the Catalan independence movement in Spain and the move for a free Quebec in Canada, are all current examples.

Giddens therefore absents himself from the proposition that the nation state is disappearing. Rather, he adapts Foucault's notion of governmentality to demonstrate that globalization is changing the configuration of power within and between nation states, in ways which are beyond the ability of any single nation state to control. However, it is also clear that he regards the central processes of the third way, namely the 'new individualism', life politics and the inclusive society, to be rampant throughout the world. Globalization is blowing a winnowing wind through the ramparts, turrets and corridors of nationalism and the nation state, culminating in a more rational, co-operative system of governance. We shall return to the question of rationality later in the discussion.

At this stage, we want to turn to the proposition that we are living through a major break or rupture in social and economic conditions. In relation to the subject of social development, both Giddens and Beck are appropriately scornful of loose postmodernism which asserts apocalyptic, thoroughgoing change (Baudrillard, 1983a and b; Lyotard, 1984). Elsewhere, Giddens (1990: 150–73) uses the term 'radicalized modernity' to distinguish his position from that of unreconstituted postmodernity. Briefly, radicalized modernity:

1  Retains commitment to espistemology and hence, to the rational adjudication of competing positions and problem solving.
2  Regards social development as producing centripetal tendencies as well as centrifugal ones.
3  Advocates an active, knowledgeable role for individual agents, rather than a passive, docile one.
4  Rejects cultural and historical relativism in favour of a modified thesis that universal truth claims are irresistible.
5  Replaces the notions of transparency and depthlessness with an approach which regards everyday life as an unfinished, complex set of initiatives and responses to abstract systems, involving appropriation as well as loss.
6  Reinforces a rationalist interventionist stance in the global world order that is committed to building reflexive, efficient, inclusive institutions of management.

While this distances Giddens from postmodern excess in relation to the question of social transformation, it also serves to accentuate the impression that he believes that 'radicalized modernity' is qualitatively distinct from earlier formations of modernity. This is particularly evident in the area of politics which, Giddens regards as a sort of weathervane of wider social, cultural and economic changes. He and Beck submit that classical social democracy (old labour) and neo-liberalism (the new right), were associated with political and class formations that have disintegrated. Both state and market models of government and society proved to be incapable of responding to the complexity of challenges posed by new technologies, social movements and the general trend of globalization. The appeal of the third way is that it claims to have retreated from custom and tradition and to offer a pragmatic, global, ethical set of solutions to central life problems. The new dynamic of social activism is combining left with right, and breaking the association between social democracy and labour and neo-liberalism and management, which dominated and shaped the old politics. It is, however, also conceived as something new, rather than as a temporary alliance between fractured power blocs.

The shock of the new, and the sense of moving away from tradition have, of course, long been recognized as defining features of modernity (Berman, 1982). What is refreshing and constructive about the forms of social analysis presented by Giddens and Beck is that they seek to go beyond a thesis that recognizes the omnipresence of change, to postulate the main traits of reconfiguration in society. However, several studies of lifestyle and power suggest that Giddens and Beck overstate the case that there has been a fundamental break with the past and this raises questions of the salience of the concepts of life politics and the pure relationship as waymarks of social reconfiguration. We will re-examine these concepts presently, but here it is necessary to summarize the case against the notion that values and lifestyle have decisively broken with the past. Three issues are at stake: the nature of discretionary time; the relationship of the new service class with prior class and status formations; and the real direction of social change. Let us examine each in more detail.

Forging life politics and pure relationships requires the reallocation of discretionary time. 'Freedom's children' as Beck (1999: 9), rather controversially, calls subjects of the third way, are people with the work flexibility or free time to participate in social activism. Yet elsewhere, sociological research insists upon the lack of discretionary time and the constraints on freedom in contemporary society. For example, Hochschild's (1997) study provides a wealth of empirical data to support the proposition that the work ethic remains pivotal in the organization of lifestyle. She researched work and leisure lifestyle in a Fortune 500 company situated in a green-field site. 'Amerco' is described by Hochschild as a thriving enterprise, with a vigorous global orientation and good labour relations. The company practises a 'family friendly' policy, offering child-care, emergency back-up child-care, before- and after-school programmes, and referral services for the elderly. Flexi-work schedules are also encouraged and paid maternity leave for up to four weeks before, and six weeks after, the birth or adoption of a child.

The company appears to be the very model of the global, flexible, mobile, inclusive entrepreneurial spirit described by Giddens (1998) as one of the keystones of the new individualism and third way politics. Yet Hochschild's (1997) study demonstrates that taking advantage of company policy, by taking the discretionary time due to the employee, was more problematic than first appearances allowed. Workers were subject to conflicting desires. On the one hand, they wanted to take advantage of flexi-time arrangements and spend more time with their families. Against this, they were committed to achieving budgetary requirements at work, by meeting delivery dates for orders and assuring well-timed and relevant marketing and production processes. Top executives saw themselves as setting an example by coming into work early and staying longer. Their bonuses were related to achieving growth targets and this translated into high undertakings to subject them-selves to the flow of work time. Workers lower down in the hierarchy faced a different set of dilemmas. Many were women, employed on part-time contracts, who were attracted to 'Amerco' by the family-friendly work policies. However, they soon realized that the extent of work required could not be absorbed by the hours of the part-time employment contract. So many found themselves staying after hours and taking work home with them. Other workers decided that they preferred to work overtime or achieve bonus targets by longer hours of unpaid work. This confirms Schor's (1992) finding, that most workers will choose longer hours and more pay over shorter hours and less pay. Research in the UK indicates that one third of men of eligible age work over 50 hours per week, a rate which is higher than in any other EC member nation (Cooper, 2000). Cooper's study of 5,000 managers, from chief executive to junior rank, found that half of them work most evenings and a third work most weekends.

Hochschild's (1997) general finding is that most workers at 'Amerco' experience 'time famine'. That is, their discretionary leisure and family time is continuously harried with work or work concerns. In trying to square the circle, many workers resort to 'time thievery' (Hochschild, 1997: 144). That is, they use vacation days to handle family emergencies rather than take time off work. The overall picture is of a conveyor belt of work-related activity and para-work relations, that leaves little time for the 'life planning', 'reflexive', 'self-monitoring' arrangements described by Giddens (1991) in his discussion of 'life politics' and the new individualism. By the term 'para-work relations', we mean the accumulation of non-work tasks that occurs in discretionary time, which are attached to the goal of supporting, enhancing and achieving work performance. Examples include socializing with import-ant clients, monitoring market changes through the information and com-munications network of TV and the internet, drafting reports and business plans at home and reading corporate strategy documents.

To be fair, Giddens acknowledges that the work ethic is tenacious. In an interview (1997: 4) he refers to the

> peculiar economy of time in the world. You have . . . people like me, who work all the time; as you know, the new technologies and the instantaneous connec-tions and the total connections they give you, mean that there is no escape. So you are caught within a system (I find it pleasurable in its way) that is a bit like endless work. That's an oppression of time it seems to me. And then at the bottom you get people who have no work at all in the global economy and that's another form of oppression of time of course.

Needless to say, Giddens is not, for a moment, implying equivalence in these two forms of experiencing time. What he is saying is that interesting, well-paid labour quickly develops into an addiction for those who have access to it, and is coveted by those from whom it is segmented. Whither the work ethic in this line of analysis? And how does it bear out the life politics thesis, which is predicated on the increase of discretionary time?

Hochschild (1997) and Schor (1992) would perhaps find much to agree with in Giddens's outline of life politics. All of these writers would concur that establishing the right balance between work, leisure and family life is desirable both for the individual and society. Yet whereas Giddens fudges the issue, by championing life politics as an immanent tendency, Hochschild and Schor maintain that the work ethic remains triumphant in the organization of everyday life. Even where companies make provision to increase discretionary time, the internal status battles of the workforce, and the pressures of market competition, produce strong pressures for workers to work longer.

The research exercise in British universities can surely be referred to in this context. Under current arrangements, every four years, the Higher Education Funding Council monitors the research output of individuals, and departments. Academics are required to present their four best pieces of work, over a four-year stretch, as part of the Department's bid for higher funding. To some extent, departments support research by giving research-active staff sabbatical leave or teaching cover. However, this is unpopular with many staff, who find themselves informally defined as 'non research active' and students who find it impossible to locate professors and research-active lecturers in term time. Research-active staff may appear to be the beneficiaries of the current system, and, certainly, many exploit it to increase discretionary time and stay away from the university for as long as possible. However, they are also under intense pressure to produce, not merely four pieces of work over a four-year period, but four pieces which are unequivocally of national or, preferably, international significance in their discipline. The research exercise compels academics to suffer the 'time bind' that Hochschild (1997) argues prevails throughout society. In sum, it is a situation which Weber (1904), who popularized sociological interest in the work ethic nearly a century ago, would find entirely familiar. It raises the concern that Giddens, Beck and Urry may, in fundamental respects, be exaggerating the thesis of a break with the past.

These concerns are fuelled if we turn to the question of the relationship between the new service class and established class and status formations. Savage et al. (1992) recognize the emergence of the new service class as a significant development. However, they urge that the proposition that this has changed pre-existing social divisions should be treated with caution. Private property remains the key to class formation and consciousness, since it provides wealth that frees the individual from the obligation to engage in pecuniary labour. While the new programmers, public relations executives, net gurus, information technicians, media and communications staff of the new service class often command high salaries and control cultural capital which is highly valued in society, their influence remains bound by the vagaries of the labour market. Workers in the new service class often exhibit a pragmatic attitude to social values and politics. The sense of common class consciousness is weak, and sentiments of collectivity are often more highly developed along functional lines. Thus, managers, designers and skilled technicians and the film and media industry may acknowledge a degree of common culture, lifestyle and value orientation, but one cannot infer from this a crossover to their counterpoints in public relations, book publishing, information technology and pop music. Savage et al. (1992) present a picture which allows for the recognition of common strategic interests between service class strata, but also posits cleavages and antinomies of interest. Neither Giddens (1998) nor Beck (1999) would necessarily dissent from this analysis. Indeed, Giddens (1998: 104–5) directly calls for increased social and economic equality and, fairly conventionally, postulates that the 'social investment' state is the key to social inclusion. Elsewhere, Giddens (1994: 98) notes that 20 per cent of the world's population live in conditions of absolute poverty and uses this to underline the profound limitations of policies of social and economic inclusion which stop short at the walls of the nation state.

Without doubt there is a consciousness, beyond rhetoric, in contemporary culture which recognizes the abomination of third world hunger. Moreover, the expansion of aid through the voluntary sector, to say nothing of the highly public ventures of Comic Relief, Red Nose Day and Live Aid, supports the view that informational capitalism can be used to achieve a measure of equitable reallocation in resource distribution. At the same time, the evidence to suggest that there has been a 'profound' structural transformation in social and cultural values is negligible. When members of the new service class or successful, upwardly mobile achievers are interviewed about their social values and deepest concerns, two things regularly emerge.

First, workers complain of being overworked and feeling insecure in their work. Cooper's (2000) study of British managers found that 50 per cent undergo major work restructuring once a year. The constant stream of new technologies and mergers makes downsizing and delayering a perpetual threat. Insecurity and overwork engender destructive relationships with families and high health risks. In January 2000, the British government sponsored a 'Work-Life Manual', published by the Industrial Society. The document exhorted employers to practise family-friendly labour policies and encourage a balanced attitude to work. All the signs are that this will be an uphill struggle. It is estimated that, at present, only 5 per cent of employers meet the manual's work-life recommendations. Furthermore, as Hochschild (1997), Schor (1992) and other writers make plain, the great enticements of consumer culture, the status distinction hierarchy and the genuine threat to employment posed by economic and technological transformation, combine to exert powerful leverage upon workers to work harder.

Secondly, among achievers, insecurity is almost matched by guilt. Pahl's (1995) study of the politics of success and identity formation in Britain found a widespread feeling that success was provisional or undeserved. Ehrenreich's (1989) study of the 'fear of failure' in American society supports this finding. In the face of significant monetary success, feelings of unworthiness and inauthenticity perhaps reflect the realization that monetary values are shallow and unstable. However, they do not seem to translate into a mass movement of management staff away from boardrooms and executive desks to voluntary work in soup kitchens and refuge centres. Both Pahl (1995) and Ehrenreich (1989) found little evidence that feelings of estrangement from work or the politics of success produce statistically significant increases in social activism. A more common response is to remain inert in a well paid job or live off capital, and to retreat from the day-to-day problems of wider society. There is a powerful sentiment among these individuals, that the problems of national and global inequality are classified as too great for any group or association of groups to solve. While they are frequently generous in making voluntary donations to private causes dedicated to combat inequality, they leave the question of more fundamental interventions to the established system of formal government.

What this research undeniably shows is that successful workers in the knowledge, information and communication sectors possess more flexibility in the allocation of time than is available to generic labour. For these workers, especially in relation to specific strategic or pragmatic work and life issues, the dividing line between paid labour and life politics may indeed be thin. However, to suggest that they constitute a first wave, or, more egregiously, a majority, which has decisively broken with the politics of individual possession and competitive advantage that characterized the past, is surely fanciful. Life politics may be an increasingly prominent feature of the rhetoric of advanced industrial society, and subpolitics has unquestionably channelled issues that emerged in the counter-culture into the arena of formal politics. However, Western society remains overwhelmingly dominated by corporate culture and business corporations. These institutions ineluctably operate to attain monopolistic or quasi-monopolistic control of market share. The greening of corporate culture, and the raising of business awareness of problems of inequality and global poverty, are undeniable facts of the last twenty years. But just as undeniable is the responsibility, perceived by most chief executives and managing directors as primary, to maximize return on investment to shareholders. Accumulation remains the overriding goal of business activity. As the demonstrations against the World Trade Organization meeting in Seattle, in 1999, highlighted, both corporations and campaigners regard business commitment to ecological and social concerns as subsidiary to the profit motive. Third way politics advances all sorts of arguments to enjoin corporations to play a more enlightened role in redistributive justice, but it cannot delink the ultimate responsibility that managers have to answer to shareholders, without prejudicing its wider commitments to enterprise initiative, and the mixed economy. So long as this remains true, doubts will always remain about the scale, drive and significance of corporate participation in social activism and equality.

This brings us to our third general criticism of the Giddens/Beck approach to action and solidarity, which has to do with the issue of the real direction of social change. For generations, a prominent theme in sociology has been the recrudescence of irrationalism in notional conditions of rationally informed administrative orders. Adorno's (1995) wonderful analysis of the *LA Times* astrology column, and its influence in manufacturing consent, is a case in point. So too is the work of Foucault (1961, 1981, 1988) on the antinomies of institutions of normative coercion, and Bauman (1989) on the fearful disjunction between means and ends in the Nazi Holocaust. Beck's (1992) study of risk society might be taken as evidence of work which deepens and enriches our understanding of this question. For what does it postulate, if not the imminence of the global catastrophe and decomposition of social order that, we argued earlier, haunted the sociological imagination, from the infant days of classical political economy? However, the thrust of the third way arguments is that human actors are reflexive and rational, and that rational solutions can be found to risk, identity crises, poverty and other current problems. We have no quarrel with the argument that human beings are rational and reflexive, although we would place a greater emphasis on unconscious influence in personal and collective life. Equally, antipathy towards the cultural relativism and passivity of some versions of post-modernism is justified (Rojek and Turner, 1993). We agree with Giddens and Beck, that contemporary conditions have not dissolved epistemology altogether and that the social construction of systematic knowledge about the human condition is not precluded by cultural difference. Having said that, we would assign a more pronounced role to irrationality in everyday life. Castells's (1997) analysis of millenarianism in the terrorist activity of the Aum Shinrikyo and the revival of the far right in the US in the form of the American Patriot and Militant movements are cases in point. In addition, the revival of Islamic fundamentalism, and the popularity of new age and spiritualist beliefs in the West, testify to the persistence of theological and Manichaean belief systems.

In stressing the growth of self-monitoring, reflexivity and rational problem solving, Giddens and Beck are perhaps pointing to a specific kind of Western rationality, one which is moreover, pre-eminent among workers in the knowledge, information, communication and administrative sectors of the economy. Indeed, one can sometimes almost detect a Hegelian tone in Giddens and Beck, regarding their hopes for the ascent of life politics. Our own emphasis would be on the proposition that social divisions still divide, albeit in modified ways. Life chances, health, income, knowledge, belief and values are enmeshed within textures of class, race, gender and status distinctions. It is in the nature of these distinctions to change. Further, we may be much more reflexive about how they operate in social life than we were even twenty years ago. However, this does not stop us from being caught up in the dilemmas which they continually pose.

### Life politics and pure relationships

Webster (1997: 120), in the context of a thoughtful and generally appreciative extended review article, inveighs against what he takes to be the imprecision in the concept of 'information' in Castells's work. Webster differentiates three usages of the term in Castells's *magnum opus*:

1  Computerized technologies that transform labour activities.
2  Systems of communication that co-ordinate labour activities.
3  Strata of specialized 'symbolic analysts' who interpret and manage flow in network society.

For Webster, communication rather than information is the key to network society – the point being, of course, that communication is inherently ambivalent, whereas the concept of information suggests hard and fast divisions. By implication Castells is criticized for oversimplifying the ambiguity and layered contextuality of life relationships in the age of informational capitalism.

It is an interesting observation, which can certainly be extended to Giddens's treatment of life politics and pure relationships. Unless it is contextualized in social, economic, cultural and psychological dimensions, 'life politics' is a fairly imprecise concept. The confrontations between the powerful and the less powerful are concrete, and our understanding of how their meanings are negotiated and applied must also be concrete. Of course this does not exclude the usage of the term 'life politics' at a metatheoretical level, to signify reflexivity, self-monitoring, flexibility and globalism. However, by limiting the concept to this level, as Giddens tends to do, the diverse and uneven forms that reflexivity, self-monitoring, flexibility and globalism assume in the social dynamics of relations of superordination and subordination, metropolis and village, office and shop floor, will be glossed over. The result is that the claim made for life politics as a harbinger of universal relationships is over-extended.

Certainly many factors in contemporary life coalesce to preclude or inhibit the reflexive, self-monitoring processes upon which, Giddens argues, life politics is predicated. For example, time famine encourages a pragmatic attitude to data. Individuals absorb information that they judge to be directly pertinent to their life and work goals, and screen out the rest. Given the data glut produced by informational capitalism, reflexivity and monitoring are inevitably partial and contingent. Perforce then, individuals are thrown back upon experts to supply specialized diagnosis of personal problems. The increasing prominence of professionals and technicians in health, financial management, therapy and impression management partly reflects the extent of time famine in the service class. Sections of this class allocate disposable income to manage life politics issues by proxy, in ways which are quite contrary to the hypothesis of life politics.

The concept of life politics implies both self-reliance and reflexive co-dependence. For it suggests that informed, responsible and rational individuals will exchange representative government for self-management and pool resources in problem solving. There are undoubtedly signs of this in public demands for new levels of openness and accountability in elected government, and in the vitality of subpolitics as a political force. Conversely, time famine pushes individuals to cede substantial power to specialists in many focal points of identity management and peaceful co-existence. In Marxist sociology, living in separation from others was a characteristic sign of alienation. In the high tech, public relations realm of informational capitalism, living *through* others, is perhaps, becoming a more significant form of self-estrangement. For, *pace* Levinas and Bauman, while you might, psychologically speaking, be able to discount the generalized and concrete other in everyday life, specialist advisers have importunate force, over-turning your serenity with a letter of bad tidings, or filling you with fore-boding about the precarious nature of your (temporarily) able-bodied and solvent status. The broader issue is this: when accountants instruct you on your financial matters, doctors issue prescriptions to help you cope, builders advise on lagging, roof repairs and preventative measures against subsidence and therapists provide a ten-step programme for getting in touch with yourself, questions of autonomy and self-direction assume an undeniably piquant quality in lifestyle management and planning. For the service class, the corollary of Bauman's *living with contingency* is the condition of *living by proxy.*

Interestingly enough, Giddens (1991) warns against leaning too heavily upon professional expertise. As he puts it:

> Expert problem-solving endeavours tend very often to be measured by their capacity to define issues with increasing clarity or precision (qualities that in turn have the effect of producing further specialization). However, the more a given problem is placed precisely in focus, the more surrounding areas of knowledge become blurred for the individuals concerned, and the less likely they are able to foresee the consequences of their contributions beyond the particular sphere of application . . . expertise is increasingly more narrowly focused, and is liable to produce unintended and unforeseen outcomes. (1991: 31)

Undeniably so, and yet where does this leave professional expertise, or the heightened reflexivity, by which Giddens sets such store, as an asset for the development of life politics? The analysis here is neo-Weberian, but the force of the third way/life politics thesis is that neo-Weberianism can be transcended through purposeful reflexive action. Our argument is that the two adjoining positions point in different directions and the concept of life politics is merely a substitute for a thoroughgoing account of concrete political values and types of social action. In particular, the new indi-vidualism and the inclusive society are presented as enabling forces which represent widespread social convictions. However, if our argument in Chapter 3, on 'Disorder' is correct, identity and civil society are vulnerable to dislocation because transgression is implicit in all human relationships. While the concept of governance figures prominently in Giddens's analysis, he rarely addresses questions of crime and deviance in any detail. In passages where he does confront these subjects his approach is generally anodyne. For example, he advocates the regeneration of the community and collaborative policing as the solution to crime (1998: 86–8), and he

reduces questions of perversion to problems of epistemology and nomenclature (1992: 32–4). Giddens has failed to provide an adequate theory of
deviance or to recognize the significance of transgression in personal and
interpersonal relations. One could develop another version of life politics in
which egoism, accumulation, possessive individualism and thrill-seeking are
pre-eminent. Katz's (1986) work on the seduction of crime can be read in
this way.

   Giddens and Beck frequently bracket life politics with the new individualism. Third way philosophy envisages committed, flexible, responsive
and reflexive individuals who recognize new forms of belonging in globalization, the inclusive society and cosmopolitan virtue. Post-Cartesian bio-
engineering extends the idea of the replaceable body, and potentially lays
the foundations for revolutionizing traditional concepts of the life cycle and
social action. It also creates enormous business opportunities for patenting
crucial technologies of cell and tissue replacement and harvesting organs in
the poorer regions of the world. Of course, Beck and Giddens are concerned to establish ethical principles that ensure that advances in bio-
engineering are applied responsibly and equably. However, their account of
the new individualism does not deal adequately with the possibilities for
new individuation and control. In their account, the new individualism
refers to reflexive, flexible and ethically responsible personal values. It is
predicated on high levels of personal autonomy. The new individuation
may be defined as the social characteristics which structure the allocation of
scarce resources of replaceable technology. Chief among these, of course, is
money, although kinship and friendship networks are also important. In
general, new individuation implies new ways of conferring status upon
individuals. Status divisions constitute a ranking system in social interaction, and this in turn functions as the basis for regulating personal autonomy. Just as Bauman's (1998) account of postmodern ethics is weakest
when it asserts that 'care for the other' should be the ethical principle
governing interpersonal relations under postmodernity, the analysis of
Giddens and Beck is most nebulous and evasive when it comes to par-
ticularizing the content of ethics in the third way. How are resources to
replacement technology to be allocated? In what ways are corporations and
governments going to ensure that those without high levels of disposable
income benefit? Can unethical practices of organ harvesting be effectively
combated? The fiscal and policing implications of these questions are
extensive and they are not satisfactorily explored by Giddens or Beck.
Again, the failure to develop an adequate theory of deviance and transgression is exposed.

   Granted, Beck (1992, 1999) might respond by arguing that the new
replacement technologies naturally give birth to new risks, and this is
exactly the point of characterizing contemporary society as risk society.
This is undoubtedly a truism. But there is reason to query its novelty.
Weberian sociology developed the metaphor of the iron cage to represent
how social actors became ensnared by the unplanned consequences of their

actions; and, more recently, Elias (1978b) observed that every intended action has unintended consequences. In each case, social action is portrayed as pregnant with risk. We have already referred to the slippage between type 1 and type 2 risks, in Beck's application of risk society. As we noted, type 2 risks are integral to the process of modernization, and have to do with the individualization of social structures and the pluralization of the life world. Beck's (1992, 1999) discussion of risk society tends to focus on what we call type 1 risks, having to do with the environmental attrition caused by the unintended consequences of scientific and industrial accumulation. Chernobyl and Bhopal certainly bear out the proposition that we live in risky societies. But his elaboration of type 2 risks is altogether more nebulous. It seems to postulate a generalized feedback loop in all social and economic relationships. In as much as this is so, it is not clear how enjoining 'new individuals' to be more reflexive and self-monitoring will expedite a solution. For the logic of type 2 analysis is that risk operates on a merry-go-round principle, with intended actions always having unintended consequences. As we noted above, Giddens (1991: 31) uses precisely this argument to attack the growth of professional advice in the presentation of identity and the management of social order.

From this apprehension a certain solace follows. Arguably, it is a dubious solace, for it is based in the realization that nothing much can be done about the problem of unintended consequences. Of course, reflexivity and monitoring can pre-empt and control some things that follow from social action. But the density and velocity of contemporary life is such that unintended consequences will always be a fact of life.

However, by the term 'life politics', Giddens and Beck mean something more decisive and momentous. We can variously describe this as 'self-mastery', 'self-knowledge' or 'self-awareness'. Thus, the practice of life politics is postulated as eliciting personal autonomy, and the coalescence of identity, around reflexively constituted personal and interpersonal pro-grammes of self-management. Life politics is fundamentally about getting more control over your own life. The purpose of this is not ego gratification, but to work towards a healthier balance between self and society, and self and nature. Above all, life politics is a movement of empowerment.

For Giddens, one important dividend of empowerment is the possibility of building the pure relationship. He presents this, overwhelmingly, in positive terms. Thus (1991: 88–98), pure relationships are depicted as 'internally referential' and free from external criteria; they are continually, reflexively organized; they are forged and developed through commitment, intimacy and trust; and finally, they exploit and develop a sense of 'shared history'. This is a peculiarly asocial conception of human relationships, and has been criticized as such by Craib (1994). The 'internally referential' relationship which is free of criteria outside the relationship itself is a hard thing to envisage. For one thing it denies indexicality and the premise that all relationships draw on common social resources and restraints. For another, and this is closer to the reservations held by Craib, the proposition that we can actually construct ourselves may conform to our wishes and fantasies, but, in practice, it typically involves foisting these wishes and fantasies onto others. The concept of the pure relationship envisages an equality of power that is scarce in human relationships.

Giddens deals with this objection by allowing that intimate relationships are often built around a dynamic of what he calls 'co-dependency', in which the participants recognize asymmetry in the relationship, resent it, but feel incapable of breaking free. In contrast, he holds (1991: 93) that the pure relationship involves a 'nexus of intimacy', in which participants are in touch with their feelings, and sustain bonds of reciprocity which enable them to open their inner desires and thoughts to the gaze of the other without fear of censure or misunderstanding. Yet this sits awkwardly with his advocacy of reflexive monitoring as a way of securing and legitimizing the relationship. Reflexive monitoring is, of course, the adjunct of Giddens's characterization of radicalized modernity as chronically unstable and insecure. However, in Craib's (1994: 169) view, reflexive monitoring can have a destructive effect, because it implies that a neurotic dynamic subsists in trust-work. He suggests that reflexive monitoring negates the leap of faith upon which trust must always rest. In a telling metaphor, he (ibid.) contends that reflexive monitoring is akin to pulling up a tree and examining its roots to see if it is still living.

Giddens (1991) himself seems uncomfortable with the finality implied in the notion of commitment underpinning the pure relationship. He conditions the principle of commitment by postulating that the possibility of 'voluntary' breakage is integral to all forms of intimacy (1991: 187). In addition, he suggests that the conditional recognition that the pure relationship is 'good until further notice', serves to morally distinguish it from traditional and hierarchical relationships of co-dependency. However, an intimate commitment which is entered into 'until further notice' might strike many readers as a fragile and problematic undertaking. In contrast, the force of parental love resides precisely in its unconditional quality. In general, parents issue no caveat of 'until further notice' to their children, and vice versa. This is not to say that there are *no* limits to what parents will do to help their children, or what children will do to support and honour their parents. Nonetheless, the principle of unconditionality is integral to the relationship. The ideology of romantic love adapts this principle, by transferring a bond of consanguinity to the market of emotions. In choosing a beloved, or in being chosen as such, unconditional commitment is implied. This is what distinguishes a 'serious' relationship, be it marriage or living together, from others. In qualifying this, by adding an 'until further notice' caveat to serious relationships, Giddens is probably accurately reflecting a change from hierarchical and traditional relations. By the same token he is rendering 'commitment' more provisional than most hierarchical or traditional readings would allow.

There are, then, problems with the solutions that Giddens proffers to the dilemmas posed by radicalized modernity. In sum, third way politics may be more strategic and provisional than his thesis of a break with the past intimates; lifestyle politics captures an important shift in identity formation and personal orientation towards globalism, flexibility and eco-consciousness, but it does not dissolve traditional problems relating to deeply rooted social divisions, deviance and transgression; and the pure relationship is attractive at a theoretical level, but it is much rarer to encounter it empirically.

Giddens (1990: 154) considers himself to be a disciple of 'utopian realism'. By this term he means a theoretical approach which is directed to the task of projecting rational, ethical solutions to the problems of radicalized modernity. As such, he would no doubt agree that his analysis of the third way and its concomitant lifestyle transformation is, in part, counter-factual. The justification is, that by proposing alternative futures and idealized constructs, one helps to create the conditions that allow these characteristics to be achieved. This is an acceptable defence of the necessity for counter-factual theory, but behind it is the question of the character and types of social values propagated. Unless one resorts to a determinist reading of globalization and its associated tendencies, the human development of the future must always involve a struggle over conflicting wants, desires and beliefs. This is certainly partly the message that Castells (1998: 360) seeks to impart when he concludes:

> There is nothing that cannot be changed by conscious, purposive social action, provided with information, and supported by legitimacy.

Giddens and Beck would hardly dissent from this statement. To be sure, the construction of life politics and the new individualism rests precisely upon the enactment of choice. Yet unless types of choices and values are investigated in concrete settings, treatment of the question of finding solutions to the problems of radicalized modernity is likely to seem abstract and unsatisfactory. In particular, the questions of who makes decisions, how decisions are made and the basis of inclusion or exclusion in the decision-making process are crucial.

In turning now to the work of Etzioni (1994, 1996a), we argue that a set of concrete, testable solutions has been produced for the perceived travails of contemporary society. The communitarian movement, of which Etzioni is a principal theorist and activist, presents a set of solutions to problems of education, the family, crime and welfare. In being more concrete, it is also more tangible about the social values which it seeks to nurture and those which it regards as negative or pernicious. By examining communitarianism, we argue, the concrete social dilemmas, value-conflicts and struggles that Giddens and Beck tend to gloss over, in confronting the problems of risk society, are thrown into sharper relief. While we find much to disagree with in the work of Etzioni, we argue that his work reveals a clear understanding that social development involves a struggle between competing value positions. By implication, we submit that this sense of continuing, unfinished struggle is marginalized in the work of Giddens and Beck.

Rather, both writers tend to present the central dilemmas facing society as posing universal threats or opportunities to personal and collective well-being. Because social actors are presupposed to be essentially rational and benign, Giddens and Beck argue that untenable value positions will be abandoned in favour of the 'radical centre'. Etzioni's work is less bland in its propositions about collective political and lifestyle realignments. Communitarians also believe that social actors are essentially rational and benign (Etzioni, 1996b, 1999). However, they maintain that 'the good society' requires the extraction or capping of problematic or 'destabilizing' social values and moral precepts.

### Etzioni and communitarianism

Communitarianism is a movement of moral reform dedicated to rehabilitating a theory of rights and responsibilities in personal and collective life. Communitarians attack the values of both the permissive society and neo-liberalism. They claim to seek a balance between the pursuit of self-interest and the reproduction of moral solidarity (Etzioni, 1993: 2). The 'new golden rule' for society is that rights always entail responsibilities (Etzioni, 1992: 9; 1996a). The diagnostic means for accomplishing this is the revitalization of the community. The core values of the community are therefore alluded to as the decisive means of conflict resolution between social actors and the foundation for moral reform.

The stress on the moral authority of the community has provoked the criticism that communitarianism is a disguised form of puritanism. Etzioni (1993: 41–3) rejects this criticism. In fact, his defence of communitarianism is most accurately classified as the reassertion of some of the principal tenets of sociological functionalism. The doctrine of functionalism proposed that society is an organic entity in which specialized institutions discharge integrative functions to elicit social harmony and order. Functionalism emphasized the reciprocity between social institutions and the collaboration of social actors in achieving organic equilibrium.

All of these features are present in Etzioni's account of communitarianism. Indeed, communitarians present their ideas as a spontaneous reaction to social and cultural disequilibrium. Thus, Etzioni (1996a, 1999) contends that 'the good society' requires an appropriate balance between individual autonomy and moral solidarity. Between 1960 and 1990, he asserts, this equilibrium was profoundly disturbed, first by the rise of the counter-culture, and then by the resurgence of neo-liberalism. It might be thought that Etzioni is trying to turn the clock back to the 1950s. However, this is not the case. He accepts (1993: 248) that the critics of the day were right to point to latent authoritarianism in the political system and inequitable treatment of women and minorities in postwar society. His point is that social criticism went too far. The counter-culture intensified social divisions, fomented a climate of moral relativism, and gave overweening powers to lobbying groups and the state to intervene in private life.

The neo-liberal backlash in the 1980s was excessive. In privileging the virtues of market freedom and individual autonomy, it signally failed to nurture the roots of community. The equilibrium, upon which the moral health of society is alleged to depend, was damaged by privileging individual rights over individual responsibilities. Communitarianism seeks to restore society to a condition of homeostasis or a dynamic balance between individual autonomy and moral solidarity. Invoking the well established functionalist dichotomy between centrifugal and centripetal forces, Etzioni (1996a and b: 46) writes:

> A society's trends may be compared to the movement of a ball in a bowl: Up to a point, swing the bowl one way, the ball will roll back to the centre (although it will overshoot the centre several times until it comes to rest), but push the ball too hard, and it will fly out of the bowl. A society, by analogy, can be pushed out of its pattern. But unlike a bowl, a society can change its specific formation while sustaining its basic pattern, to try and keep the ball of social change within its confines.

Within sociology, functionalist thought has been subjected to heavy criticism on the basis that it is over-deterministic, neutralizes the power and will of social actors and cannot satisfactorily explain change. We argue that all of these criticisms apply to communitarian thought. However, before developing these points, it is important to clarify Etzioni's analysis of the present social condition and to consider his solutions for restoring equilibrium.

Etzioni's analysis of the present social condition relies heavily on caricature. For example, he refers to the world of 'massive street violence, the unfailing war against illegal drugs and unbridled greed' (1993: 248) as the normative culture in many sections of society. Elsewhere (1996a: 37, 10; 1999: 88–9) he describes the 'malaise' and 'rising moral anarchy' afflicting contemporary moral life. Ironically, given the strong emphasis he places upon the necessity for balance in social life, this is a peculiarly unbalanced analysis of current conditions. It presents social breakdown and moral disorder as rife, and calls for new realism about personal and collective responsibilities. Further, it depicts transgression as a monolithic tendency in society and therefore neglects the nuances of transgression and the processes of criminal sequestration that we pointed to above, in the discussion of disorder. Leaving that aside for the moment, Etzioni (1996a and b: 52) advocates four principles of moral reconstruction:

1  The establishment of effective mechanisms of regulation to deal with types of social value and behaviour that constitute a 'clear and present danger' to the common good.
2  The generalized reform of personal and collective life to restore moral values which contribute to the appropriate equilibrium of individual autonomy and social order.
3  The commitment to a minimally intrusive state and maximally self-reliant and autonomous citizens.

4   The expansion of public information and communication systems, to
    enable citizens to utilize and practise their common rights and discharge
    their moral responsibilities, effectively and amicably.

According to Etzioni, the key to realizing these principles is not the
invention of new social institutions, but the regeneration of existing ones. In
particular the family, schooling and informal community associations are
nominated as the chief engines of moral reform (Etzioni, 1992; 1993: 248–
9). Their resources are seen as more relevant and dynamic in the programme of grassroots moral re-education than the assets of the state. In
general, communitarianism favours a minimalist role for state intervention.
The cultural capital of the community is privileged over the government
powers of the state. For example, Etzioni (1992) advocates that communities should take care of their own members in respect of welfare
provision, education, policing and family relations. The state exists as a
resource of last resort, to be mobilized only when the resources of the
community prove, demonstrably, to be insufficient.

The strategic moral aim of communitarianism is to enhance individual
self-reliance and social responsibility. Specific policy measures imply the
curtailment of civil liberties as they are presently constituted. For example,
Etzioni (1992) argues that the community should have the right to claim the
organs of all persons who die without formally contracting out of the
approved system of donation. Further, communities are encouraged to
practise 'suspicionless searches' in criminal detective work, so long as the
intrusion is judged to be 'minimal', and the danger to the public 'substantial'. Communities will 'encourage' 'likely' HIV carriers to be tested,
and if found to be infected with the virus, to disclose all sexual contacts to
the health authorities or to inform the people concerned unilaterally.
Campaign contributions to political parties should be strictly regulated, and
Political Action Committees (PACs) should be 'abolished' on the grounds
that they generate obligations for candidates aiming for political office
which are 'inimical' to democratic representation (Etzioni, 1992: 9–11).

In our vocabulary, this form of social transformation is designed to
replace cool/thin identities and relationships with hot/thick alternatives.
Etzioni (1996a: 12) wants to substitute the thin social order of radicalized
modernity, in which individuals are notionally free agents, with 'a social
order that contains a set of shared values, to which individuals are taught
they are obligated'. The legitimation for this is the utilitarian principle of
'the common good' which, by implication, is held to be threatened by loose
associations and flexible, mobile orientations. This does not signify the
recrudescence of puritanism. Etzioni (1993: 196–202) is notably liberal on
the question of so-called 'hate speech'. He rejects the argument that
behaviour which is verbally abusive to women, ethnic minorities or any
other group should be made illegal, because to do so would infringe the
right of free speech. He argues that the correct remedy to hate speech is low
key, voluntary counter-activity, such as the establishment of courses on

tolerance and one-on-one interracial lunches and dinners. Given a choice between voluntarism and coercion as a method of regulating social conduct, communitarians will always choose voluntarism.

However, Etzioni's arguments do signify the resurgence of nostalgia as a primary component in civil society. They posit the core values of the moral majority as the vanguard of decency, goodness and common sense and that communities have the fundamental right to protect their distinctive ways of life. These ways of life have been partly suffocated by the values of pluralism and cosmopolitanism. The remedy is to go back to the core values that inspired the founding fathers and to use these values as the new basis for social reintegration.

This is an old argument in international relations which is perhaps, most closely associated with Hegel (1952, 1956). Hegel rejected the Kantian vision of a 'world republic' consisting of a society of co-legislators. Instead, he argued that the sovereign state, understood as the ultimate expression of rooted community values and rights, is the only plausible institution capable of delivering individual freedom. However, there are numerous difficulties with this argument. First, it does not empirically demonstrate whether core community values actually exist. Rather, it attributes them to a territorially rooted people. Secondly, it fails to show how community values can be insulated from the various processes of globalization. Thirdly, it cannot explain how community values change or how hybrid social formations and value positions emerge. All of these points can be summarized by the observations that the Hegelian and communitarian traditions do not offer a defensible moral basis for social exclusion or a tenable principle of moral unity in states or communities.

In fact both traditions are versions of the dominant ideology thesis. Commentators have pointed to severe structural defects in this thesis (Abercombie et al., 1980). In particular, it exaggerates the pre-eminence of the dominant ideology or the core values in society; overstates the unity of the social strata which are nominally in control; and understates the interpretive and transformative powers of the social strata that are, theoretically, controlled by dominant or core constructs. In the case of communitarian arguments, where secondary empirical data is used – as in the case of proposals to tighten up the family, reform the schools, extend community service, or advance the number of suspicionless searches – it generally reinforces designated arguments rather than tests them (Etzioni, 1993: 62, 91, 114, 167, 171). Thus, the 'core values' of society are asserted, not demonstrated.

The communitarian case is vulnerable to the serious general charge that it misconstrues the character of society and the condition of culture. For example, Smart (1999: 168–70) argues that Etzioni assigns a false sense of value-unity to society and culture by misreading the challenges posed by multiculturalism and multi-ethnicity to the ideology of geo-political homogeneity. The point connects up with the arguments made by Giddens and Beck, that nationalism is a declining force in the organization of emotional attachments, and that it is being replaced by cosmopolitan attachments to environmentalism, human rights, world aesthetics and flexible identity.

Without doubt, Etzioni's handling of multiculturalism, multi-ethnicity and value diversity is clumsy. For example, although he pays lip service to the vitality and energy of heterogeneous ethnic and cultural influences in American society (1993: 155; 1996a: 191–2), he proposes that their fate must be assimilation rather than co-dependence. Moreover, it is assimilation of a specific type, which prioritizes a specific set of anthropological and historical values over others, rather than recognizes the need for hybrid formation and accommodation. For example, in his critique of the pitfalls of multicultural education he is quite explicit about the nature of the value struggle involved here. He declares (1992: 10):

> Universities should welcome courses that add to the European tradition as well as information about other cultures. However, neither the federal government nor local ones should provide public support to colleges that eliminate European elements from their core curricula or required courses, to the extent that they exist. Our values – the constitution, our democratic tradition and our values of mutual tolerance – come to us from our European heritage, not from other cultures; eliminating them from the university undermines our national strength and unity.

This is an explicit statement in support of policies of social exclusion, which resides in some tension with the communitarian claim to embrace difference and diversity. Postcolonialism has now developed a large battery of concepts demonstrating how the Eurocentric tradition of statecraft has institutionalized subaltern communities, opposed hybridity and repressed difference. This tradition warns against universalizing discourses of identity and argues for respecting the 'idiosyncrazies' of others. It rejects the defence that certain discourses of identity are natural and universal on the grounds that discourse is the product of history. Conceptions of universality are therefore tainted by their origins. In contrast, communitarianism holds that cultural and ethnic minorities have the right to practise a distinctive way of life, but that their ultimate responsibility is to show allegiance to the values of the 'encompassing' host community. On this account, migration carries inalienable duties which subsume ethnic and subcultural particularity beneath the universalism of the nation state. Set against much current political and ethical theory, these are questionable arguments. They suggest a limited, non-dialogic, reading of tolerance, belonging and respect for difference.

Perhaps Bauman (1997, 1999) is right in his proposition that communitarianism should ultimately be understood as the reaction of conservative formations whose identity is threatened by the homogenizing forces of globalization. Bauman's sociology recognizes moral universalism, but it does so on the basis of individual choice, rather than community fiat or *a priori* loyalties which predispose individuals to a preceding set of community values. Since the option of withdrawal is a basic constituent of personal choice, his reading emphasizes that moral universalism is inherently contingent and 'burdened with the same anxieties of risk-taking as all other aspects of life' (Bauman, 1997: 195). For Bauman, globalization divides as much as it unites, and it does so automatically, spontaneously and in perpetuity. Thus, the advocation of a foundational set of core values is beside the point. The present condition requires new forms of reflexive, ethically sensitive citizenship, which recognize the nuances of pluralism, diversity and transgression. In contrast, communitarianism represents the return of neo-tribalism and fundamentalism. As such, Bauman (1998: 3) believes it is fatally flawed.

## Conclusion

In this chapter we have explored several leading positions in contemporary political economy which argue that a new form of capitalism is emerging in our midst. All of the positions recognize these forms as a new development in a social formation which continues, in all essential respects, to be capitalistic. For much of the last two centuries, the vision of a socialist alternative inspired transformative thought and practice. It is now clear that this vision has receded, and that strategies of moral reform, environmentalism and redistributive justice are now waged in a context which presupposes the continuation of capitalism.

Of course, this does not mean that criticism of capitalism is over. The notions of the 'black holes' of informational capitalism, 'risk society' and 'life politics' all articulate moral and practical objections to capitalist forms of organization. Further, the proposition that subpolitics is now a vital element in the body politic expresses the significance of micro-politics in the reproduction and development of everyday life. The capillaries of sub-politics are perfectly capable of challenging capitalist hegemony, as the civil disturbances which occurred at the World Trade Organization meeting in Seattle at the end of the last century demonstrated. Most critics accept that if capitalism is to be changed, it must be reformed from within, rather than transcended. The old book-ends of debate, between the 1950s and 1980s, which regarded the fate of Modernity to be precariously poised between 'two systems' have been dismantled.

In part, this reveals the remarkable fecundity and flexibility of the capitalist form of organization. The rise of informational capitalism has shifted primary political struggle from the factory floor to the internet and from the nation state to the global order; it has contributed to the agglomeration of belonging around the virtual images and calculated representations of mass communications and weakened identification with community and region. It is not surprising that many of the old forms of solidarity with which we grew up now appear to be rickety and untenable.

But this does not mean that the goal of building solidarity is now *passé*. We accept the argument of Deleuze and Guattari (1980) and Virilio (1980, 1995), that the acceleration of velocity in the lifeworld under capitalism has contributed to deterritorialization. Identity is now layered and cross-cut into many divisions. But we stop short of declaring, with them, the arrival of a state of nomadism. Nomads wander the earth with a sense of the primordial boundaries of the cosmos as their ontological context. Now, the peoples of advanced modernity are not orphans or refugees from the ontology of primordial wonder. The popularity of new age spiritualism, and the durability of other irrational belief systems, supports the conclusion that the desire to experience the other side of the world is both deeply rooted and widespread. However, the other is posited and mediated through the habitual lifeworld of advanced modernity. This is the world in which man-made social divisions and values predominate. It is a world in which all are enmeshed in a struggle for scarce resources, funnelled into the public domain by precarious social institutions. The peoples of advanced modernity are 'bearers' of social divisions in the Althusserian (1966, 1971) sense of the term. While we wish to absent ourselves from the structuralist implications of the Althusserian position, his idea of 'calling forth' subjectivity, through interpellation, continues to be fruitful. It is necessary to couple the concept of interpellation with that of governmentality. Foucault's sociology emphasizes the pluralized, processual form of governmentality in late modernity, and this is an emphasis that we wish to support. We retain an emancipatory interest in eliminating the surplus social and economic constraints which prevent human subjects from 'making the most of their own history' and removing the emotional and psychological barriers that deform identity. The resurgence of capitalism in recent years has not left us with a sense of defeat, but with the conviction that, while circumstances have changed, there is still much for critical sociology to do. Sociology *après* the collapse of the 'presently existing alternative to capitalism' (Bahro, 1978), is not sociology without solidarity. In the next chapter we seek to oppose idealism, in the form of communitarian core values, pure relationships and nomadism, with a materialist account which predicates solidarity on the frailty of the body, the precariousness of the normative social and ecological environment and the sensuality of human interaction and communication.

# 11

# CONCLUSION: SOCIOLOGY AND COSMOPOLITAN VIRTUE

In this analysis of sociology and modern society we have been concerned to understand the dynamic between scarcity and renewal of solidarity in a world of rapid technological and scientific change. Our approach to the disciplinary divisions in the social sciences has been to argue that economics is the study of scarcity in human societies, that is a science of the allocation of means to the achievement of ends in a condition of limited resources. Whereas classical economics treated scarcity as a consequence of natural scarcity, classical sociology argued that the problem of scarcity was a social not a natural state of affairs: the solution of the problem of human scarcity was presumed to lie in the constitution of solidarity. If economics was a science of economizing behaviour, politics was the study of the means of violence. In Hobbesian society, both scarcity and violence required the social regulation of the conflict of interests through shared culture and institutions to regulate the conflict of interests. The emergent social sciences of the nineteenth and early twentieth centuries required this triangulated picture of the social – scarcity (money/exchange), violence (blood) and solidarity (bread) – in order to study the trajectory of capitalist society.

If sociology is to remain a creative vision of modern society and make a contribution to politics and moral debate, it requires a new vision of how social solidarity is possible in postmodern society. In part, this is a matter of recognizing that existing discourses which appeal to 'place' or 'collective interest' are unlikely to succeed. There are good practical reasons why individuals no longer feel rooted to place or bound together by common interests. Globalization has transformed the popular conception of the relationship between place and identity. The increase in the rate of divorce erodes the principle of stable family life, and the mechanization of labour through automated and micro-chip processes transforms industrial notions of work and career. Bio-medical engineering presents radical challenges to notions of bounded identity and the life cycle. In the West, these developments are unravelling in the midst of declining central institutions that in former times were capable of curtailing anomic tendencies. The family, organized religion and the nation state are in decline. Following the postmodern critique of grand narratives, the emphasis in social theory is upon living with contingency and living for the moment, rather than proceeding to 'higher', 'universal' social forms.

### Antinomies of globalization and sociology

We argue that the traditional framework of (national) citizenship does not offer a form of social membership that can respond to globalization. Post-national ways of conceiving solidarity are already recognized. Urry (2000: 210) argues that a 'reconstituted sociology' should be founded around 'mobilities' rather than 'societies'. Leaving aside the rhetorical resonance of this argument with the emergence of 'networld', and the reputed replacement of face-to-face contact with digital communication, we wish to retain the concept of society as the centre of sociological activity. The velocity of mobility has unquestionably increased since the start of the industrial revolution. Equally, one might posit the democratization of mobility. In the eighteenth century, by and large, it was the sons of the aristocracy and later the *nouveaux riches* that engaged in long distance travel. The European Grand Tour was valued as a rite of passage in elite circles. Properly executed, it conferred cultural sophistication, political awareness, increased business knowledge and a network of continental contacts upon the traveller. By the late twentieth century, travel had become almost a citizenship right in the mass democracies. The decline in the cost of air transport, relative to real incomes, since the 1950s has magnified the numbers of ordinary people who travel around the world. The World Tourist Origanization estimates that as many as 700 million people engage in travel for pleasure every year. Compared with the size of the total world population, this is still an elite. However, it is one that is clearly growing.

It is easy to see why mobility, contingency and velocity are currently 'in the air' for social and cultural theorists. Our argument is that there are obvious dangers in identifying mobility as the primary defining feature of being in the world today. Marx and Simmel both attributed motive power to capital and money. In their sociologies, capital and money are conceptualized as real agents which compel humans to act in certain ways. At the same time, they never speculated on the 'post-humanism' that now accompanies much theorizing on globalization and the new technologies (Latour, 1987, 1993). For Marx and Simmel, capital and money are inherently social constructions which derive from the unintended consequences of countless, reciprocally related intentional actions, which occur both contemporaneously and over long spans of time.

Perhaps somewhat against the grain of fashion, we insist on the necessity of developing a reconstituted sociology with the embodied actor at its centre. There are serious dangers in responding to the challenges posed by new technologies with a post-human sociology. Our critique of decorative sociology is precisely that, through creating a privileged position for the cultural and the aesthetic, it has undermined the significance of the economic, political and social dimensions of life. Questions of style and symbol have been permitted to overshadow matters of money (exchange), blood and bread. We contend that these matters are the indispensable foundations of being in the world at all times and in all places.

Decorative sociology cannot offer any critical perspective on modern society – let alone provide a political vision of the future. The fascination with consumer society has taken the implicit view that there is no problem of scarcity, or that scarcity is a short-term tension between 'desire' (needs) and 'lack' (demand). Politics in decorative sociology has become a problem of subjectivities, usually conceived as 'split' or 'floating', and cultural definition in a 'politics of difference and recognition'. The violent division between friend and foe in political space has been reduced primarily to psychological questions of tolerating difference and recognizing the 'other'. The politics of velocity has been presented as an alternative to the politics of place and blood (Virilio, 1999). We have argued in this critique of the decorative sociology of consumer society that without a robust political economy of social organization there can be no rebuilding of the sociological imagination. Although we find much to disagree with in Giddens's (1998, 2000) 'third way' (see pp. 175–9), we share his interest in a theoretical engagement with actual practical issues, especially policy issues. Indeed, we go further by insisting that social citizenship is nothing but the applied side of social theory. We will return to this point later when we discuss 'cool/thin citizenship' and cosmopolitan virtue.

We propose that the interest in aesthetic and philosophical questions, rather than empirical work, is in part a response to management processes within universities to increase output. The research exercise in the UK and Australia was intended to increase academic productivity and provide an 'objective', comparative basis for evaluating the quality of research. Empirical work has suffered in this climate. Given the long payload between collecting data and publication, there has been pressure on academics to switch to commentaries on secondary texts or aesthetic and technological 'revolutions' so as to produce research ratings by increasing output. Doubtless, we ourselves have been caught up in this. Writing too much, too quickly is in danger of becoming the characteristic vice of the professional sociologist in a context of research measurement.

Publishers have colluded in this by becoming more intrusive in the content of books and journals. Outside the USA, where the domestic market is sufficiently large to bolster the demands of shareholders for ever-increasing year-on profit margins, publishers are faced with producing books for an international English speaking market. The reason for this is starkly simple. Companies like Routledge, Blackwell, Verso, Polity and Sage are unable to sell enough copies of works in their frontlist which focus on national data, in their domestic markets. Empirical studies of cults, families, crime, education and other institutions in social life do not 'travel well'. On the whole publishers are not commissioning books in these areas, and are encouraging aspiring authors working in these fields to turn their work into journal articles. Instead, the incentive in academic publishing is to find topics that will be meaningful throughout the English speaking world. Not unreasonably, books dealing with pure social theory, global consumer culture, research methods and textbooks on 'Society', have been identified as having wider international appeal than empirical research monographs.

The climate contributes to frenetic publishing, which revolves around fads and fashions, and supermarket research which is devoted to the latest aesthetic or technological dispute or 'revolution'. The elevation of the 'other' and abstract 'difference' is a perfectly reasonable response to these various changes in the international academic market place. It signifies a recognition of social differentiation and change without requiring analysis of the many-layered and often very complex character of differentiation and change.

The shift of focus to the level of ideas *per se*, rather than the empirical testing of ideas, has palpable and far reaching consequences for the quality of intellectual activity. Bursts of momentary enthusiasm and passion replace stable research and theory traditions. The classical end of sociology, which is to explore the basis for solidarity in the midst of conflicts over the allocation of scarce resources and the legitimate use of the means of violence, is replaced with the rhetorical study of texts in the search for postmodern culture. There is an overheated quality about sociological debate today, and this has been the case for over a quarter of a century. Sudden ideas buttonhole debate for a few years, to be followed by general apathy and indolence. Multiparadigmatic complexity is played out in a gladiatorial framework of the sociology of knowledge, namely an orientation to argument and debate which is accusative rather than interrogative. The purpose of argument and debate is to overcome competing positions so as to command pre-eminence. The result of this orientation is to polarize competing arguments, and to foment stereotyping and caricature. The commonalities between competing positions are undertheorized. Instead, the emphasis is upon separation, division and winning. The condition breeds *ressentiment* and gestural outbursts which reject entire research traditions in a few confident sentences.

### Kierkegaard and the present age

In struggling to explain the condition of contemporary social theory, we have found it helpful to return to a neglected work in sociological circles, Kierkegaard's *The Present Age*. Written in 1846, just before the revolutionary 'moment' of 1848, the book is a commentary upon intellectual life and the ideas of the day. Early on (1846: 35), he makes a distinction between a 'revolutionary age' and a 'passionless age'. The former is regarded as thoroughly transformative, taking questions of scarcity, violence and solidarity and recasting them. In contrast, Kierkegaard (1846: 35, 40) notes that a passionless age revolves around 'advertisement' and 'publicity' rather than action and transforms everything into 'representational ideas'. Kierkegaard continues by arguing that a genuine revolutionary age overthrows everything. In contrast a *faux* revolutionary age which purports to be addressing action, but which in reality is fundamentally reflective and passionless,

> transforms that expression of strength into a *feat of dialectics: it leaves everything standing but cunningly empties it of significance. Instead of culminating in a rebellion it reduces the inward reality of all relationships to a reflective tension which leaves everything standing but makes life as a whole ambiguous: so that everything continues to exist factually whilst by a dialectical deceit*, privatissime, *it supplies a secret interpretation that it does not exist.* (Kierkegaard, 1846: 42–3, emphasis in original)

We find these words helpful in thinking about the current state of sociology, for we are struck by the same 'reflective tension' in much sociological debate and a similar 'feat of dialectics' which purports to reveal fundamental transformation, but leaves everything standing. Kierkegaard (1846: 64) further points out, in what is perhaps a notable *aperçu*, that 'the fewer ideas there are at any time, the more indolent and exhausted by bursts of enthusiasm will it be'. The exaggerated enthusiasms which surrounded postmodernism, deconstructionism and the third way are thrown into relief, when considered from the perspective of Kierkegaard's comment.

We refer to Kierkegaard here, not because we want to suggest that he has the answers to the challenges of the decorative but, we contend, fundamentally passionless sociology of the present age, but rather to re-emphasize the importance of classical perspectives in contemporary debate. Lyotard's (1984) thesis of the collapse of 'grand narratives' melted many frozen positions in social and cultural theory. However, to the extent that it implied a break or rupture with the ideas of the classical tradition, its effects can now be seen as rather harmful. We can illustrate this by exploring the relationship between social theory and social citizenship.

## Social theory and social citizenship

In our analysis of the scarcity–solidarity dynamic of social order, we submit that the issue of citizenship and the construction of human rights has played and will play a major role in providing a viable politics of modernity. For Marxist sociology, class conflict was an inevitable outcome of the structure of ownership and interests in industrial capitalism. These conflictual relationships in Marxism were seen to be constrained by the dominant ideology of capitalism, namely possessive individualism. One sociological response to Marxist theory came from T.H. Marshall's analysis of citizenship as a reform of capitalism and as a basis of social solidarity through common membership. Citizenship modifies the negative impact of the capitalist market by a redistribution of resources on the basis of rights. In Marshall's well known formula, legal rights in the seventeenth and eighteenth centuries were associated with the growth of a range of juridical institutions that provided some important forms of protection. In the nineteenth and twentieth centuries, the growth of political rights created a public arena of debate through such mechanisms as parliament, freedom of association, and the secret ballot. Finally in the twentieth century, the welfare state was the expression of a growth of social rights.

Criticisms of the Marshallian model are, perhaps, now well known, so there is no need to do anything more than list them here. To begin with, one should say that in the twentieth century there was a growth of educational and economic rights through an expansion of higher education and trade union participation in the management of the economy. Marshall failed to provide a clear view of the mechanisms that produced various expansions of citizenship.

Marshall's model also failed to recognize different types of citizenship. The comparative sociology of citizenship has identified significant differences between various traditions. For example, there was an important liberal model of citizenship that emphasized the virtues of the property-owning citizen who remained passive on the assumption that the state would not interfere too vigorously in society and that the market remained a free arena of exchange. This pattern of individualistic citizenship had its roots in the Lockean settlement of the late seventeenth century. A sharp contrast is to be found in the doctrines of the Federalist papers and the American war of independence, which created a political ideology of freedom from aristocratic powers and the rights of citizens to challenge the state. This secular view of the powers of citizens was inherited by the French revolution, which established the core of modern secular political cultures – liberty, equality and fraternity. The Lutheran legacy of Germany represents yet a third alternative in which anxieties about the moral standing of the citizenship created in ideological terms a role for the state and the Church in the spiritual regulation of citizens. The freedom of the citizen was expressed as actions in conformity with the state. This doctrine found its modern expression in Weber's analysis of plebiscitary democracy and power politics.

A further problem with the Marshallian sociology of citizenship was that it assumed the existence of a homogeneous society in which ethnic and cultural divisions were not important when compared which social class divisions. By contrast, the American debate about citizenship was primarily concerned with immigration, ethnic identity and nation-building. The central issue in modern citizenship is the relationship between ethnicity, residence and nationalism. The old pattern of national citizenship is being challenged by the possibilities of dual citizenship, multiple citizenship and hence post-national citizenship. In this respect, the rates and patterns of naturalization are an effective measure of the openness and tolerance of modern democracies.

Finally, Marshall's theory was primarily a theory of entitlement, and had little to say about duties and obligations. As such the theory envisaged a passive citizenship in which the state protected the individual from the uncertainty of the market through a system of rights. These rights often retrospectively compensated for existing deprivations of unemployment and sickness in the form of benefits to acquire welfare restitution. One criticism of Marshall, for example the Marxist critique of reformism, has been that where citizenship rights are merely formal, they do not dramatically reduce social inequalities. The sociological question is: how do citizenship rights become effective forms of entitlement?

In all of this we are intent on using classical sociology as a living resource in sociological explanation and argument. Of course, the material and historical contexts in which these ideas are propagated is not the same. Perhaps some sociologists have been too prone to believe that the essentials have remained intact since the days of Marx or Marshall. But that is no justification for regarding the classical tradition as a mere period piece. The questions of how we should live with others, and what the proper ends of life should be, have faced all cultures, be they mobile or governed by the *taedium vitae*. What, in the current condition, constitute the foundations of effective entitlement? And how does sociological theory contribute to conceptualizing them correctly?

## Effective entitlement

Historically speaking, there are three important foundations of effective entitlement: work, warfare and reproduction. In terms of social theory, it is helpful to think of this model as Fordist. Principally through the experience of full employment, the worker gains an effective claim on resources through wages, savings and superannuation. The worker-citizen is the basic foundation of a Fordist democracy.

The second road to effective participatory citizenship was warfare. As Titmuss realized, it was the ability of the returning serviceman to make claims on the state in terms of housing, land and education for services rendered that gave a powerful stimulus to postwar British society and the welfare state of the Beveridge report. Alongside the worker-citizen, we can locate the warrior-citizen. In many societies, but Australia in particular, ex-servicemen's associations (such as the Return Servicemen's League) played an important part in the politics of postwar civil society, often in conservative defence of postwar settlements.

These trajectories of effective entitlement are largely masculinist. The Fordist model of Marshallian citizenship assumed that women would stay at home to reproduce, manage domestic space and service their husbands (thereby reducing the costs of servicing labour). In return, husbands' retirement packages were intended to provide for the couple in old age. This produced our third foundation of effective citizenship, namely reproductive citizenship, in which parenthood was seen to be a social contribution to the reproduction of society. The final citizenship role is the citizen-as-parent.

It is possible to argue that these conditions of effective entitlement also established a pattern of active participation in society, which in turn contributed to civil society. Active citizenship supported work-related associations such as working men's clubs, trade union organizations and guilds, and political organizations such as the traditional Labour Party. These guilds, clubs and collectivities correspond to what Durkheim called 'intermediary associations'. In British social and literary theory, this feature of society was analysed by Leavis, Williams and Hoggart as an essential foundation of British communal cohesiveness (as a defence against barbarian consumer culture).

Following Titmuss, we have already noted that the history of mass warfare in the twentieth century has been tragically destructive of traditional society, but one unintended consequence of these conflicts was to produce a multitude of (male) associations that provided support and services to ex-soldiers. Rituals of male solidarity (ANZAC parades and other services of remembrance) kept alive the comradeship of war. In Britain, the Dunkirk spirit continued to be a norm of service and sacrifice for generations who were born after the war. In the US, days of remembrance for the fallen continue to be presented as binding the nation together. Finally, parenthood has traditionally provided solidaristic linkages to the wider community through women's groups, child-care associations, school-related groups, neighbourhood groups, and church-based groups such as the Mothers' Union. The growth of postwar active citizenship was also associated with activities that contributed to social solidarity.

Of course, much contemporary sociological and cultural theory is concerned to maintain that the Fordist model has disintegrated. This pattern of citizenship has broken down because the three foundations of effective entitlement have been transformed by economic, military and social changes. Economic changes, especially in the labour market (job sharing, casualization, flexibility, downsizing and new management strategies), have disrupted work as a career. With the disappearance of careers, there is also an erosion of commitment to both the company and labour unions. Workers can no longer depend on a stable life course or life cycle. In addition, there has been a major decline in trade union membership and work no longer so clearly defines identity. Class-based identities have disappeared along with class-based communities. There has in short been an erosion of citizenship through the erosion of work-based entitlemennts. The decline in 'unionateness' has coincided with the privatization of many services, such as health. We broadly agree with Sennett (1998) in his analysis of the social and moral consequences of the new economy in terms of a 'corrosion of character'.

The Titmuss mechanism of war-related claims to entitlement has also disappeared with the end of mass warfare. In the post-Cold War environment, nuclear disarmament has meant that the traditional role of the citizen-soldier has disappeared. It is inconceivable that a modern democracy would commit millions of conscripted soldiers to conventional ground warfare in defence of a nation. Modern warfare is typically short, intense, technological and conducted by professional soldiers against dissident ethnic minorities, freedom fighters, terrorists and bandits. Democracies have difficulty in fighting protracted conflicts because media coverage tends to alienate the support of citizens for conflicts in remote regions where the reasons for engagement are disputed. Vietnam proved to be expensive not only in lives but in political careers. In Britain, media coverage of the 1982 conflict with Argentina in the South Atlantic could not be easily managed by the government and led to accusations that the BBC was a treasonous institution. The ageing of First and Second World War soldiers has resulted in a decline of servicemen's clubs and military ritualism is no longer so central to the display of authority in civil society. Of course, this argument is largely about British society, but, given the technological character of modern warfare, military conflicts in Korea, Vietnam, Afghanistan and Kosovo appear to fragment democracies rather than cement them.

Finally, the transformations of parenthood in modern society have also raised difficult issues for reproductive citizenship. Women have entered the labour force in large numbers and the traditional pattern of female reproduction and disrupted work careers has been transformed by delayed and controlled pregnancy, serial monogamy, and reduced fertility. The demographic structure of modern societies is no longer a pyramid, because lower fertility and increasing life expectancy have brought about a dramatic greying of the population. We are familiar with both the development of single parent households and the extreme isolation of the elderly. Citizenship has expanded to include increasing rights for gay and lesbian parents, and has given rise to debates about sexual citizenship. In a liberal democracy, sexual citizenship would allow gay marriages and, with the appropriate technology, gay and lesbian parenting.

These changes have major consequences for the development of post-Fordist citizenship, but we should also recognize that modern medical technology has not, generally speaking, been widely available to unmarried couples, gay households or elderly women. New reproductive technologies have generally had conservative social consequences in reasserting the view that heterosexuality and marriage are the ideal framework within which stable parenting can take place. As a result, reproduction through marriage and the formation of a heterosexual household remain the bedrock of traditional patterns of citizenship entitlement.

These social changes lead us to the conclusion that there has been an important erosion of effective citizenship entitlement in modern society, and as a result there has also been an erosion of social solidarity. The new consumer society was perhaps first clearly identified by writers like Benjamin in the Arcades Project. With mass consumerism, society became a voyeuristic experience in which the new 'cathedrals of consumption' have replaced the traditional centres of worship and sociality. Society has become increasingly a spectacle in which citizenship is passive. Participation in economic production has for many sections of society been replaced by passive consumption. Postmodern sociology is in many respects not an analysis of consumerism but a product of it; the concentration on the aesthetic qualities of everyday life produces a surface view of consumer-driven capitalism.

At the same time, the role of the citizen-soldier was an aspect of 'national manhood' (Nelson, 1998), which was the foundation for traditional patterns of citizenship inclusion. The professional soldier, while commanding some degree of status honour, does not provide a mass basis for modern forms of inclusion. In Western elites, military service may have some electoral advantages, but it has declined as a significant aspect of elite membership. We do not see militarism as an important feature of the social bond, but it may continue as a feature of male bonding, where militia groups offer a reactionary answer to the complexities of modernity. In modern society, especially for young poorly educated girls, reproduction is probably the only remaining basis of social recognition. Hence the prevalence of teenage pregnancy. But where does this leave young men without jobs or careers to build up resources, or military opportunities to establish an identity as a warrior-citizen, and without the capacities for building households and funding romantic love (Ilouz, 1997)?

The erosion of citizenship through the transformations of work, war and parenthood also corrodes the possibilities of participatory or associative democracy. The decline of social capital is an index of the erosion of citizenship. In this study, we have criticized the notion that the 'third way' could provide an effective and comprehensive channel for rebuilding active citizenship. For example, the ongoing enthusiasm for voluntary associations and the third sector, as a platform for activism and social participation, receives some degree of support from the literature. However, voluntary associations can only play a limited role in Britain where, for example, the laws surrounding charity status preclude the political involvement of the voluntary sector. In any case, voluntary associations are under great pressure to raise their own revenue competitively and while they are not-for-profit institutions they are constrained by the economic logic of input maximization. While the third sector has avoided the centralization and bureaucratization of the traditional welfare state, it cannot provide a universalistic service accountable to government and there are no accepted guides to enforce quality of service. Voluntary associations can make an important contribution to active citizenship and social capital, but we remain sceptical about the larger claims of associative democracy (Brown et al., 2000).

## Human rights and post-national citizenship

In retrospect, while Marshall's work on citizenship was a major intellectual contribution to the sociological analysis of postwar society, his theory is now challenged by the growth of global society. The Marshallian model, as Parsons and Bendix realized, provided a model of nation building through citizenship building. In the modern world, the scope for government action with respect to its own citizens is constrained by globalization and the changes that globalism implies for sovereignty. Nation state citizenship was an exclusionary model of welfare reform that protected citizens from claims to resources by immigrants. It created a distinctive inside/outside category. In this sense, citizenship is a specifically political category. In the modern world economy, immigration and multiculturalism become a serious challenge to national citizenship. In addition, something like 700 million people are engaged in tourism each year. Together with the expansion of mass communications, this erodes the concept of the bounded nation state.

Our argument is that frameworks for modern solidarity will involve a merging of human rights and citizenship legislation to reflect greater degrees of labour mobility, migration and inter-civilizational contact. We submit that this will occur through bilateral and multilateral agreements between nation states, rather than through moves to construct a world government. In the current situation, it is probably very fanciful indeed to posit the imminent emergence of world government. On the other hand, there are already economic and human rights agreements, produced by governments and NGOs, which have a global impact.

In contemporary sociology, there are special difficulties in analysing actions and trends which have a universal impact. The decorative turn has magnified the politics of difference as the centre-point of sociological concerns. This has led to a commitment to cultural relativism which, *a priori*, problematizes notions of human rights. In order to support the idea of human rights as an important source of social solidarity in modern politics, it will be necessary to challenge the conventional wisdom about relativism in the social sciences.

We recognize that human rights codes, especially the Universal Declaration of Human Rights (1948), have been persistently criticized as Western visions of rights discourse and enactment. They are seen to be both individualistic and inappropriate in the context of the economic and political need for Asian development. Criticism of Western models of rights has looked towards reformed versions of Confucian and Buddhist ethics as a model of justice and solidarity. Critics of Western individualism have noted the growing importance of the East Asian discourse on Human Rights following from the Bangkok Declaration on human rights (1993). This emerging interest in an Asian alternative has been stimulated by the need to protect civil society against growing global economic competition and the challenge to social solidarity from increasing income inequality and poverty. A variety of non-Western governments have simultaneously been under pressure to enforce international human rights agreements in their region. Political resentment of what is seen as Western interference has been orchestrated publicly by Lee Kuan Yew of Singapore and Mahatir Mohamad of Malaysia. In 1999 these tensions between United Nations resolutions on human rights enforcement and Asian politics were further intensified in the case of East Timor and the political crisis of Indonesia, with growing violence between Christian and Muslim communities. Many Asian leaders have subsequently been influenced by the so-called 'Lee Thesis' that Western-style human rights legislation is incompatible with and irrelevant to the economic and political needs of developing societies in Asia. More positively, it is argued that 'the Asian Way' has a strong communitarian tradition which is incompatible with and superior to the underlying individualism of the (Western) human rights tradition. There is a clear resonance between Western communitarianism and Asian communitarianism as the foundation for a critique of economic individualism and liberalism.

Against the Lee Thesis, it is certainly the case that some authoritarian regimes (South Korea, Singapore and China) have enjoyed higher rates of economic growth than many less authoritarian regimes (India, Costa Rica or Jamaica), but the issue is more complex than a simple set of highly selective comparisons. Even if a causal relationship could be identified between authoritarianism and sustained economic growth, there is still an argument to be made in favour of the intrinsic value of human rights. More significantly, no substantial famine has ever occurred in a society with a democratic form of government and a relatively free press (Sen, 1999). Authoritarianism may survive paradoxically in a context of economic success, but few governments can survive a catastrophe like a substantial famine. Elected governments have to be sensitive to popular pressure. Any simple picture of the Oriental East–West dichotomy should be questioned because for example the natural law tradition had a strong communitarian dimension. Social philosophers like Charles Taylor (1999) have explored restatements of the Buddhist traditions for a moral and political view of the connections between human rights and environmentalism. The contemporary reform of Theravada Buddhism in Thailand has attacked the corruption of the principles of Enlightenment and responsibility in popular forms of Buddhism; it is equally critical of consumerism, environmental pollution and political corruption. Such a Buddhist tradition would provide opportunities for cross-cultural understandings (overlapping consensus) of human rights legislation (Gombrich and Obeyesekere, 1988).

**Women's rights under Islam**

One of the critical issues in contemporary human rights theory is the question of women's rights, especially women's rights in Muslim societies. The debate about women can only be understood in the context of religious reform. Reform Islam has required true Muslims to explore the Qur'an and the hadith for passages that encourage hard work, frugality and diligence. From the perspective of Reformers a correct interpretation of the Qur'an showed that it was compatible with modern science, democracy and rational thought, but that Islam had become corrupted by the importation of folk beliefs and by the survival of pre-Islamic practices in the popular movements of Sufism. In this sense, the fundamentalism of Islam was a necessary step towards its modernization. Contemporary fundamentalism has accepted this model of modernization with a supplementary formula, namely anti-Americanism, and in particular an official hostility to the Western media. The challenge to the individual rights of women in religious fundamentalism may be a paradoxical consequence of a modernization movement that is driven by religious beliefs. These arguments are important, partly because they illustrate the polyvalent nature of traditional religious texts and their openness to divergent interpretations, especially in religions that subscribe to the authority of the revealed word. Fundamentalists are not traditionalists in the sense that a traditionalist response would involve an assertion of the value of local customary practice. The attempt to impose an Islamic orthodoxy raises problems where the text is silent or divergent. This textual strategy makes it difficult to impose religious norms as a response to the secularization of religion as a matter of private practice.

The case of women's rights in Malaysia and Indonesia is interesting as an illustration of the debate over Qur'anic textual authority. The problem in East Asia is that in addition to struggles over modernist and traditionalist readings of the Qur'an, women's lives have traditionally also been regulated by local custom or *adat* that affirms women's public roles in a positive and non-hierarchical way. The rule of *hijab* (covering and seclusion) is not deeply embedded in the 'Malay world'. Throughout the 1980s and 1990s local ulema in several of the Malay states attempted to encourage polygamy. Women's groups in Malaysia and other Islamic societies have often been successful in challenging the argument that the right of polygamy is enshrined in the Qur'an. The traditionalist view of the Qur'an has been that women are a secondary creation (from the rib of Adam) and that they exist to satisfy men's needs. Women have challenged these arguments on the grounds that these anachronistic elements are not essential or compatible with the theme of gender equality in the Qur'an, the anachronistic verses are products of local historical circumstances (a principle of Islamic historicism) and the Qur'an expects that a husband will protect his wife and promote her welfare – marital goals that are difficult to reconcile with polygamy. The most sophisticated defence of women's equality has involved an appeal to a common ontology and has argued that Islamic law is not opposed to human rights because it supports the notion of a shared ontology. This awareness is by no means alien to Islam. It is grounded in the Qur'anic notion of a common ontology (*fitna*) and couched in an Islamic idiom of moral universalism that predates much of the Western discourses about human rights. It is thus, doctrinally, a part of the Qur'anic worldview itself. The quest to impose polygamy on a community that has traditionally operated as much by local customary practices as by Islamic norms has produced a reflexive reaction: what is tradition? what is orthodoxy? The idea that 'regressive' norms are the product of the historical specificity of the Qur'anic teachings raises difficult issues about what teachings are in fact *not* historically specific.

In these conflicts over history, authority and interpretation, the veil in Islam has assumed considerable cultural significance. The marriage contract in Islamic belief is a so-called 'root paradigm' that provides people with a cultural map for everyday behaviour. In its legal form, marriage is a contract involving a sale of goods and services. In exchange for a bride-price and maintenance, a husband gains exclusive rights to a woman's sexual services and thus over her personality. As a contractual relationship, it has to be entered into voluntarily and assumes consent on the part of the woman. The tension in this traditional formula is that the woman is both a legal person and an object, but the consequence of marriage is to impose on the woman a duty of obedience. According to Islamic convention, the disobedience of women is simultaneously an erosion of male privilege and an attack on the social order. Of course, within this normative framework, there is much scope for everyday negotiation of the mundane practice of marriage.

Let us briefly take the case of Iran. At various stages in Iranian modernization women had been encouraged to unveil: for example the Unveiling Act (1936) and the Family Protection Law (1967). During the secularization of Iranian society under Reza Shah, Muslim women had unveiled as they entered new urban occupations and interacted with Western culture. With the growth of religious opposition, Ayatollah Khomeini had encouraged women to adopt the veil as a protest against the Shah and as a symbol of their religious commitment. Fundamentalists supported protests of veiled women against the Pahlavi regime and cultivated respect for and identification with Zainab the granddaughter of the Prophet. In short, women were politically motivated to form a mass movement against a nationalist and secularist regime, and were organized around a set of religious symbols that did not always and necessarily coincide with the official theology of the ayatollahs.

Islamic fundamentalists have to confront the unintended consequences of their success as revolutionaries. One consequence is a heightened political consciousness amongst women. Having been exposed to radical Shi'ite discourse, urban women have engaged with the clerics over the interpretation of religious law and custom. The situation of women has been compounded by the consequences of the war with Iraq when, with the decline in the number of young men available for marriage, men were encouraged to engage in polygamy. Iranian women have replied by arguing that only in a true Muslim society can men maintain justice between several wives and thus under present circumstances women can only suffer from neglect and brutality. In both Iran and Pakistan, the nervousness of the authorities is illustrated by edicts to regulate the nature of veiling and to ensure that 'bad veiling' is avoided.

Contrary to the legacy of Orientalism, these examples also point to the fact that (in all religious cultures) with modernization the status of women, the family and sexual relationships become problematic, and traditional values no longer provide unambiguous guides for action. The demand for homosexual male couples to reproduce through surrogacy is a rights issue for which many traditional religious cultures have no immediate answer. The notion that there is a clearcut division between Western and Asian value systems when it comes to communitarian versus individualistic values is not convincing (DeBary, 1998). Although there is clear evidence that Confucianism embraces a communitarian tradition, it is ironic that in the early twentieth century radical Chinese leaders were anxious to overthrow Confucian values that were seen to be feudal in favour of the liberation of the individual from the constraints of Confucian traditionalism. The real point is that the notion of the sovereign individual of capitalism is relatively modern and not all forms of Western individualism endorse the notion of a rugged and independent individual (Abercrombie et al., 1986). Confucianism also taught respect for the value of the individual, but 'Confucian individualism' is better described as 'personalism' to distinguish this tradition from Western utilitarianism. The neo-Confucian ideal of self-cultivation provided the basis for opposition to Ming despotism with the aim of protecting personalism. Finally, the contemporary effort to claim Confucian communitarianism for state purposes contradicts the core Confucian tradition which saw voluntary co-operation within civil society as its ideal against the efforts of authoritarian states to appropriate or to co-opt Confucianism.

While cultural and moral relativism are views generally shared by intellectuals, we live in a period when theories of globalization are widely entertained by social scientists. Of course, an assumption that the modern world is subject to global pressures in economics, politics and culture does not necessarily mean that there is any corresponding set of assumptions that the social world is becoming more uniform. A global age does not automatically result in McDonaldization, because there can be equally powerful pressures towards localism and hybridity. The 'Reclaim the Streets' protests against global capitalism in 1998, and the disruption of the World Trade Organization conference in Seattle at the end of 1999, revealed the potential of the internet in the politics of resistance. Against the Bolshevik model of prominent cadres of leadership, the political organization of 'Reclaim the Streets' makes a virtue of opacity. While the protests are highly visible, using a mixture of situationist spectacles and new age symbolism to jam economic, industrial, political and civic activity, the political and communication structure is opaque and evasive, making it very difficult for the police to anticipate or curb anti-corporatist disruption. The success of this decentralized politics of resistance is a phenomenon of our time and perhaps hints at a new direction in how the struggle over scarcity and injustice might be waged in the future. At the same time it exposes the speciousness of globalization rhetoric which emphasizes the transcendentalism of global processes of communication. Globalization always involves specific networks of people, caught up in particular flows of power, which results in a variety of responses and formations.

Nevertheless, there is a widespread view in sociology that there are powerful pressures towards the experience of 'one world' solidarity. The rise of global tourism, world sport, communication networks, agencies like WHO and UNESCO, and the experience of common medical crises such as AIDS and HIV are features of globalism which result in a common experience of social change. Optimistic globalization theory may lull us into a false vision of the world as culturally relative and thus as having the potential for cultural integration. This form of cultural relativism (everything is relative and paradoxically everything is the same) precludes any serious debate about justice and suffers from the same dilemma as conventional liberalism. What does a liberal do in a world which is inhabited by people who don't accept liberalism? A liberal has problems with Fascism, when Fascists do not accept norms about freedom of speech. Cultural relativists have similar problems when fundamentalists regard relativism as an aspect of the disease of secularism. Anthony Woodiwiss's outstanding study on the sociology of law (1998) takes on the question of globalization in connection with the debate about liberal, social and Confucian moral codes.

### Globalization and labour

One crucial aspect of globalization has been the spread of common standards of employment and work conditions through enforceable inter-national legislation. Labour law is additionally important to our argument since the solidarity of labour has been a crucial source of social solidarity. Labour laws are fundamental conditions of positive notions of rights and freedoms. Those rights that are most pertinent to labour are rights to freedom of association, rights to work, just and favourable conditions, trade union membership, collective bargaining and a living wage. Because the capitalist economy produces class inequalities, as illustrated by systematic income inequality, the rights of citizenship have been regarded as basic to a rights regime. While the Lee Thesis argues that emergent capitalism cannot afford the luxury of Western-style human rights, Marxist legal theory claims that capitalism is intrinsically subversive of respect for human rights.

In Pacific Asia, labour is undertaken in conditions that are determined by the globalization of the world economy, and within this economy labour relations are modelled on Japanese industrial relations regimes. Whereas in the West, human rights have been pursued primarily as liberties or immuni-ties, in the patriarchal East they have been pursued as claims. Because activists in Asia are unlikely to win support for individualistic versions of human rights, they are better advised to follow neo-Confucianism and the more liberal tendencies within Buddhism and Islam in the context of 'enforceable benevolence' (Woodiwiss, 1998).

With the ending of the Cold War and the maturation of the economic take-off of Pacific Asia, a third force has erupted within global society as an alternative to liberalism and socialism, namely patriarchalism. These regimes are patriarchal in the Weberian sense that they adopt a familialist discourse that assumes the naturalness of inequalities and justifies them by reference to the respect due to a benevolent father-figure (such as the state) who exercises a joint right (in the interests of all members). Such a political relationship might not be thought compatible with the exercise of human rights. However, within patriarchal conditions there is always the possibility of 'enforceable benevolence', that is a mode of governance where, while hierarchy is maintained, the content of benevolence is democratically decided and legally enforced. Within these regional forms of patriarchalism there are specific opportunities for the production of human rights frameworks that are better adapted to indigenous traditions of Confucianism, Islam and Buddhism.

The greater levels of mobility and flexibility required by globalization introduce a new, or perhaps one might say, a heightened dynamic in labour relations. As the accumulation of surplus becomes more transnational, the challenges facing organized labour cease to be confined to the national level. The decision of the German car manufacturer BMW to divest itself of the British Rover car group in 2000 underlined the mobility and unsentimentality of capital. Anger in Britain led to consumer groups and trade unions urging consumers to 'buy British', a strategy that had been unsuccessfully tried before in the 'I'm Backing Britain' campaigns of the 1960s. What the BMW episode illustrated, in relation to consumer culture, is that consumers are every bit as mobile and unsentimental in their wants as capitalist suppliers. The futility of counting on rigidity or loyalty in consumer markets is reinforced by the switch of retailing to the internet. Faced with the choice of financing the retailer's display mark-up, or buying at a cheaper price, consumers are increasingly opting to buy at a cheaper price. The globalization of the market is a real phenomenon and persists irrespective of cultural or religious barriers.

These arguments suggest that we should not seek to replace Occidentalism with Orientalism in claiming the superiority of the Confucian or Buddhist traditions over Western cultures. We perceive opportunities for a more hybrid approach to human rights discourse that draws on many reformed traditions. One thing often missing, however, is a critical discussion of rights regimes: they have typically nothing to say about obligations. If we are to continue to embrace the notion of human rights, we need to spell out a corresponding set of obligations. For what are we responsible and how is that responsibility to be expressed? One possible answer that we wish to propose here is the notion of 'cosmopolitan virtue' as a companion to cosmopolitan democracy. The agenda for a new pattern of social solidarity involves a critical assessment of sources of solidarity in modern society through the ideas of the vulnerability and sensuousness of the body and the precariousness of the physical and institutional environment. On this basis, we argue, it is possible to attempt an assessment of the conditions for cosmopolitan virtue as a moral foundation for respect of others.

**Post-Cartesian capitalism?**

Throughout this discussion we have argued that as a social fact, the human body has become increasingly significant in the politics and economics of modern societies. The political prominence of the body is a product of various causes: the greying of the population, medical (reproductive) technology, social movements that are concerned with many dimensions of the human body (women's movements, gay and lesbian liberation, environmental and right-to-life movements), the impact of microbiological innovations and inventions on medicine, food production and warfare, and the consequences of sexual liberalization (including pornography and sexual tourism).

The apex of these concerns is located at the industrial and military – the interface between body and technology in the cyborg. These are manifestations of the medical-industrial complex of capitalism, of what we might call corporeal capitalism. The transformation of medical sciences and the capacities of medical technology have in principle created the conditions for, at the very least, the radical reassembly of familial and kinship relationships. While these issues are part of the historical development of capitalism as such, there are a number of more enduring and permanent questions about the relationship between embodiment, meaning and selfhood that will occupy us in the twenty-first century. The first question – the place of the body in social structure – is primarily a sociological problem. The second question – the place of embodiment in the formulation of a meaningful perspective on consciousness and identity – is, for want of a better expression, a religio-phenomenological problem. Economics, politics and sociology are intimately and irrevocably bound up with questions of corporeality. Money (exchange), blood and bread are common to all human groups: they unite individuals and form the basis of conflict.

The sociology of the body and the phenomenology of embodiment are two separate lines of enquiry, but we attempt to bring them into a critical conjunction. The connections are partly provided by Michel Foucault's seminal contrast between 'the anatomo-politics of the human body' and the 'bio-politics of the population' (Foucault, 1981: 139). This discussion is an attempt to elaborate further the notion of a 'somatic society', that is 'a social system in which the body, as simultaneously constraint and resistance, is the principal field of political and cultural activity . . . the dominant means by which the tensions and crises of society are thematized' (Turner, 1992: 12).

The growth in the prominence of the body in an advanced technological society is brought about by socio-technical developments that simultaneously erode the natural and comfortable intimacy of body and self. One sign of the transformations of the relationships between body, self and society is the obsolescence of effective corporeal metaphors as conduits of significance, meaning and emotion. The elementary corporeal foundations of society are being erased, and given the particularly close or binding relationship between body, self and religion, these changes are incompatible with the metaphorical frameworks of religious cultures.

Our embodiment is the basis on which our perceptions of the world are constructed, and the stuff from which our identities are framed. Consider the hand. Things are dextrous, handy and handsome, but also high handed, a handful or handicapped. The fact that the body is somehow important to the metaphors we use to think with has been commonly recognized in social anthropology. Consider religious mythology. Because the body is traditionally always the nearest-to-hand source of metaphors for understanding society, it is hardly surprising that for example the Abrahamic faiths are constructed around body metaphors: virgin births, charisma as blood, Adam's rib, incarnations, resurrections, and the Eucharistic feast. Elementary social theories have also been dependent on corporeal metaphors. The homology between body, house and cosmos has provided the building blocks of traditional mythologies (Eliade, 1959).

The feast provided the most basic model of society as a pattern of exchange, sacrifice and consumption; the Church is an institution that was conceptualized as a body. From the idea of the Church as the Body of Christ came early models of trading groups as corporations. The body of Mary, especially in her role as provider of the milk of paradise and as a model of religious humility, has been a rich source of metaphors about nurturing, suckling and caring. Patriarchalism was and remains a persistent component of theories of power as a generative force. The body is however more than a rich source of metaphor. It is constitutive of our being-in-the-world. This is why we have identified the sensuousness of the body as a foundation of our approach. It is because the human senses provide a common grid of experience, that notions of sympathy and sentiment have purchase in sociology.

A general sociological theory must seek to connect our embodiment to the building of social institutions and social interdependency. In many respects, this sociological argument returns to the critical philosophy of the young Marx's concepts of practice and alienation as embodied activities in the Paris Manuscripts. Humans are 'self-mediated beings of nature' in the sense that they produce themselves through their own practical activity as an encounter with their environment (Meszaros, 1970: 162). Human beings create their world through sensuous practical engagement with it so that Nature and their nature are effects of collective and practical activities or mediations (Schmidt, 1971). The question is: how are these necessary connections between embodiment, practice and environment dissolving in advanced technological civilizations?

There are three components to our argument: as sensuous creatures, we are ontologically frail; the institutions that we create to compensate for this frailty are also precarious; but there is a sociological compensation for frailty and precariousness in the interconnected and interdependent social world. The theory is neo-Hobbesian because it recognizes that life is nasty, brutish and short. However, the bleakness of the Hobbesian position is modified by the Feuerbachian premise of the pleasurable engagement with reality through the sensuous character of this practical embodiment, and further, by the assumption that humans are always and already social.

Our sensual apprehension of the world (for example through eating it) is a sensuous experience, driven by necessity and pleasure. Our adult response to the delight and fear that infants show in being in the world, is a sensuous reaction based upon genetics and memory. Human sympathy is the corollary of human sensuousness. Weber's writing on the method of *Verstehen* has been influential in sociology, precisely because we have the capacity to empathize with others as a corollary of the socialization process. Of course, one must also be aware of the Nietzschean Dionysian argument, that human sensuousness is also connected to violence and appropriation. The desire to make ourselves drunk with sensual pleasure, to cancel personal invalidity with overwhelming bodily gratification, is a common theme in human history. We could summarize by saying that social life is always a contingent or shifting balance between the rigours and constraints of (natural) scarcity, the pleasures and frailties of our embodiment, and the precarious comforts of human solidarity. These notions about self, practice and embodiment are developed to provide a theory and defence of human rights as a universalized system of (legal) protection against threats to our ontological frailty; an analysis of risk and regulation in modern society; and a commentary on the estrangement of the body from traditional systems of meaning and significance.

There is a dialectical relationship between these three components that becomes obvious when one thinks about modernization. The medical and technological revolutions of the twentieth century have encouraged us to believe that we are less frail and our world less precarious. Everywhere we are surrounded by the promise of a deathless existence, the final elimination of infectious disease and the ability to design our own children. Against this 'mirage of health' (Dubos, 1960), we need to recognize for example that by living longer, a larger proportion of our lives is spent in disability and dependency. Our naïve over-dependence on antibiotics has now made our hospitals precarious in the face of super-bugs (such as streptococcus aureus bacterium). Globalization has indeed made the world a single disease space not only for influenza but also for TB. The outbreak of 'old' infectious diseases in New York and London proves that new varieties of disease are multi-drug resistant. As the institutions of 'governmentality' (Foucault, 1991) increase to monitor risk, so our lives become politically more precarious. A decrease in (ontological) frailty produces an increase in (political) precariousness. The growth of a 'risk society' (Beck, 1992) means that modern societies are increasingly regulated and controlled: social life comes increasingly under a system of governmentality.

It is within this dialectical balance of frailty, precariousness and interconnectedness that modern medical technologies are powerful and far reaching. If our embodiment is the real source of our commonality and our community, then changes to our embodiment must have significant but uncertain implications for both frailty and interconnectedness. The new microbiological revolution is Cartesian (in separating mind and body), that is driven by a powerful commercial logic, and it has (largely unrecognized) military uses and implications. Cloning, reproductive technology and organ transplants both express and enhance social inequalities (especially between societies) and they have the potential to transform our human identity. Paradoxically the more powerful medicine becomes, the more the patient disappears behind the disease. As the disease entity dominates the patient, medicine becomes more fragmented and specialized in terms of disciplines that compete for funding and pre-eminence.

Consider religious mythology. *Religio* is that which binds and disciplines a community whose humanity is a function of a shared set of experiences of birth, maturation, procreation and death. It is difficult to see how this *communitas* could survive the medical rationalization of our world or how anything could replace or stand in for this *religio*. This loss is one sense in which we can speak of the 'end(s) of "man"'. The implication of philosophical anthropology would be that identity, especially gender identity, is embodied and that the transformation of our traditional *habitus* must include the transformation of identities or sexualities. The twentieth-century philosopher who perhaps saw this coming most clearly was Martin Heidegger (1977) who believed that modern technology would come between our being and the world. Does this Heideggerian critique of modernity as the end of man necessarily entail Fascism?

As the body becomes the real material of economic and technological growth, we are increasingly alienated from our own bodies. The body (or at least body parts) becomes a commodity within a global network of exchange, a commodity in the exchange between North and South that potentially leaves donors and recipients in debt. One measure of this alienation can be seen in the exhaustion of corporeal metaphors to express our connectedness with our environment through practical activity. This situation offers a remarkably ironic reflection on the origins of Marx's critique of alienation in capitalist society, where 'critical criticism' engaged with capital via a preliminary and necessary onslaught against religion. While Ludwig Feuerbach's *The Essence of Christianity* (1957) had exposed the inverted world of Christianity in which human powers were mistakenly ascribed to sacred powers, Marx's political economy explored the real basis of social reality in the practical (economic) activities of human beings. Although Christianity, especially Protestant Christianity, was a mythological parallel of human alienation in capitalism, religion remained the sign of the oppressed creature and the heart of a heartless world. What best expresses metaphorically the nexus between frailty, precariousness and interconnectedness? One answer would be the crucified Christ, the Lamb of God, who gave his body that we might have eternal life. In short, Christianity reversed the ancient sacrifice in which human life was destroyed to placate the gods, by the sacrifice of the Son to create a community between humanity and the God.

These metaphors of exile (from the Garden), sacrifice and God's redemptive work (the Christ figure) were not peculiar to Christianity. On the contrary, they form a segment of a much more general vocabulary of human salvation through a theology of birth, exile and restoration. The metaphors of birth and rebirth formed part of a comprehensive discourse of sacred mythology. Of course, there were profound changes in primitive mythology, for example with the rise of agrarian societies that made possible the cults of Mother Earth as a cosmic figure of fecundity (Eliade, 1958). These metaphors of human religion are now largely obsolete, with the medicalization of life through technical innovation. They are specifically redundant as the possibilities of natural reproduction by a sexual act are replaced by artificial means of reproduction. However, the transformations of reproductive relationships mask a more profound erasure, namely the gradual disembodiment of life. These (secular) transformations are the new (religious) alienation. In order to clarify these relations between technology, body and society, we need to tell a sociological story about the strange connections between rites and rights.

These arguments from philosophical anthropology are relatively well known and understood, especially since the legacy of Arnold Gehlen (1988) has recently become more widely recognized and acknowledged. In order to put this philosophical argument into a more definite sociological and political framework, we will direct the discussion towards legal questions about human and social rights, and thereby map out a set of connections between the body and citizenship. Within the framework of human rights and social citizenship, we are concerned to examine the embodiment of individuals and the reproduction of populations. Some examples are drawn therefore from the impact of medical innovation on human reproduction. Human reproduction has been fundamental to human society, not simply because populations need to be replaced over time, but because the institutions that surround reproduction (patriarchy, kingship, religion and the family) are basic to the exercise of power in human societies. Medical innovations in the conditions of reproduction transform (in principle) the basis of human embodiment and identity, but these transformations have social consequences that are poorly understood and health consequences that are unpredictable. Although sociologists have probably overused, exploited and debased the expression 'social revolution', it is clear that the transformation of microbiological sciences and their technological applications are bringing about a massive and revolutionary transformation of human societies. The danger is that we do not fully understand the immediate implications of these changes, especially with respect to reproduction. However, the medical revolution in reproductive technologies, cloning, the Human Genome Project and bio-cybernetics, in addition to their potential social benefits, do open up huge opportunities for the commodification of the body and its militar-ization. We do not understand the long-term consequences of these changes for human ontology.

Sociologists have attempted to understand the social implications of these scientific changes in terms of a theory of risk. The paradoxical consequence of the attempt to regulate reproduction by medical rationalism is the proliferation of risk. As the social risks of artificial reproduction increase, the state will need to intervene to regulate the medical profession and the national market in body parts. However, state regulation of the (public) conditions of (private) reproductive activities cannot be easily or effectively secured, because medical establishments and medical markets are unregulated, partly because they are global. State legislative regulation of scientific innovations will be typically retrospective, reluctant and ineffectual. It is difficult to see how the state could effectively monitor the behaviour of scientists in corporate laboratories, where the incentives of economic profit and scientific fame are so potent. There are important variations in government policy on the management of these medical innovations, but it is unlikely that deregulation and market forces will be the optimal solution. The current attempts of the British government to regulate the spread of GM products and to carry out controlled experiments of GM crops illustrate the difficulties that confront governments attempting to regulate global corporations. British government responses have been driven partly by the erosion of consumer trust, but these responses developed after GM products such as modified soya bean had already been widely adopted in North America and continental Europe. These problems with GM foods followed the disasters of 'mad cow disease' and provided a classic illustration of the difficulties faced by governments confronted with contradictory expert knowledge. Although the problems of enforcing regulation are significant, the national consequences of not regulating are equally obvious.

This criticism provides the basis for a discussion of the medical and commercial processes by which the human body is treated as a collection of manageable and marketable parts – a set of processes which we can for convenience refer to as McDonaldization (Ritzer, 1993). The rise of McSociety is a product of the application of Fordism and Taylorism to the management cultures of a variety of institutions – the food industry, hotels, health services and universities. It is plausible to think of the management of the human body in a variety of settings as McDonaldization. For example, the delivery practices and processes of maternity units in British public hospitals are McDonaldized, because there is an expectation that a cohort of women will deliver babies of a certain weight and at specific times determined by the hospital management. The labour of mothers is often still induced in order to create an orderly queue of births out of a disruptive assembly of people. In medical science, the female body is regarded as an inefficient machine for reproduction that requires significant management and, if possible, re-engineering.

Although these processes are the result of twentieth-century management strategies, the philosophy underlying these procedures is Cartesian in the sense that the body can be treated as a machine. With the development of a global market for organs, the collection of organs from donors is referred to as 'harvesting' and the price of spare body parts is determined by a global market that is morally and legally questionable. One could develop another version of *The Protestant Ethic and the Spirit of Capitalism* (Weber, 1930) in which Descartes's separation of the mind and the body in 'Cogito ergo sum' paves the way towards an elective affinity between Cartesian objective rationalism and the economic cultures of global capitalism. Cartesianism found an elective affinity with possessive individualism, accumulation and discipline.

This new social environment of biological experimentation vividly confirms the social developments that are registered in the notion of risk society. Risks associated with the new biology are an inevitable aspect of the processes of modernization. As the risks of medical experimentation increase, we can detect an expansion of the regulative technologies of society, namely 'governmentality', whereby the state is harnessed to increasing the productive powers of populations through for example eugenic policies. There is a dialectical relationship between the growth of medical risks and the development of new regimes of regulation. The rationalization processes that make possible a precise and detailed regulation of society can be employed to understand for instance the growing medicalization of birth through such techniques as contraception, *in vitro* fertilization, new reproductive technologies and cloning. More generally, the new relationships between the economy, society and the body in terms of organ transplants, global organ marketing, surrogacy and internet donorships can be described as a process of rationalization or McDonaldization. One can already anticipate a reaction to McDonaldized bodies or McBody in terms of a quest for authentic embodiment. We envisage this conflict between McDonaldization and the authentic body as a further elaboration of the critical debate between the rational defence of technology and Martin Heidegger's attack on modern science.

## Cool citizenship and thin solidarity

Religion was a powerful force of social solidarity in traditional society, but these sacral bonds have been weakened by secularization and industrialization. Citizenship offers the possibility of a secular foundation for solidarity. However, because the citizenship tradition, like the human rights tradition, has concentrated on the problem of rights, it has not developed a rich language of obligation. We have also noted that historically there was a powerful relationship between religious and nationalistic patterns of solidarity. These systems were typically exclusive and the core problem of modern politics is to develop more inclusive criteria. The distinction between hot and cool loyalties and thick and thin patterns of solidarity can provide a useful framework for thinking about identity and membership in modern society (Turner, 1999). This fourfold property space enables us to develop a view of cosmopolitan identity that incorporates an ironic distance from one's own culture and develops an ethic of care for others. These ideas about membership can usefully draw on the legacy of Durkheim. The distinction between hot/cool loyalties is taken from McLuhan's (1964) analysis of modern communication; for example, the telephone offers a unidimensional communication with high definition. It is a cool medium, whereas the tribal mode of communication of tradition by oral and ritualistic means is hot. This distinction in McLuhan's theory of the media is redeployed in this conclusion to talk about modes of loyalty in the modern state. Hot personalities are intensely attached to local central value systems and view hybridity and globalization with suspicion. They provide insulation and support for themselves by building or reinforcing thick layers of kith, kin and community ties around them. Hot/thick types reject the proposition that the world is changing and stress instead the historical continuities in social life. Often, they treat the challenge of globalization as a problem of social inequality. Not everyone engages in long distance travel, not everyone has access to the internet. Look at India and Africa where most people do not have a telephone, let alone a computer, and where a bicycle is a more common means of transport than an aeroplane. Hot/thick types acknowledge the rise of a cosmopolitan vernacular in respect of the analysis of contemporary forms of identity, practice and association. But they reject the thesis that the vernacular translates into new ways of being.

In contrast cool/thin types are more mobile, both in their physical patterns of movement and their social and cultural perspective. Their 'coolness' does not refer to their sense of personal cachet, but rather to their qualified connection to solid, coherent value positions. Cool personalities regard the world as inherently contradictory. This may not mean that they take the road to moral relativism. On the contrary, cool types often insist on the moral importance of equality and freedom. However, their commitment tends to be at an abstract level, rather than at the level of continuous micro-politics. Cool types are typically situated in long networks of communication. It is not unusual for them to feel closer to people who correspond with them on the internet, than to colleagues in the same workplace or neighbours in the same street or apartment block.

Now in a system of global cultures, postmodern or cosmopolitan citizenship will be characterized by cool loyalties and thin patterns of solidarity. Indeed we could argue that the characteristic mode or orientation of the cosmopolitan citizen would in fact be one of Socratic or ironic distance. An ironist always holds her views about the social worlds in doubt, because they are always subject to revision and reformulation. Her picture of society is always provisional or temporary and she is sceptical about grand narratives, because her own 'final vocabulary' is always open to further inspection and correction. Her ironic views of the world are always 'for the time being'. If the cosmopolitan mentality is cool, the social relationships of the ironist will of necessity be thin; indeed email friendships and electronic networks will constitute the new patterns of friendship in a postmodern globe. In our account of Muslim women asking questions about the marriage contract, Indonesian women raising issues about female judges or Iranian women challenging the injunction of Hashemi Rafsanjani for men to adopt polygamy, we can see a reflexivity that suggests irony in Rorty's sense: namely, are these practices useful in promoting a good society? Ironists are people who are in some sense dislodged from their traditional worlds and find themselves in new situations where old answers no longer work. They are inclined towards reflexivity, because they get the point of hermeneutic anthropology. In this anthropologically reflexive context, the world is a site of contested loyalties and interpretations.

Given the complexity and the hybridization of modern society, there is no convenient place for hot emotions. Intercultural sensitivities and the need to interact constantly with strangers promote irony as the most prized norm of wit and principle of taste. Irony is sensitive to the simulation which is necessary for interaction in multicultural societies (Rorty, 1989). In such a world, ironic distance is functionally compatible with globalized hybridity, because we have all become strangers in the Simmelian City. Hot emotions and thick solidarities are dysfunctional to social intercourse, which has to take place on a mobile, and often artificial, plane. Although there has been much criticism of the emotional barrenness of the City of Artifice, post-emotionalism (Meštrović, 1997) may be functionally necessary for modern society to exist as a social system.

Perhaps it is not too fanciful to believe that, precisely because of their exposure to global concerns and global issues, the cool/thin type, in recognizing the ubiquity of hybridization, rejects all claims to cultural superiority and cultural dominance. Precisely because we are exposed to global forces of postmodernization, the cool/thin personality should welcome a stance which supports postcolonial cultures and celebrates the teeming diversity of human cultures. In their awareness of the tensions between local cultures and global processes, cosmopolitan virtue might come to include stewardship over and for cultures which are precarious. Cool/thin types, being convinced of the evolutionary importance of bio-diversity, would be equally careful in their support of cultural hetero-geneity.

In order to avoid being misunderstood, it is perhaps necessary to state again that moral indifference is not the necessary condition of cool/thin types. In academic life, we often think of the intellectual as the cultural hero, who is passionately committed to social and political causes. However, care for other cultures might be conceptualized in terms of the psychoanalytic relationship, in which the neutral analyst has to listen carefully to what the other is saying. Moral responses to pain may require not passion but care as a controlled emotional engagement. One could imagine that cosmopolitan virtue will take on a careful engagement with cultural issues such as the protection of so-called primitive cultures and Aboriginal communities which are clearly threatened by the globalization of tourism, and responsibility for advocacy in a world of collapsing environments and endangered languages. Cool/thin types do not argue that fundamentalism is, in some simple sense, false. Rather, they join with local voices to probe and if necessary to problematize debate. But only rarely do they make these debates a life cause or mission. It is plausible to regard cool/thin types as heralding a new kind of cosmopolitan virtue. We consider the features of this construct below.

This discussion has attempted to follow that recommendation in not dismissing fundamentalists as misguided traditionalists or anti-modernists, and in arguing that, because traditional texts are always and already open to question, there are in that sense no final vocabularies. Equally it may mean that one cannot take automatically a wholly critical view of nationalism as a basis for personal identity. Nationalism is clearly on the increase in European societies, where the demise of communism has left an identity vacuum. Intellectuals have been generally hostile to nationalism, but it is important to distinguish between its liberal and illiberal versions, and between the idea of nation as cultural identity and nationalism as a political movement. The assertion of belonging to a nation does not automatically involve commitment to an illiberal nationalist movement.

## Cosmopolitan virtue

We suggest that the components of cosmopolitan virtue are as follows:

1  Irony, both as a cultural method and as a contemporary mentality, in order to achieve some emotional distance from our own local history and culture.
2  Reflexivity with respect to other cultural values and a recognition that all perspectives are culturally and historically conditioned and contingent.
3  Scepticism towards the grand narratives of modern ideologies.
4  Care for other cultures, especially Aboriginal cultures, arising from an awareness of their precarious condition and hence acceptance of cultural hybridization.
5  An ecumenical commitment to dialogue with other cultures, especially religious cultures.
6  Nomadism, in the sense of never being fully at home in cultural categories or geo-political boundaries, and constant awareness of the difference and otherness that these categories and boundaries exclude.

Cosmopolitan virtue is generally incompatible with nostalgia, because it recognizes that our modern dilemmas cannot be solved simply by a naïve return to origins. Cosmopolitanism is specifically a product of globalization and modernity, but it also has much in common with Stoic cosmopolitanism that, among other things, attempted to come to terms with the cultural diversity of classical times (Hill, 2000). Cosmopolitan virtue is not offered here as the basis for a new political party. In so far as it is translated into the sphere of party politics it is likely to break down under the weight of its own contradictions. We suggest that this is what is already occurring with 'third wayism' which, unlike the hot/thick approach of communitarianism, is perhaps one of the primary exponents of cool/thin values. Nonetheless, in terms of identity formation and political *orientation*, cosmopolitan virtue is already very significant. Arguably, in academic circles, politics and the multimedia it has become pre-eminent in the last two decades. Whereas the hot/thick values of 'old Labour' proved to be electoral poison, at least in terms of securing a majority vote, the cool/thin values of 'new Labour' have proved to be peculiarly successful in securing power. They parallel Clinton's 'pact with America', in prioritizing mobile, fluid, energy over deep, methodical planning and diversified, decentralized social entrepreneurship over centralized state intervention.

Our attempt to develop an outline of cosmopolitan virtue follows directly from Edward Said's critique of Orientalism. For Said, homelessness, nostalgia and being 'out of place' (Said, 1999) have been dominant aspects of his literary studies. Said's sense of homeless is germane to our analysis of modern society as a nomadic existence. In Said's case, there was, so to speak, a triple exile – national, familial and personal. The nationalistic exile is obvious. Said inherited American citizenship from his father Wadie Said, who acquired his US passport from service in the American Expeditionary Force under General Pershing in 1917, but his ethnic and social roots were in Arab culture. His childhood experiences were formed by the evolution of this sense of exile from the culture of English preparatory schools, remoteness from American school culture and alienation from the nationalism of American universities. Then there was a familial exile from the dominating figure of his father, whose commercial success and regimented asceticism represented a permanent challenge to Said's identity. The patriarchal father was, so to speak, offset by the sympathetic and intellectual figure of his mother. The personal exile is the contradiction between his cultural roots and his educational experiences, between the first name of 'Edward' and the family name of 'Said'. These contradictions are explored in *Out of Place* as a series of tensions between 'Edward' and 'Said'. 'Edward' was the creation of his parents who were themselves self-creations – two Palestinians with dramatically different backgrounds and temperaments living in colonial Cairo as members of a Christian minority within a large pond of minorities, with only each other for support, without any precedent for what they were doing except an odd combination of prewar Palestinian habit.

Said, in his subtle and painstaking unpicking of Orientalism, has always been conscious of the paradoxical relationships between Western hostility to 'Arabs' and anti-Semitic notions of the 'Jews'. The study of Orientalism must logically include an analysis of anti-Semitism, because the negative view of Islam is part of a larger hostility towards Semitic cultures in the West. There has been a general anti-Semitism in Europe, in which antagonism to Jews has often accompanied hostility to Muslims. Generally speaking, the academic critique of Orientalism has not noticed the ironic connection between these two forms of racism, namely against Arabs and against Jews. In his Introduction to *Orientalism*, Said writes that in 'addition, and by an almost inescapable logic, I have found myself writing the history of a strange, secret sharer of Western anti-Semitism. That anti-Semitism and, as I have discussed it in its Islamic branch, Orientalism resemble each other very closely is a historical, cultural and political truth that needs only be mentioned to an Arab Palestinian for its irony to be perfectly understood' (Said, 1978: 27–8). In replies to his critics, Said has emphasized the parallels between what he calls 'Islamophobia' and anti-Semitism. Because Said has been sensitive to the exile of both religious communities in his overtly academic work on colonialism and literature, the irony of the Palestinian Diaspora dominates his overtly political writing.

There is a strange parallel between Walter Benjamin's 'A Berlin Chronicle' (Benjamin, 1978) and *Out of Place*. Benjamin's *Berliner Chronik*, published in Germany in 1970, was sketched out in his first stay in 1932 in Ibiza and explores the Berlin of his childhood and youth, but the real topic is the act of memory itself, the techniques of remembering. The two memories come together as works of generic melancholy. We know that Benjamin, remembering in 1932 the comforts of his middle-class background and his excursions to the Zoo and Tiergarten with nursemaids, was to face death at the hands of Fascists. We know that Said, remembering the comforting intimacy of the relationship with his mother and the caring relationship with Auntie Mela, will face the evolving tragedy of Palestine against the background of his illness and isolation. But this is merely to say that all acts of memory are melancholic practices, and that most of the time we are, if not out of place, than at least out of joint. We cannot fashion the history of our times to satisfy the needs of our own biographies. Hence the tendency of human life to exhibit the debris of an exile experience.

## Conclusion: intimacy against nostalgia

Cosmopolitan virtue is a function of the globalization of society and the need for more inclusive and flexible models of citizenship. It reflects the increase in the numbers of people throughout the world with dual citizenship; and the tendency of governments to reduce the residential criteria of citizenship to facilitate membership; the rise of the transnational corporation and the growth of multinational work patterns; and the ubiquity of the multimedia in challenging 'received' models of family, community and nationalism with data reflecting difference and otherness (Clarke et al., 1998). In as much as this is so, we expect the number of cool/thin types to increase with a corresponding decline in hot/thick types. Of course, this process will never be absolute and we would disagree with the inference that cool/thin types will *replace* hot/thick types. We are referring here to contexts of being, primary compulsions in the organization of identity, practice and association, rather than an absolutist numbers game. Globalization, the spread of the transnational corporation and the increase in travel, will exert more pressure on the viability of hot/thick forms of being.

One sign of this increasing pressure is the intense, but sporadic, anti-capitalist protests that became a feature of *fin-de-siècle* capitalist culture and, for the foreseeable future, seem set to continue. The 'guerrilla gardening' or 'avant-gardening' that disrupted London in 2000 is a case in point. The daubing of paint on the Cenotaph and the statue of Winston Churchill in Parliament Square, and the planting of marijuana plants on the green, attracted considerable media coverage. What was ignored in the reports is the profoundly nostalgic character of the riot. Without a plausible alternative to advanced capitalism, the protesters resorted to elemental metaphors in antinomian politics – clearing the soil, planting seeds, shedding blood (red paint). This was an example of the anti-modern writ in Parliament Square, overlooked by the mother of all parliaments. Amid the McDonald's chains (the Whitehall branch was trashed in the riots), the Starbuck's coffee houses, the All Bar One pubs, some kind of halt to the 'madness' of capitalism was demanded. Of course, it failed. Klein's (2000) sharp analysis of the revolt against logo culture proposes the possibility of an anti-logo social movement as the spearhead of a genuinely new revolutionary politics. This argument fails too. Since Marx, we have known that capitalism is a seductive as well as a brutal mode of production. The theory of surplus value demonstrated how wealth is extracted from wage labour and how ideology functions to regulate populations. For much of the last century, the possibility of overturning capitalism in the advanced industrial countries was real. But with the collapse of statism in Eastern Europe, and the postmodern turn which highlighted social differentiation, the limitations of dominant ideology theories and the flexibility and mobility of lifestyles, the possibility of transformation has receded. Hobsbawm (1961) wrote of social banditry in the rise of industrial society. Interestingly, his argument was mainly directed against the factory system and it privileged the sphere of production as the trigger for change. Against capitalist control, are offered various versions of the thesis that society should be controlled by associated labour practising non-hierarchical relations. The guerrilla gardeners or avant-gardeners of the twentieth century direct their attacks against high finance (the World Trade Organization, the Stock Exchange) and the brain-washing processes of commodity consumption. Three changes in the composition of advanced capitalist society combine to restrict the transformative potential of these processes.

First, the collapse of statism in Eastern Europe has removed society-wide experiments in socialist engineering from the doorstep of Western Europe and from the immediate sphere of interests of North America. The recognition that statist regimes were not morally superior to the market, and the widespread consensus that they were economically inferior to the capitalist mode, has diminished popular interest in the state-centred revolt against capitalism. The traditional aims of socialism – greater equality and more justice – have not disappeared. They are now spread out between social movements and lifestyles rather than centred on party and state.

Secondly, the denationalization of publicly owned companies in the 1980s, and the expansion of relatively low risk share options like unit trusts, Personal Equity Plans and Individual Savings Accounts, significantly increased the shareholding element in wage labour. One can argue about the character of this shift. For example, in the UK there is probably a North/South divide among wage-labourer shareholders, with the higher incomes of the south, or more particularly, the south-east, producing a higher propensity for shareholding. Equally, share issues from privatized public companies may not be retained. There is some evidence that neo-phyte shareholders have sought quick profits, rather than an immediate or long-term return. However, what is not in dispute is that the numbers with exposure to shareholding increased appreciably in the Thatcher–Reagan years, and that the trend has been maintained under subsequent admin-istrations.

Thirdly, the globalization of capital and the intensification of mass communications have given a more pronounced role to the sign economy in the organization of everyday life. The ubiquity of advertising and the accessibility of the multimedia have partly decoupled the aesthetics of commodity culture from the accumulation process. Of course, capitalists expect their advertising campaigns and product design to translate into increased sales. But the sophistication of advertising aesthetics disables the traditional call for the transcendence of commodity culture. Goldman and Papson (1998) describe the layers of complexity surrounding the com-modity form today, and demonstrate how commodities are routinely appreciated as popular works of art and accessories of aestheticized lifestyles. Faced with the world of Apple Mac, Nike, Calvin Klein, DKNY and even McDonald's, how many really want to follow the anti-capitalists and wage war against the logos in pursuit of an inchoate alternative of recognition and belonging?

The prominence of the metaphor of the soil and the plea for 'self-sufficiency' in the ideology of the avant-gardeners is revealing. Decorative sociology would have us believe that people are moving towards a state of post-humanism, in which email communication replaces face-to-face contact and velocity replaces blood and place as the new (mobile) locus of belonging. Yet the statistics on leisure pastimes suggest more rooted notions of identity and belonging. In Britain today 60,000 people are employed in the gardening industry and the industry is growing at a rate of 20 per cent per year. Three out of every four Britons – a higher percentage than any industrial country – possess a garden or outdoor space for cultivation. Two out of every three identify gardening as a hobby, making it, in statistical terms, the most popular national pastime. More visit garden centres than all of the National Trust properties and theme parks combined. In 1999, £3 billion was spent on plants alone, and a further £3 billion on deckchairs, irrigation systems, ponds, pesticides and conservatories (*Guardian*, 24 May 2000). Britain seems to be a country in which the garden gnome possesses more cultural resonance than the cyborg.

In turning towards the ancient metaphor of the soil for their protests, and in berating corporate capitalism, the avant-gardeners were highlighting continuities in how people think about identity, solidarity and oppression. On the whole, decorative sociology emphasizes the discontinuities of change and, arguably, exaggerates the significance of developments which are relatively marginal to the consciousness of collective life. Without wishing to minimize their significance, we believe it is probably unrealistic to posit that a viable politics of change can be built upon Web-world or cyborg culture. We may have entered a stage in which the dialectic between home and homelessness is a more accentuated feature of public and private life. But for the time being, blood, place and soil remain at the forefront of social consciousness, just as they continue to dominate personal self-consciousness.

# REFERENCES

Abell, P. (1996) 'Rational Choice Theory' in B.S. Turner (ed.) *The Blackwell Companion to Social Theory*. Oxford: Blackwell. pp. 252–273.

Abercrombie, N. (1980) *Class Structure and Knowledge*. Oxford: Blackwell.

Abercrombie, N., Hill, S. and Turner, B.S. (1980) *The Dominant Ideology Thesis*. London: Allen & Unwin.

Abercrombie, N., Hill, S. and Turner, B.S. (1986) *Sovereign Individuals of Capitalism*. London: Allen & Unwin.

Abercrombie, N., Hill, S. and Turner, B.S. (eds) (1990) *Dominant Ideologies*. London: Unwin Hyman.

Abu-Zahra, N. (1997) *The Pure and the Powerful. Studies in Contemporary Muslim Society*. Reading: Ithaca Press.

Adorno, T. (1995) *The Stars Come Down to Earth*. London: Routledge.

Adorno, T. and Horkheimer, M. (1944) *Dialectic of Enlightenment*. London: Verso.

Adriaansens, H. (1980) *Talcott Parsons and the Conceptual Dilemma*. London: Routledge & Kegan Paul.

Ahmed, A. (1992) *Postmodernism and Islam*. London: Routledge.

Alatas, S.H. (1977) *The Myth of the Lazy Native*. London: Frank Cass.

Alexander, J. (1984) *Theoretical Logic in Sociology, Talcott Parsons*, Vol. 4. London: Routledge & Kegan Paul.

Alexander, J. (ed.) (1985) *Neofunctionalism*. Beverly Hills, CA: Sage.

Alexander, J. (1987) *Twenty Lectures, Sociological Theory since World War II*. New York: Columbia University Press.

Alexander, J. (1988) *Neofunctionalism and After*. Oxford: Blackwell.

Althusser, L. (1966) *For Marx*. London: Allen Lane, The Penguin Press.

Althusser, L. (1971) *Lenin and Philosophy and Other Essays*. London: New Left Books.

Anderson, B. (1983) *Imagined Communities. Reflections on the Origin and Spread of Nationalism*. London: Verso.

Anderson, P. (1974a) *Passages from Antiquity to Feudalism*. London: New Left Books.

Anderson, P. (1974b) *Lineages of the Absolutist State*. London: New Left Books.

Antoni, C. (1962) *From History to Sociology. The Transition in German Historical Thinking*. London: Merlin Press.

Arberry, A.J. (1960) *Oriental Essays. Portraits of Seven Scholars*. London: George Allen & Unwin.

Arendt, H. (1958) *The Human Condition*. Chicago: Chicago University Press.

Arendt, H. (1996) *Love and Saint Augustine*. Chicago and London: University of Chicago Press.

Arkoun, M. (1998) 'Islam, Europe, the West. Meanings-at-Stake and the Will-to-Power' in J. Cooper, R.L. Nettler and M. Mahmoud (eds) *Islam and Modernity. Muslim Intellectuals Respond*. London and New York: I.B. Tauris. pp. 172–215.

Armstrong, D. (1983) *Political Anatomy of the Body. Medical Knowledge in Britain in the Twentieth Century*. Cambridge: Cambridge University Press.

Arnold, M. (1969) *Culture and Anarchy*. Cambridge: Cambridge University Press.

Aronowitz, S. and Di Fazio, W. (1994) *The Jobless Future*. Minneapolis: University of Minnesota Press.

Aronowitz, S. and Cutler, J. (eds) (1998) *Post-Work*. London and New York: Routledge.

Asad, T. (1993) *Genealogies of Religion. Discipline and Reasons of Power in Christianity and Islam*. Baltimore and London: Johns Hopkins University Press.

Atchley, R.C. (1989) 'A Continuity Theory of Normal Aging', *The Gerontologist*, 29 (2): 183–190.

Auerbach, E. (1953) *Mimesis. The Representation of Reality in Western Literature*. Princeton, NJ: Princeton University Press.

Ayers, R. (2000) 'Serene and Happy and Distant: an Interview with Orlan' in M. Featherstone (ed.) *Body Modifications*. London: Sage. pp. 171–184.

Bahro, R. (1978) *The Alternative in Eastern Europe*. London: Verso.

Barbalet, J.M. (1998) *Emotion, Social Theory and Social Structure. A Macrosociological Approach*. Cambridge: Cambridge University Press.

Baring, E. (1908) *Modern Egypt*. London: Macmillan.

Barry, B.M. (1977) 'Justice between Generations' in P.M.S. Hacker and J. Raz (eds) *Law, Morality and Society. Essays in Honour of H.L.A. Hart*. Oxford: Clarendon. pp. 268–284.

Barthes, R. (1973) *Mythologies*. London: Paladin.

Barthes, R. (1977) *Image-Music-Text*. London: Fontana.

Bataille, G. (1985) *Visions of Excess. Selected Writings 1927–1939*. Minneapolis: University of Minnesota Press.

Bataille, G. (1987) *Eroticism*. London: Marion Boyars.

Bataille, G. (1991) *The Accursed Share, Vols 2 and 3*. New York: Zone Books.

Baudrillard, J. (1983a) *In the Shadow of the Silent Majorities*. New York: Semiotext(e).

Baudrillard, J. (1983b) *Simulations*. New York: Semiotext(e).

Baudrillard, J. (1987) *The Evil Demon of Images*. Sydney: Power Institute.

Baudrillard, J. (1989) *America*. London: Verso.

Baudrillard, J. (1990) *Cool Memories*. London: Verso.

Bauman, Z. (1987) *Legislators and Interpreters. On Modernity, Post-modernity and Intellectuals*. Cambridge: Polity.

Bauman, Z. (1993) *Postmodern Ethics*. Oxford: Blackwell.

Bauman, Z. (1995) *Life in Fragments. Essays in Postmodern Morality*. Cambridge: Polity.

Bauman, Z. (1997) *Postmodernity and its Discontents*. Cambridge: Polity.

Bauman, Z. (1998a) *Work, Consumerism and the New Poor*. Buckingham: Open University Press.

Bauman, Z. (1998b) *Globalization. The Human Consequences*. Cambridge: Polity.

Bauman, Z. (1999) *Culture as Praxis*. London: Sage.

Bauman, Z. (2000) *Liquid Modernity*. Cambridge: Polity.

Beck, U. (1992) *Risk Society. Towards a New Modernity*. London: Sage.

Beck, U. (1995) 'Die irdische Religion der Liebe' in *Die feindlose Demokratie*. Stuttgart: Philipp Reclam. pp. 42–64.

Beck, U. (1999) *World Risk Society*. Cambridge: Polity.

Beck, U. and Beck-Gernsheim, E. (1995) *The Normal Chaos of Love*. Cambridge: Polity.

Beck, U., Giddens, A. and Lash, S. (1994) *Reflexive Modernization*. Cambridge: Polity.

Becker, G. (1997) *Disrupted Lives: How People Create Meaning in a Chaotic World*. Berkeley: University of California Press.

Becker, H.S. (1963) *Outsiders. Studies in the Sociology of Deviance*. New York: Free Press.

Bell, D. (1976) *The Cultural Contradictions of Capitalism*. New York: Basic Books.

Benedict, A. (1983) *Imagined Communities: Reflections on the Origin and Spread of Nationalism*. London: Verso.

Benjamin, W. (1978) *Reflections*. New York: Schocken Books.

Berger, P.L. (1980) 'Foreword' to A. Gehlen, *Man in the Age of Technology*. New York: Columbia University Press.

Berger, P.L. and Luckmann, T. (1967) *The Social Construction of Reality*. Garden City, NY: Doubleday.

Berman, M. (1982) *All That is Solid Melts into Air: The Experience of Modernity*. New York, Simon & Schuster.

Bhabha, Homi K. (1994) *The Location of Culture*. London: Routledge.

Blau (1964) *Exchange and Power in Social Life*. New York: Wiley.

Bogner, A. (1986) 'Zivilisation und Rationalisierung, ein Vergleich: der Zivilisation Theorien Max Webers, Norbert Elias, Max Horkheimers und Theodor W. Adornos', dissertation, Universitat Bielefeld.

Bogner, A. (1987) 'Elias and the Frankfurt School', *Theory, Culture & Society*, 4 (2–3): 249–286.

Bohman, J. and Lutz-Bachmann (eds) (1997) *Perpetual Peace. Essays on Kant's Cosmopolitan Ideal*. Cambridge, MA: MIT Press.

Bourdieu, P. (1977) *Outline of a Theory of Practice*. Cambridge: Cambridge University Press.

Bourdieu, P. (1984) *Distinction: A Social Critique of the Judgement of Taste*. London: Routledge.

Bourdieu, P. (1988) *Homo Academicus*. Cambridge: Polity.

Bourdieu, P. (1990a) *The Logic of Practice*. Cambridge: Polity.

Bourdieu, P. (1990b) *In Other Words: Essays Towards a Reflexive Sociology*. Cambridge: Polity.

Bourdieu, P. (1991) *The Political Ontology of Martin Heidegger*. Cambridge: Polity.

Bourdieu, P. (1993) *Sociology in Question*. London: Sage.

Bourricaud, F. (1981) *The Sociology of Talcott Parsons*. Chicago and London: University of Chicago Press.

Boyne, R. (1996) 'Structuralism' in B.S. Turner (ed.) *The Blackwell Companion to Social Theory*. Oxford: Blackwell. pp. 160–190.

Brachin, P. (1985) *The Dutch Language. A Survey*. Cheltenham: Stanley Thornes.

Braidotti, R. (1991) *Nomadic Subjects*. New York: Columbia University Press.

Brown, K., Kenny, S. and Turner, B.S. (2000) *Rhetorics of Welfare*. Basingstoke: Macmillan.

Bryant, C. and Jary, D. (eds) (1991) *Giddens' Theory of Structuration*. London: Routledge.

Burgess, E.W. and Cottrell, L.S. (1939) *Predicting Success or Failure in Marriage*. New York: Prentice-Hall.

Butler, J. (1990) *Gender Trouble*. London: Routledge.

Buxton, W. (1985) *Talcott Parsons and the Capitalist Nation State*. Toronto: University of Toronto Press.

Camic, C.C. (1991) *The Early Essays of Talcott Parsons*. Chicago: University of Chicago Press.

Cancian, F. (1960) 'Functional Analysis of Change, *American Sociological Review*, 25: 118–127.

Carrier, J.G. (ed.) (1995) *Occidentalism. Images of the West*. Oxford: Clarendon Press.

Castells, M. (1996) *The Rise of Network Society*. Oxford: Blackwell.

Castells, M. (1997) *The Power of Identity*. Oxford: Blackwell.

Castells. M. (1998) *The End of the Millennium*. Oxford: Blackwell.

Certeau, M. de (1984) *The Practice of Everyday Life*. Berkeley: University of California Press.

Chamberlain, C. (1983) *Class Consciousness in Australia*. Sydney: Allen & Unwin.

Chaqnon, N. (1968) *Yanomamo: The Fierce People*. New York: Holt, Rinehart & Winston.

Cheah, P., Fraser, D. and Grbich, J. (eds) (1996) *Thinking through the Body of the Law*. St Leonards: Allen & Unwin.

Clarke, P.B. (1996) *Deep Citizenship*. London: Pluto Press.

Clarke, J., van Dam, E. and Gooster, L. (1998) 'New Europeans: Naturalisation and Citizenship in Europe', *Citizenship Studies*, 2 (1): 43–68.

Clifford, J. and Marcus, G.E. (eds) (1986) *The Poetics and Politics of Ethnography*. Berkeley: University of California Press.

Cloward, R. and Ohlin, L. (1960) *Delinquency and Opportunity*. New York: Free Press.

Cohen, S. (1972) *Folk Devils and Moral Panics*. London: Paladin.

Connell, R.W. (1977) *Ruling Class, Ruling Culture*. Cambridge: Cambridge University Press.

Connor, S. (1989) *Postmodern Culture: An Introduction to Theories of the Contemporary*. Oxford: Blackwell.

Coser, L. (1977) *Masters of Sociological Thought*. New York: Harcourt Brace Jovanovich.

Craib, I. (1992) *Anthony Giddens*. London: Routledge.

Craib, I. (1994) *The Importance of Disappointment*. London: Routledge.

Crook, S., Pakulski, J. and Waters, M. (1992) *Postmodernization: Change in Advanced Society*. London: Sage.

Dahrendorf, R. (1968) *Essays in the Theory of Society*. London: Routledge & Kegan Paul.

DeBary, W.T. (1998) *Asian Values and Human Rights. A Confucian Communitarian Perspective*. Cambridge, MA: Harvard University Press.

Deleuze, G. and Guattari, F. (1987) *A Thousand Plateaus: Capitalism and Schizophrenia*. Minneapolis: Minnesota University Press.

Denzin, N.K. (1991) *Images of Postmodern Society. Social Theory and Contemporary Cinema*. London: Sage.

Denzin, N.K. (1992) *Symbolic Interactionism and Cultural Studies*. Oxford: Blackwell.

Denzin, N.K. (1995) *The Cinematic Society. The Voyeur's Gaze*. London: Sage.

Derrida, J. (1991) *A Derrida Reader*. Hemel Hempsead: Harvester Wheatsheaf.

Djilas, M. (1957) *The New Class*. London: Thames & Hudson.

Dubos, R. (1960) *Mirage of Health*. London: George Allen & Unwin.

Duby, G. (1978) *Medieval Marriage. Two Models from Twelfth-Century France*. Baltimore and London: Johns Hopkins University Press.

Duby, G. (1983) *The Knight, the Lady and the Priest*. New York: Pantheon Books.

Duncan, G. (1995) 'The Commercialization of the Humanities in the United Kingdom and Australia' in D. Myers (ed.) *Re-Inventing the Humanities. International Perspectives*. Kew: Australian Scholarly Publishing. pp. 11–17.

Durkheim, E. (1952) *Suicide: A Study in the Sociology*. Glencoe, IL: Free Press.

Durkheim, E. (1954) *The Elementary Forms of the Religious Life*. London: Allen & Unwin.

Durkheim, E. (1958) *The Rules of Sociological Method*. Glencoe, IL: Free Press.

Durkheim, E. (1992) *Professional Ethics and Civic Morals*. London: Routldege.

Ehrenreich, B. (1989) *Fear of Failing*. New York: Pantheon.

Eliade, M. (1958) *Rites and Symbols of Initiation*. New York: Harper & Row.

Eliade, M. (1959) *The Sacred and the Profane*. New York: Harper & Row.

Elias, N. (1956) 'Some Problems of Involvement and Detachment', *British Journal of Sociology*, 7 (3): 226–252.

Elias, N. (1978a) *What Is Sociology?* London: Hutchinson.

Elias, N. (1978b) 'The Changing Balance of Power between the Sexes – a Process-sociological Study: the Example of the Ancient Roman State', *Theory, Culture & Society*, 4 (2–3): 287–316.

Elias, N. (1978c) *The Civilizing Process, Vol. 1, The History of Manners*. Oxford: Blackwell.

Elias, N. (1982) *The Civilizing Process, Vol. 2, State Formation and Civilization*. Oxford: Blackwell.

Elias, N. (1985a) *The Loneliness of the Dying*. Oxford: Blackwell.

Elias, N. (1985b) *Humano Conditio. Beobachtungen zur Entwicklung der Menschheit am 40. Jahrestag eines Kriegsendes*. Frankfurt: Suhrkamp.

Elias, N. (1987a) 'On Human Beings and their Emotions: a Process-sociological Essay', *Theory, Culture & Society*, 4 (2–3): 339–365.

Englehardt, D.V. (1988) 'Romanticism in Germany' in A.R. Porter and M. Teich (eds) *Romanticism in National Context*. Cambridge: Cambridge University Press. pp. 109–133.

Erchak, G.M. (1992) *The Anthropology of Self and Behaviour*. New Brunswick, NJ: Rutgers University Press.

Eribon, D. (1991) *Michel Foucault*. London: Faber & Faber.

Etzioni, A. (1992) 'Communitarian Solutions/What Communitarians Think', *Journal of State Government*, 65 (1): 9–11.

Etzioni, A. (1993) *The Spirit of Community*. New York: Touchstone.

Etzioni, A. (1996a) *The New Golden Rule*. New York: Basic Books.

Etzioni, A. (1996b) 'A Moderate Communitarian Proposal', *Political Theory*, 24 (2): 155–171.

Etzioni, A. (1999) 'The Good Society', *Journal of Political Philosophy*, 7 (1): 88–103.

Falk, P. (1994) *The Consuming Body*. London: Sage.

Featherstone, M. (1995) *Undoing Culture. Globalization, Postmodernism and Identity*. London: Sage.

Featherstone, M., Hepworth, M. and Turner, B.S. (eds) (1991) *The Body. Social Process and Cultural Theory*. London: Sage.

Femia, J. (1975) 'Hegemony and Consciousness in the Thought of Antonio Gramsci', *Political Studies*, 23 (1): 29–48.

Ferguson, M. and Golding, P. (eds) (1997) *Cultural Studies in Question*. London: Sage.

Ferri, E. (1895) *Criminal Sociology*. London: Longman.

Ferri, E. (1901) *The Positive School of Criminology*. Chicago: Kerr & Co.

Ferry, L. and Renaut, A. (1990) *Heidegger and Modernity*. Chicago and London: University of Chicago Press.

Feuerbach, L. (1957) *The Essence of Christianity*. New York: Harper & Row.

Fiske, J. (1989a) *Understanding Popular Culture*. Boston: Unwin Hyman.

Fiske, J. (1989b) *Reading the Popular*. Boston, Massachusetts, London: Unwin.

Fitzgerald, T.K. (1993) *Metaphors of Identity: A Culture-Communication Dialogue*. New York: State University of New York Press.

Foucault, M. (1965) *Madness and Civilisation. The History of Insanity in the Age of Reason*. New York: Random House.

Foucault, M. (1970) *The Order of Things*. London: Tavistock.

Foucault, M. (1972) *The Archaeology of Knowledge*. London: Tavistock.

Foucault, M. (1973) *The Birth of the Clinic. An Archaeology of Medical Perception*. London: Tavistock.

Foucault, M. (1977) *Discipline and Punish. The Birth of the Prison*. London: Allen Lane.

Foucault, M. (1978) *The History of Sexuality, Volume 1: An Introduction*. New York: Random House.

Foucault, M. (1980a) 'The Politics of Health in the Eighteenth Century' in C. Gordon (ed.) *Power/Knowledge. Selected Interviews and Other Writings 1972–1977*. Brighton: Harvester Press. pp. 166–182.

Foucault, M. (1980b) *Herculine Barbin. Being the Recently Discovered Memoirs of a Nineteenth Century French Hermaphrodite*. Brighton: Harvester Press.

Foucault, M. (1985) *The History of Sexuality, Volume 2: The Use of Pleasure*. New York: Random House.

Foucault, M. (1986) *The History of Sexuality, Volume 3: The Care of the Self*. New York: Random House.

Foucault, M. (1988) 'Social Security' in L.D. Kritzman (ed.) *Michel Foucault. Politics Philosophy, Culture. Interviews and Other Writings 1977–1984*. New York and London: Routledge. pp. 159–177.

Foucault, M. (1991) 'Governmentality' in G. Burchel, C. Gordon and P. Miller (eds) *The Foucault Effect*. Brighton: Harvester Wheatsheaf, pp. 87–194.

Foucault, M. (1981) *The History of Sexuality. Volume One*. Harmondsworth: Penguin.

Freud, S. (1936) *Civilisation and its Discontents*. London: Hogarth.

Freund, L. (1968) *The Sociology of Max Weber*. London: Allen Lane.

Friedan, B. (1993) *The Fountain of Age*. New York: Simon & Schuster.

Frisby, D. (1985) *Fragments of Modernity*. Cambridge: Polity.

Frisby, D. and Sayer, D. (1986) *Society*. London: Tavistock.

Fugen, H.N. (1985) *Max Weber*. Hamburg: Rowohlt.

Fukuyama, F. (1992) *The End of History and the Last Man*. New York: Free Press.

Game, A. (1992) *Undoing the Social. Towards a Deconstructive Sociology*. Milton Keynes: Open University Press.

Gansmann, H. (1988) 'Money – a Symbolically Generalised Medium of Communication', *Economy and Society*, 17 (3): 285–316.

Garfinkel, H. (1967) *Studies in Ethnomethodology*. Englewood Cliffs, NJ: Prentice-Hall.

Gartman, D. (1994) *Auto-Opium*. London: Routledge.

Gehlen, A. (1980) *Man in the Age of Technology*. New York: Columbia University Press.

Gehlen, A. (1988) *Man. His Nature and Place in the World*. New York: Columbia University Press.

Gellner, E. (1969) *Saints of the Atlas*. London: Weidenfeld & Nicholson.

Gellner, E. (1970) 'Concepts and Society' in D. Emmet and A. MacIntyre (eds) *Sociological Theory and Philosophical Inquiry*. London: Macmillan. pp. 115–149.

Gellner, E. (1981) *Muslim Society*. Cambridge: Cambridge University Press.

Gellner, E. (1992) *Postmodernism, Reason and Religion*. London: Routledge.

Gellner, E. (1997) *Nationalism*. London: Weidenfeld & Nicholson.

Gerhardt, U. (ed.) (1993) *Talcott Parsons on National Socialism*. New York: Aldine de Gruyter.

Gibb, H. (1949) *Mohammedanism. An Historical Survey*. New York: Henry Holt.

Giddens, A. (1971) *Capitalism and Modern Social Theory*. Cambridge: Cambridge University Press.

Giddens, A. (1976) *New Rules of Sociological Method*. London: Hutchinson.

Giddens, A. (1982) *Profiles and Critiques in Social Theory*. London: Macmillan.

Giddens, A. (1984) *The Constitution of Society: an Outline of the Theory of Structuration*. Cambridge, Polity.

Giddens, A. (1990) *The Consequences of Modernity*. Cambridge: Polity.

Giddens, A. (1991) *Modernity and Self-Identity. Self and Society in the Late Modern Age*. Cambridge: Polity.

Giddens, A. (1992) *The Transformation of Intimacy. Sexuality, Love & Eroticism in Modern Societies*. Cambridge: Polity.

Giddens, A. (1998) *The Third Way*. Cambridge: Polity.

Giddens, A. (2000) *The Third Way and its Critics*. Cambridge: Polity.

Gierke, O. (1990) *Community in Historical Perspective*. Cambridge: Cambridge University Press.

Gieysztor, A. (1992) 'Management and Resources' in H. de Ridder-Symoens (ed.) *A History of the University in Europe*. Cambridge: Cambridge University Press, Vol. 1, pp. 108–143.

Gitlin, T. (1995) *The Twilight of Common Dreams*. New York: Owl Books.

Godbout, J.T. (1992) *L'Esprit du don*. Paris: Editions la découverte.

Goffman, E. (1959) *The Presentation of Self in Everyday Life*. New York: Doubleday Anchor.

Goffman, E. (1967) *Interaction Ritual. Essays in Face-to-face Behavior*. Chicago: Aldine.

Goffman, E. (1971) *Relations in Public*. Harmondsworth: Penguin Books.

Goffman, E. (1974) *Frame Analysis*. New York: Harper & Row.

Goldman, H. (1992) *Politics, Death and the Devil. Self and Power in Max Weber and Thomas Mann*. Berkeley: University of California Press.

Gombrich, R. and Obeyesekere, G. (1988) *Buddhism Transformed in Sri Lanka*. Princeton: Princeton University Press.

Goode, W.J. (1959) 'The Theoretical Importance of Love', *American Sociological Review*, (1): 38–47.

Gorz, A. (1982) *Farewell to the Working Class*. London: Pluto.

Gorz, A. (1983) *Paths to Paradise*. London: Pluto.

Gorz, A. (1989) *Critique of Economic Reason*. London: Verso.

Gorz, A. (1994) *Capitalism, Socialism, Ecology*. London: Verso.

Goudsblom, J. (1987) 'The Sociology of Norbert Elias', *Theory, Culture & Society*, 4 (2–3): 323–328.

Goudsblom, J. (1987) 'The Sociology of Norbert Elias – its resonance and significance', *Theory, Culture & Society*, 4 (2–3): 323–338.

Gouldner, A.W. (1970) *The Coming Crisis of Western Sociology*. New York: Basic Books.

Groves, E.R. and Ogburn, W.F. (1928) *American Marriage and Family Relationships*. New York: Henry Holt.

Guha, R. and Spivak, G.C. (eds) (1988) *Selected Subaltern Studies*. New York: Oxford University Press.

Gutman, H., Hutton, P. and Martin, L. (1988) *Technologies of the Self*. London: Tavistock.

Gutting, G. (1989) *Michel Foucault's Archaeology of Scientific Reason*. Cambridge: Cambridge University Press.

Habermas, J. (1976) *Communication and the Evolution of Society*. London: Heinemann.

Habermas, J. (1981) *The Theory of Communicative Action Vol. 2*. Cambridge: Polity.

Habermas, J. (1987) *The Philosophical Discourse of Modernity*. Cambridge: Polity.

Habermas, J. (1988) *On the Logic of the Social Sciences*. Cambridge: Polity.

Habermas, J. (1996) *Between Facts and Norms. Contributions to a Discourse Theory of Law and Democracy*. Cambridge: Polity.

Hagstrum, J.H. (1989) *Eros and Vision. The Restoration to Romanticism*. Evanston, IL: Northwestern University Press.

Haines, V.A. (1987) 'Biology and Social Theory: Parsons's Evolutionary Theme', *Sociology*, 21 (1): 19–39.

Hall, S. (1988) 'New Ethnicities' in K. Mercer (ed.) *Black Film, British Cinema*. London: BFI/ICA Documents. pp. 27–31.

Hall, S., Critcher, C., Jefferson, T., Clarke, J. and Roberts, R. (1978) *Policing the Crisis*. London: Macmillan.

Halliday, F. (1997) 'Neither Treason nor Conspiracy: Reflections on Media Coverage of the Gulf War 1990–1991', *Citizenship Studies*, b1 (2): 157–172.

Hayner, N.S. (1927) 'Hotel Homes', *Sociology and Social Research*, 12: 124–131.

Hechter, M. (1975) *Internal Colonialism. The Celtic Fringe in British National Development 1536–1966*. London: Routledge & Kegan Paul.

Hegel, G.W.F. (1952) *Phenomenology of Spirit*. Oxford: Oxford University Press.

Hegel, G.W.F. (1956) *Philosophy of History*. New York: Dover.

Heidegger, M. (1962) *Being and Time*. Oxford: Blackwell.

Heidegger, M. (1977) *The Question concerning Technology and Other Essays*. New York: Harper & Row.

Held, D., McGrew, A., Goldblatt, D. and Perraton, J. (1999) *Global Transformations*. Cambridge: Polity.

Hennis, W. (1988) *Max Weber, Essays in Reconstruction*. London: Allen & Unwin.

Hepworth, M. and Turner, B.S. (1982) *Confession. Studies in Deviance and Religion*. London: Routledge & Kegan Paul.

Herzlich, C. and Pierret, J. (1987) *Illness and Self in Society*. Baltimore, MD and London: Johns Hopkins University Press.

Heywood, L. (1996) *Dedication to Hunger. The Anorexic Aesthetic in Modern Culture*. Berkeley: University of California Press.

Hill, C. (1975) *The World Turned Upside Down*. Harmondsworth: Penguin Books.

Hindess, B. and Hirst, P.Q. (1975) *Pre-Capitalist Modes of Production*. London: Routledge & Kegan Paul.

Hobsbawm, E. (1964) *Labouring Men*. London: Weidenfeld & Nicolson.

Hobsbawm, E. (1969) *Bandits*. London: Weidenfeld & Nicolson.

Hochschild, A. (1997) *The Time Band*. New York: Metropolitan Books.

Hofheinz, T.C. (1995) *Joyce and the Invention of Irish History*. Cambridge: Cambridge University Press.

Hofstadter, R. (1955) *Social Darwinism in American Thought*. Boston: Beacon Press.

Hoggart, R. (1957) *The Uses of Literacy*. Harmondsworth: Penguin Books.

Holmwood, J. (1996) *Founding Sociology? Talcott Parsons and the Idea of General Theory*. London and New York: Longman.

Holton, R.J. (1991) 'Talcott Parsons and the Integration of Economic and Sociological Theory', *Sociological Inquiry*, 61 (1): 102–114.

Holton, R.J. and Turner, B.S. (1986) *Talcott Parsons on Economy and Society*. London and New York: Routledge & Kegan Paul.

Howard, R.E. (1995) *Human Rights and the Search for Community*. Boulder, CO: Westview Press.

Huff, T.H. (ed.) (1981) *On the Roads to Modernity: Conscience, Science and Civilizations*. Totowa, NJ: Rowman & Littlefield.

Hughes, H.S. (1959) *Consciousness and Society*. London: Paladin.

Hunnicutt, B.K. (1988) *Work Without End*. Philadelphia: Temple University Press.

Ilouz, E. (1997) *Consuming the Romantic Utopia. Love and the Cultural Contradictions of Capitalism*. Berkeley: University of California Press.

Inwood, M. (ed.) (1992) *A Hegel Dictionary*. Oxford: Blackwell.

James, P. (1996) *Nation Formation. Towards a Theory of Abstract Community*. London: Sage.

Japp, K.P. (1996) *Soziologische Risikotheorie. Funktionale Differenzierung, Politisienierung and Reflexion*. Wienheim and Munich: Juventa.

Jay, M. (1984) *Marxism and Totality*. Berkeley: University of California Press.

Jenkins, R. (1992) *Pierre Bourdieu*. London: Routledge.

Jones, C. and Porter, R. (eds) (1998) *Reassessing Foucault. Power, Medicine and the Body*. London and New York: Routledge.

Katz, J. (1988) *Seductions of Crime*. New York: Basic Books.

Kerr, C., Dunlop, J., Harbison, F. and Meyers, C. (1962) *Industrialism and Industrial Man*. Harmondsworth: Penguin Books.

Kelsky, K. (1996) 'Flirting with the Foreign: Interracial Sex in Japan's "International" Age', in R. Wilson and W. Dissanyake (eds) *Global/Local. Cultural Production and the Transnational Imaginary*. Durham, NC and London: Duke University Press. pp. 179–192.

Kelsall, R.K. (1955) *Higher Civil Servants in Britain*. London: Routledge & Kegan Paul.

Kierkegaard, S. (1846) *The Present Age and Other Essays*. New York: Basic Books.

Klein, N. (2000) *No Logo*. London: Flamingo.

Krieger, L. (1957) *The German Idea of Freedom*. Chicago: University of Chicago Press.

Kristeva, J. (1986) 'Stabat Mater' in T. Moi (ed.) *The Kristeva Reader*. Oxford: Basil Blackwell. pp. 160–186.

Kristeva, J. (1987) *Tales of Love*. New York: Columbia University Press.

Kroker, A. (1984) *Technology and the Canadian Mind. Innis/McLuhan Grant*. Montreal: New World Perspectives.

Kuhn, T. (1962) *The Structure of Scientific Revolutions*. Chicago: University of Chicago Press.

Kumar, K. (1995) *From Post-Industrial to Post-Modern Society. New Theories of the Contemporary World*. Oxford: Blackwell.

Laing, R.D. (1964) *Sanity, Madness and the Family, Volume 1: Families of Schizophrenics*. London: Tavistock.

Lane, E.W. (1836) *The Manners and Customs of the Modern Egyptians*. London: Charles Knight.

Laqueur, T. (1990) *Making Sex. Body and Gender from the Greeks to Freud*. Cambridge, MA: Harvard University Press.

Laroui, A. (1976) *The Crisis of the Arab Intellectual*. Berkeley: University of California Press.

Lash, S. and Urry, J. (1987) *The End of Organized Capitalism*. Cambridge: Polity.

Latour, B. (1995) *We Have Never Been Modern*. Cambridge, MA: Harvard University Press,

Lawson, A. (1988) *Adultery. An Analysis of Love and Betrayal*. Oxford: Blackwell.

Lear, J. (1990) *Love and its Place in Nature. A Philosophical Interpretation of Freudian Psychoanalysis*. New York: Farrar, Straus & Giroux.

Le Bon, G. (1901) *The Crowd: A Study of the Popular Mind*. New York: Viking.

Lebow, R. (1976) *White Britain, Black Ireland. The Influence of Stereotypes on Colonial Policy*. Philadelphia: Institute for the Study of Human Issues.

Leder, D. (1990) *The Absent Body*. Chicago and London: University of Chicago Press.

Lee, H. (ed.) (1995) *The Secret Self: A Century of Short Stories by Women*. London: Phoenix Giants.

Lepenies, W. (1992) *Melancholy and Society*. Cambridge, MA: Harvard University Press.

Lewis, C.S. (1936) *The Allegory of Love. A Study in Medieval Tradition*. London: Oxford University Press.

Leyton, E. (1986) *Hunting Humans*. Toronto: McLelland & Stewart.

Leyton, E. (1995) *Men of Blood*. London: Constable.

Lidz, C.W. and Lidz, V.M. (1976) 'Piaget's Psychology of Intelligence and the Theory of Action', in J.L. Loubser, R.C. Baum, A. Effrat and V.M. Lidz (eds) *Explorations in General Theory in Social Science. Essays in Honor of Talcott Parsons*. New York: Free Press. Vol. 1, Chapter 8.

Lock, M. (1993) *Encounters with Aging. Mythologies of Menopause in Japan and North America*. Berkeley and Los Angeles: University of California Press.

Lockwood, D. (1992) *Solidarity and Schism: 'The Problem of Order' in Durkheimian and Marxist Sociology*. Oxford: Clarendon Press.

Lombroso, C. (1911) *Crime: its Causes and Remedies*. Boston: Little Brown.

Luhmann, N. (1986) *Love as Passion. The Codification of Intimacy*. Cambridge: Polity Press.

Luhmann, N. (1995) *Social Systems*. Stanford, CA: Stanford University Press.

Lupton, D. (1965) *The Imperative of Health. Public Health and the Regulated Body*. London: Sage.

Lyng, S. (1990) 'Edgework: a Social Psychological Analysis of Voluntary Risk Taking', *American Journal of Sociology*, 95: 887–921.

Lyotard, J.-F. (1984) *The Postmodern Condition. A Report on Knowledge*. Manchester: University of Manchester Press.

Lyotard, J.-F. and Thebaud, J.-L. (1985) *Just Gaming*. Manchester: Manchester University Press.

Macey, D. (1993) *The Lives of Michel Foucault*. London: Hutchinson.

MacIntyre, A. (1981) *After Virtue*. South Bend, IN: University of Notre Dame Press.

MacIntyre, A. (1999) *Dependent Rational Animals. Why Human Beings Need the Virtues*. London: Duckworth.

Maffesoli, M. (1996) *The Time of the Tribes. The Decline of Individualism in Mass Society*. London: Sage.

Malthus, T.R. (1976) *An Essay on the Principle of Population*. New York: Norton.

Mann, M. (1973) *Consciousness and Action among the Western Working Class*. London: Macmillan.

Mann, M. (1986) *Social Sources of Power*. Cambridge: Cambridge University Press.

Mann, M. (1988) *States, War and Capitalism Studies in Political Sociology*. Oxford: Blackwell.

Marcuse, H. (1964) *One Dimensional Man*. London: Abacus.

Margoliouth, D.S. (1911) *Mohammedanism*. London: Williams & Norgate.

Marlow, L. (1977) *Hierarchy and Egalitarianism in Islamic Thought*. Cambridge: Cambridge University Press.

Marshall, T.H. (1964) *Class, Citizenship and Social Development*. Chicago: University of Chicago Press.

Marshall, T.H. (1981) *The Right to Welfare and Other Essays*. London: Heinemann Educational Books.

Martin, E. (1987) *The Women in the Body. A Cultural Analysis of Reproduction*. Milton Keynes: Open University Press.

Martin, L.H., Guttman, H., and Hutton, P.H. (eds) (1988) *Technologies of the Self. A Seminar with Michel Foucault*. London: Tavistock.

Marx, K. (1847) *The Poverty of Philosophy*. Paris: A. Franck.

Mason, H. (ed.) (1989) *Testimonies and Reflections. Essays of Louis Massignon*. Notre Dame, IN: University of Notre Dame Press.

Massignon, L. (1962–63) *Opera Minora*. Beirut: Dar el-Maaref, 3 volumes.

Matar, N. (1998) *Islam in Britain 1558–1685*. Cambridge: Cambridge University Press.

Matza, D. (1969) *Becoming Deviant*. Englewood Cliffs, NJ: Prentice-Hall.

Mauss, M. (1954) *The Gift*. New York: Free Press.

Mauss, M. (1973) 'Techniques of the Body', *Economy & Society*, 2: 70–88.

McClintock, A. (1995) *Imperial Leather. Race, Gender and Sexuality in the Colonial Contest*. London and New York: Routledge.

McGuigan, J. (1996) *Culture and the Public Sphere*. London: Routledge.

McGuigan, J. (1999) *Modernity and Postmodern Culture*. Buckingham: Open University Press.

McLuhan, M. (1964) *Understanding the Media. The Extension of Man*. Toronto: McGraw-Hill.

Mead, G.H. (1934) *Mind, Self and Society: From the Standpoint of a Social Behaviourist*. Chicago: University of Chicago Press.

Merton, R. (1968) *Social Theory and Social Structure*. New York: Free Press.

Meštrović, S.G. (1991) *The Coming Fin de Siecle. An Application of Durkheim's Sociology to Modernity and Postmodernism*. London: Routledge.

Meštrović, S.G. (1997) *Postemotional Society*. London: Sage.

Meszaros, (1970) *Marx's Theory of Alienation*. London: Merlin Press.

Miller, D. (1987) *Material Culture and Mass Consumption*. Oxford: Blackwell.

Miller, J.H. (1998) 'Literary and Cultural Studies in the Transnational University', in J.C. Rowe (ed.) *'Culture' and the Problem of the Disciplines*. New York: Columbia University Press. pp. 45–67.

Mills, C.W. (1959) *The Sociological Imagination*. New York: Oxford University Press.

Milner, A., Thomson, P. and Worth, C. (1990) *Postmodern Conditions*. Oxford and Munich: Berg.

Minichiello, V., Plummer, D., Waite, H., and Deacon, S. (1996) 'Sexuality and Older People: Social Issues' in V. Minichiello, N. Chappell, H. Kendig and A. Walker (eds) *Sociology of Aging. International Perspectives*. ISA: Research Committee on Aging. pp. 93–111.

Miyoshi, M. (1996) 'A Borderless World? From Colonialism to Transnationalism and the Decline of the Nation-State' in R. Wilson and W. Dissanayake (eds) *Global/Local. Cultural Production and the Transnational Imaginary*. Durham, NC and London: Duke University Press. pp. 78–107.

Moore, B. (1966) *Social Origins of Dictatorship and Democracy*. Boston: Beacon.

Moorhouse, H.F. (1973) 'The Political Incorporation of the British Working Class: an Interpretation', *Sociology*, 7 (3): 341–359.

Moorhouse, H.F. and Chamberlain, C. (1974) 'Lower-class Attitudes to Property', *Sociology*, 8 (3): 387–405.

Morris, D.B. (1996) 'About Suffering: Voice, Genre and Moral Community', *Daedalus*, 125: 25–45.

Morrison, K.F. (1988) *'I Am You'. The Hermeneutics of Empathy in Western Literature, Theology and Art*. Princeton, NJ: Princeton University Press.

Munch, R. (1981) 'Talcott Parsons and the Theory of Action', *American Journal of Sociology*, 86: 709–740.

Murphy, B. (1993) *The Other Australia. Experiences of Migration*. Cambridge: Cambridge University Press.

Nagel, E. (1956) 'A Formalization of Functionalism' in *Logic without Metaphysics*. New York: Free Press. pp. 247–283.

Nelson, D.D. (1998) *National Manhood. Capitalist Citizenship and the Imagined Fraternity of Men*. Durham, NC and London: Duke University Press.

Nerval, G. de (1980) *Voyage en Orient*. Paris: Flammarion, 2 volumes.

Nettleton, S. and Watson, J. (eds) (1998) *The Body in Everyday Life*. London and New York: Routledge.

Nisbet, R. (1966) *The Sociological Tradition*. New York: Basic Books.

Newby, H. (1996) 'Citizenship in a Green World: Global Commons and Human Stewardship' in M. Bulmer and A.M. Rees (eds) *Citizenship Today: The Contemporary Relevance of T.H. Marshall*. London: UCL Press. pp. 209–221.

Niethammer, L. (1992) *Post Histoire. Has History Come to an End?* London: Verso.

Nietzsche, F. (1968) *Twilight of the Idols. The Anti-Christ*. Harmondsworth: Penguin Books.

Nimkoff, M.F. and Ogburn, W.F. (1934) *The Family*. Boston: Houghton Mifflin.

Nisbet, R.A. (1966) *The Sociological Tradition*. London: Heinemann Educational Books.

O'Neill, J. (1989) *The Communicative Body. Studies in Communicative Philosophy, Politics and Sociology*. Evanston, IL: Northwestern University Press.

Oxaal, I. (1990) 'Die Juden im Wien des jungen Hitler: Historische und soziologische Aspekte' in G. Boltz, I. Oxaal and M. Pollak (eds) *Eine zerstoerte Kultur. Juedisches Leben und Antisemitismus in Wien seit dem 19. Jahrhundert*. Buchloe: Druck & Verlag Obermayer. pp. 29–60.

Pahl, R. (1995) *After Success*. Cambridge: Polity.

Parsons, T. (1929) '"Capitalism" in Recent German Literature: Sombart and Weber', *Journal of Political Economy*, 36: 641–661 and 37: 31–51.

Parsons, T. (1937) *The Structure of Social Action*. New York: McGraw-Hill.

Parsons, T. (1942) 'Democracy and the Social Structure of pre-Nazi Germany', *Journal of Legal and Political Sociology*, 1: 96–114.

Parsons, T. (1949) *Essays in Sociological Theory*. New York: Free Press.

Parsons, T. (1950) 'The Prospects of Sociological Theory', *American Sociological Review*, 15: 3–16.

Parsons, T. (1951) *The Social System*. London: Routledge & Kegan Paul.

Parsons, T. (1959) 'An Approach to Psychological Theory in terms of the Theory of Action' in S. Koch (ed.) *Psychology: a Study of a Science*. New York: McGraw-Hill, Vol. 3, pp. 612–711.

Parsons, T. (1960) *Structure and Process in Modern Society*. Chicago: Free Press.

Parsons, T. (1963) 'Christianity and Modern Industrial Society' in E.A. Tiryakian (ed.) *Sociological Theory, Values and Sociocultural Change: Essays in Honor of Pitrim A. Sorokin*. New York: Free Press. pp. 33–70.

Parsons, T. (1964) *Social Structure and Personality*. New York: Free Press.

Parsons, T. (1967) *Sociological Theory and Modern Society*. New York: Free Press.

Parsons, T. (1971) *The System of Modern Societies*. Englewood Cliffs, NJ: Prentice-Hall.

Parsons, T. (1973) 'Clyde Kluckhohn and the Integration of the Social Sciences' in W.W. Taylor, J.L. Fischer and E.Z. Vogt (eds) *Culture and Life. Essays in Memory of Clyde Kluckhohn*. Carbondale and Edwardsville: Southern Illinois University Press. pp. 30–57.

Parsons, T. (1975) 'The Sick Role and the Role of Physician Reconsidered', *Milibank Memorial Fund Quarterly*, 53 (3): 257–278.

Parsons, T. (1978) *Action Theory and the Human Condition*. New York: Free Press.

Parsons, T. (1981) 'Revisiting the Classics throughout a Long Career' in B. Rhea (ed.) *The Future of the Sociological Classics*. London: George Allen & Unwin. pp. 183–194.

Parsons, T. and Bales, R.F. (1956) *Family, Socialization and Interaction Process*. London: Routledge & Kegan Paul.

Parsons, T. and Clark, K.B. (eds) (1966) *The Negro American*. Boston: Houghton Mifflin.

Parsons, T. and Fox, R.C. (1953) 'Illness, Therapy and the Modern Urban American Family', *Journal of Social Issues*, 8: 31–44.

Parsons, T. and Shils, E.A. (eds) (1951) *Toward a General Theory of Action*. New York and Evanston, IL: Harper & Row.

Parsons, T. and Smelser, N. (1956) *Economy and Society*. London: Routledge & Kegan Paul.

Parsons, T., Bales, R., Olds, J., Zelditch, M. and Slater, P.E. (1955) *Family, Socialization and Interaction Process*. Chicago: Free Press.

Pearce, L. and Stacey, J. (eds) (1995) *Romance Revisited*. London: Lawrence & Wishart.

Pearson, G. (1983) *Hooligan: A History of Respectable Fears*. London: Macmillan.

Peel, J.D.Y. (1971) *Herbert Spencer: The Evolution of a Sociologist*. London: Heinemann Educational Books.

Perry, N. (1998) *Hyperreality and Global Culture*. London: Routledge.

Pevsner, N. (1955) *The Englishness of English Art*. London: The Architectural Press.

Polanyi, K. (1944) *The Great Transformation*. Boston: Beacon.

Popper, K. (1962) *Conjectures and Refutations*. New York: Basic Books.

Popper, K. (1964) *The Poverty of Historicism*. New York: Harper & Row.

Quint, D. (1998) *Montaigne and the Quality of Mercy. Ethical and Political Themes in the Essais*. Princeton, NJ: Princeton University Press.

Radzinowicz, L. (1966) *Ideology and Crime*. London: Heinemann.

Rajan, R.S. (ed.) (1992) *The Lie of the Land. English Literary Studies in India*. Delhi: Oxford University Press.

Reich, R. (1991) *The Work of Nations. Preparing Ourselves for 21-st Century Capitalism*. New York: Random House.

Renan, E. (1890) *L'Avenir de la science*. Paris: Calmann-Lévy.

Renaut, A. (1997) *The Era of the Individual. A Contribution to a History of Subjectivity*. Princeton, NJ: Princeton University Press.

Rex, J. (1981) *Social Conflict. A Conceptual and Theoretical Analysis*. London: Longman.

Riggs, A. and Turner, B.S. (1996) 'Healthy Ageing and the Embodied Self', *Health Education Association of Victoria Quarterly*: 12–14.

Ritzer, G. (1993) *The McDonaldization of Society*. Thousand Oaks, CA: Pine Forge Press.

Ritzer, G. (1999) *Enchanting a Disenchanted World.* Thousand Oaks, CA: Pine Forge Press.

Robertson, R. (1992) *Globalization. Social Theory and Global Culture.* London: Sage.

Robertson, R. and Garrett, W.R. (eds) (1991) *Religion and Global Order. Religion and the Political Order.* New York: Paragon House, Vol. 6.

Robertson, R. and Turner, B.S. (eds) (1991) *Talcott Parsons: Theorist of Modernity.* London: Sage.

Rojek, C. (1998) 'Stuart Hall and the Antinomian Tradition', *International Journal of Cultural Studies,* 1 (1): 45–66.

Rojek, C. (2000) *Leisure and Culture.* London: Macmillan.

Rojek, C. and Turner, B.S. (eds) (1993) *Forget Baudrillard?* London: Routledge.

Rojek, C. and Turner, B.S. (eds) (1998) *The Politics of Jean-François Lyotard. Justice and Political Theory.* London and New York: Routledge.

Rorty, R. (1989) *Contingency, Irony and Solidarity.* Cambridge: Cambridge University Press.

Rose, A.M. (ed.) (1962) *Human Behavior and Social Processes: An Interactionist Approach.* London: Routledge & Kegan Paul.

Ross, A. (1989) *No Respect. Intellectuals & Popular Culture.* London: Routledge.

Rougemont, D. de (1983) *Love in the Western World.* Princeton, NJ: Princeton University Press.

Rousseaux, A. (1956) 'Raymond Schwab et l'humanisme intégrale', *Mercure de France,* 1120: 663–671.

Rowse, T. and Moran, A. (1984) '"Peculiarly Australian" – the Political Construction of Cultural Identity', in S. Encel and L. Bryson (eds) *Australian Society.* Sydney: Longman Cheshire. pp. 229. 247.

Rudé, G. (1985) *Revolutionary Europe: 1793–1815.* London: Fontana.

Russell, S. (1996) *Jewish Identity and Civilizing Processes.* London: Macmillan.

Ryan, M. and Gordon, A. (1994) *Body Politics. Disease, Desire and the Family.* Boulder, CO: Westview Press.

Rybczynski, W. (1987) *Home. A Short History of an Idea.* Harmondsworth: Penguin Books.

Sahlins, M. (1974) *Stoneage Economics.* London: Tavistock.

Said, E. (1978) *Orientalism.* London: Routlege & Kegan Paul.

Said, E.W. (1981) *Covering Islam. How the Media and the Experts Determine How We See the Rest of the World.* New York: Pantheon Books.

Said, E.W. (1984) 'Foreword' in R. Schwab, *The Oriental Renaissance. Europe's Rediscovery of India and the East 1680–1880.* New York: Columbia University Press. pp. vii–xx.

Said, E.W. (1985) 'Orientalism Reconsidered', *Race and Class,* 27 (2): 1–15.

Said, E.W. (1991) *The Word, the Text and the Critic.* London: Vintage.

Said, E.W. (1993) *Culture and Imperialism.* London: Chatto & Windus.

Said, E.W. (1994) *Reflections on the Intellectual.* London: Vintage.

Said, E.W. (1999) *Out of Place. A Memoir.* London: Granta.

Sarsby, J. (1983) *Romantic Love and Society. Its Place in the Modern World.* Harmondsworth: Penguin Books.

Savage, M., Barlow, J., Dickens, P. and Fielding, J. (1992) *Property, Bureaucracy and Culture.* London: Routledge.

Saxonhouse, A.W. (1992) *Fear of Diversity. The Birth of Political Science in Ancient Greek Thought.* Chicago and London: University of Chicago Press.

Scarry, E. (1985) *The Body in Pain. The Making and Unmaking of the World.* New York: Oxford University Press.

Schapiro, B.A. (1983) *The Romantic Mother. Narcissistic Patterns of Romantic Poetry.* Baltimore and London: Johns Hopkins University Press.

Schmidt, A. (1971) *The Concept of Nature in Marx.* London: NLB.

Schnabelbach, H. (1984) *Philosophie in Deutschland, 1831–1933.* Frankfurt: Suhrkamp.

Scholem, G. (1973) *Sabbatai Sevi, the Mystical Messiah.* Princeton, NJ: Princeton University Press.

Schor, J. (1992) *The Overworked American.* New York: Basic Books.

Schwab, R. (1934) *Vie d'Amquetil-Duperron, suivie des usages civils et religieux des Parses par Anquetil-Duperron.* Paris: Leroux.

Schwab, R. (1950) *La Renaissance orientale.* Paris: Payot.

Sciulli, D. (1992) *Theory of Societal Constitutionalism. Foundations of a non-Marxist Critical Theory.* Cambridge: Cambridge University Press.

Scott, J.F. (1963) 'The Changing Foundation of the Parsonian Action Scheme', *American Sociological Review,* 29: 716–735.

Sen, A. (1999) 'Human Rights and Economic Achievements', in J.R. Bauer and D.A. Bell (eds) *The East Asian Challenge for Human Rights.* Cambridge: Cambridge Universiy Press. pp. 88–102.

Sennett, R. (1998) *The Corrosion of Character. The Personal Consequences of Work in the New Capitalism.* New York: W.W. Norton.

Seymour, W. (1989) *Bodily Alterations. An Introduction to a Sociology of the Body for Health Workers.* Sydney: Allen & Unwin.

Seymour, W. (1998) *Remaking the Body. Rehabilitation and Change.* Sydney: Allen & Unwin.

Sharafuddin, M. (1994) *Islam and Romantic Orientalism. Literary Encounters with the Orient.* London and New York: I.B. Tauris.

Shilling, C. (1993) *The Body and Social Theory.* London: Sage.

Shoshan, B. (1993) *Popular Culture in Medieval Cairo.* Cambridge: Cambridge University Press.

Siikala. A.-L. and Vakimo, S. (1994) *Songs of the Kalevala.* Studia Fennica, Folkloristica 2. Tampere: Tammer-Paino Oy.

Simmel, G. (1978) *The Philosophy of Money.* London: Routledge.

Simons, J. (1995) *Foucault & the Political.* London: Routledge.

Singer, I. (1994) *The Pursuit of Love.* Baltimore and London: Johns Hopkins University Press.

Sjoberg, G. and Vaughan, T.R. (1993) 'The Ethical Foundations of Sociology and the Necessity for a Human Rights Alternative' in T.R. Vaughhan, G. Sjoberg and L.T. Reynolds (eds) *A Critique of Contemporary American Sociology.* New York: General Hall. pp. 114–159.

Slater, D. (1997) *Consumer Culture and Modernity.* Cambridge: Polity.

Smart, B. (1999) *Facing Modernity.* London: Sage.

Smith, W.R. (1889) *Lectures on the Religion of the Semites.* Edinburgh: Adam & Charles Black.

Sohn-Rethel, A. (1978) *Intellectual and Manual Labour. A Critique of Epistemology.* London: Macmillan.

Spivak, G. (1990) *The Post-Colonial Critic.* London: Routledge.

Stauth, G. and Turner, B.S. (1988) *Nietzsche's Dance. Resentment, Reciprocity and Resistance in Social Life.* Oxford: Blackwell.

Stedman Jones, G. (1971) *Outcast London.* Harmondsworth: Penguin Books.

Stenberg, L. (1996) *The Islamization of Science. Four Muslim Positions Developing an Islamic Modernity.* Lund: Novapress.

Stevens, J. (1998) 'The Uses and Disadvantages of Feminist (Political) Theory', *Political Theory,* 26 (5): 725–747.

Stoner, C. (1993) *Reinventing Love.* Harmondsworth: Penguin Books.

Strauss, L. (1950) *Natural Right and History.* Chicago and London: University of Chicago Press.

Striker, H.-J. (1982) *Corps infirmes et sociétés.* Paris: Aubier Montaigne.

Swedberg, R. (1986) 'Introduction' in T. Parsons, *The Marshall Lectures.* Uppsala: Uppsala University Department of Sociology Research Reports Vol. 4, pp. i–xxxiv.

Synnott, A. (1993) *The Body Social. Symbolism, Self and Society.* London and New York: Routledge.

Szasz, T.S. (1971) *The Manufacture of Madness. A Comparative Study of the Inquisition and the Mental Health Movement.* London: Routledge & Kegan Paul.

Tarde, G. (1895) *La Logique sociale.* Paris: Alcan.

Taylor, C. (1989) *Sources of the Self.* Cambridge: Cambridge University Press.

Taylor, C. (1999) 'Conditions of an Unforced Consensus on Human Rights' in J.R. Bauer and

D.A. Bell (eds) *The East Asian Challenge for Human Rights*. Cambridge: Cambridge University Press. pp. 124–146.

Thomas, W.I. (1908) 'The Older and Newer Ideals of Marriage', *The American Magazine*, 67 (April): 548–552.

Tibi, B. (1995) 'Culture and Knowledge. The Politics of Islamization of Knowledge as a Postmodern Project? The Fundamentalist Claim to De-westernization', *Theory Culture & Society*, 12 (1): 1–24.

Tillyard, E.M.W. (1958) *Shakespeare's Last Plays*. London: Chatto & Windus.

Titmuss, R.A. (1963) *Essays on the Welfare State*. London: Unwin University Books.

Tocqueville, A. de (1968) *Democracy in America*. Glasgow: Collins.

Todd, J. (1986) *Sensibility. An Introduction*. London and New York: Methuen.

Tönnies, F. (1957) *Community and Association*. East-Lansing: Michigan State University Press.

Touraine, A. (1971) *The Post-Industrial Society*. New York: Random House.

Traugott, M. (1978) *Emile Durkheim on Institutional Analysis*. Chicago: University of Chicago Press.

Tregaskis, H. (1979) *Beyond the Grand Tour*. London: Ascent Books.

Troeltsch, E. (1931) *The Social Teaching of the Christian Churches*. New York: Macmillan.

Tucker, K. (1998) *Anthony Giddens and Modern Social Theory*. London: Sage.

Turner, B.S. (1974) *Weber and Islam, a Critical Study*. London: Routledge & Kegan Paul.

Turner, B.S. (1978) *Marx and the End of Orientalism*. London: Allen & Unwin.

Turner, B.S. (1982) 'The Government of the Body: Medical Regimens and the Rationalisation of Diet', *British Journal of Sociology*, 33: 254–269.

Turner, B.S. (1984) *The Body and Society. Explorations in Social Theory*. Oxford: Blackwell.

Turner, B.S. (1986) *Citizenship and Capitalism. The Debate over Reformism*. London: Allen & Unwin.

Turner, B.S. (1987a) 'The Rationalisation of the Body. Reflections on Modernity and Discipline' in S. Lash and S. Whimster (eds) *Max Weber, Rationality and Modernity*. London: Allen & Unwin. pp. 222–241.

Turner, B.S. (1987b) 'A Note on Nostalgia', *Theory, Culture & Society*, 4 (1): 147–156.

Turner, B.S. (1988) *Status*. Milton Keynes: Open University Press.

Turner, B.S. (1990a) 'Outline of a Theory of Citizenship', *Sociology*, 24 (2): 189–217.

Turner, B.S. (1990b) 'The End of Organised Socialism?' *Theory, Culture & Society*, 7: 133–144.

Turner, B.S. (ed.) (1990c) *Theories of Modernity and Postmodernity*. London, Sage.

Turner, B.S. (1991) *Religion and Social Theory*. London: Sage (2nd edition).

Turner, B.S. (1992) *Regulating Bodies. Essays in Medical Sociology*. London and New York: Routledge.

Turner, B.S. (1993) 'Outline of a General Theory of Human Rights', *Sociology*, 27 (3): 489–512.

Turner, B.S. (1994a) 'The Postmodernisation of the Life Course: towards a New Social Gerontology', *Australian Journal of Ageing*, 13: 109–111.

Turner, B.S. (1994b) 'Lebensphilosophie und Handlungstheorie. Die Beziehungen zwischen Talcott Parsons und Max Weber innerhalb der Entwicklung der Soziologie' in G. Wagner and H. Ziprian (eds) *Max Webers Wissenschaftslehre. Interpretation und Kritik*. Frankfurt: Suhrkamp. pp. 310–331.

Turner, B.S. (1994c) *Orientalism, Postmodernism and Globalism*. London: Routledge.

Turner, B.S. (1995a) 'Aging and Identity: Some Reflections on the Somatisation of the Self' in M. Featherstone and A. Wernick (eds) *Images of Aging: Cultural Representation of Later Life*. London: Routledge. pp. 245–260.

Turner, B.S. (1995b) *Medical Power and Social Knowledge*. London: Sage (2nd edition).

Turner, B.S. (ed.) (1996a) *The Blackwell Companion to Social Theory*. Oxford: Blackwell.

Turner, B.S. (1996b) 'Talcott Parsons on Economic and Social Theory: the Relevance of the Amherst Term Papers', *The American Sociologist*, 27 (4): 41–47.

Turner, B.S. (1996) *The Body and Society*. London: Sage (2nd edition).

Turner, B.S. (1997) 'Citizenship Studies: a General Theory', *Citizenship Studies*, 1 (1): 5–18.

Turner, B.S. (1998) 'Postmodernisation of Political Identities: Solidarity and Loyalty in

Contemporary Society' in B. Isenberg (ed.) *Sociology and Social Transformation*. Lund University, Research Report. pp. 65–79.

Turner, B.S. (1999) 'McCitizens: Risk, Coolness and Irony in Contemporary Politics' in B. Smart (ed.) *Resisting McDonaldization*. London: Sage. pp. 83–100.

Turner, B.S. and Hamilton, P. (eds) (1994) *Citizenship. Critical Concepts*. London and New York: Routledge, 2 volumes.

Turner, B.S. and Riggs, A. (1994) 'In Sickness and in Health: Intimacy and Health in the Ageing Process', *Annual Review of Health Social Sciences*, 4: 42–56.

Ullmann, W. (1977) *Medieval Foundations of Renaissance Humanism*. London: Paul Elek.

Underdown, D. (1985) *Revel, Riot & Rebellion*. Oxford: Oxford University Press.

Urry, J. (1990) *The Tourist Gaze. Leisure and Travel in Contemporary Societies*. London: Sage.

Urry, J. (2000) *Sociology beyond Societies*. London: Routledge.

Vandermeersch, P.A. (1996) 'Teachers' in H. de Ridder-Symoens (ed.) *A History of the University in Europe*. Cambridge: Cambridge University Press, Vol. 2, pp. 210–255.

Vattimo, G. (1988) *The End of Modernity. Nihilism and Hermeneutics in Postmodern Culture*. Cambridge: Polity.

Veblen, T. (1953) [1899] *The Theory of the Leisure Class*. New York: Mentor.

Virilio, P. (1986) *Speed and Politics*. New York: Semiotext(e).

Virilio, P. (1995) *The Vision Machine*. London: BFI.

Wallerstein, I. (1974) *The Modern World System*. New York: Academic Press.

Wartofsky, M.W. (1977) *Feuerbach*. Cambridge: Cambridge University Press.

Waters, M. (1996) 'Human Rights and the Universalisation of Interests: Towards a Social Constructionist Approach', *Sociology*, 30: 593–600.

Watt, W.M. (1972) *The Influence of Islam on Medieval Europe*. Edinburgh: Edinburgh University Press.

Watt, W.M. (1991) *Muslim–Christian Encounters. Perceptions and Misperceptions*. London and New York: Routledge.

Wearne, B. (1989) *The Theory and Scholarship of Talcott Parsons to 1951. A Critical Commentary*. Cambridge: Cambridge University Press.

Weber, A. (1950) *Kultur-Geschichte als Kultur-Soziologie*. Munich: R. Piper.

Weber, M. (1930) *The Protestant Ethic and the Spirit of Capitalism*. London: Allen & Unwin.

Weber, M. (1952) *Ancient Judaism*. Glencoe, IL: Free Press.

Weber, M. (1958) *The City*. New York: Free Press.

Weber, M. (1962) *Basic Sociological Concepts*. New York: Free Press.

Weber, M. (1968) *Economy and Society. An Outline of Interpretive Sociology*. Berkeley: University of California Press.

Weber, M. (1989) 'The National State and Economic Policy' in K. Tribe (ed.) *Reading Weber*. London and New York: Routledge, pp. 188–209.

Webster, F. (1997) 'Information, Urbanism and Identity: Perspectives on the Current Work of Manuel Castells', *City*, 7: 105–121.

Wernick, A. (1961) *Promotional Culture*. London: Sage.

Williams, R. (1958) *Culture and Society*. Harmondsworth: Penguin Books.

Williams, R. (1961) *The Long Revolution*. Harmondsworth: Penguin Books.

Williams, R. (1973) *The Country and the City*. London: Chatto & Windus.

Williams, R. (1979) *Politics and Letters*. London: New Left Books.

Willis, P. (1978) *Profane Culture*. London: Routledge & Kegan Paul.

Willis, P. (2000) *The Ethnographic Imagination*. Cambridge: Polity.

Wittfogel, K. (1957) *Oriental Despotism, a Comparative Study of Total Power*. New Haven, CT: Yale University Press.

Wolferen, K. van (1990) *The Enigma of Japanese Power*. New York: Vintage Books.

Wolin, S.S. (1961) *Politics and Vision. Continuity and Innovation in Western Political Thought*. London: George Allen & Unwin.

Woodiwiss, A. (1998) *Globalisation, Human Rights and Labour Law in Pacific Asia*. Cambridge: Cambridge University Press.

Wrong, D. (1961) 'The Oversocialized Conception of Man in Modern Sociology', *American Sociological Review*, 26: 183–193.

Young, R.J.C. (1995) *Colonial Desire. Hybridity in Theory, Culture and Race*. London and New York: Routledge.

Yuval-Davis, N. (1997) *Gender & Nation*. London: Sage.

Zenos, N. (1989) *Scarcity and Modernity*. London and New York: Routledge.

# AUTHOR INDEX

# SUBJECT INDEX